An Introduction to Linguistics and Language Studies

Equinox Textbooks and Surveys in Linguistics
Series Editor: Robin Fawcett, Cardiff University

Published titles in the series:

Analysing Casual Conversation
Suzanne Eggins and Diana Slade

Multimodal Transcription and Text Analysis: A Multimodal Toolkit and Coursebook with Associated On-line Course
Anthony Baldry and Paul J. Thibault

Meaning-Centered Grammar: An Introductory Text
Craig Hancock

Language in Psychiatry: A Handbook of Clinical Practice
Jonathan Fine

The Power of Language: How Discourse Influences Society
Lynne Young and Brigid Fitzgerald

Genre Relations: Mapping Culture
J.R. Martin and David Rose

Writing Readable Research: A Guide for Students of Social Science
Beverly A. Lewin

Intonation in the Grammar of English
M.A.K. Halliday and William S. Greaves

Invitation to Systemic Functional Linguistics through the Cardiff Grammar: An Extension and Simplification of Halliday's Systemic Functional Grammar. Third edition
Robin Fawcett

The Western Classical Tradition in Linguistics. Second edition
Keith Allan

An Introduction to Irish English
Carolina P. Amador Moreno

Forthcoming:

An Introduction to English Sentence Structure: Clauses, Markers, Missing Elements
Jon Jonz

Text Linguistics: The How and Why of Meaning
M.A.K. Halliday and Jonathan Webster

Learning to Write/Reading to Learn: Scaffolding Democracy in Literacy Classrooms
J. R. Martin and David Rose

Multimodal Corpus-Based Approaches to Website Analysis
Anthony Baldry and Kay O'Halloran

Functional Syntax Handbook: Analysing English at the Level of Form
Robin Fawcett

Corpora and Meaning
Steven Jones and Howard Jackson

An Introduction to Linguistics and Language Studies

Anne McCabe

LONDON   OAKVILLE

Published by Equinox Publishing Ltd.

UK: 1 Chelsea Manor Studios, Flood Street, London, SW3 5SR
USA: DBBC, 28 Main Street, Oakville, CT 06779

www.equinoxpub.com

First published 2011

British Library Cataloguing-in-Publication Data
A catalogue record for this book is available from the British Library.

ISBN   978 1 84553 425 7 (hardback)
          978 1 84553 426 4 (paperback)

Library of Congress Cataloging-in-Publication Data
McCabe, Anne.
  An introduction to linguistics and language studies / Anne McCabe.
    p. cm.
  Includes bibliographical references and index.
  ISBN 978-1-84553-425-7—ISBN 978-1-84553-426-4 (pbk.)
  1. Linguistics. 2. Language and languages. I. Title. P121.M344 2010
  410—dc22
                                 2010026352

Typeset by S.J.I. Services, New Delhi
Printed and bound in Great Britain by Lightning Source UK Ltd, Milton Keynes

Contents

Acknowledgments

I am very grateful

to Peter Fries for his encouragement and guidance at the genesis of this book project, to Michael Cummings for his suggestions, and to the cross-disciplinary research group at Saint Louis University in St. Louis, especially Georgia Johnston, for their enthusiasm and critique of my ideas.

to Mark Hancock for suggesting the Turkish examples, and to Güner Çelik and Elisa Hidalgo for developing them. Thanks also to Isabel Alonso Belmonte, Hamish Binns, Daniel Chornet-Roses, Catriona Fox, Gwyneth Fox, Diana Hidalgo, Cristina Matute, Annie McDonald, Marjory Hutchison, Myra Palmer, Hilary Plass, Rachel Whittaker and Paul Vita for providing other examples of language use sprinkled throughout the book. Also, I am grateful to Cary Barney for the exercises on prominence in Chapter 3.

to Nathan Burdick for his work on the glossary.

to Hamish Binns for his drawings.

to the contributors in Chapter 8.

to Tom Bloor, Michael Busch, Mark Hancock, Elisa Hidalgo, Julianne Hixson, Marjorie Hutchison, Maura Tarnoff and Whit Wirsing for their careful reading and comments.

to all of my students for their enthusiasm and interest over the years, and for their examples that come through in the book, especially to Alex Ocasio, Julianne Hixson, Ed Burt, Elizabeth Swackhammer, Rebecca Rice, Adeola Epega, Cat, Kelsey, Kirsten, and the rest, from whom I have learned so much about linguistics and language studies.

to Janet Joyce and Valerie Hall, of Equinox Publishing, for their support, and to George Moore for his cheerful and dedicated editing.

to my family, and especially to Luis Miguel, for all of their patience and support.

While all of the above have helped in shaping this book, the final shape is my own, for which I take full responsibility.

The author and publishers would like to thank the following copyright holders for granting permission to reproduce their material:

The parody of a rejection letter (Chapter 3) is reprinted by permission of John Kador (Retrieved 1 January 2010 from http://www.jkador.com/letter.htm)

'Question: What Is The Best Type Cardiovascular Exercise Machine For Losing Fat Weight?' (Chapter 3) is reprinted with permission of Hugo Rivera (Retrieved on 1 January 2010 from (http://bodybuilding.about.com/od/bodybuildingfaq/f/bestcardio.htm)

'Motorcycle Cancer Seat Patent Granted' (Chapter 3) is reprinted with permission of Randall Dale Chipkar (Retrieved on 3 January 2010 from http://www.motorcyclecancer.com/)

The recipe review for Adrienne's Tom Ka Gai, posted 4 July 2005, by reviewer MUMCADEN, (Chapter 3) is reprinted with permission from Allrecipes.com (Retrieved on 1 January 2010 from http://allrecipes.com/Recipe/Adriennes-Tom-Ka-Gai/Reviews.aspx?Page=5)

The So Good advertisement is reprinted with permission of Sanitarium Health Food Company, Auckland, New Zealand. (Retrieved on 4 January 2009 from http://www.sogood.co.nz/)

'Parenting tips for your 6 month old baby' (Chapter 3) is reprinted with permission of eXtension Foundation (Retrieved on 1 January 2010 from http://www.extension.org/pages/Your_Baby's_First_Tooth_May_be_Causing_Her_Some_Pain)

'Eruption of the primary dentition in human infants: a prospective descriptive study' is from © 2000 American Academy of Pediatric Dentistry and is reprinted with their permission.

'"Hypnotist" thief hunted in Italy' (Chapter 3) is reprinted with permission from © BBC.

The cartoons 'Inclinationship' (Chapter 4), 'Outimacy' (Chapter 5) and 'Big talk' (Chapter 7) are reprinted with permission from Peter Kohlstaat.

The *Dilbert* cartoons (Chapter 6) are reprinted with permission from © United Features Syndicate.

While the author and publishers have made every effort to contact copyright holders of the material used in this volume, they would welcome hearing from anyone they were unable to contact.

To Tom Bloor, linguist and educator

1 An Introduction to Linguistics and Language Studies

I find it helpful to think of linguistic form as if it were located in a pane of glass through which ideas are transmitted from speaker to listener. Under ordinary circumstances language users are not conscious of the glass itself, but only of the ideas that pass through it. The form of language is transparent, and it takes a special act of will to focus on the glass and not the ideas. Linguists undergo a training that teaches them how to focus on the glass ... the experience of becoming conscious of previously unconscious phenomena is one of the principal joys of linguistic work. (Wallace Chafe 1994: 38)

Wallace Chafe's image of language as a pane of glass which linguists are trained to turn their attention on brings to mind another possible metaphor for thinking about the work of linguists. CSI criminologists, in order to uncover clues not visible to the eye, use specialized tools, such as luminal, a liquid that reacts with the hemoglobin in blood to illuminate previously invisible blood stains. In much the same way, linguists use a variety of methods of analyzing language in order to illuminate many different aspects of language: how we acquire it, how and why we pronounce it the way we do, how we string words together to make meaning, how we understand meaning, how and why we are effective in using language for communication in some situations but perhaps not in others, how and why it changes, why languages disappear (and if we can prevent a complete loss) ... You will have your own reasons for wanting to learn more about linguistics and about principled ways of studying language, as you join the legions of linguists, past and present, around the world and provide your contributions to the study of language.

Often, people approach the study of linguistics with a feeling of great awe, perhaps because they feel that the terminology is difficult. However, terminology is rife in any field of activity (witness the proliferation of new words related to new technologies). As with other fields, linguistics needs terms in order to delineate its concepts, yet often people are put off by the technical jargon. Tom and Meriel Bloor (2004: 16) provide an interesting parable when writing about terminology in linguistics; they ask us to imagine a dictator who prohibits all use of technical terms in garages, so those involved in motor vehicle maintenance would not be able to use terms such as 'reverse gear selector pivot pin' or even 'brake' for that matter. Instead of the technical term 'brake', mechanics would have to say something like 'the thing that puts pressure on the wheels to stop them turning', which with time might be shortened to 'wheelstopper'. Then, Bloor and Bloor ask, would that be considered a technical term, and need to be banned? The point is that every field has its terms to refer to the activity and concepts involved in its realization. The odd thing about linguistics, perhaps, is that it needs a language to talk about itself, to talk about language; in other words, it needs a **meta-language**. Linguistics shares this meta-language with the type of prescriptive grammar book which tells people what is 'right' and what is 'wrong' in language use, through the use of terms such as *subject, verb, adjective, noun*, etc. This sharing of terms is rather unfortunate, as it leads to the notion that linguistics is about correctness in language use. However, this is far from the reality of linguistic study.

EXERCISE 1.1

Make a list of word classes[1] as you know them. Do not worry about being 'right' or 'wrong' about the terms. Now analyze the sentence 'CSI criminologists, in order to uncover clues not visible to the eye, use specialized tools, such as luminal, a liquid that reacts with the hemoglobin in blood to illuminate previously invisible blood stains,' assigning each of the words to a word class.

In doing Exercise 1.1, you have been involved in a theoretical task: that of classifying words into categories. You may have found some of the words easier to categorize than others. Words like *CSI, criminologists, clues, eye, tools, luminal, liquid, hemoglobin, blood* and *stains* you may have labeled as **nouns**. Perhaps you learned in school that nouns refer to people, places and things, as these words do. However, linguists would not attempt to define nouns by reference to what they refer to, but rather by how they can be used in phrases, clauses and sentences, in terms of how they can be strung together to form acceptable syntactic strings and also how they can function to create meaning. The same is the case for all linguistic categories, as we will be seeing throughout the book, especially in Chapters 3 and 4. Also perhaps not difficult to categorize are **verbs**, the category in which

1.   Linguists prefer the term 'word class' to the more traditional 'part of speech', as 'word class' is a more accurate term for what is essentially the practice of dividing up words into different types or classes. If you would like more practice on placing words into classes, the webpage by Dick Hudson, University College London, designed for middle school English teachers in the UK is very helpful: http://www.phon.ucl.ac.uk/home/dick/tta/wc/wcall.htm

perhaps you included *uncover, use, reacts,* and *illuminate,* **adverbs,** such as *previously,* and **adjectives,** such as *visible, specialized,* and *invisible.* Nouns, verbs, adjectives and adverbs form the **content words** of language, those that refer to something in our experience (whether real or imagined).

Perhaps more difficult to categorize are **function words,** or words which allow us to connect the different parts of phrases, clauses and sentences, or to convey another type of meaning, such as **polarity** (referring to the 'yes/no' dimension of clauses and sentences) in the case of *not,* **prepositions** and **prepositional phrases** such as *in* (as in *in blood*), *to* (as in *to the eye*), and *with.* The *to* in *to uncover* and *to illuminate* is not a preposition, but is needed in English to form the infinitive of the verb, and when it is used for this purpose, it is often called a 'particle', and not included in a traditional word class category. Other function words include *the* and *a,* labeled 'articles' by some and 'determiners' by others; *that* is a relative pronoun in this context, as it introduces a relative clause describing the type of liquid (although it sometimes has other functions, such as in *Give me that book* or *She said that she would call*). *Such as* functions to introduce an example, and would fit with other phrases, like *in order* (*to*), which serve as discourse markers to signal relationships between ideas, but not all of these words are considered to belong to the traditional word classes. Thus, linguists may not always agree on the exact categories to work with in describing language; however, while there is some disagreement on how to classify some bits of language (and we will study different theoretical perspectives on grammar in Chapters 3 and 4), they would agree on major classes such as noun, verb, adjective, adverb, and preposition.

EXERCISE 1.2

Make a list of utterances which you have heard or have used yourself which you consider bad usage, or incorrect language. Can you identify why you consider them incorrect?

Linguistic work is about describing language, not about prescribing what people should do. The items in the list you created for Exercise 1.2 may be illustrations of the fact that language is constantly changing (see Chapter 5) or they may illustrate dialectal differences (see Chapter 6). A fundamental prerequisite for approaching linguistic study is an understanding that all languages and dialects are equal from a descriptive linguistic point of view. In this perspective, no language or dialect is more elegant, more sophisticated, or more correct than any other language or dialect. All languages and dialects have the necessary resources to draw upon to create new meanings in a systematic way, in order to match the communicative needs of the community which speaks the language or dialect. That is from a linguistic, and a linguist's, point of view. However, from a social perspective, there are differences in how languages and dialects are perceived. It is much the same as with ways of dressing. There is no reason to think that wearing a suit and tie is somehow objectively superior to wearing sweatpants, or that wearing a space suit is more sophisticated than wearing a bikini. Decisions as to the appropriateness of a way of dressing has everything to do with context, and people will make judgments on ways of dressing depending on their social position and on pre-existing views of what that way of dressing represents.

It is the same with language and dialects. Certain ways of speaking are considered more appropriate in given contexts and situations, and people attach judgments to different ways of speaking which in some settings are deemed as not appropriate or which one might not usually encounter in a given situation or context. At the same time, a sociologist simply describing different manners of dress would not make judgments in terms of what the *best* form of fashion is *outside of a context*. In the same vein, a linguist would not make judgments as to which is the best language or which is the best dialect, which is the 'correct' way of speaking. It is the business of linguists to describe language. In this book, we study many different methods that linguists and those involved in the study of language use to undertake this description, commenting on the theoretical perspectives underpinning those methods.

There is a common misconception that a linguist is someone who speaks many different languages. While there are many linguists who can speak more than one language, there are also those who feel comfortable mainly in one language. After studying linguistics they do have a general understanding of how language works, a knowledge which can be applied to other languages. However, prior knowledge of other languages is certainly not a prerequisite for undertaking linguistic study. After all, we all speak a language and have spent years studying it in school and using it to get on with our daily lives. The study of linguistics has a further benefit: working with multiple perspectives concerning the nature of language and how it works differently in different contexts can provide an understanding which can help us be more successful in using our first language in a range of situations.

Another possible misconception about linguistics, which can make it seem like a daunting study to more artistic minds, is that it is the *scientific* study of language. It is the case that linguistics involves the principled study of an object of inquiry known as human language. The 'principled' part is informed by differing theoretical perspectives on that object of study. In this introduction, we look at some of those perspectives in their historical contexts, in order to prepare for the chapters ahead. There are three linguists whom I would like to introduce in this opening chapter, as their work has motivated vast areas of linguistic work and legions of people whose passion is an understanding of language. The innovative theoretical perspectives of these three people underpins much of twentieth–twenty-first-century linguistics, and some broad brushstrokes on their beliefs and insights into language provide a good introduction to the chapters ahead.

1.1   Ferdinand de Saussure

While this is a gross oversimplification about centuries of language study, much of what happened in the eighteenth and nineteenth centuries in linguistics (at a time when the field was more often referred to as *philology*) was mainly historical or comparative in nature. Of pressing concern to those involved in the study of language was an understanding of the history of a language, in order to discover relationships amongst languages, and to highlight regularities in language change. Also, there existed a number of grammars of different languages, describing their pronunciations, rules for forming words (e.g. noun and verb declensions) and sentences, and vocabularies, often to aid those wishing to learn another language (perhaps for commercial and/or scholarly purposes) or for translation of documents and literary texts.

In the twentieth century, the work of **Ferdinand de Saussure**, a Swiss linguist widely considered to be the father of modern linguistics, brought about a change in the field. While he himself published very little, after his death in 1913, his colleagues and students published notes from his teachings as a book entitled *Cours de linguistique générale*, in which Saussure defines the field of linguistics. Several of Saussure's revelations about the nature of language revolutionized the way that this object of inquiry was viewed, and thus have had a profound impact on language study up to this day.

First of all, Saussure eschewed a diachronic approach, or a study of language over time, as he placed little importance on understanding how languages came to be as they were, emphasizing instead a synchronic approach, one which focuses on describing language at a given point in time as it exists as a system. Saussure viewed language as a system of **signs**, which consist of two parts: **signified** and **signifier**. The signified is the concept which is referred to, and the signifier is the label used for that concept (see Figure 1.1).

Figure 1.1 Sign

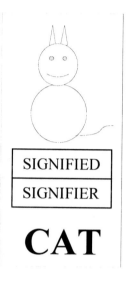

SIGNIFIED

SIGNIFIER

CAT

There are several principles of Saussure´s theory of signs which are important of an understanding of his view of language. First of all, the relationship between a given signified and its signifier is arbitrary. There is nothing in the essence of the signified in the rough diagram above which would lead one to utter the string of sounds spelled by 'c-a-t'. Second, while we might think of language as a naming game, with signifieds being assigned to already existing signifiers, this is far from the case, as evidenced by differences across languages, dialects, and registers in what is named; that is, different languages carve up experience in different ways. For example, Arabic has different words for a mother's sister (khala) and a father's sister (ama), while English uses *aunt* for both. There is further evidence for language not being a system which names already-existing concepts: there are differences across time in relationships between signifieds and signifiers. For example, *meat* during the seventeenth century referred to *food* in general, and in the present time, in food terms, it refers only to the *flesh of an animal*. Thus, signs are not stable in terms of the relationship between signified and signifier.

So, if language is not a fixed nomenclature for pre-existing concepts, how do we use it to mean anything? Saussure's efforts to define linguistics led him to a further key principle: language is a set of signs which are: (a) members of a system; and (b) defined by their relationships to each other. We know what something <u>means</u> by knowing also <u>what it does not mean</u>. We know that *pat* and *bat* are different from each other because /p/ is not /b/. Both /p/ and /b/ are consonants, and both are articulated by bringing the lips together and allowing sound to explode its way through, as it were (more in Chapter 2 on how these sounds are articulated, in the sections on phonetics and phonology). However, there is a major difference in that with /b/ we vibrate our vocal cords, and with /p/ we do not. We can also contrast *meat* with both *flesh* and *food* and understand how these signs are conceptually alike and conceptually different.

Furthermore, elements of language stand in relationship to each other in two important ways. First of all, they are in relationship to each other in the ways in which they can string together on the **syntagmatic** dimension; for example, 'p' is followed by 'a' and then by 't' to make *pat*; another example of the syntagmatic dimension is that in English we put the adjective before the noun, as in 'black cat'. Elements of language also relate to each other on the **paradigmatic** dimension; for example we understand *pat* as differentiated from *bat*, *cat*, *sat*, etc. because we can substitute *p* with *b*, *c*, and *s*. To illustrate the paradigmatic set of choices further, we can consider 'black' in its relationship to other colors, and 'cat' in its relationship to other animals, or, more generally, we know that 'black' belongs to a set of words known as adjectives and 'cat' to that of nouns.

For Saussure, linguistics then is the study of the system of a language in order to articulate the elements which distinguish one functional form from another. This understanding of the differences is what constitutes the meaning-making capability of language. What is of interest to linguists, in Saussure's view, is the system of forms, or **la langue** as Saussure termed it, rather than **la parole**, or the actual use of language by individual speakers. *Langue* refers to the "hoard deposited by the practice of speech in speakers who belong to the same community, a grammatical system which, to all intents and purposes, exists in the mind of each speaker" (*Course*, 13–14). *Langue* belongs to all of us, as it is a collective social product.

Saussure's ideas about linguistics have influenced generations of linguists, including the **structuralists**, who focused a great deal of effort on describing the systems of many different languages. Structuralists make inventories of *parole* in order to delineate *langue*. Thus, structuralists created descriptions of the sound and meaning units of a great number of languages by collecting data (recording large amounts of actual speech) and analyzing the component parts of the data into smaller units (phonemes, morphemes, groups and phrases), and by relating these units into a system of paradigms and syntagms. (In the sections on phonology – Chapter 2 – and morphology – Chapter 3 – in this textbook, you will be involved in carrying out these types of analyses.) Indeed, the work of American structuralists, led by the great American structuralist Leonard Bloomfield, especially during the 1930s and 1940s, has been of great importance in leaving us a legacy of inventoried languages which have since been lost or which are endangered.

Discussion question: When we learn another language, we sometimes discover words and phrases that do not have an exact counterpart in our own language. Discuss Saussure's notion that there is no signified without a signifier, especially in terms of translating terms for more abstract notions.

1.2   Noam Chomsky

Noam Chomsky's work in linguistics was both a reaction against certain theories about language and an acceptance of other perspectives at the same time. At the time of Chomsky's early thinking and writings on linguistics (in the middle of the twentieth century), linguistics had only experienced about a half a century of existence as a field more or less resembling what we think of today. Chomsky was trained in structuralist theory, and while structuralist analysis was, in Chomsky's view, adequate for descriptions of phonemes, morphemes, and clause constituents (such as noun phrases, verb phrases, prepositional phrases, etc.), it was not robust enough to account for syntax, especially the ability of syntax to generate an infinite number of sentences (see Chapter 4). Furthermore, structuralism focused on actual speech, and used real data for its analysis; in essence, large amounts of language were collected in order to analyze how language worked, how it behaved. Speech patterns were seen as an example of behavior;[2] in the behaviorist view of study of human practices, such as language, the object of study is that which can be overtly observed and described.

Chomsky's linguistics is considered a revolution against the behavioral view of language. For Chomsky, actual language use, or **performance**, is only the tip of the iceberg of linguistic **competence**, or the underlying mental processes which we carry out in our production of language. Each one of

2.   Structuralism has provided support for some second language teaching methods. The audiolingual method, for example, drew on structuralism to devise drills (which are still used in language classes today) which would reinforce correct use of the language.

us has a mental repository of the rules by which our language or dialect organizes linguistic elements into well-formed strings; that is, each one of us holds in our heads syntactic expertise in terms of a set of finite rules which allows us to generate an infinite number of sentences, many of which we have never heard before. Syntactic theories attempt to make transparent that mental knowledge by modeling it, and in many cases by showing how language might be generated by a computer if programmed to have the same kind of rule-based knowledge. Indeed, the growth of Chomskyan mentalist syntactic theory was contemporary to the growth of computer technology and capabilities, which added a dimension to the study of syntax: a desire to be able to replicate the ability of humans to produce language. This desire calls for a theory of language which is precise and explicit, and Chomsky used formulas and definitions in the style of mathematics to describe and model linguistic competence, and thus his theory (and other related theories) have come to be called 'formal' (which are often contrasted with 'functional' theories). Furthermore, because of the interest in underlying mental structures rather than on actual performance, Chomskyan theory focuses attention on idealized utterances, or instances of language which are considered to be well-formed according to the syntactic rules of a language, rather than on real language in use. We will revisit Chomsky's linguistic theory in Chapter 4.

Chomsky later moved from the terms competence and performance to using the terms **I-language** and **E-language** (Chomsky 1986), I-language being the internal set of linguistic rules that children develop over their early years. A further motivation in Chomsky's work in linguistics was the observation that children develop this rule-governed notion of language simply from hearing language, language that is not always presented to them in an ideal syntactically-ruled way. E-language, or external language, is often incomplete and thought of as rather messy, especially in certain contexts such as informal conversation. The point that Chomsky makes is that the data available to a child is often more limited than the I-language that the child develops out of this data. Thus Chomsky posited that humans have an innate faculty for acquiring the idealized I-language, a point which we return to in Chapter 7.

1.3   M. A. K. Halliday

Michael Halliday became interested in the study of language because of his own experiences first learning and then later teaching Chinese. He writes that his motivation for developing a way of analyzing language:

> was driven by the need to solve particular problems in teaching the language
> and to explain features of the language to the learners. And that could mean
> everything from, say, the Chinese tone system, the nature of Chinese writing,
> and therefore of writing systems in general, to the relations between grammar
> and vocabulary. (Halliday and Hasan 2006: 16)

Thus, he set about developing descriptions of language and its workings which formed the bases for **systemic functional linguistics (SFL)**. While working on his linguistic theory, Halliday was commissioned to create methods and materials to help much needed school-based literacy programs in England. Halliday explains further that his early work was influenced by J. R. Firth, a linguist who drew attention to the relationship between meaning and context, including the surrounding co-text that a bit of language participates in. This co-text lends meaning to words, as Firth famously pointed out by saying: 'You shall know a word by the company it keeps' (Firth 1957: 11) (a notion we will come back to in Chapter 8 on corpus linguistics). A description of language in this view needs to take into account the context for which language is used. Furthermore, Firth paid heed to Saussure's project of focusing on both the syntagmatic and paradigmatic dimensions of language, and this led Halliday to posit a systemic framework of functional choices in his linguistic theory. Thus, language is a system of choices at different levels, and each choice provides an aspect of meaning. When we revisit SFL in greater depth in Chapter 3, we will focus on the functional part of the theory; in other words, we will focus on how clauses function to create meaning at the same time in three broad ways: interpersonally: by establishing and maintaining relationships between people, and by allowing us to express opinions about propositions; ideationally: by construing the world, whether real, invented, or abstract; and textually: organizing the interpersonal and the ideational into coherent texts. We will not focus on the systemic part, which refers to the construction of the systemic networks of choices available to users of language at different levels. Figure 1.2 demonstrates this aspect of the theory.

In Figure 1.2 we see that a choice of **mood** is available to us when we open our mouths to speak, or pick up a pen or sit at a keyboard to write. We can choose to use the **imperative** mood, in which case we are making demands on people, such as in *Write me! Call me! Leave me alone!*. Or we can choose the **indicative** mood, which involves a further choice; we can either make statements, through the **declarative** mood, such as in *He wrote me a letter,* or we can ask questions, through the **interrogative** mood; if we choose the interrogative mood, we have the further choice of WH-type (*Who wrote you a letter?*) or yes/no questions (*Did he write you a letter?*).

Figure 1.2 Systemic Network of Mood Choices

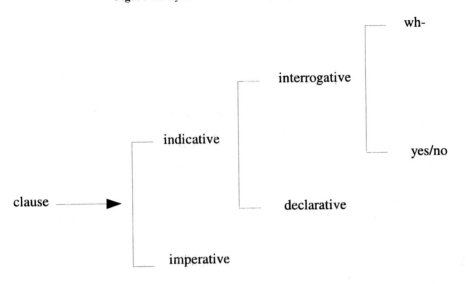

These mood choices provide a layer of meaning related to the relationship between the people involved in the speech exchange, as we can think about *who can demand things of whom, who can make statements to whom,* and *who can ask questions of whom, about what and in what context.*

A key term in Halliday's theory is that of **register**. Register refers to the linguistic choices made in given contexts of situation; i.e. in a particular situational context, people will tend to make meanings appropriate to the situation through appropriate **lexico-grammatical** choices (that is, choices related to both vocabulary and grammar). The variables which determine the register of a given text are **field** (the subject matter at hand, what it is the people involved are referring to in terms of experience, real or imagined), **mode** (the channel of communication, e.g. written or spoken, or, more delicately, a textbook, a sermon, a conversation, an e-mail, etc.), and **tenor** (the relationship between interlocutors, e.g. symmetrical, as between friends, or asymmetrical, as between a boss and an employee, a teacher and a student). If we take the history textbook as an example, and examine its register, we could say that in terms of field, the nature of the social action centers on historical events, on what happened in the past. The mode is written, with a pedagogical function; in other words, written to be assimilated for study purposes. The tenor is asymmetrical: the writer is the one who is in possession of historical information which the reader presumably does not know but needs to learn.

EXERCISE 1.3

Analyze the following texts in terms of field, mode and tenor. Explain your choices.
1. Keep out!
2. Whatcha doin'? Wanna get a burger or somethin'?
3. I am writing to enquire about the position in sales advertised in the Saturday August 12 edition of *The Times*.
4. Shadows covered wide areas of European life in the fourteenth and fifteenth centuries. The vigorous expansion into bordering areas that had marked European history since the eleventh century came to an end. The Christian West fought to halt the expansion of the Muslim Turks. Plague, famine, and recurrent wars decimated populations and snuffed out their former prosperity. The papacy and feudal government struggled against mounting institutional chaos. Powerful mystical and heretical movements and new critical currents in Scholasticism rocked the established religious and philosophical equilibrium of the thirteenth century.

1.4   Conclusion

We have seen in this introductory chapter that linguistics is a field of study that examines language in a principled way. There are various theoretical perspectives from which that object of study can be analyzed, as language is multi-faceted; language is influenced by our physiological make-up, by our brains and by our speech organs, by how we use it to achieve that which we wish to achieve in carrying out communicative acts. Thus, it can be examined using different lenses. In the rest of this course, we will learn to use some of the different lenses available to those involved in linguistics and the study of language.

We have left out here the scores of linguists who have helped to further the projects of the linguists mentioned in this chapter and who have created perspective and projects of their own. A number of other linguists will be mentioned throughout the book, but, unfortunately, it is not possible to mention all whose work has added to our ever-growing understanding of language. You will notice that Saussure, Chomsky and Halliday came to develop their theories of linguistics based on compelling questions for which they could not find answers in existing ways of analyzing and explaining language. What burning questions do *you* have about language?

EXERCISE 1.4

Attribute each of the following phrases to either Ferdinand de Sausurre, Noam Chomsky, or Michael Halliday. What motivates your response? What does the quote tell you about their perspective on the study and analysis of language?

1. 'If we could embrace the sum of word-images stored in the minds of all individuals, we could identify the social bond that constitutes language. It is a storehouse filled by the members of a given community through their active use of speaking, a grammatical system that has a potential existence in each brain, or, specifically, in the brains of a group of individuals. For language is not complete in any speaker; it exists perfectly only within a collectivity.'

2. 'It seems clear that we must regard linguistic competence – knowledge of a language – as an abstract system underlying behavior, a system constituted by rules that interact to determine the form and intrinsic meaning of a potentially infinite number of sentences.'

3. 'Every text – that is, everything that is said or written – unfolds in some context of use; furthermore, it is the uses of language that, over tens of thousands of generations, have shaped the system. Language has evolved to satisfy human needs; and the way it is organized is functional with respect to these needs.'

4. 'Linguistic theory is concerned primarily with an ideal speaker-hearer, in a completely homogeneous speech community, who knows its language perfectly and is unaffected by such grammatically irrelevant conditions as memory limitations, distractions, shifts of attention and interest, errors (random or characteristic) in applying his knowledge of the language in actual performance.'

5. 'Language is a system of interdependent terms in which the value of each term results solely from the simultaneous presence of the others ... [for example]. To determine what a five-franc piece is worth one most know: (1) that it can be exchanged for a fixed quantity of a different thing, e.g. bread; and (2) that it can be compared with a similar value of the same system, e.g. a one-franc piece, or with coins of another system (a dollar, etc.). In the same way a word can be exchanged for something dissimilar, an idea; besides, it can be compared with something of the same nature, another word. Its value is therefore not fixed so long as one simply states that it can be 'exchanged' for a given concept.'

6. 'Spoken and written language, then, tend to display different KINDS of complexity; each of them is more complex in its own way. Written language tends to be lexically dense but grammatically simple; spoken language tends to be grammatically intricate but lexically sparse' ... 'The value of having some explicit knowledge of the grammar of written language is that you can use this knowledge, not only to analyze the texts, but as a critical resource for asking questions about them.'

1.5   References and further reading

Bloor, Thomas and Bloor, Meriel (2004) *The Functional Analysis of English. Second Edition*. London: Arnold.

Chafe, Wallace (1994) *Discourse, Consciousness, and Time: The Flow and Displacement of Conscious Experience in Speaking and Writing*. Chicago, IL: University of Chicago Press.

Chomsky, Noam A. (1965) *Aspects of the Theory of Syntax*. Cambridge, MA: MIT Press.

Chomsky, Noam A. (2006) *Language and Mind. Third Edition*. Cambridge: Cambridge University Press.

Crystal, David (2009) *Just a Phrase I'm Going Through: My Life in Language*. London: Routledge.

Firth, J. R. (1957) *Papers in Linguistics 1934–1951*. London: Oxford University Press.

Halliday, M. A. K. (1987) Spoken and written modes of meaning. In R. Horowitz, and S. J. Samuels (eds) *Comprehending Oral and Written Language*. Orlando, FL: Academic Press.

Halliday, M. A. K. and Hasan, Ruqaiya (2006) Language and literacy. In R. Whittaker, M. O'Donnell, and A. McCabe (eds) *Language and Literacy: Functional Approaches* 15–44. London: Continuum.

Labov, William (1997) How I got into linguistics, and what I got out of it. Retrieved on February 24, 2010 from http://www.ling.upenn.edu/~wlabov/Howlgot.html .

de Saussure, Ferdinand (1959) *Course in General Linguistics*. New York: McGraw-Hill Publishers.

1.6 Some answers to the exercises

Exercise 1.1

Answers may vary. See section in chapter immediately following the exercise for a discussion of possible answers.

Exercise 1.2

Answers will vary. An example: some people point out that 'less' is now used where 'fewer' was considered 'correct' (with plural count nouns, such as *people* or *chairs*).

Exercise 1.3

1. Field of trespassing or of danger; mode probably a sign, possibly a shouted warning; tenor possibly of authority warning the general public, or private enterprise warning the general public.
2. Field of negotiating free time or getting something to eat; mode probably spoken, as it calls for an immediate response, but is too long for an SMS, and the tenor is symmetrical, probably between friends.

3. Field of job application; mode of written letter; the tenor is asymmetrical – writing to someone in a position of power.

4. Field is history; mode is textbook, tenor is asymmetrical – writer has knowledge that the reader needs or wants.

Exercise 1.4

1. De Saussure, Ferdinand (1959) *Course in General Linguistics*. New York: McGraw-Hill Publishers, pp. 13–14.

2. Chomsky, Noam (2006) *Language and Mind. Third edition.* Cambridge: Cambridge University Press, p. 62.

3. Halliday, M. A. K. (1985) *An Introduction to Functional Grammar*. London: Edward Arnold, xiii.

4. Chomsky, Noam A. (1965) *Aspects of the Theory of Syntax*. Cambridge, MA: MIT Press, p. 3.

5. de Saussure, Ferdinand (1959) *Course in General Linguistics*. New York: McGraw-Hill Publishers, pp. 114–115.

6. Halliday, M. A. K. (1987) Spoken and written modes of meaning. In Horowitz, R. and Samuels, S. J. (eds) *Comprehending Oral and Written Language*. Orlando, FL: Academic Press, 66.

2 A Focus on Spoken Interaction

A linguistic system is a series of differences of sound combined with a series of differences of ideas. (Ferdinand de Saussure 1959: 120)

In this unit, we focus on ways of describing language which will help us to understand how we make sense of the world and communicate through language in spoken contexts. Obviously, many of the theoretical perspectives on language that we look at in this unit can also apply (and indeed have been applied) to written language contexts; however, these perspectives have had their genesis in attempts to explain spoken interaction. Much of what we study in this unit falls under the field of **pragmatics**, or the study of meaning in use; that is, pragmatics provides tools to help us understand the meaning of language in a given social context, including the effect that language has on those involved in the speech situation. We can compare it to the field of **semantics**, the study of meaning outside of its contextualized use with a focus on the literal meaning of words and phrases, which we will delve into in Chapter 4. To grasp the difference of meaning in a semantic sense and meaning in a pragmatic sense, think of what it <u>means</u> when you hear someone utter *jump*. If you look up the word in a dictionary in an attempt to discover what the word means in the semantic sense, you might get something like 'move off the ground by propulsion through use of the legs'. However, the pragmatic sense would look at who is uttering *jump* to whom and in what context, e.g. a boss barking at his employees after chewing them out for not working fast enough. Pragmatics also attempts to explain why we have many different ways of saying the same thing. If I would like someone to give me something to drink, I can say *Could I have a glass of water, please,* or *Gosh, I'm so thirsty!* or *Give me something to drink!*

Language has the ability to achieve many things under many guises; this ability is explained through the field of pragmatics. Pragmatics is a vast field of its own, and its theoretical perspectives are informed by linguistics and philosophy; here we will focus on **speech act theory, conversational implicature, politeness**, and **conversation analysis**. Along the way, we will look at **spoken discourse markers, vague language, ellipsis** and **intonation**, all of which are features that help us to achieve our communicative needs in spoken interactive situations. We will then go on to look at **phonetics** and **phonology**, two traditional areas of study within modern linguistics, which help us focus on the ways in which we make meaning based on the physical sounds which we produce and string together in significant ways.

EXERCISE 2.1

List several phrases which would allow you to achieve the following:
1. A $100 loan
2. An apology
3. A lunch date
4. A sympathetic ear

For each of the above, explain in what specific ways the language used would change depending on whether you were speaking to:
1. a) a parent b) a sibling c) a friend d) your boss
2. a) a parent b) a stranger you bump into c) a sibling d) a friend
3. a) someone you are interested in b) a parent c) a friend d) your boss
4. a) a counselor b) a friend c) a parent d) your boss

2.1 Speech act theory: Doing things with words

People often think of language as representing our experience: that is, we often think that the role of language is to explain, inform, describe, and say something relevant (or not!) about the world. *The world is round, It's Tuesday today,* and *Water boils at 100° Celsius* all seem to fit that use of language. Indeed, language is certainly used in the sense of *saying something*, but it is also used to *do* things, such as promise, bet, request, threaten, warn, apologize, put a hex on someone, and swear (as in court).[1] Furthermore, sometimes we use the same language (i.e. language that at first glance seems to be representing the same experience) to do different things. For example, if I say *It's cold in here*, you might interpret that as a simple comment on my part on the state of atmospheric conditions in a particular room. However, if you have just opened a window, and while I am saying it, I look accusingly at you, then you will probably understand that I am asking you to close the window.

While the notion of speech act goes back further, its prominence in linguistics is attributed to J. L. Austin's 1955 William James' lectures, which were published posthumously as a book entitled *How to do Things with Words*. Austin questioned the contemporary philosophical focus on the truth value of statements, a view which centered on the conditions of an utterance

1.   Whether that utterance be in speech or in writing. Speech act theory is included in this chapter on the spoken language, as it will help us understand how conversation works. However, speech acts also happen through writing.

or sentence that can be declared true or false. In his book, Austin begins by examining what he called **performatives**: sentences that are used to *do* things, rather than declare or state something. Performatives include such utterances as *I now pronounce you man and wife*. Obviously, only certain people in certain conditions can do this kind of pronouncing (for example a minister, priest or public official, with two people present who agree to the ceremony, and further witnesses). Furthermore, when children at play utter the words *I now pronounce you man and wife*, no real marriage takes place. However, if the conditions *are* right, then a change has taken place through the uttering of the words.

EXERCISE 2.2

Make a list of performative utterances, such as *I now pronounce you man and wife*, *Tag! You're it!* What new state of affairs do the utterances create? What conditions must be present for the new state of affairs to come about?

Performatives are speech acts which in themselves constitute an action. Austin refers to this aspect of language as its **illocutionary** force. The illocutionary force of an utterance refers to the ability of the utterance to carry out an act. As *How to do Things with Words* unfolds, and Austin attempts to pin down just what it is that constitutes a performative utterance, he reveals to us that in essence *all* utterances are doing something, whether it is to inform, persuade, regulate, promise, etc. For example, if I state *My name is Anne*, obviously I am not naming myself Anne, as that was done some years ago by my parents. However, if I am uttering that statement so that you may know my name, the intention behind that statement is one of informing. Actually, I could say: *I hereby inform you that my name is Anne*. Thus, the illocutionary act is one of informing in this case.

Austin actually distinguished three kinds of acts:

> **Locutionary act**: the act of saying something
> **Illocutionary act**: the act of doing something by saying something
> **Perlocutionary act**: the act of achieving something by saying something.

The locutionary act is simply the physical act of uttering the words. We have seen with the example above of *My name is Anne* that the illocutionary act is that of what the utterance is doing (in that example, bringing about a change in a state of information). The perlocutionary act, however, is what we actually achieve through utterance; I could achieve less formality from you if you call me Anne, or perhaps you have just called me Susan and what I achieve is that you now call me by my right name.

EXERCISE 2.3

For each of the pairs of scenarios below, write the common locutionary act of the underlined words, the different illocutionary act being carried out (informing, persuading, warning, advising, etc.), and what you think the perlocutionary act (or effect) might be.

Scenario 1: (in an elevator, 3 people. A and B know each other, C is smoking:

A (to B): *Ahem, did I ever tell you that I am allergic to cigarette smoke?*

Scenario 2: (A is filling in a form for a dating service):

A (writing on form): *(I am) allergic to cigarette smoke.*

common locutionary act: both are saying that the person in question has an allergy to cigarette smoke.

illocutionary act in scenario 1: A is making a veiled request for C to stop smoking, and we cannot know if C will react favorably (and stop smoking) or unfavorably (and blow smoke towards A!).

illocutionary act scenario 2: A is informing; the perlocutionary effect should be that A is provided with a date who does not smoke.

1. Pair 1:
   Scenario 1: (in a club, the night before an assignment is due; A and B are friends and classmates)
   A (to B): *I haven't done my homework.*
   Scenario 2: (in the classroom; A is a student, B a teacher)
   A (to B): *I haven't done my homework.*

2. Pair 2:
   Scenario 1: (in an airport parking lot; A has just met B, a good friend who has just arrived off a plane)
   A (to B): I don't see my car anywhere!
   Scenario 2: (in the street, next to an empty parking spot, B is a police officer)
   A (to B): I don't see my car anywhere!

3. Pair 3:
   Scenario 1: (a teacher A talking to a class about their recent exam)
   A: In this section, a lot of mistakes were made.
   Scenario 2: (government leader A giving a speech on the radio)
   A: Mistakes were made.

4. Now, invent a pair of scenarios of your own.

John Searle took work on speech acts further by introducing the difference between **direct** and **indirect** speech acts. Searle noted that there are speech acts which are so fundamental to communication that they are captured through the **mood** of our utterance. Thus, **indicative mood** signals that we are giving information, **interrogative mood** signals a request for information or goods, and **imperative mood** signals a command to do something:

(a) **Indicative:** *There's a serious problem outside.*
(b) **Interrogative:** *Are the papers here?*
(c) **Imperative:** *Marry me!*

In these examples, the mood of each utterance signals its illocutionary force. Or does it? As we will be seeing throughout this unit on the spoken language, context is key in explaining what it is people are trying to do with the language they use. Imagine this context for (a) above: A is a security guard for a business, and B is the manager of the business, and B says to A *There is a serious problem outside.* We might then want to interpret the illocutionary force of (a) not as an informative, but rather as an imperative, as a indirect order to the security guard to go take care of the problem. Likewise, (b) could be an indirect order from a boss to a worker to fetch the papers. In many cultures, (c) can hardly be seen as a direct command for someone to do something; it is rather considered to be a request. Thus, the mood of an utterance may not always indicate its illocutionary force.

EXERCISE 2.4

For each utterance, state the mood (indicative, interrogative, or imperative). Then state the direct speech act which it could represent, and the indirect speech act which it more likely represents.

E.g. *There's the door.* Mood = imperative. Direct speech act = informing. Indirect speech act = commanding or requesting someone to answer the door.

1. *Would you mind handing me the salt?*
2. *Go ahead, try it. See where that'll get you!*
3. *Honey, the phone's ringing!*
4. *I have always wanted to have a pair of earrings just like those.*
5. *I'm sure I must look awful.*

2.2   Grice's conversational maxims

Imagine you overhear the following conversation:

A: *Are John and Mary back together again?*
B: *I saw a red Porsche parked outside 1128 Green Street last night ... and it was still there this morning!!*

In this example, A asks a question which elicits a *yes* or *no*, or perhaps an *I don't know*, response. There is nothing in B's response to connect it to A's question, unless, of course, we know something about John and Mary; that is, we need to bring our knowledge of the context to an understanding of how B might be interpreted as a response to A.

In order to help us understand how context works in deciphering meaning in a given situation, we can look to Paul Grice's **Cooperative Principle**, which explains how people act in conversation: 'Make your conversational contribution such as is required, at the stage at which it occurs, by the accepted purpose or direction of the talk exchange in which you are engaged' (Grice 1975: 45–46). Note that Grice here is not telling us what to do, but rather providing an explanation for *how we behave in communicative situations and how we assume other people behave*; we behave as if people are adhering to the Cooperative Principle. In the exchange above, we might assume that B's response is indeed providing A with the information requested. We can make the connection between the question and the answer by relying on **presupposition**: B presupposes that A also knows the following:

✓ John has a red Porsche
✓ Mary lives at 1128 Green Street

In this scenario, John and Mary are back together, and so B's answer to A's question is *yes*. In another scenario, perhaps they both know that <u>Bill</u> has a red Porsche, and thus John and Mary are NOT back together, as Mary is seeing someone else; or perhaps both know that <u>Jill</u> lives at 1128 Green Street, and thus the gossip is that John is seeing someone else ... Whatever the case, the point is that in conversation we assume that people are adhering to the Cooperative Principle, and interpret their responses accordingly.

Grice further divided the Cooperative Principle into sub-principles of Quantity, Relation, Quality, and Manner:

Quantity:
Maxim 1. Make your contribution as informative as is required
Maxim 2. Do not make you contribution more informative than is required

Relation:
Maxim 1. Be relevant.[2]

Quality: (super-maxim – try to make your contribution one that is true)
Maxim 1. Do not say what you believe to be false
Maxim 2. Do not say that for which you lack adequate evidence

Manner:
Maxim 1. Avoid obscurity of expression
Maxim 2. Avoid ambiguity
Maxim 3. Be brief
Maxim 4. Be orderly

The sub-principles are not something that we always adhere to, obviously. However, given that, for purposes of exchanging information in the most straightforward way, we normally assume that interactants adhere to the Cooperative Principle and its sub-principles. When we do (usually clearly and obviously) break any of the sub-principles, we create an instance of **conversational implicature**. For example, if you say *I heard you did well on the exam* and I respond *Yes, and pigs fly*, I flout the maxim of quality, as I am telling an obvious untruth. However, in doing so I create an implicature which you will interpret as me letting you know that I did not do well on the exam. In order to work out these conversational implicatures, we rely on the conventional meanings of words used along with the context in which they are uttered, any background knowledge that we have of the situation, the Cooperative Principle and its maxims, and finally the fact that all of this knowledge is shared by both interlocutors.

Thus, in an exchange, with respect to the maxims, we have the options of:

- ✓ Observing the maxims (adhering to them)
- ✓ Violating one or more maxims (i.e. secretly not adhering – perhaps to achieve some benefit, e.g. in the case of lying or cheating)
- ✓ Opting out (making clear that there is an unwillingness to adhere, e.g. in refusing to answer a direct question)
- ✓ Not fulfilling one maxim because of a clash with another (e.g. *A: Do you know where Sally is from? B: Somewhere in the US.* B violates the maxim of Quantity – providing A with the specific information

2. Sperber and Wilson (1995) challenge Grice's theory, suggesting that the single cognitive concept of relevance accounts for pragmatic phenomena, thus shying away from Gricean social underpinnings.

requested – in order to avoid violating the maxim of Quality – inventing something that B does not know)

✓ Flouting a maxim (i.e. clearly and purposefully failing to fulfill a maxim) in order to make a conversational implicature.

EXERCISE 2.5

For each utterance or exchange, suggest which maxim is being flouted, and what is being communicated through that flouting. For example:

A: How's your work coming along?

B: It sure is sunny outside.

In this exchange, B is flouting the maxim of relevance. Given that B responds to A's question with an utterance which is clearly irrelevant, A can assume that the work is NOT coming along.

1. In a recommendation letter for a sales job:

   A: *Dear Sir, I have been asked to write a few lines in support for John Smith's application for work in sales within your company. What perhaps is most impressive about John is that his appearance is impeccable, and his class attendance has been faultless. Sincerely, A.*

2. A: *Do you like Anne's new shoes?*   B: *I can't imagine where she got them from.*

3. A: *Do you think the kids would like some of that freezing cold creamy concoction that could be served in an edible cylinder-like container?*

4. A: *How did Mary and John do on their exams?*   B: *Mary did just fine.*

5. A: *Were you invited to John's party?*   B: *Were you?*

6. A: *Are you free this evening?*   B: *I have had so much work lately! I had to finish a 20-page paper, my dog has been sick and I had to take him to the vet, and now my mother says she's coming to visit this weekend!*

EXERCISE 2.6

Observation:

Jot down some examples of implicature that you hear in conversations around you. What maxim is flouted? What does that flouting communicate?

Jot down some examples of implicature that you see on TV or in movies. What maxim is flouted? What does that flouting communicate?

EXERCISE 2.7

Question for relection. Why do we use implicature, instead of adhering to the maxims, in order to communicate our meanings and intentions? Why also do we use indirect speech acts (e.g. questions for commands)?

The last option, flouting a maxim, is perhaps the most interesting, as it is what we use to communicate meanings beyond the literal or conventional meaning of the words we use.

2.3   Politeness

We can see from Exercise 2.5 that we often flout the maxims of conversation in order to avoid insulting someone or perhaps in order to avoid disagreement. When we interact with others, we do much more than simply communicate information: we also work toward establishing and maintaining social relationships. An important part of that work involves **face**, which Erving Goffman defined as 'the positive social value a person effectively claims for himself by the line others assume he has taken during a particular contact' (1955: 13). Thus, in a given interaction, we project an identity which we wish others to respect and protect, as we do likewise for them. To do otherwise is to create a situation in which someone might have their face publicly diminished, with its consequent humiliation and awkwardness. Penelope Brown and Stephen Levinson use Goffman's concept of face to explain **politeness**, and divide it into two types: positive and negative face. Positive face is related to our desire to be liked, and to create bonds with others. Negative face is our desire not to be imposed upon, and to not impose on others. In interaction, we are constantly attempting to balance our need for privacy and autonomy with others' need for the same, our need for being liked and respected with others' need for the same, while at the same time trying to achieve our goals in interacting. In these attempts, there are occasions when a face-threatening act (FTA) looms. In these situations, we have several options open to us:

1. Do an FTA bald-on-record and with no mitigation: *Move over. You're taking up too much room.*
2. Do an FTA on record, with **positive politeness strategies** for mitigation: *I always like sitting next to you! So would you mind moving over just a bit?*
3. Do an FTA with **negative politeness strategies** for mitigation: *I'm sorry, I hate to bother. Could I trouble you to move over a little?*
4. Do an FTA off-record, or implicitly: *I wish they had provided more space. My legs are tired.* This gives the speaker the chance to deny the FTA if pressed: e.g. *Are you saying that I'm taking up too much room? No, no, I'm just commenting on how badly the organization anticipated the number of people...*
5. Opt out – do not do the FTA (and just stand there quietly!!).

'Piled Higher and Deeper' by Jorge Cham
Retrieved February 21, 2010 from www.phdcomics.com

Thus **positive politeness strategies** are instances of communication in which interlocutors attempt to mitigate face-threatening acts by appealing to the others' desire to be liked and accepted, while **negative politeness strategies** appeal to others' need for their own space and their desire to avoid being imposed upon.

EXERCISE 2.8

We move away here for a moment from the spoken language to analyze politeness strategies in written language, albeit in what is thought of as a more informal context. Look at the two e-mail messages below, and describe for each one:

(a) what it is the writers are attempting to achieve
(b) what the FTAs are
(c) what politeness strategies the writers use to achieve their goals and mitigate the FTAs.

1. E-mail 1: *My name is John Smith and I am a doctoral student at the University of Indiana, and am doing my dissertation research on issues related to writing at the University. As I was not able to attend your presentation at the recent writing conference, I wondered if you wouldn't mind forwarding to me a copy of the handout from your presentation on nominalized writing. As you can imagine, I am very interested in your topic for my dissertation research, and I'd love to be able to take a look at your findings and methodology.*

> *If this would be possible, I would greatly appreciate it. Perhaps, the easiest way would be just to send it as an attachment via e-mail. Otherwise, I would be happy to send you a self-addressed and stamped envelope.*
> *Thank you for your help with this.*
> Sincerely,
> 2. E-mail 2: *Hello! Well, I am quite a relieved, happy, though rather tired, little bunny – I have finished college! That feels pretty good to say. Obviously now the scary part comes cuz I really don't know what I'll be doing next but at the moment I'm just enjoying doing very little! I am going to do the TEFL course in July but Mom said that you were hardly going to be in Madrid then, most inconsiderate of you! So, instead, I'm going to Barcelona for the month. But, I really want to see you all, so I was wondering if there was a weekend in July that you were around so that I could come and visit, as long as you want me, obviously! I'd love to see you, it's been so long and I miss you all.*
> *Hope everything is ok with you and everyone. Say hello to them from me. Let me know all the news.*
> *Take care of yourself, love*

In this chapter, we have seen so far how we use language to achieve our goals in spoken interaction through the use of speech acts (direct and indirect), how we understand and expect others to be taking part in spoken interaction through the Cooperative Principle (and can use that knowledge to create meanings which go beyond the words spoken), and how we use positive and negative politeness strategies to mitigate possible face-threatening acts, as interaction involves a balance between our own needs and those of our interlocutors. We now can move deeper into the language itself, into the words and grammar (the lexicogrammar) we choose (and leave out) in spoken interaction.

2.4   The lexicogrammar of casual speech

2.4.1 Discourse markers

Before moving on to conversation analysis, we need to focus in on some of the particular aspects of the lexicogrammar of spoken language, of more casual speech. Many people cringe when they hear themselves on tape, in part because the quality and timbre of their voice sounds different to their ears, but also because they hear themselves saying things like *um, er, well, like, you know, I don't know* and *oh*. People sometimes think of language which incorporates these features as somehow deficient, as these bits of language are often not included in grammar books (which tend to focus on the written language). However, these **discourse markers** have their function in the spoken language, as they often signal the flow of the discourse; they provide hints as to how what is coming up can be related to what has been said before, or orient the listener/reader as they raise expectations of what is coming next. In this sense, they are similar to the discourse markers which are more typical of formal written language, such as *nevertheless* and *in addition*. In spoken interaction, discourse markers also serve an interpersonal function, as they allow us to preface something that perhaps we think our interlocutor might not want to hear, as in the following example, in which *well* prefaces disagreement:

> <u>Well</u>, *maybe that's not exactly what she said.*

We often find discourse markers occurring at the beginning of a turn, marking a boundary between topics:

> <u>Okay</u> <u>so</u> *that is one opinion about the economic impact.*
> <u>Now</u>, *how do you want to continue?*
> <u>Right</u>. *That's the end of that section.*

Discourse markers can also indicate a logical or temporal sequence (*'cos, then*), exemplification (*like*), reported speech (*like*), or that the speaker assumes shared knowledge (*you know*). Discourse markers also serve to soften the impact of what is being said, so that the speaker does not sound too definite or sure of him/herself (*well*). Sometimes they can serve more than one function simultaneously. While the functions of discourse markers in the written language are arguably more stable, in the spoken language we very much need to look at the discourse in order to determine the function of the marker within the context. A large number of studies have been carried out on discourse markers and their function in spoken interaction, so we will look at only a few here. In her seminal book entitled *Discourse Markers*, Deborah Schiffrin (1988) analyzes exchanges which include the marker *oh*, and suggests that this marker has a range of information management functions, showing speaker orientation to information, such as:

(a) Focusing attention (*Oh, would you just listen to this!*)
(b) Indicating repair (*Oh, wait a minute. I was wrong about that.*)
(c) Suggesting a reorientation in knowledge/marking receipt of new information (A: *They have the best ice creams.* B: *Oh, I didn't know that they served ice cream!*)

(d) Correcting a misassumption (A: *Could you drop me off on your way?* B: *Oh ... I didn't drive today.*)

While *oh* serves to indicate information state, *well*, according to Schiffrin (1987) serves to frame participation. *Well* tends to indicate that what is coming up is probably not in accord with what has been previously stated. Halliday and Hasan (1976: 269) suggest that *well* 'serves to indicate that what follows is in fact a response to what has preceded; in other words, it slips in quietly the respondent's claim to be answering the question'. It also serves to indicate a shift in topic.

Giuliana Diani examines *I don't know* and describes four different functions (usually in combination with other markers):

(a) Mitigating disagreement (A: *John's a pig, isn't he?* B: *Oh, I don't know ... he isn't always this out of control*).
(b) Indicating uncertainty, often because speakers are unwilling to commit themselves to a particular proposition. (A: *Do you agree with the change in policy?* B: *I don't know ... it might not be easy to follow ...*)
(c) Providing a filler, allowing speakers to hold the floor while organizing their thoughts. (*The problem is... I don't know... it's not been thought out as well as it could have been.*)
(d) Minimizing compliments (A: *You're looking so good these days.* B: *Oh, I don't know. I should really do something about my hair...*)

Simone Muller (2005) surveys several studies on *like*, and describes the following functions:

(a) Introducing something said previously, although not usually the direct words, but perhaps the thought or feeling behind the words (*And then she was like 'ohmigod! I love that movie!'*); this is often called the **quotative** function of like.
(b) Conveying approximation (*I finished it in like 5 minutes*)
(c) Introducing examples (*I prefer to watch team games, like basketball or hockey*).

We could further add that *like* serves to suggest openness in options, that what one is putting forward is just a possibility (*We could, like, paint it green*). We do need to distinguish the function of *like* as a discourse marker from its function as a preposition (*He's like a little kid*). This distinction in function underscores the importance of examining what the linguistic item in question is doing in the discourse in order to determine its function.

Muller also describes the functions of *you know*:

(a) Mitigating a face-threatening act
(b) Suggesting common ground or shared knowledge between speaker and listener
(c) Shifting to a new topic

Another function of discourse markers is to indicate that attention is being paid to the speaker, and to acknowledge that hearer has indeed listened and heard something. This is often the function of DMs such as *yeah* and *uh huh*.

Schiffrin (1988: 102) suggests that *well, okay* and *so* also serve to signal that closure is approximate, in case the hearer wishes to retrieve a previously instated topic, or to get something else in before the end of the conversation. Ute Lenk discusses the function of *anyway* and suggests that it serves to close down one topic and lead to a previously included topic or a completely new one. Thus, it is important to look at the role these markers play in the interaction taking place, in terms of information management, turn-taking and floor-holding, as well as interpersonal positioning.

If we look at the functions of discourse markers in the spoken language mentioned so far, perhaps we can stop feeling that their use is extraneous to our attempts to communicate!

EXERCISE 2.9

What is the function of the words in bold in the following text? Suggest the functions of these discourse markers in the context of the conversation.

1. Carol: **Oh** ... um, no, Mom.. *I was thinking about actually staying a little bit longer in Rome.. an ... or maybe* **like** *traveling around Europe for a little bit.. umm*
2. Mom: **o:kay:**[3] ... *How long would you be planning on this trip being? And how are you planning on paying for it?*
3. Carol: *umm ... umm..* **well** *I don't know,* **like**, *it depends on how long we want to stay here.. maybe,* **like**, *a couple weeks or so?. And..* **I dunno like** *I can pay you back?* **Like, I dunno** *I probably need some money.* **But** *I would..* **like***.. maybe I could get some here.*
4. Mom: **Yeah, OK** ...
5. Carol: *Or umm* ...
6. Mom: **Ok well** *are you just planning on making these trips alone?* **I mean**, *Europe isn't your backyard. You can get lost. I need to know plans here, Carol.*

---

3.   : means that the syllable is lengthened.

7. Carol: *No I don't think I'd be alone.* **I mean**, *I'd have,* **you know** *...
there's a couple other girls ... that would wanna travel. And* **I dunno**
*... an there's like some guys there too so it's not like I'm gonna be
dangerous in the city or anything.* **But yeah, you know**.. *I'd be fine.*

EXERCISE 2.10

Analyze the following extract and suggest possible meanings of the
discourse markers in bold

'You know, we're Harvard. We're **like** the most prominent national
institution. And I think we should be entitled to ... we should be able
to get anyone. And in my opinion, we're settling here.' (From Smith,
Tovia 'Rowling's Harvard Speech Doesn't Entrance All', *The Morning
Edition*, NPR Radio, June 6, 2008, which reported on reactions to J.
K. Rowling's selection as commencement speaker).

EXERCISE 2.11

A search online for TV scripts provides a wealth of data for the analysis
of spoken discourse markers. While they are scripted data, they can still
provide us with contextualized examples of their use. Search online for a
TV script, perhaps one of your favorites, and choose a passage of dialogue
(a complete scene or 12–14 turns). Print or copy the passage, highlight
any discourse markers, and explain their function in the exchange.

EXERCISE 2.12

Take some time to listen to some conversations this week (real or scripted)
and jot down any discourse markers that you notice. Take note of the
context of use as well.

All of these examples illustrate the many functions discourse markers
serve in helping us to make meaning when interacting with others, and
naturally spoken discourse sounds empty without them. To test this, remove
all of the discourse markers from the script you analyzed for Exercise 2.11
and say the dialogue out loud. Much of the interpersonal work that happens
in conversation gets lost without the discourse markers. We move on now
to another feature of naturally spoken discourse which adds to the creation
of jointly constructed conversation.

2.4.2 Vague language

In casual conversation, we often use less precision, and thus we can sound vague. Maryann Overstreet and George Yule in their (1997) article 'On being inexplicit and stuff in contemporary American English', draw on Homer Simpson's imitation of young people for an example of this kind of language: 'It's like, they're all stupid and stuff'. Indeed, often the younger generation is perceived as being rather less than articulate because of this feature of informal spoken language. However, Overstreet and Yule go on to point out that vague language helps create solidarity, shared experience, and social connectedness.

2.4.3 Ellipsis

What do you notice about the following conversations?

1. A: *Going to the game?* B: *Dunno, depends on the weather.*
2. A: *Gotta sec?* B: *Sure*
3. A: *Good to see you!* B: *yeah...*
4. A: *Gotta run.* B: *Okey dokey. Talk to ya later.*

In addition to the contracted versions of *don't know* and *got to*, you might notice the lack of subjects and sometimes verbs, as in *(Are you) going to the game? (I) don't know, (it) depends on the weather.* According to Shigeko Nariyama (2006), this kind of ellipsis is characteristic of informal spoken English, with some differences across dialects (e.g. it is more common in British English), and it exists not just because of economy or speed of delivery. Rather ellipsis, as with other features of language, serves to aid in conveying certain kinds of meaning, such as establishing an informal interaction with familiar participants, while also allowing for indeterminacy, and thus a sense that the interlocutors are jointly constructing knowledge.

2.4.4 Intonation

How we say what we say in terms of length and pitch of syllables conveys as much, if not more, meaning as what we say. In all languages, natural speech has rhythm, which allows us to perceive some languages as being more staccato and others more melodic. This is because extended speech tends to have a regular beat. Different languages fit their syllables into the beat in different ways. Some languages are called **syllable-timed**, where all the syllables tend to be more or less of the same length (e.g. French, Spanish, Chinese). In other languages, known as **stress-timed** (or **foot-timed**) languages, there tends to be a regular length of time between *stressed* syllables, and thus the length of the syllables varies, since a **foot** can consist of varying numbers of syllables. English is a noticeably stress-timed language. We **stress** our syllables by varying the pitch, length and/ or loudness.

In English, each foot begins with a stressed syllable, and contains any number of following unstressed syllables. A foot can begin with what is known as a **silent ictus**, which indicates a lack of a stressed syllable, indicated by a caret (^).

^ she /	turned her /	gaze onto the /	fabulous /	red /	Porsche.
1	2	3	4	5	6

In this example, we see that the first foot contains a silent ictus and 1 unstressed syllable, the second contains 2 syllables, the third foot contains 4 syllables, the fourth foot contains 3 syllables, and the fifth and sixth feet contain 1 syllable each. In English, we vary which syllable receives the salient stress; usually it is the **content words** (or words which express something related to experience) whose syllables are stressed, while **function words** (or words which convey grammatical relationships) are often weakened, which explains the lack of stress on *she, her, onto,* and *the* in the above utterance. At the same time, we tend to stress the words which are most important in conveying our message. The following message might receive a different stress pattern:

^ she /	turned her /	gaze onto /	my /	fabulous /	Porsche.
1	2	3	4	5	6

Thus, we weaken syllables by shortening their length, and we stress syllables by lengthening them and increasing pitch. The decision to do so depends somewhat on the grammaticality of the words involved: lexical items with experiential content tend to receive stress, while the functional words do not. However, the decision of what is stressed depends very much on the intent of the speaker. Look at the difference in stress of *that* in the following:

(a) Mary thinks that reading is difficult.
(b) Mary thinks THAT reading is difficult.

In (a) *that* is a function word which introduces a noun clause (*Mary thinks reading is difficult*); *that* is not stressed and actually the vowel is pronounced as a **schwa** (an unstressed vowel – see Section 2.6.2.3). In (b), *that* is a determiner which refers to a particular reading (*that reading, not this one*), a specific text, and therefore is stressed, and the vowel is pronounced fully (as in *bat*). Thus, the content which the word is intended to convey in the utterance within a given context will determine whether or not it is stressed. Part of the decision is related to a need for contrast, as happens with *can/can't* in English; think of how you might utter the following B responses:

> A: *Can someone give me a hand this weekend either on Saturday or Sunday? I'm moving house.*
> B: *I can do it either day.*
>   or
> B: *I can't do it this weekend.*

In this situation, we tend to stress the negative form in the second response.

It is clear, then, that part of the function of intonation in English is to package information in a way that makes the intended message as clear as possible to our interlocutors. Information, when taken in a technical grammatical sense (Halliday 1995), refers to the tension between what the speaker assumes can be taken as known or predictable (Given) and what the speaker assumes is not known, unpredictable, or worthy of special focus (New).

Is your name Susan?

No, it's	*Anne*
Given	New

Normally, but not always, the Given precedes the New, and the New is marked by tonic prominence; that is there is one element in each information unit which receives the greatest pitch movement, and this element is said to be carrying the information focus (marked in bold in the example here):

> *In this job, Anne, we're working with silver. Now silver needs to have love.*

// ^ *now / silver /*	*needs to have / **love** //*
Given	New

(Halliday 1995: 297)

EXERCISE 2.13

Prominence. On which word would the stress go in each of the following examples, depending on the question or situation? Underline the word. 1(a) has been done for you as an example.

1. *This is my new black leather jacket.*
   (a) Is that your old black leather jacket? *This is my **new** black leather jacket.*
   (b) Is that my new black leather jacket?
   (c) Is that other jacket your new black leather jacket?
   (d) Is that your new black naugahyde jacket?
   (e) That isn't your new black leather jacket.

2. *My sister lives in Chicago, but she has a house in Florida.*
   (a) Does your sister live in Florida?
   (b) Where does your sister live?
   (c) Do you know anyone who lives in Chicago?
   (d) Does your sister have a house in Chicago?

3. *Both of my parents were photographers.*
   (a) Who was a photographer, your mother or your father?
   (b) What did your parents do?
   (c) Neither of your parents was a photographer.
   (d) Both of your wife's parents were photographers, right?

EXERCISE 2.14

Prominence. On which word would the stress go in the question below, depending on the different scenarios in 1–4?
Do you have a pen I could borrow?
1. I'm asking you for the first time.
2. I've asked you ten times, and you won't give me a clear answer.
3. I've asked a lot of other people.
4. You were going to give me a pen, but you can't find one.

EXERCISE 2.15

New Information: Stress is usually given to new, and not repeated, information. Where would the stress go in each line of the following dialogue? Rewrite the dialogue in your exercise notebook, underlining the word you think would be stressed in conversation.
1. A: *Let's go to a restaurant.*
2. B: *Which restaurant?*
3. A: *An Italian restaurant.*
4. B: *We went to an Italian restaurant yesterday.*

> 5. A: *No, yesterday we went to an Argentinian restaurant.*
> 6. B: *But they served Italian food.*
> 7. A: *I thought you liked Italian food.*
> 8. B: *I do, but I don't want to eat it every day.*
> 9. A: *Okay. What kind of restaurant do you want to go to?*
> 10. B: *A Japanese restaurant.*

2.4.5 Intonation patterns

In using intonation, we create **contours** or **patterns** that allow us to make clear what we want our listeners to focus on; we also use intonation to convey our communicative function. Consider the difference between:

> *You're going.* (statement)
> *You're going?* (question)

The rise and fall of pitch throughout is called its intonation contour. Researchers on intonation in English identify four main patterns of ending a tone group:

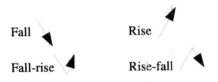

Often, meanings are expressed through conventional uses of intonation contours. Thus we can interpret meaning according to the final intonation contour of the clause, as the examples illustrate:

You're going (there's no two ways about it!)   *You're going* (what?? so soon??)

I can't believe it!   *I can't believe it!*
What?   *What?*
Spain won!   *I said I can't believe it!*

The two examples ending in rise contours seem to suggest a more open-ended tentative nature to the utterance, and the two ending in fall, a more closed, final tone. Research into how we use intonation suggests that when disagreeing with someone, speakers of English tend to use a more open tone, a rising tone, to avoid sounding too overtly in disagreement with their speaker. Thus, a falling tone often makes a person sound rude or harsh.

EXERCISE 2.16

Map the possible final intonation contours with which you could imagine yourself saying the following. What different meanings would you convey? Rewrite the statements, indicating the ending pitch of the utterances along with differences in meaning, as shown in this example:

Yeah, Right   sarcasm: I disagree with what you are saying

Yeah... Right growing understanding. 'Ah, I see...'

Yeah. Right?   on second thought, I'm not sure I think so...

1. John loves Mary.
2. Mary's studying medicine.
3. You're not wearing that.

Now that we have a set of linguistic tools available to us which we can apply to natural spoken discourse in order to discover how we use language to create different kinds of meanings and relationships, we move on to a specific way of analyzing talk in interaction.

2.5   The analysis of talk in interaction (conversation analysis)

2.5.1 Background

Conversation analysis (CA) took its inspiration from ethnomethodology, a field of sociology, developed initially by Harold Garfinkel, which examines how people make sense of their lived experience, how they demonstrate that sense, and how they create shared orderliness. Ethnomethodologists see social order as something built up by people through their participation in interactive events, yet it is something that we take for granted. Thus we often cannot see the ways in which our recurring social events are constructed, and ethnomethodologists collect data in order to focus on not so much *what* it is that participants do, but rather *how* they do it: how they demonstrate understanding of a situation through their involvement in furthering procedures and providing different kinds of responses as events unfold.

Through work by leaders in the field of CA, Harvey Sacks, Emmanuel A. Schegloff and Gail Jefferson, in the 1960s and 1970s, CA became established as a field of study in its own right. Talk in interaction is very different from written academic discourse (or even speeches) in that it is jointly constructed by the participants involved (although we will examine the interactive nature of written language in Chapter 3), and it does not follow a pre-set script, as we cannot predict (usually!) the ways in which our interlocutors are going to respond, nor how we will then respond to their conduct and intentions. We are creating social action as we interact, and we constantly analyze our interlocutors' conduct as we participate; that we are analyzing as we interact is actually evidenced by the ways in which we respond. At the same time, when we are involved in a conversation, we are usually quite orderly about it, as we follow a set of unspoken guidelines. CA analyzes and describes the sequential patterns of interaction, whether in institutional settings (in the school, doctor's surgery, courts or elsewhere) or in casual conversation, as it unfolds. It analyzes responses to turns according to what these responses suggest about the speakers' understanding of the social event, of the intentions of their interlocutors and of the goals of the particular interactive event.

2.5.2 Turn allocation

One aspect of talk in interaction that CA has focused on is the allocation of turns, as it seems speakers surprisingly know most of the time when they can take the floor or when it is their turn to speak. CA focuses on two components in turn-taking: the **turn constructional component** and the **turn allocational component** (see Sacks *et al.* 1974). The turn constructional component consists of the basic units which comprise turns and which are known as **turn constructional units (TCUs)**. TCUs are recognizable as carrying out a social action within a given context, and may be composed of different elements, linguistic or non-linguistic (whole sentences, words, shoulder shrugs). Usually, a speaker gets one TCU, at the end of which a **transition relevance place (TRP)** occurs. The **turn allocational component** describes how turns are allocated among participants: whether current speaker selects next speaker, current speaker selects self, or next speaker selects self.

Often, the utterance of one speaker conditions in some way the response of another speaker. These TCUs are known as **adjacency pairs**; in this type of TCU, the utterance of one speaker makes a particular kind of response likely. There are several types of adjacency pairs, for example:

greeting–greeting
question–answer
apology-acceptance/rejection
compliment-acknowledgment/rejection
offer-acceptance/rejection
request-acceptance/refusal
opinion-agreement/disagreement
invitation-acceptance/rejection
comment-acknowledgment

Adjacency pairs thus typically consist of **first-pair parts** and **second-pair parts**. Second-pair parts can be **preferred** or **dispreferred**. Preferred responses are usually brief and straightforward (because they are expected):

A: *Can you do it?*
B: *Sure.*

In this exchange, A puts forth a request, and B responds with the second part of the adjacency pair in what we know is a preferred response type to the request because it is brief and unmitigated. We know something is being put forth as a dispreferred response, on the other hand, when the second-pair part is delayed or qualified in some way. Our discourse markers come into play here, because dispreferred responses often make recourse to them, in order to express token agreement, apology, etc.

A: *Can you do it?*
B: *Well, um (2) no, sorry!*

The number in the brackets in B's response indicates a 2-second pause (see below for transcription conventions). There are other TCUs which can put off the second-pair part, such as **insertion sequences, side sequences, gist**, and **upshot**. We begin by looking at an example of an insertion sequence, the content of which relates to the social action which is taking place:

Insertion sequence:
T1   A: *You going to the party?*
T2   B: *You?*
T3   A: *Yes.*
T4   B: *Yes.*

B's final response in Turn 4 is to A's question in Turn 1. However, B's final response is conditioned by the insertion sequence in 2 and 3.

In a side sequence, on the other hand, the social action is different from the talk in which it is embedded (note that overlap in talk is indicated through the use of square brackets):

Side sequence:
1. A: *oh, Sally told me that her dog*   [*died*
2. B: [*where's the peeler?*
3. A: *In the top*   [*drawer over there*
4. B: [*Oh, that's too bad.*

Turns T1 and T4 form an adjacency pair of comment-acknowledgment about the death of a friend's dog, while turns T2 and T3 have nothing to do with that exchange, but rather have to do with the event of preparing food that is taking place alongside of the talk.

Gist allows for clearing up any possible misunderstanding in terms of the semantic meaning of the language used, in order for the social action to continue unfolding:

Gist:
1. A: *Can you help me next weekend?*
2. B: *um, do you mean this coming weekend, as in the day after tomorrow, or the following weekend?*
3. A: *the following one*
4. B: *sure, not a problem!*

In this exchange, note that the side sequence does set up a possible dispreferred response in Turn 4. In Turn 1, A requests help. B's request for clarification in Turn 2 allows him to possibly say 'No' in Turn 4, with the explanation for that refusal residing in his possibly not being free on a given weekend.

Upshot allows for clarification of the pragmatic meaning behind the language used:

Upshot:
1. A: *My back's killing me (1.0) and I uh I gotta get my stuff moved by Sunday at the latest.*
2. B: *Hey, you mean you might need some help with that?*
3. A: *Well, yeah, if maybe you could?*
4. B: *Sure, not a problem!*

Note how the indirect speech act in T1 allows for different possibilities in this conversation. For example, if as the action unfolds, A becomes concerned with B's negative face (B's desire not to be put out in any way), then A can always say in Turn 3 something like 'Naw, I just want to gripe a bit'. Or if B wants to avoid A making a direct request, B could, in Turn 2, say something like 'B: I'm sorry to hear that. If I weren't going away this weekend, I'd offer to help'. This desire to avoid face-threatening acts often is evident in the use of **presequences**:

> **Presequence:**
> 1. A: *You busy?*
> 2. B: *Fraid so. Why?*
> 3. A: *Just wondering ... I'll come back later ...*

The presequence in Turn 1 allows A not to have to request an invasion of B's time or privacy.

Another concept which conversation analysts focus on is **repair**, or the way in which interlocutors work towards solving problems in understanding in conversation. Repair can be **self** or **other** initiated; Schegloff, Jefferson and Sacks point out that there is a preference for self-initiated repair, such as in:

> **Repair:**
> Roger: *We're just workin on a different*
> →   *thing, the same thing.*
> (from Schegloff *et al.* 1977: 370)

2.5.3 Transcription conventions

Conversation analysts follow a set of conventions in an attempt to capture relevant features of conversations. Keep in mind that (as we will also see with phonetics) the map is never the territory: a written down conversation misses much of the whole action that is taking place, especially with respect to tone of voice, gaze, speed of talk, etc. A very full set of transcription symbols exists in order to convey as much information as possible so that we can study talk in interaction. We will only mention a few here (for more information, see the references listed at the end of this chapter):

Table 2.1: Transcription symbols

(.)		very brief pause
(.3) (2.6)		pauses of a specific length (.3 seconds, 2.6 seconds)
A: *word*	[*word*	aligned square brackets indicate overlapping talk
B:	[*word*	
.hh		in-breath
hh		out-breath
wo(h)*rd*		(h) suggests that the word 'laughter' bubbling within it
wor-		dash indicates truncated word
(*word*)		parentheses around words indicate an estimate if sound is unclear
A: *word*=		equal sign indicates no discernible pause between two speakers' turns
B: =*word*		

We can also map on the intonation contours to provide fuller information of the communicative intention of the speaker, and CA has its own set of conventions for this purpose:

Table 2.2: Transcription symbols: Intonation

word	underlined sounds are stressed
WORD	talk that is markedly louder than surrounding talk is in all caps
:	colon indicates lengthening of previous sound
hello:	underlining of letter before colon indicates rise
.	period indicates falling intonation
?	question mark indicates rising intonation
,	comma indicates slightly rising, but suggests an incomplete intonation contour
¿	upside-down question mark indicates more than a slight rise, but not as high as ?
↑↓	arrows are used to indicate sudden rises and falls

Thus, we can indicate different intonation contours by combining these symbols:

Hello:. (Liddicoat 2007: 22)

In this example, a rise happens on the 'o' (indicated by the underlining of that sound followed by the colon, which indicates lengthening) and then a fall (indicated by the period).

Not all transcribers include information on all of the intonation contours in the utterances, and often only those that deviate from expectations are included. We can use symbols to add on more layers of contextual information, such as gaze, and, indeed, transcription symbols exist to capture when someone focuses their gaze on an interlocutor (often at a TRP) or when they focus their gaze elsewhere (often while holding the floor).

This section on conversation analysis has described some of the findings of conversation analysts who have focused on English. Different languages and cultures may organize their talk in interaction in different ways; aspects of interaction, such as intonation, silence, and gaze, for example, may be interpreted in different ways. Only by focusing on how the participants respond and jointly construct the social action can we know what implicit rules people follow in order to maintain the social order accepted by the speech community to which they belong.

EXERCISE 2.17

Conversations for analysis: analyze the following conversations in terms of CA, explaining the understanding of the different turns by the speakers involved.

Example Conversation

T1 C: *So I was wondering would you be in your office on Monday (.) by any chance?*

T2 (2.0)

T3 C: *Probably not.*

T4 R: *Hmmm yes =*

T5 C: *= You would?*

T6 R: *Ya*

T7 C: *So if we came by could you give us ten minutes of your time?*
(Levinson 1983: 320)

C initiates by asking a question (obviously the start of a presequence as C wants to ask a favor). Given that R does not respond in turn 2, C assumes that R is pausing because he is going to give a dispreferred response to the question; that is, C assumes R will say 'no'. T4 is a preferred response to the presequence question in T1. T5 and T6 are a repetition of this presequence, allowing C to ask the favor in T7. Note: based on the conversation, we can not explain why R did not answer right away. Conversation analysis only accounts for what can be inferred from the way the interactants respond and interact, not based on frames of minds of speakers or any other contextual factors.

1. (overheard as C and D looked at a painting in an art gallery)

    C: *i really like that*

    (3.0)

    C: *well i mean i think it's the type of work that kinda grows on you*
    (Turnbull, 2003: 153)

2.

    T1 A: *May I have a bottle of Mich?*

    T2 B: *Are you twenty one?*

    T3 A: *No*

    T4 B: *No*
    (Merritt 1976: 333)

3.

    T1 C: *How ya doin =*

    T2   *=say what 'r you doing?*

    T3 R: *Well we're going out. Why?*

    T4 C: *Oh, I was just gonna say come out and come over here an' talk this evening, but if you're going out you can't very well do that*
    (Atkinson and Drew 1979: 143)

4.

> T1 L: *But y'know single beds 'r awfully thin ta sleep on.*
> T2 S: *What?*
> T3 L: *Single beds//they're-*
> T4 S: *Y'mean narrow?*
> T5 L: *They're awfully narrow//yeah*
> (Roger and Bull 1989: 253)

2.6   Speech sounds

2.6.1 Introduction

Take a few moments to listen to a conversation or a radio or TV program without focusing on the meaning but rather on the sounds being emitted. You will obviously hear strings of sounds which add up to form words, and you may also hear clicks, sighs and exclamations, such as 'ow!', 'wow!' and 'uh oh'. Not all of these sounds are considered part of the English language; clicks, for example, do not take part in the formation of strings of sounds which add up to meaningful expression. They do, obviously, create meaning, as anyone on the receiving end of a disapproving click knows. However, they do not form part of the English language system; that is, in English, they do not combine with other sounds to form significant meaningful patterns. Here, we will leave aside for now clicks and sighs and focus on those speech sounds which we use, in conjunction with other sounds, to create meaning through the English language system. **Phonetics** is the study of these speech sounds, which are called **phones**.

Our vocal apparatus is capable of making an incredible number of different kinds of sounds. UCLA's Phonological Segment Inventory Database (UPSID) contains data on 451 of the world's languages and has inventoried more than 600 consonants and more than 200 vowel sounds. Obviously, no one language draws on all of these speech sounds; however, the number may vary widely. For example, the Khoisan language !Xu, spoken in southern Africa, draws on over 100 sounds (including clicks, which are meaningful speech sounds in !Xu) while the South-American language Múra-Pirahã, uses just a dozen. The number of sounds available has no effect on the possibilities for meaning, as the sounds can be combined in any number of complex ways.

Our first step in thinking about speech sounds is to try to step away from thinking about sounds as letters of the alphabet. We can do this in a playful way by looking at **mondegreens**, homophonic phrases which are heard as a different set of words and meaning than that originally intended. The word comes from the American writer Sylvia Wright, who, as a child, heard the line 'and laid him on the green', from Percy's *Reliques*, as 'Lady Mondegreen'. These lines can be quite entertaining, and there is actually a game in English called Mad Gabs, in which players are given a mondegreen and have to guess what its phonetic counterpart might be (e.g if you repeat 'Dew wino hue' out loud over and over, you might start hearing 'Do I know you').

EXERCISE 2.18

Many times we mishear lyrics from songs, such as 'outright offensive' for 'out riding fences' (Eagles, 'Desperado') or 'round John Virgin' for 'round yon Virgin' (Silent Night). List some of your own misheard lyrics, and explain why you think we hear what is not actually being sung in these cases.

Mondegreens highlight the fact that English spelling and pronunciation have a very tentative relationship with each other. Alphabetic writing systems are designed to capture sound; that is individual letters are used to represent sounds, and those sounds (and, by correspondence, letters) are strung together to form words which represent objects and concepts. We can compare this type of system to others, such as hieroglyphics or other types of representational pictographic systems, where symbols represent objects and concepts, rather than sounds. However, in alphabetic systems, our graphic symbols are not always representative of the sounds we utter, as we know from words such as 'cough', 'bough', 'tough' and 'through', to mention just a few. In a perfect phonological alphabet, each sound would correspond directly with one symbol, in which case we would be able to predict the exact pronunciation of a word we saw written, and the exact spelling of a word we heard spoken.

For this purpose, linguists have designed a phonetic alphabet, in which one symbol represents one sound. The alphabet, called the **International Phonetic Alphabet**, contains symbols for all of the language sounds of the world. By focusing on how these sounds are produced and then represented through the IPA, we can illustrate the differences in pronunciation between different dialects (what we often call *accents*). For example, while British, American and Australian speakers might all write 'latter' in the same way, the way the sounds uttered differ. That difference cannot be caught through our standard spelling system (especially if we wish to differentiate that word from 'ladder'). It can by using the IPA.

Here, for now, we will only concentrate on the sounds used in the English language, pointing out some broad dialectal differences along the way (and we will return to dialects in Chapter 7). We will first analyze the sounds by examining how they are physically produced, which places us in the realm of **articulatory phonetics**.

2.6.2 Articulatory phonetics

The study of how we use physiological process in order to make speech sounds is called articulatory phonetics. We produce speech sounds by moving air about our bodies. In English, the sounds we make are **egressive pulmonic sounds**, egressive because we push air *out* of the body, and pulmonic because the air is produced from the lungs. The **egressive pulmonic** airstream mechanism is responsible for producing the majority of the world's language sounds, and all of the sounds in English. There are other airstream mechanisms; for example, we can move air around in our mouths. When we inhale while making a speech sound, such as in the case of **implosives** and **clicks**, the sound is classified as **ingressive**.

In the case of our egressive pulmonic speech sounds, as we take a breath, the vocal folds (or vocal cords), the two bands of muscular tissue located directly above the trachea, come together. As the air that is held in the lungs is gradually released, it passes through the lightly closed vocal folds, causing vibration and producing the voice. Most of the sounds of the voice pass through the throat and then into the mouth, while others pass into the nose for nasal sounds such as 'm,' 'n' and 'ng'. The lips, tongue, palate and jaw come into play in precise ways to produce our distinct speech sounds.

For example, try to produce the sound that we associate with the letter 'p', but without any other sound attached to it (that is, no vowel sound before or after). As you move air out of your lungs and then through your mouth, you will feel your lips come together and apart very quickly, and you will probably feel a puff of air escape from your lips as you force them apart (you can also try this while at the same time holding a piece of paper in front of your mouth, in which case you will see the paper move). Obstruction of the air flow in some way is what defines a **consonant** in language.

Obviously, there are different ways of stopping the air flow, depending on which part(s) of your vocal tract you use to stop it, in other words the point or place of articulation, as well as on the manner in which you stop it. Focusing on points and manners of articulation give us the **phonetic features** of the sounds we make in producing spoken language.

Before going on to look at phonetic features, it is worth pointing out again that it is important to try to think in *sounds*, and not in *letters*. As we have seen with attempting to represent spoken conversation in writing, producing the way we articulate speech sounds in a highly exact way in written form is essentially an impossible task. A string of written symbols representing someone's spoken words will never give us every single nuance as when we hear them utter those words. At the same time, the IPA does provide highly valuable information through its standardization of all the world's speech sounds into a comprehensive set. This information can then be used by speech pathologists and therapists, foreign language teachers and learners, lexicographers, actors, singers, and interpreters, and by linguists who strive to inventory the speech sounds of rapidly disappearing languages.

The IPA gives us a way to write down sounds using symbols which attempt to capture the phonetic features of each sound. Our alphabet also attempts to do that, although, as we have seen, not always very efficiently! As an example, think of the sound at the beginning of 'cell'. It is the same as the sound at the beginning of 'sell', and both of those sounds are represented in the IPA as [s]. Think also of the sound at the beginning of 'chill' and of 'cello'. We use two letters (or a digraph) to represent that sound in '**c h** ill'; however, it is only one sound, and is represented in the IPA as [tʃ] (note that we use [ ] to enclose speech sounds as represented in the IPA). We will strive to inventory the sounds of English in the upcoming sections. Along the way, we will at times make reference to dialectal differences between General American (GA, or broadcast American English – that standard mid-western accent, which many people feel is the most 'neutral' of American accents), Received Pronunciation (RP – what many perceive to be the most prestigious British accent), and other national varieties and regional varieties. The following exercise will help you get started.

EXERCISE 2.19

You say 'tomaydo' and I say 'tomahto'. Make a list of words which you have heard others pronounce differently from you.

2.6.2.1 Features of consonants in English: Point of articulation

Consonants are produced by airflow being obstructed through two articulators coming into contact with each other at a point of articulation. For example, in producing the sound [p], you bring your lips together. Thus, [p] is a bilabial consonant. Before continuing, try this exercise. Look at the diagram and try

EXERCISE 2.20

Analyze Figure 2.3 to determine the various points of articulation of the consonants. Then, match the consonant with its point of articulation by completing 1–6 below with the corresponding sounds. The exercise has been started for you.

Figure 2.3 Vocal Apparatus

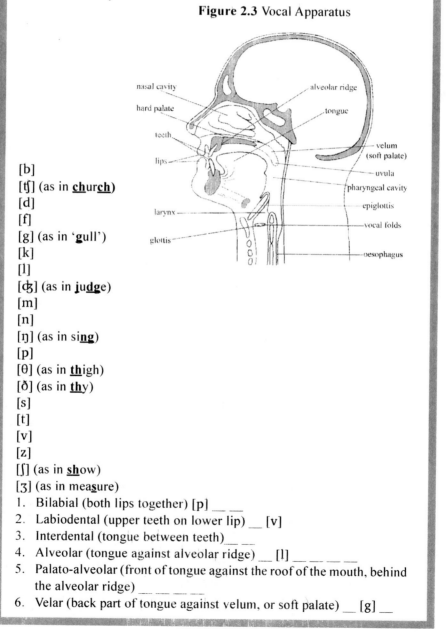

[b]
[tʃ] (as in **chur<u>ch</u>**)
[d]
[f]
[g] (as in '**g**ull')
[k]
[l]
[ʤ] (as in **ju<u>dg</u>e**)
[m]
[n]
[ŋ] (as in si**ng**)
[p]
[θ] (as in **th**igh)
[ð] (as in **th**y)
[s]
[t]
[v]
[z]
[ʃ] (as in **sh**ow)
[ʒ] (as in mea**s**ure)

1. Bilabial (both lips together) [p] ___ ___
2. Labiodental (upper teeth on lower lip) ___ [v]
3. Interdental (tongue between teeth) ___ ___
4. Alveolar (tongue against alveolar ridge) ___ [l] ___ ___ ___ ___
5. Palato-alveolar (front of tongue against the roof of the mouth, behind the alveolar ridge) ___ ___ ___ ___
6. Velar (back part of tongue against velum, or soft palate) ___ [g] ___

to pinpoint the place where air flow is obstructed in order to produce each consonant sound you make in your language.

There are other consonant sounds which we produce in English, such as [h], which is a glottal fricative, and [ɹ], as in *red*, [j] (as in *y*our), and [w]. Along with [l], these are called **approximants**. In making these sounds, we only partially obstruct the air flow, creating some turbulence. Thus, in order to describe them, we must move on to discussing **manner of articulation**, and our discussion of approximants will continue in the next section.

2.6.2.2 Features of consonants in English: Manner of articulation

The point at which we produce our consonant sounds, or the point of articulation, combines with other features involving *how* the sounds are produced to give us our distinct speech sounds, which we call the manner of articulation. We begin our discussion of manner of articulation with the approximants.

Approximants

> [w] made by rounding the lips, for example in **w**itch (so it is also known as a <u>bilabial</u> approximant)
> [j] made by flattening the lips, almost in a smile, as in **y**ear, as the blade of the tongue moves up towards the palate (so it is also known as a <u>palatal</u> approximant)
> [ɹ] in American English, this sound is articulated with either the tip or the blade of the tongue against the alveolar ridge, partially obstructing the air flow, as in **r**eal (an <u>alveolar</u> approximant)
> [l] produced by placing the tongue at the alveolar ridge, while letting air go around its sides, such as in **l**ip (a <u>lateral</u> approximant)

We have seen that, with the approximants, air is partially obstructed as it flows through the vocal tract. Think about how air flow is obstructed in the case of [p], [f], [m], and [tʃ] (as in *pill, fill, mill* and *chill*). You might notice the following:

> [p] air is completely stopped and then released; this type of consonant is called a **plosive**, or a **stop**.
> [f] air flow is never completely obstructed, as the air is forced steadily through the articulation point; this type of consonant is called a **fricative**. Note that the sound [h] is produced by tightening the glottis slightly while the air flows through (a glottal fricative, although many linguists feel that it has lost it fricative nature, and thus is more of an approximant)

[tʃ]: (as in *chill*) it begins as a plosive, and ends as a fricative: this type of consonant is called an **affricate**.
[m]: air flow is redirected through the nose; this type of consonant is called a **nasal**.

EXERCISE 2.21

Classify the sounds according to their manner of articulation.
(P = Plosive, F = Fricative, A = Affricate, N = Nasal
1. [b] _____
2. [d] _____
3. [f] _____
4. [g] (as in 'gull') _____
5. [k] _____
6. [ʤ] (as in judge) _____
7. [m] _____
8. [n] _____
9. [ŋ] (as in sing) _____
10. [θ] (as in thigh) _____
11. [ð] (as in thy) _____
12. [s] _____
13. [z] _____
14. [ʃ] (as in show) _____
15. [ʒ] (as in measure) _____

As we produce these sounds, there are further differences in the manner in which they are articulated. Take the sounds [p] and [b], for instance. They are both bilabial plosives, so why do we hear 'bill' and 'pill' differently? Take also [f] and [v], both labiodental fricatives, or [tʃ] and [ʤ], both palatal affricates, yet we can distinguish the final sounds if someone says 'Mitch' or 'midge'. This is because in the second set of each of these pairs, the vocal cords are vibrating, producing **voicing**. Sounds like [b], [v] and [ʤ] are **voiced consonants**.

Nasals are voiced consonants, as are some of our approximants such as [j], [l], [ɹ], and [w]. However, in the case of the latter, voicing is not always the case for all speakers of English. In some dialects, the initial sound in the words 'wine' and 'whine', 'witch' and 'which' are pronounced the same; this sound [w] is voiced. In other dialects, they are pronounced differently. If you pronounce the initial sound of 'whine' or 'which' while blowing air through your lips, then you produce the unvoiced counterpart, or [ʍ].

EXERCISE 2.22

Fill in the chart.
For each consonant, give its point and manner of articulation, and then give its voiced counterpart.

Sound	Point of articulation	Manner of articulation	Voiced counterpart
[p]	bilabial	plosive	[b]
[f]			
[k]			
[t]			
[s]			
[ʃ]			
[tʃ]			
[θ]			

Our inventory of English consonant sounds is not quite complete, as there are other sounds which we produce in uttering words and phrases. One of these sounds is that which is produced at the beginning of words like 'hue' and 'human', in many dialects of English. Pronounce those words and try to isolate that beginning sound, and think about what you are doing with your mouth. Some people pronounce that initial sound in 'hue' (or 'huge') the same as they would for the initial sound of 'yew', which is represented in the IPA as [j]. Others pronounce the initial sound as two sounds, [h j]. For others, the tongue goes up towards the palate, while the air is forced through the area between. This produces a palatal fricative, represented in the IPA as [ç].

Another consonant sound which we produce in some varieties of English is the alveolar flap [ɾ]. This is the middle consonant sound in the words 'latter' and 'ladder', which are homophones for many speakers of North American English. It is also used in American English instead of [t] in words like 'bottle'.

Another sound that you may not be aware that you produce is the glottal stop [ʔ]. Think of the sound you make before the vowel sounds in the exclamation 'uh oh', or before the initial vowel sound in 'apple'. This is produced by closing the glottis tightly, which creates a brief silence followed by a slight choke or cough-like explosive sound when released. In some varieties of British English, the glottal stop is the sound produced instead of a [t] or the flap [ɾ] in words like 'bottle'.

EXERCISE 2.23

You can now fill in the chart below with the consonant sounds of English discussed so far. Include a word which exemplifies the given sound. (A few have been done for you.)

Figure 2.4 English Consonants

| place→ ↓manner | LABIAL | | CORONAL | | | DORSAL | | Glottal |
	Bilabial	Labio-dental	Inter-dental	Alveolar	Palato-alveolar	Palatal	Velar	
Nasal								
+voice	[ ]			[ ]			[ ]	
-voice	[ ]			[ ]			[ ]	[ʔ] ʔapple
Plosive								
+voice	[ ]			[ ]			[ ]	
-voice		[ ]	[ ]	[ ]	[ ]			[h] hill**
Fricative								
+voice		[ ]	[ ]	[ ]	[ ]	[ç] huge*		
-voice	[ ]*							
Approximant								
+voice	[w] witch			[ ]		[ ]		
-voice					[ ]			
Affricate								
+voice					[ ]			
Flap								
+voice				[ ]*				
Lateral approximant +voice				[ ]				

That completes our description of the consonant sounds of English for the moment. Before going on to the vowels, and in order to review the sounds in terms of their points and manner of articulation, fill in the chart in Exercise 2.23 to use later in transcribing words and phrases.

We have now compiled a list of the consonant sounds used in the English language, based on their place and manner of articulation. You might notice two things about chart in Exercise 2.23. The first is that we have added a categorical level at the top, dividing the points of articulation into broader categories: labial (involving one or more of the lips), coronal (involving the front part of the tongue), and dorsal (involving the middle part of the tongue). This allows us to make generalizations about how we combine sounds in meaningful ways. Second, there are a number of blank cells in the chart. The shaded cells are those deemed impossible to articulate. However, the white cells indicate the possibilities for further meaning-making resources through language sounds. For example, many languages have a palatal nasal consonant represented as [ɲ]; in Spanish, this sound is represented in the alphabet as the letter 'ñ', and is used in words like *enseñar*, 'to teach'. Note that in some dialects of English it is used for words like 'onion', and for borrowed Spanish words, like 'piñata', while other dialects of English use two sounds when producing the 'ny' of these words and words like 'canyon'.

Also on the full IPA chart are columns, or points of articulation, which are not included in the chart in Exercise 2.23. English does not make use of uvular consonants (which are articulated by moving the back of the tongue near or against the uvula), pharyngeal consonants (in which the back part of the tongue comes in contact with the pharynx) or epiglottal consonants (articulated by contact between the aryepiglottic folds and the epiglottis). We have also left off all of the non-pulmonic consonants, such as clicks and implosives. However, other languages do make use of these language sounds. Knowing how the vocal tract is put to work to produce these sounds can help us to articulate sounds in languages other than our own. We now move on to how we produce the sounds we know as vowels.

2.6.2.3 Features of vowels in English

In school we learn that the vowels of English are 'a', 'e', 'i', 'o', 'u', and sometimes 'y'. That is the case for written English, and in terms of the graphemes of our alphabet. However, the vowel sounds we produce in English are far more than those six. Vowels are also more complicated to describe than the consonants. We saw that consonants are defined as such because of some obstruction to the air as it is being pushed out of the body. With vowels, there are no obstructions; thus, they are described by phoneticians in terms of the **height of the tongue** at the moment of production, **frontness**, or whether the tongue is positioned farther forward or farther back in the mouth, and **roundedness**, which refers to the shape of the lips.

Tongue height: Try producing the [æ] sound in 'ch<u>a</u>t', and compare it to the [i] in ch<u>ea</u>t. You might notice that your jaw drops to let your tongue fall in producing [æ]. Thus, the tongue is farther from the roof of the mouth when pronouncing [æ] than when pronouncing the vowel sound in ch<u>ea</u>t. Thus, vowels can be divided according to the closeness of the tongue to the roof of the mouth. **Close** vowels (also referred to as '**high**' vowels, especially in American phonetics) are those whose pronunciation means that the tongue comes closest to the roof of the mouth, without coming in direct contact (in which case a consonant would be produced!). An **open** (or **low**) vowel is one in which the tongue is farthest from the roof of the mouth, while **mid**

vowels, as the name suggests, are neither close nor open. Table 2.3 shows examples from English; it is worth pointing out now that the open vowels in English tend to be rather unstable. These are the vowels that have a major role to play in the different varieties of spoken English. I attempt to point out some of the differences here; in order to understand these differences, try to concentrate on the position of the tongue.[4]

Table 2.3: Vowels according to tongue height

Close:	[i] b<u>ee</u>t	[u] b<u>oo</u>t
Near-close:	[ɪ] b<u>i</u>t	[ʊ] w<u>oo</u>d
Close-mid:	[e] b<u>e</u>d[1]	[o] h<u>o</u>pe[2]
Mid:		
Open-mid:	[ɛ] b<u>e</u>t	[ʌ] p<u>u</u>tt [ɔ] t<u>au</u>ght
Near-open	[æ] ch<u>a</u>t	[ɑ] h<u>o</u>p
Open:	[a]sp<u>a</u>[3]	

[1] As this word is pronounced by speakers from Australia. This is close to the sound speakers of American English make in words such as *mate*, which in American English is more of a diphthong [eɪ], as seen at the end of this section on vowels. [e] is also the sound pronounced by Spanish speakers in words such as *bebe*.
[2] Actually, in English, most speakers do not pronounce this clipped [o] sound, but rather the diphthong [oʊ], as explained at the end of this section on vowels.
[3] As this word is pronounced by speakers from New England, Australia, and New Zealand.

It is worth pointing out here that in dictionaries of English which include pronunciation, you will often see the long vowels written with the symbol : as in [biːt]. The symbol : indicates lengthening of the vowel quality; for our purposes in this chapter, we will only focus on quality, and not on length. In transcribing speech, you might want to use this **diacritic** for greater accuracy in reflecting the string of sounds you hear. Indeed, the International Phonetic Alphabet includes a set of diacritics, or symbols/markings which can be added to the basic symbols to indicate some kind of alteration or greater specificity in the pronunciation of the sound. Another example of a diacritic is [h], which indicates aspiration of the preceding consonant sound, such as [pʰ] in [pʰɪt] (compare to [spɪt], where the [p] is not aspirated – try pronouncing the two words *pit* and *spit* with a piece of paper held close to your mouth). Another diacritic that is frequently used in transcription is the symbol ' to indicate that the syllable following the symbol receives the primary stress in the word, as in ['pɛnsəl] (pencil). For a full set of diacritics, see the IPA chart.

4. To match your perception of imagining the sound through tongue position to the physical pronunciation of the sound, you can hear the vowels (and consonants) pronounced by Peter Ladefoged, one of the foremost phoneticians of recent times, at http://hctv.humnet. ucla.edu/departments/linguistics/VowelsandConsonants/vowels/contents.html.

EXERCISE 2.24

Transcribe the following words according to how you pronounce them. If you have access to someone who speaks a different dialect, ask him/her to pronounce the words. See if you can capture the difference in pronunciation using the IPA.

> *E.g. pen [pɛn] is how I pronounce this word; my mother is from southern USA, and pronounces it [pɛn]*

1. caught
2. cot
3. car
4. merry
5. marry
6. Mary
7. stock
8. creek

Another feature of vowels can be thought of horizontally with respect to the above chart. Let's look at our two close vowels: as you pronounce b**ee**t and b**oo**t, think about how the tongue is positioned in terms of whether it is more towards the **front** or the **back** of the mouth. We can now add this feature onto our chart:

Table 2.4: Vowels according to tongue height and vertical position

	Front	*Central*	*Back*	
Close:	[i] b**ee**t		[u] b**oo**t	
Near-close:	[ɪ] b**i**t		[ʊ] w**oo**d	
Close-mid:	[e] b**e**d		[o] h**o**pe	
Mid:				
Open-mid:	[ɛ] b**e**t		[ʌ] p**u**tt	[ɔ] t**au**ght
Near-open	[æ] ch**a**t		[ɑ] h**o**p	
Open:	[a]sp**a**			

Now try producing an [u] sound (as in 'c**oo**l') and an [i] sound as in 'ch**ee**se'. You will probably notice that your lips draw together and are rounded in the first case, and your mouth opens into a smile in the second, which explains the popularity of that word in photo opportunities. We can now add that feature to our chart:

Table 2.5: Vowels according to tongue height, horizontal position and lip roundedness

	Front	*Central*	*Back*	
Close:	[i] b<u>ee</u>t		[u] b<u>oo</u>t	ROUNDED
Near-close:	[ɪ] b<u>i</u>t		[ʊ] w<u>oo</u>d	
Close-mid:	[e] b<u>e</u>d	[ɚ] s<u>ir</u>	[o] h<u>o</u>pe	
Mid:				
Open-mid:	[ɛ] b<u>e</u>t	[ə] <u>a</u>bout	[ʌ] p<u>u</u>tt	[ɔ] c<u>au</u>ght
Near-open:	[æ] ch<u>a</u>t			
Open:	[a] sp<u>a</u>		[ɑ] h<u>o</u>p	[ɒ] B<u>o</u>ston[1]

[1] As pronounced by speakers from the Boston area; also pronounced in South African park, and British RP *hot*. In most of North America, these two open back vowels have merged into [ɑ]. To pronounce *hot* with a Boston accent, pronounce the vowel with the lips rounded, and you should feel and hear the difference.

There are two mid-central vowel sounds that are worth highlighting. The first is [ə], commonly known as the schwa. This vowel sound is the sound we hear in unstressed syllables, like the 'a' in about [əbaʊt]. Any of our vowel graphemes can be articulated as a schwa if they form part of an unstressed syllable (e.g. 'e' in synthesis [sɪnθəsɪs], 'i' in pencil [pɛnsəl], the 'o' in harmony [hɑɹməni] 'u' in supply [sə'plaɪ], 'y' in syringe [səɹɪndʒ]), which means that the schwa actually has a range of spellings. Indeed, most words in English which consist of more than one syllable contain at least one unstressed syllable, thus the great importance of the schwa in English.

The other sound, [ɚ], refers to 'r-colored vowel', or **rhoticized** vowel sounds. Perhaps you have heard how someone from Boston or the American South, or someone who speaks in an RP accent in England pronounces words like 'heard' or 'bird'. These are non-rhoticized dialects; rather than produce an 'r' sound, they stretch out the vowel, ending in a schwa. However, in standard American dialect, an approximation of [ɹ] occurs after a vowel sound, such as in 'her' [hɚ] and 'bird' [bɚd].

EXERCISE 2.25

For each of the set of vowels, list the features that they have in common. e.g. [u] [o] [u] [ʊ] all are vowels which are pronounced with the tongue in the back of the mouth and the lips rounded; they are back rounded vowels.

1. [i] [ɪ] [u] [ʊ]
2. [i] [e] [ɛ] [æ]
3. [u] [ʊ] [ʌ] [ɔ] [ɑ]
4. [æ] [a] [ɑ] [ɒ]

Diphthongs

Diphthongs are combinations of vowel sounds; they are sounds that begin in one place and positioning in the mouth and glide towards another. The word 'low', for example, after the initial consonant sound [l], has a vowel sound in which the tongue starts out in a mid-back position and ends in a high back position in American English; thus, it is rendered as: [oʊ].[5] In RP British English, the same word 'low' starts out with a mid-central unstressed unrounded vowel and ends at a high back rounded vowel, thus [əʊ]; the dipthongs of American, Australian and British English are included in Table 2.6 and its accompanying notes.

Table 2.6: Dipthongs

hi<u>gh</u> [aɪ][1]	n<u>ear</u> [ɪə][6]
c<u>ow</u>: [aʊ][2]	b<u>oy</u> [ɔɪ]
m<u>a</u>ne [eɪ][3]	l<u>ow</u>: [oʊ][7]
c<u>are</u> [eə][4]	b<u>ore</u>: [ʊə][8]
l<u>ow</u> [əʊ][5]	

[1] As pronounced in British and American English; in Australian English [ɑe]
[2] As pronounced in British and American English; in Australian English, [æɔ].
[3] As pronounced in British and American English; in Australian English, [æɪ].
[4] Pronounced in British RP English.
[5] Pronounced in British RP English.
[6] Pronounced in British RP English and Australian English.
[7] Pronounced in Standard American English
[8] Pronounced in British RP English.

2.6.3 Articulatory processes

When transcribing words using the IPA, you might notice that you carefully enunciate as you work out the sounds. However, as we all know, when we are speaking naturally, we are not so careful; hence we say *gonna* for 'going to' and *dunno* for 'don't know'. There are various articulatory processes which occur in all languages which help explain the ways in which we adapt sounds as we speak; for instance, in speaking at a natural rate, we often go for ease of articulation, and thus sounds can be affected by the surrounding sounds through a process called **assimilation**. For example, fully pronouncing *don't know* means that the tongue is the alveolar position for the stop [t] at the end of *don't*, and then we put it back in the same place nasal [n] at the beginning of *know*. Many people, when pronouncing this phrase, articulate [t] in this particular context in a way which is much more similar to the articulation

5. Most speakers of English produce this blend rather than a pure [o] sound, although [o] is included in the tables of vowels in English.

of [n]. Others may employ **deletion** or **elision** and do away with sounding the [t] altogether. Amongst Spanish speakers, deletion happens with past participle endings; so, instead of *hablado*, often [ablao] is what is heard. We also employ deletion with vowel sounds sometimes in rapid speech with words like *suppose*, which can come out sounding as [spoʊz].

Epenthesis involves inserting a sound within a string of sounds. For example, try to pronounce the word *something* as you would in casual speech. You might notice that you insert a [p] sound, making for the string [sʌmpθɪŋ]. To explain why this might happen, we need to further classify consonants into the categories of **obstruent** and **sonorant**. Obstruents, as the name implies, are all those consonants, such as plosives, fricatives and affricates, whose articulation implies an obstruction of the air flow which causes friction. Sonorants are those consonants whose articulation allows for a freer airflow, without friction; in English, the sonorants are the nasal consonants [m], [n] and [ŋ], and the approximants [l], [ɹ], [w], and [j]. Now, it seems that the movement from a sonorant such as [m] to an obstruent such as [θ] is made easier by inserting [p], given that [p] shares with [m] the property of bilabial articulation. The shared point of articulation further helps in the transition from a voiced consonant to an unvoiced one. Thus, epenthesis allows for ease of articulation. Vowel epenthesis happens as well. For example, in Spanish, [s] never occurs at the beginning of a word immediately followed by a consonant. Thus, in adapting the word *stress* to the Spanish language, an epenthetic vowel has been added before the initial *s*, creating the word *estrés*. In parts of the English-speaking world, as in Newcastle and the surrounding area, vowel epenthesis occurs in words like *film*, pronounced [fɪləm].

The process of **dissimilation** involves pronouncing sounds in a way which creates a contrast with other sounds. This occurs for example with words like *can* and *can't*. In some parts of North America, in normal spoken speech, we pronounce *can* with an unstressed schwa [kən] in front of another word and its negative counterpart with a stressed front vowel [kæn] sometimes articulating lightly the [t]. In many forms of British English, the schwa is also used in the positive form, and a stressed back vowel in the negative: [kɑn].

These articulatory process not only affect the way we pronounce, but also the way we hear. That is, in our attempts to make sense of the utterances we hear, we will impose our own understanding of sounds, including by changing our understanding a sound to match preceding sounds we think we have heard, and inserting or deleting sounds. This adaptation of hearing is what caused Sylvia Wright, to hear 'Lady Mondegreen' instead of 'and laid him on the green'.

Further Exercises in Phonetics

EXERCISE 2.26

Look at these misheard lyrics, on the one hand, and what is actually sung, on the other. Highlight and explain the difference in terms of the sounds the person hears/does not hear.

e.g. *sensitive manatee* for *sense of humanity* (Bob Dylan, "Not Dark Yet")

[sɛnsətɪvmænəti]   [sɛnsəvjumænəti]

Explanation: The sounds the person hears/doesn't hear: after the first schwa, in the misheard version the person hears an epenthesized unvoiced alveolar stop, followed by a high front vowel and a voiced labiodental consonant. In the real version, the voiced labiodental comes first, followed by a palatal approximant (slightly aspirated to give the impression of an [h]) and a high back vowel.

1. *outright offensive* instead of *out riding fences* (Eagles, 'Desperado')
2. *round John Virgin* instead of *round yon Virgin* (Silent Night)
3. *there's a bathroom on the right* instead of *there's a bad moon on the rise* (Creedence Clearwater Revival, 'Bad Moon Rising')
4. Supply 2 or 3 of your own misheard lyrics, and explain the differences. Try also to account for why you might have heard what you think you heard.

EXERCISE 2.27

More mondegreens: Write the phonetic transcription of the lines below to see if you can come up with a homophonic equivalent, or very near homophonic equivalent. The trick is to not put spaces between the words, and read the transcription quickly, to see if you can come up with a meaningful alternative.

e.g. laid him on the green [ledəmɑnðəgrin] [ledəmɑndəgrin] Lady Mondegreen

In this example, the only difference is the voiced interdental consonant [ð] and the voiced alveolar stop [d].

1. wreck a nice beach
2. ice cream
3. kiss this guy
4. fork handles
5. point of you

2.7 Phonology: Meaningful sounds across languages

2.7.1 From speech sounds to meaningful sounds

As we have seen, there are many sounds that we produce when we speak, all of which rely on several physical properties in terms of what we do with the various parts of our bodies involved in the speech apparatus. We have seen, for example, that in English, we distinguish the sounds [b] and [p], both bilabial stops, through voicing the former, that is, by vibrating our vocal cords. This simple difference of vibrating the vocal cords when bringing our lips together and forcefully stopping the air that comes through is an important difference in English, and we know that it is an important distinction because it allows us to distinguish words such as *bat* and *pat*, *cap* and *cab*, *amble* and *ample*, etc. Not every language finds this voiced-voiceless distinction meaningful for bilabial stops. For example, in Standard Arabic, there is no corresponding graphic symbol for [p]. There is for [b], yet Arabic speakers do not make a distinction between these two sounds, and thus there are no words, or **minimal pairs**, which can be distinguished based on the voicedness of the bilabial stop (although the voiceless biliabial stop is produced in Arabic before other voiceless consonants).

Thus, not all of the physical properties of sound which we produce as we articulate our speech sounds are actually meaningful. For example, try saying these pairs of words as naturally as possible while holding a piece of paper in front of your mouth:

pit spit   pat spat

What you may notice is a much stronger puff of air when you pronounce the first sound of the first word in each pair. This is because the voiceless stop [p^h] (note that the superscript ^{h} indicates aspiration) is aspirated when it is word initial. However, when it is not, the aspiration is greatly reduced (test this also with a word like *peeper*).

Thus, the phonetic transcription of these words is:

[p^{h}ɪt] [spɪt]   [p^{h}æt] [spæt]

Another example of a physical difference in speech production is vowel nasalization. Try pronouncing these pairs of words several times out loud, and then try pronouncing them as if you were going to pronounce the whole word, but leave off the final consonant:

bead beam   road roam   slipper slimmer   heck hen

What you may notice in this experiment is that you lower the velum in the second pair in each word, as more air passes through the nose in pronouncing the vowel. When this happens, the vowel is nasalized (indicated by the diacritic ˜ over the vowel). Thus, the phonetic transcription for these words is:

[bid] [bĩm]   [ɹoʊd] [ɹõʊm]   [slɪpɚ] [slĩmɚ̃]   [hɛk] [hẽn]

While we do produce this sound when we speak, vowel nasalization is *not* a distinctive feature of English, and so usually we are not even aware that we are pronouncing a sound in a different way. That is, we have no two words, say *be* and *bee,* pronounced, for example, [bi] and [bĩ], which would mean we would hear vowel nasalization as **contrastive**. However, other languages do use vowel nasalization to contrast minimal pairs. Akan Twi, a Ghanian language, for instance, has the following pairs:

[ka] 'bite'   [kã] 'speak'
[fi] 'come from'   [fĩ] 'dirty'
[tu] 'pull'   [tũ] 'hole/den'
[nsa] 'hand'   [nsã] 'liquor'

Knowing which sounds are distinctive in our own language is part of our underlying phonological knowledge of that language. These distinctive sounds are called **phonemes**. Given that they are the distinctive sounds that allow us to make meaningful strings of sound, they are also **contrastive**. That is, we know that the sounds contrast meaning as evidenced by **minimal pairs** that exist in the language. Minimal pairs are strings of sound, or words, that have meaning, and that differ in only one sound, as for example *pit* and *bit, sing* and *zing,* or *taped* and *tapped.* Thus substituting one of these sounds for another creates a new meaning, and it is in this sense that phonemes are contrastive, as opposed to **noncontrastive** sounds, such as [p] and [pʰ] in English: there are no two words in the language which differ only in those two sounds. We can think of plenty of words in English which contrast only because of /p/ and /b/: *pit* and *bit, pat* and *bat, pelt* and *belt, peas* and *bees, cup* and *cub,* etc. Note that phonemes are encoded within slashes (while phones, or speech sounds are in square brackets [ ]), and the minimal pairs *pit* and *bit, sing* and *zing,* or *taped* and *tapped.* differ in the following phonemes: /p/ and /b/, /s/ and /z/, /eɪ/ and /æ/.

EXERCISE 2.28

Make three lists of minimal pairs; in the first list, include pairs which differ only in the initial sound, in the second, only a sound in the middle of a word, and in the third only a word's final sound. Try to use as many speech sounds as you can, to come up with a complete inventory of phonemes in English. Try also to include sounds which have similar points and/or manner of articulation:

Initial sounds		Middle sounds		Final sounds	
pat	bat	lazy	lacy	road	wrote
/p/	/b/	/z/	/s/	/d/	/t/

2.7.2 Phonemes and allophones

Revisiting our examples of [pʰɪt] and [spɪt], we know that [p] and [pʰ] are *not* two distinct phonemes in English, as there are no minimal pairs in our language which differ only in the aspiration of the [p]; obviously, *pit* and *spit* differ because of the added sound at the beginning of *spit*. When we have a case where two sounds differ but they are *not* **distinctive**, or **contrastive**, then we have a situation of allophony; that is, [p] and [pʰ] are allophones of the same phoneme /p/. When a speech sound is **noncontrastive**, as in the case of [pʰ] in English, it is also known as **redundant**, as it adds nothing in the sense of meaning. Thus, phonemes are the underlying abstract mental representations that we hold in our linguistic repertoire of meaningful sounds, and allophones are the actual soundings of those representations.

It is also the case that **allophones of the same phoneme** never occur in the same phonetic environment, that is, they are in **complementary distribution**. We have seen that vowels are nasalized in the environment of nasal consonants, just as in Arabic /b/ becomes voiceless [p] in the environment of other voiceless consonants. So nasal vowel allophones in English are predictable, as are voiceless bilabial stops in Arabic; we can predict when they will occur based on the surrounding speech sounds. The surrounding speech sounds, because of their articulatory features, impact certain features of other sounds, which creates the slight, noncontrastive differencs in the production of these allophones.

In carrying out a **phonemic inventory** for a language, our goal is to determine which speech sounds are **phonemic** (or contrastive) and which are **allophonic** (or redundant). In order to do this inventory, we:

1. Look for minimal pairs in which the speech sounds we are interested in are contrasting; once we find these minimal pairs, then we know we are dealing with different phonemes.

2. If we do not find any minimal pairs, then we look for regularities of environments in which the sounds occur: can we predict the occurrence of the speech sound based on the environment? Then we are dealing with different allophones. Once we determine that the sounds under analysis are allophones, then we need to describe the rule that governs the allophonic variation. Aspects of the environment that determine the allophone are the surrounding sounds (as with nasalized vowels), the position in the word (as with the aspirated [pʰ]), and the stress of the syllables in which it appears or those which surround it.

Let's look at the following data set in English, focusing on the velar stops [k] and [g]

[kɛg] keg	[kɪn] kin
[kɪl] kill	[dʒɪn] gin
[gæg] gag	[koʊld] cold
[goʊld] gold	[gɪl] gill

We can see that we do have minimal pairs – [goʊld] and [koʊld], [gɪl] and [kɪl]. Thus, we know that in English the voiced velar stop /g/ and the voiceless velar stop /k/ are distinct phonemes.

Let us now look at the following data for English focusing on the speech sounds [k] and [kʰ] (remember that superscript ʰ indicates that we aspirate the consonant):

[kʰoʊld] cold	[ɹɪski] risky
[kʰræʃ] crash	[kʰæʃ] cash
[skoʊld] scold	[bikɚ] beaker
[kʰræks] cracks	[beɪkəri] bakery

In this data set, there are no minimal pairs which differ only in the sounds [kʰ] and [k]. Furthermore, [kʰ] occurs in environments in which [k] never occurs, and vice versa. Thus, these two sounds are allophones of /k/. We see that when /k/ is word-initial, then we pronounce the allophone [kʰ], and in all other environments, we sound the unaspirated [k].

/k/ → [kʰ] when word initial.

We have seen this phenomenon before, with [pʰɪt] vs. [spɪt]). What phonetic features do the phonemes /p/ and /k/ have in common? They are both voiceless stops.

EXERCISE 2.29

We have a third voiceless stop in English, which is /t/. Can we extend this aspiration rule to that voiceless stop? Explain your answer.

Indeed, we can make a more general rule to account for the surface soundings in our spoken language:

Aspiration rule: Aspirate a voiceless stop when it is word initial.

How is it that speakers of English agree on this rule? It is not an arbitrary rule (as are the rules which determine which sounds become phonemic in a language). Rather, the physical properties of the sounds themselves may drive the phonetic rule. We have seen a rule earlier with reference to vowels in the environment of nasalized consonants: *nasalize a vowel before (and after) a nasal consonant ([m], [n], and [ŋ])*. This is because assimilation is at play in these contexts: it is easier to pronounce the vowel with the air passing through the nose either in preparation for or immediately following a nasal consonant.

EXERCISE 2.30

Flap [ɾ].
When we did our phonetic inventory for English, we saw that many dialects use the voiced alveolar flap (represented as [ɾ]). Let us look at how that sound contrasts with [t] and [d] in American English in the following data:

[læɾɚ] latter	[mʌstɚ] muster
[læɾɚ] ladder	[mʌɾɚ] mutter
[ətʰempʰtʰ] attempt	[bɛd] bed
[ədæpʰtʰ] adapt	[bɛt] bet
[bæd] bad	[bɛɾɚ] better
[bæɾɚ] batter	

Now, answer the following questions:
1. Are [t] and [d] separate phonemes? What is the evidence for your answer?
2. What is the situation for [ɾ]? Is it a phoneme or an allophone? If the latter, describe the rule for its use.

EXERCISE 2.31

Look at this data set for Castilian Spanish, and focus on the speech sounds [d] and [ð]:

[deðo] 'finger'	[andar] 'to walk'
[meðir] 'to measure'	[andando] 'walking'
[kaldo] 'broth'	[ablaðo] 'have talked'
[karðo] 'thistle'	[falda] 'skirt'
[deuða] 'debt'	[niðo] 'nest'

Are [d] and [ð] separate phonemes or allophones of the same phoneme? Describe the steps you took in arriving at your conclusion.

EXERCISE 2.32

The data below are also taken from Castilian Spanish. In this case focus on the speech sounds [b] and [ß]. [ß] is a voiced bilabial fricative, pronounced by bringing the lips together, as in the case of the plosive [b], but then allowing the air to escape more slowly, as we do when we pronounce the labiodental [v].

[batʃe] 'pothole'	[sußir] 'to go up'
[buθo] 'scuba diver'	[embaraθo] 'pregnancy'
[deßer] 'to owe'	[umbral] 'threshold'
[aßaniko] 'fan'	[ambar] 'amber'
[beße] 'baby'	[oßispo] 'bishop'
[beso] 'kiss'	[saßer] 'to know'

Are [b] and [ß] separate phonemes or allophones of the same phoneme? Describe the steps you took in arriving to your conclusion.

2.7.3 Phonemic tone and length

Earlier in this unit on the spoken language we saw that intonation, or contours of pitch and lengthening of syllables, is used to convey a range of meanings, from informational to interpersonal. There are languages which use pitch phonemically; these languages are known as **tone** languages. Many of the world's languages are tone languages; however, most Indo-European languages do not use tone phonemically. In a tone language, relative pitch is used to contrast meaning. For example, Thai distinguishes five linguistic tones: low, middle, high, falling and rising, each tone indicated by a different diacritic symbol (except middle tone, which is unmarked). The string of sounds [mai] takes on different meaning depending on the relative pitch at which it is uttered:

[mai] (middle tone) 'mile'

[mài] (low tone) 'new'
[mái] (high tone) 'wood'
[mâi] (falling tone) 'not'
[mǎi] (rising tone) 'silk'

Some languages use length of vowels and consonants phonemically. This involves, in essence, repeating the same sound twice, or doubling it. Italian, for example, lengthens consonants, and these are realized graphically (in writing) as double consonants. Thus, in Italian, we have the following minimal pairs (among others):

[sete] 'thirst'   [sette] 'seven'
[andremo] 'we will go'   [andremmo] 'we would go'

EXERCISE 2.33

Pohnpeian is a Micronesian language spoken mainly in the Federated States of Micronesia and its surrounding islands. Is vowel length (also known as double vowels) phonemic in Pohnpeian?
    [paa] 'to fight'
    [pa] 'under'
    [tool] 'mountain'
    [tol] 'to mix'

EXERCISE 2.34

Look back on the exercises carried out for this section on phonology, especially at those involving languages other than those you are comfortable speaking. What phonemes and allophones would you find most difficult to hear and to articulate? Why? What do you think might cause difficulty for speakers of other languages in learning English?

2.8   Further exercises

EXERCISE 2.35

Loan words
There are many loan words in language. For example, in English, we speak of *siestas* and *coyotes*, and Spanish speakers send *emails* to each other, and can ride in their friend's motorcycle *sidecar* (pronounced [siðekar]. Choose some loan words in two languages. Get an informant from each language and ask them to pronounce the words as they would naturally say them. Transcribe the data in phonetic script. What kind of alterations

happen when words are borrowed? What do these alterations tell you about the phonology of the host, or target, language?

EXERCISE 2.36

Tongue twisters

Make a list of three or four tongue twisters in two languages. Get an informant from each of the languages, and have them try both those of their own language and those of the other language. Transcribe the data into the IPA, and analyze what features change in cases of mispronunciation. What do these difficulties tell you about the phonology of each language?

EXERCISE 2.37

Poems

Choose a couple of short poems in two languages. Have a native speaker of each language read the poem in their own language. Transcribe the poems using the IPA. After transcribing the lines into the IPA, analyze the sounds in the excerpts. Are there interesting patterns of consonant sounds? Are there interesting patterns of vowel sounds? What sounds and patterns of sound in the lines make some lines easy to read aloud and others difficult? Why do some lines read quickly and others slowly? What comparisons can you make across the two languages?

EXERCISE 2.38

Intonation patterns

Tape some naturally occurring conversations in two languages. Choose some excerpts from the data and transcribe them, clearly demonstrating the stress and intonation patterns (using the transcription conventions included in Section 2.5.3). What similarities and differences do you find?

EXERCISE 2.39

Conversation analysis

Tape some naturally occurring conversations in two languages. Choose some excerpts from the data and transcribe them, clearly identifying the pauses, overlaps, etc. (using the transcription conventions included in Section 2.5.3). Compare and contrast the conversations, using Conversation Analysis methods in your explanations.

EXERCISE 2.40

Spoken grammar

Tape some naturally occurring conversation. Transcribe the data. Analyze the transcript for use of ellipsis and discourse markers such as *well, ok., like,* and *I mean.* Compare your findings to the types of discourse markers you find in a written text.

2.9   Chapter outcomes

After having read this chapter carefully, discussed with others the content, and carried out the exercises, you should assess your ability to:

✓ Briefly explain pragmatics and how it differs from semantics.
✓ Explain some of the basic tenets of speech act theory, such as performatives, locutionary, illocutionary and perlocutionary force, and direct and indirect speech acts.
✓ Give the functions of indicative, interrogative and imperative mood, providing examples.
✓ State what Paul Grice's Cooperative Principle consists of; list each of Grice's conversational maxims (Quality, Quantity, Relevance and Manner), explaining each one.
✓ Explain what happens when we flout a maxim (conversational implicature).
✓ Explain politeness, including the concepts of face (positive and negative) and of face threatening acts, using examples.
✓ Analyze spoken interaction for discourse markers (such as *oh, I don't know, like, I know, well,* etc.) for functions such as:
  – preparing for possible disagreement
  – marking boundaries between topics
  – focusing attention
  – indicating logical or temporal sequences
  – signaling exemplification
  – signaling reported speech
  – signaling assumed shared knowledge
  – marking receipt of new information
  – softening the impact of what is being said
  – indicating repair
  – correcting a misassumption
  – indicating uncertainty
  – providing a filler while holding the floor
  – minimizing compliments
  – conveying approximation
  – mitigating a face-threatening act
  – suggesting common ground/shared knowledge.
✓ Describe ellipsis and vague language in spoken conversation, and explain what their function might be.
✓ Explain the functions of intonation in English, including word stress and intonation contours or patterns.

✓ Provide a brief background to Conversation Analysis.

✓ Explain how turn-taking works (including in your explanation the turn constructional component, the turn allocational component, and transition relevance places).

✓ Explain what adjacency pairs consist of (first-pair parts and second-pair parts) and the different types, providing examples of each; explain the different types of responses (preferred and dispreferred), showing the ways in which interlocutors determine whether the response which they are about to get or which they have already received is one or the other.

✓ Explain the special types of sequences that can disrupt or alter an adjacency pair, giving examples of each (insertion sequence, side sequence, gist, upshot, repair, and presequence).

✓ Briefly define phonetics, and explain how it differs from phonology.

✓ Explain the difference between phones, allophones and phonemes, using examples.

✓ Define articulatory phonetics.

✓ Explain point and manner of articulation.

✓ Describe the International Phonetic Alphabet (IPA) and its purpose.

✓ Use the IPA to capture language sounds, and show how it can illustrate differences in how words are sounded across dialects.

✓ Describe the articulatory processes of assimilation, deletion (or elision), epenthesis, and dissimilation.

✓ Explain the notion of minimal pairs, using examples.

✓ Explain the role of minimal pairs in determining the phonemic inventory of a language, using examples.

✓ Explain what it means to say that a phonetic feature is contrastive or distinctive (in other words phonemic), as opposed to redundant or noncontrastive (in other words allophonic), using examples.

✓ Explain complementary distribution and its relevance to phonology, using examples.

2.10 References and further reading

Antaki, Charles (no date) *An Introduction to Conversation Analysis: Main Menu.* Retrieved 20 February 2010 from http://www-staff.lboro.ac.uk/~sscal/notation. htm

Atkinson, J. Maxwell and Drew, Paul (1979) *Order in Court.* London, Macmillan.

Austin, John L. (1962) *How to Do Things with Words: The William James Lectures delivered at Harvard University in 1955* J. O. Urmson (ed.). Oxford: Clarendon.

Bowles, Hugo and Seedhouse, Paul (2007) *Conversation Analysis and Language for Specific Purposes*. Bern: Peter Lang AG.

De Saussure, Ferdinand (1959) *Course in General Linguistics*. New York: McGraw-Hill Publishers.

Diani, Giuliana (2004) The discourse functions of I don't know in English conversation. In K. Aijmer and A. B. Stenström (eds) *Discourse Patterns in Spoken and Written Corpora* 157–171. Amsterdan: John Benjamins.

Eggins, Suzanne and Slade, Diana (1997) *Analysing Casual Conversation*. London: Equinox Publishing.

Goffman, Erving (1955) On face-work: an analysis of ritual elements of social interaction, *Psychiatry: Journal for the Study of Interpersonal Processes* 18(3): 213–231.

Grice, H. Paul (1975) Logic and conversation. In P. Cole, and J. Morgan (eds) *Syntax and Semantics, Volume 3* 41–58. New York: Academic Press.

Halliday, M. A. K. and Hasan, Ruqaiya (1976) *Cohesion in English*. London: Longman.

Hutchby, Ian and Wooffitt, Robin (2008) *Conversation Analysis*. Cambridge: Polity.

Ladefoged, Peter and Maddieson, Ian (1996). *The Sounds of the World's Languages*. Oxford: Blackwell.

Lenk, Ute (1998) *Marking Discourse Coherence: Functions of Discourse Markers*. Tubengen: Gunter Narr Verlag.

Liddicoat, Anthony J. (2007) *An Introduction to Conversation Analysis*. London: Continuum.

Merritt, Marilyn (1976). On questions following questions (in service encounters). *Language in Society*, 5: 315–357.

Muller, Simone (2005) *Discourse Markers in Native and Non-Native English Discourse*. Amsterdam: John Benjamins.

Nariyama, Shigeko (2006) Pragmatic information extraction from subject ellipsis in informal English. *Proceedings of the 3rd Workshop on Scalable Natural Language Understanding* 1–8. Association for Computational Linguistics, New York City, June 2006.

Overstreet, Maryann and Yule, George (1997) On being inexplicit and stuff in contemporary American English. *Journal of English Linguistics* 25(3), 250–258.

Roger, Derek and Bull, Peter (1989) *Conversation: An Interdisciplinary Perspective*. Clevedon: Multilingual Matters.

Sacks, Harvey, Schegloff, Emanuel A. and Jefferson, Gail (1974) A simplest systematics for the organization of turn-taking for conversation. *Language*, 50(4), 696–735.

Schegloff, Emanuel A., Jefferson, Gail and Sacks, Harvey (1977) The preference for self-correction in the organization of repair in conversation. *Language*, 53(2), 361–382.

Schiffrin, Deborah (1988) *Discourse Markers*. Cambridge: Cambridge University Press.

Sperber, Dan & Wilson, Deirdre (1995) *Relevance: Communication and Cognition*. 2nd edition. Oxford: Blackwell.

Ten Have, Paul (1999) *Doing Conversation Analysis: A Practical Guide*. London: Sage.

Turnbull, William (2003) *Language in Action: Psychological Models of Conversation*. Hove: Psychology Press.

Some websites of interest

Emanuel A. Schegloff's web page on Conversation Analysis, including access to sound
   files: http://www.sscnet.ucla.edu/soc/faculty/schegloff/
The Wikipedia website on the International Phonetic Alphabet is quite complete. It
   contains detailed descriptions of each of the language sounds, along with a recording
   of each.
For information on American English phonology, see George Dillon's page on the vowel
   sounds of American English: http://faculty.washington.edu/dillon/PhonResources/
   newstart.html
See http://www.cs.niu.edu/~freedman/courses/cogs/rf-phon01.pdf

2.11 Some answers to the exercises

Exercise 2.1

Open-ended. Some possible answers below:

1. *I would like to apply for a $100 loan* (in a bank). *Could you possibly
   lend me $100?* (perhaps to a parent) *You got a hundred bucks you
   could spare me?* (to a friend or sibling). *I was wondering if I could
   get a cash advance ...* (to a boss).
2. *I really didn't mean ...* (to a parent) *I'm so sorry!!* (in all situations)
   Oops! (to a friend or sibling).
3. *You are cordially invited to lunch next ...* (formal invitation, perhaps
   to a boss). *Would you like to have lunch together some time?* (someone
   you'd like to impress). *Come on ... let me treat you to lunch* (to a
   parent). *Let's get some grub* (to a friend).
4. *I would like to set up an appointment as I've been going through a
   difficult time* (to a counselor). *Do you have a few minutes? I really
   need someone to talk to ...* (to a parent). *I'm so upset!* (to a friend).
   *I've got something important on my mind that I would like to share
   with you ...* (to a boss).

The language differs in several ways. With friends and siblings, there
are fewer instances of words and phrases that suggest more politeness, such
as *would like, could, would, possibly, cordially, etc.* Requests directed to
friends are shorter. Also, the vocabulary is different, as in *$100 loan* or *a
cash advance* vs. *a hundred bucks*.

Exercise 2.2

Open-ended. These are some possible answers:

   You're fired!
   You're grounded!

You're under arrest!
I do.
I baptize you ...
I christen this ship ...
I bet you $5 it rains again today.
I swear to tell the truth ...
Safe!
Out!
Goal!
Tag! You're it!

Exercise 2.3

Open-ended. Possible answers:

1. Pair 1: The common locutionary act is that of an action that has not been done, namely that of doing homework. In scenario 1, the illocutionary act could be explaining (e.g. why s/he has to leave early), boasting, complaining, or asking for help, and the perlocutionary effect could be that B does A's homework or takes A home early. In scenario 2, the illocutionary act perhaps is one of apologizing, and perhaps the perlocutionary effect could be that the teacher forgives A, or reprimands.

2. Pair 3: The common locutionary act is that of an inability to see the car. In scenario 1, the illocutionary act could be one of apologizing for not finding the car, in which case the perlocutionary act we hope is that B lessens A's anguish by saying something like 'oh, don't worry'. In scenario 2, A is informing the police (lamenting the loss of the car – illocution) in hopes that action will be taken (perlocution).

3. Pair 4: The common locution is the statement that mistakes were made. In Scenario 1, the teacher is warning/advising the students perhaps, telling them they must study more, in which case the perlocutionary act could be one of students studying more or dropping out of the class. In scenario 2, the government leader is perhaps deflecting blame, in which case the hoped for perlocutionary act is that people will vote for that leader again.

4. Open-ended.

Exercise 2.4

(DSA = direct speech act; ISA = indirect speech act)

1. DSA = requesting information ISA = commanding or requesting service
2. DSA = commanding ISA = warning
3. DSA = informing ISA = requesting or commanding a service
4. DSA = informing ISA = requesting (a gift?)
5. DSA = informing ISA = fishing for a compliment/apologizing for state

Exercise 2.5

Possible answers:

1. A is flouting the maxim of Quantity, as the letter of reference is not very informative. This seems to communicate that A does not have very much to say that is positive about John Smith, and to avoid violating the maxim of Quality and lying, and to avoid attacking Smith, A is not as informative as the situation requires.
2. B flouts the maxim of Relation, as the utterance does not answer A's question, perhaps to avoid either disagreeing with A or violating the maxim of Quality and lying about liking the shoes.
3. A flouts the maxim of Manner, as it would be much clearer and briefer to say 'ice cream'. The hearer can thus understand that A does not want the kids to know that ice cream is a possibility.
4. B flouts the maxim of Quantity, as no information is provided about John. Thus A will assume that John did not do well, and that B does not want to provide displeasing information.
5. B flouts the maxim of Relevance in not providing an answer to A's question. A might thus understand that B does not want to hurt his/her feelings.
6. B flouts the maxim of Quantity/Manner – the answer is more informative than required, and it is not brief. A will probably get the picture that B is not free that evening, and will probably not follow through with a suggestion or invitation.

Exercise 2.6

Open-ended.

Exercise 2.7

Open-ended. Some points for discussion might include: striving to help everyone feel comfortable, not put down, and respected; giving people an out – so not forcing them to say 'no'. The next section on Politeness will help answer this question.

Exercise 2.8

FTA = face threatening act

1. Email 1: a. writer wants a copy of the handout. b. FTA on receiver's negative face, as receiver has to take action. c. Strategies to address the FTA involve mainly negative politeness, and include explaining self and purpose, making a polite request (*I wondered if you wouldn't mind ...*), making it easy for receiver to comply with request (*just send it ... I would be happy to send you ...*), and an appeal to the receiver's positive face via complimenting the receiver (I am very interested in your topic ...).
2. Email 2: a. Writer wants to come and stay. b. FTA on receiver's negative face, as having an extra person around the house can perhaps be an imposition. c. Writer uses irony to turn the situation around and suggest that the receiver is threatening her face (*most inconsiderate of you!*), and positive politeness strategies by indicating her desire to see receiver (*I really want to see you all, I'd love to see you, I miss you all*) and a negative politeness strategy by making a polite request *I was wondering ....*

Exercise 2.9

Possible answers (functions are open for discussion)

1. *oh* = prefacing a remark which will alter the listener's knowledge state; *like* = suggesting a possibility
2. *o:kay* = Mom indicates that she knows that the next move is hers.
3. *well* = indicates that what follows may not be what is expected; *like* serves to indicate possibility in the first instance, and approximating in the second. *I dunno like* and *like, I dunno* shows that Carol is open to other possibilities, in case Mom disagrees with what Carol suggests. *But* indicates an adversative relationship with what has come before, and the last *like* again indicates possibility.
4. *Yeah* serves to acknowledge that Mom is listening, and encourages Carol to continue talking.
5. (Carol doesn't really take turn.)
6. *Ok* (brief) frames Mom's move, and *well* signals that what follows may not be what Carol wants to hear. *I mean* serves to justify her question to Carol.

7. *I mean* serves to explain further the phrase *I don't think I'd be alone.* *You know* suggests that speaker and hearer share knowledge, and thus Carol conveys that she never would have thought of going alone. *I dunno* may be allowing Carol to hold the floor while she gathers her thoughts on reasons why her mother should not worry. *But yeah* shows that Carol hears her mother's worry, and the final *you know* may be attempting to create solidarity between the two positions.

Exercise 2.10

You know suggests common knowledge. *Like* suggests approximation, so mitigates a possible boast.

Exercise 2.11

Answers will vary. A sample response:

I analyzed a passage from an episode of *Frasier* (available at http://reocities.com/Hollywood/derby/3267/424.html; I analyzed Scene 1, which has the following discourse markers: *oh* in Frasier's first line (to attract attention and introduce new topic); *oh* in Roz's response (to preface a remark which will alter Frasier's state of understanding of the situation, given that Roz is turning down his offer); *Well* from Frasier in Line 5 of exchange (to mitigate Roz's face-threatening act of turning down his offer); Roz says *you know* in Line 6 of the interaction, to suggest shared knowledge between Frasier and herself about his social life; Line 8 of the interaction has Frasier using a discourse marker which is also used in more formal discourse *in other words* (to recast what Roz says through exaggeration, in essence turning down her suggestion as impossible). Roz in Line 9 prefaces her response with *Well* (which mitigates Frasier's face-threatening act of refusing the offer of a life like hers). In Line 10, Frasier uses *Oh* (to indicate receipt of new information ... that she was sick, when, according to the rest of his response, he thought she was just having a good time); Roz follows this with *Well* in Line 11 (again to mitigate the face-threatening act from Frasier, suggesting that she missed work for a frivolous reason). In this script, all of the discourse markers are at the beginning of the utterances, and there is no stammering or interruption, which contrasts with the real spoken data in Exercise 2.9.

Exercise 2.12

Open-ended

Exercise 2.13

(stressed word is underlined)

1. (a) *This is my <u>new</u> black leather jacket.*
   (b) *This is <u>my</u> new black leather jacket.*
   (c) *<u>This</u> is my new black leather jacket*
   (d) *This is my new black <u>leather</u> jacket*
   (e) *This <u>is</u> my new black leather jacket*

2. (a) *My sister lives in <u>Chicago</u>, but she has a <u>house</u> in Florida.*
   (b) *My sister <u>lives</u> in Chicago, but she has a house in <u>Florida</u>.*
   (c) *My <u>sister</u> lives in Chicago ....*
   (d) *My sister <u>lives</u> in Chicago, <u>but</u> she has a house in Florida.*

3. (a) *<u>Both</u> of my parents were photographers*
   (b) *Both of my parents were <u>photographers</u>.*
   (c) *Both of my parents <u>were</u> photographers*
   (d) *Both of <u>my</u> parents were photographers*

Exercise 2.14

(stressed word is underlined)

1. Do you have a <u>pen</u> I could borrow?
2. <u>Do</u> you have a pen I could borrow?
3. Do <u>you</u> have a pen I could borrow
4. <u>Do</u> you have a pen I could borrow

Exercise 2.15

(stressed word is underlined)

1. Let's go to a restaurant.
2. <u>Which</u> restaurant?
3. An <u>Italian</u> restaurant.
4. We went to an Italian restaurant <u>yesterday</u>.
5. No, yesterday we went to an <u>Argentine</u> restaurant.
6. But they served <u>Italian</u> food.
7. I thought you <u>liked</u> Italian food.
8. I do, but I don't want to eat it every <u>day</u>.
9. Okay. What kind of restaurant <u>do</u> you want to go to?
10. A <u>Japanese</u> restaurant.

Exercise 2.16

(some possibilities)

1. *John loves Mary* (that's a fact)

John loves Mary. (Who? I can't believe it!)

John loves Mary (What a nice surprise!)

2. *Mary's studying medicine.* (that's a fact)

Mary's studying medicine.. (Really? I can't believe it!)

Mary's studying medicine.. (Hmmmm...now that's interesting)

3. You're not wearing that (No way. It looks awful.)

You're not wearing that.. (I'm surprised! I thought you liked it...)

You're not wearing that. (But I thought you were going to...)

Exercise 2.17

Possible answers:

1. C puts forth an assessment to another person. C interprets the silence as prefacing a dispreferred response, as a disagreement of his assessment, and then qualifies his first utterance to mitigate the disagreement between the two interlocutors.
2. A makes a direct request, using a polite form. An insertion sequence follows. This insertion sequence serves as a delay for the dispreferred response to A's initial request, which is why no prefacing or other typical markings of a dispreferred response are needed.
3. C's utterance in T2 is a presequence to the invitation in T4, which saves R from having to justify not being able to respond positively to the invitation.
4. S asks for clarification in Turn 2. L understands it to be a request for repetition (as if S had not heard). Actually, S is surprised by L's word choice, as is apparent in Turn 4, when S repairs L's 'thin' with 'narrow', which L accepts in Turn 5.

Exercise: 2.18

Answers will vary.

Exercise: 2.19

Answers will vary.

Exercise: 2.20

1. Bilabial [p] [b] [m]
2. Labiodental [f] [v]
3. Interdental [ð] [θ]
4. Alveolar [d] [l] [n] [t] [s] [z]
5. Palato-alveolar [ʧ] [ʤ] [ʃ] [ʒ]
6. Velar [g] [k] [ŋ]

Exercise 2.21

Key: P = plosive, F = fricative, A = affricate, N = nasal

1. [b] P
2. [d] P
3. [f] F
4. [g] (as in 'gull') P
5. [k] P
6. [ʤ] (as in judge) A
7. [m] N
8. [n] N
9. [ŋ] (as in sing) N
10. [θ] (as in thigh) F
11. [ð] (as in thy) F
12. [s] F
13. [z] F
14. [ʃ] (as in show) F
15. [ʒ] (as in measure) F

Exercise 2.22

Sound	Point of articulation	Manner of articulation	Voiced counterpart
[p]	bilabial	plosive	[b]
[f]	labiodental	fricative	[v]
[k]	velar	plosive	[g]
[t]	alveolar	plosive	[d]
[s]	alveolar	fricative	[z]
[ʃ]	palato-alveolar	fricative	[ʒ]
[ʧ]	palato-alveolar	affricate	[ʤ]
[θ]	interdental	fricative	[ð]

Exercise 2.23

Note: examples will vary

place→ ↓manner	LABIAL		CORONAL			DORSAL		
	Bilabial	Labio-dental	Inter-dental	Alveolar	Palato-alveolar	Palatal	Velar	Glottal
Nasal +voice	[m] mail			[n] nail			[ŋ] sing	
-voice Plosive	[p] pill			[t] till			[k] kill	[ʔ] ʔapple
+voice	[b] bill			[d] dill			[g] gill	
-voice Fricative		[f] fat	[θ] thigh	[s] sip	[ʃ] show	[ç] huge*		[h] hill**
+voice		[v] vat	[ð] thy	[z] zip	[ʒ] azure			
-voice Approximant	[ʍ] which*							
+voice	[w] witch			[ɹ] red*		[j] your		
-voice Affricate					[tʃ] chip			
+voice					[dʒ] jeep			
Flap +voice				[ɾ] latter*				
Lateral approximant +voice				[l] lip				

Note: *Indicates that the sound is not produced in all varieties of English. **Some linguists classify [h] as an approximant. Shaded areas indicate articulations which are deemed impossible.

Exercise 2.24

Answers will vary according to dialect: these answers are from author's dialect.

1. [kɔt]
2. [kɑt]
3. [cɑɹ]
4. [mɛɹi]
5. [mɛɹi]
6. [mɛɹi]
7. [stɑk]
8. [krik]

Exercise 2.25

1. Vowels pronounced with the tongue close to the roof of the mouth; they are close or near close vowels.
2. Vowels pronounced with the tongue close to the front of the mouth; they are front (or near front) vowels.
3. Vowels pronounced with the tongue near the back of the mouth. They are back (or near back) vowels.
4. Vowels pronounced with the tongue far from the roof of the mouth. Thus they are open (or low in American terminology) or near open vowels.

Exercise 2.26

1. *outright offensive* for *out riding fences* (Eagles, 'Desperado')

   [auɹɹaɪɹəfɛnsəv] [auɹɹaɪɹənfɛnsəs]

   Explanation: The sounds the person hears/doesn't hear: after the second dipthong [aɪ] followed by the flap [ɾ], the person misses the nasal alveolar; then, at the end of the word, the listener substitutes the labiodental [v] for the silibant [s]. This may be because in the song, the word 'fences' is followed by the word 'for', the initial consonant of which is also a labiodental consonant, and thus assimilation explains the mishearing.

2. *round John Virgin* for *round yon Virgin* (Silent Night)

   [ɹaunʤɔnvəʤən] [ɹaundjɔnvəʤən]

   Explanation: The sounds the person hears/doesn't hear: Instead of an alveolar stop followed by a palatal approximant, the person assimilates them into a palatal fricative.

3. *there's a bathroom on the right* instead of *there's a bad moon on the rise* (Creedence Clearwater Revival, 'Bad Moon Rising')

   [ðɛɹzəbæθɹumɑnðəɹaɪt] [ðɛɹzəbædmunɑnðəɹaɪz]

   Explanation: the person first hears an interdental fricative followed by an alveolar approximant, instead of an alveolar stop followed by a bilabial nasal (difficult to explain why!). Then, probably in order to make sense of the phrase, the person hears a bilabial nasal instead of an alveolar nasal. Then at the end of the phrase, the person hears an alveolar plosive, rather than an alveolar fricative, again probably in order to make sense of the phrase as a whole.

4. Answers will vary.

Exercise 2.27

1. *wreck a nice beach* [ɹɛkənaɪsbitʃ] is very close to [ɹɛkəgnaɪs:pitʃ] or *recognize speech*. In fast speech, we delete the [g] in *recognize*, and given that both bilabial plosives in both phrases ([b] and [p] respectively) are preceded by a voiceless sibilant [s], they assimilate means of articulation that make for greater resemblance between them: the [b] becomes less voiced and the [p] loses its aspiration.

2. *ice cream* [aɪskrim] has the same phonetic representation as that for *I scream*.

3. *kiss this guy* [kɪsθəsgaɪ] sounds like [kɪsθəskaɪ] or *kiss the sky*. The [g] in *guy* assimilates the voicelessness of the sibilant [s].

4. *fork handles* [fɔɹkʰændəlz] has the same phonetic representation as *four candles*. As explained in the next section, stops, such as [k] are aspirated when they are word initial; thus *candles* is pronounced [kʰændəlz], which sounds very much like the sequence of sounds [kh].

5. *point of you* sounds as [pɔɪntʌvju] or *point of view*; the [f] in *of* is pronounced as [v] and this is assimilated into the *view*, and the final glide in *view* calls for an assimilation of the vowel sound towards [j].

Exercise 2.28

Answers will vary. Some possibilities:

Initial sounds		Middle sounds		Final sounds	
pat	bat	lazy	lacy	road	wrote
/p/	/b/	/z/	/s/	/d/	/t/
thigh	thy	real	rail	pick	pig
/θ/	/ð/	/i/	/eɪ/	/k/	/g/
chin	gin	lit	light	peer	peel
/tʃ/	/dʒ/	/ɪ/	/aɪ/	/ɹ/	/l/
yell	well	cool	coal	late	laid
/j/	/w/	/u/	/ou/	/t/	/d/
sip	zip	mesher	measure	coy	cow
/s/	/z/	/ʃ/	/ʒ/	/ɔɪ/	/au/
hill	will	bat	bet	belief	believe
/h/	/w/	/æ/	/ɛ/	/f/	/v/
ill	all	putt	pot	sin	sing
/ɪ/	/ɔ/	/ʌ/	/a/	/n/	/ŋ/

Exercise 2.29

/t/ → [tʰ] when word initial

Exercise 2.30

1. There are minimal pairs for [t] and [d]: [bɛd] and [bɛt], so they are separate phonemes
2. [ɾ] is an allophone.
   /t/ and /d/ → [ɾ] when intervocalic, following a stressed vowel

Exercise 2.31

[d] and [ð] are allophones of the same phoneme. There are no minimal pairs. [ð] occurs between vowels. Note that it even occurs across words, as in [aðaðo] *ha dado* or 'has given'.

Exercise 2.32

[b] and [ß] are allophones of the same phoneme. There are no minimal pairs. [b] occurs word initially and following a nasal consonant. [ß] occurs in all other contexts.

Exercise 2.33

Vowel length is phonemic in Pohnpeian, as there are minimal pairs [paa] and [pa], and [tool] and [tol].

Exercise 2.34

Answers will vary. It might be difficult for speakers of English who are learning Spanish to hear the allophonic variation with [d] and [ð] and [b] and [ß], meaning that they might pronounce 'finger' as [dedo] and 'baby' as [bebe] (a pronunciation which causes Spanish speakers to know that they are speaking with a learner!) Probably speakers of English would have difficulty hearing and learning the differences between tones and vowel length, in languages where these features are phonemic. Learners from other languages would probably have difficulty with the allophonic alveolar flap [ɾ] in English.

3 Analyzing written language

The value of having some explicit knowledge of the grammar of written language is that you can use this knowledge, not only to analyse the texts, but as a critical resource for asking questions about them.

(M. A. K. Halliday, 1966: 350)

In this chapter, we focus mainly on analyzing the written language through perspectives that allow us to understand why language is the way it is because of the context for which it has been produced. As with Chapter 2, on the spoken language, where we included ways of looking at language that can also be applied to the written language, the types of linguistic analysis included in this chapter are relevant not only to the written language, and, indeed, some have their genesis in the analysis of spoken language, so they can well be applied to oral, and indeed, multimodal texts as well; however, we draw on them here in order to focus on the analysis of more formal, written language. In the opening quote above by Michael Halliday, we can note the words 'the grammar of written language', which suggests that it is different from the grammar of spoken language; in Chapter 2, we referred to some differences, for example in the types of discourse markers typically used, the greater use of ellipsis, and the use of intonation, pitch and stress to help convey meaning when we are engaged in using language in the spoken mode. In this chapter, in order to focus the spotlight on language in written modes, we turn to methods of text and discourse analysis, which help explain language in its context of use. **Discourse** refers to the totality of interaction between humans within a given sphere or context. Thus, we can talk of 'political discourse' or 'discourse about education'. Political discourse, for example, includes everything from speeches, political cartoons, editorials in newspapers, books about politics and comments by politicians in public arenas. It includes the gestures they use, symbols which refer to political parties and movements, statistics, slogans, etc. A **text** is the linguistic outcome of a specific interaction, such as a particular speech (or part of a speech), a book (or a chapter or a paragraph from a book). In discourse analysis, usually the analyst will look not just at the text, but will also bring in relevant background from the wider discourse, such as what other texts have had to say, what the current political situation is like, what the relationships among participants are, etc. The methods explained in this chapter focus on text, although they in no way confined to it, and include ways of analyzing how text is organized beyond the level of the sentence as well as at the level of the sentence and below. Here we will begin at a more macro-level, at the level of genre; from there we will move to a more micro-level, to the level of the lexicogrammar.

3.1   Genre and text analysis

3.1.1 Genre

Genre analysis attempts to explain variation in texts (and not necessarily written texts) by referring to the context, by linking features of the text to variables of the social and cultural context in which it takes place. It is an analysis which looks beyond written words on the page, or the spoken words in a taped exchange, beyond the text itself, to the social event underlying its production. This type of analysis of language in use is very different from the type of syntactic analysis which we will see in Chapter 4, which looks to model language in terms of mental representations and processes. Genre analysis, along with other perspectives on language, such as systemic functional linguistic theory, which we become familiar with later in this chapter, describes and explains language use in social contexts.

Genre analysis examines texts which are considered members of a genre in order to describe their typical configuration in terms of their features, such as layout and organization of concepts, and their use of vocabulary and grammar (their **lexicogrammar**). We can see clearly that texts do take on certain characteristics which allow us to identify whom they were written for and for what purposes, when we realize how easy it is to place a text from simply reading an excerpt. For example, it may not take you long to figure out the context of this text: 'wer 2.don't go out 2 l8. it takes m 4evr 2 get a cab after 9'. If you are familiar with the genre, you probably recognize that it is an SMS message, more fully spelled out as 'Where to? Don't go out too late. It takes me forever to get a cab after 9'. The most telling feature is probably the abbreviations, especially *l8* for 'late' and *4evr* for 'forever'. The mode, or channel of communication, calls for abbreviated messages, not just in terms of the time it would take to spell out all of the words on a cell phone, but also because of the cost. Another clue is the subject matter of the text: arranging to go out for the evening is a common topic in text messages. We also have clues as to the relationship between the interlocutors in the very direct imperative *don't go out*, suggesting either an imbalance in the relationship, with the sender of the message in a position to order the receiver about, or an equal and close relationship. The justification of the direct speech act in the last line *it takes me 4evr to get a cab after 9* suggests the latter interpretation. Indeed, the SMS message is one written from a young woman to a close friend.

EXERCISE 3.1

Identify each of the following texts in terms of where you think it would be found, what its purpose is, who is writing for whom, what might have come immediately before it and what might come immediately after.

1. **Text 1**

   Preheat oven to 350 degrees F (175 degrees C). Grease one 9 × 13 inch pan.

   Mix the flour, baking soda, baking powder, white sugar, brown sugar, cinnamon, cloves, nutmeg, and salt in a large bowl until well blended. Beat the eggs, oil, and vanilla in a separate bowl until smooth. Fold in the flour mixture, then stir in the pumpkin. Pour the batter into the prepared pan.

2. **Text 2**

   Mary has also been involved this year as a volunteer ESL teacher in our Community English Language program. This program provides free English language instruction for members of the community, and classes are taught by our university students; the only pre-requisite for teaching on the program is a strong command of English, and a desire to provide a service to the host community while learning about teaching and about Spanish culture through interaction with the community students. Mary has brought to the program an incredible amount of enthusiasm and insight, and her students enjoyed having her as a teacher, and also felt that they had learned quite a bit of English.

   Mary's enthusiasm, willingness to work hard, and ability to communicate with people are all qualities which have been of great benefit to our campus.

3. **Text 3**

   Step 1. Bolt together all three of the column assemblies. To do this, lay two assemblies down together as shown in Figure 1. Lay one coupler plate across the joint and bolt together using two 2 3/4" long bolts and lock nuts per plate. See Figure 2. Repeat for the other side. Step 2. Repeat this process again so that you have a total of 3 column assemblies bolted together. Set this assembly aside.

4. **Text 4**

   Last summer, I worked as a receptionist at the Northern Hospital Health Clinic. My position involved me in greeting and helping patients, scheduling appointments, and handling insurance billing under the guidance of the office manager.

   I hope you find that my background and skills would be beneficial to your practice.

5. Text 5

Once upon a time, there was a little girl who lived on the edge of the forest.

6. Text 6

Discussion

Ellis and Mellsop (1985) concluded that de Clérambault's syndrome is an aetiologically heterogeneous disorder. Theories of aetiology have encompassed alcoholism, abortion, post-amphetamine depression, epilepsy, head trauma and neurological disorders. None of these is relevant in this case. Reviewing various descriptions of the pre-morbid personality in pure cases, Mullen and Pathe (1994: 101) summarise by invoking 'a socially inept individual isolated from others, be it by sensitivity, suspiciousness or assumed superiority. These people tend to be described as living socially empty lives ... the desire for a relationship is balanced by a fear of rejection or a fear of intimacy, both sexual and emotional.'

We can recognize texts as belonging to a specific genre, as we can identify who is writing to whom, when and where, and for what purpose in much the same way that we know to respond to a 'hello' with another 'hello'. This ability to recognize a typified response exists most probably because, in order to aid in the achievement of our communicative purposes, a **genre** is a 'staged, goal-oriented, purposeful activity in which speakers engage as members of our culture' (Martin, 2001: 155). While there is variation within a given genre, as genres are not fixed, they tend to follow a series of 'moves' (a term used in genre analysis to refer to a staged maneuver in a text) as in Text 6 in Exercise 3.1, taken from a scholarly journal of psychiatry. Indeed, academic articles of this kind are often organized into the stages, or moves, of:

Introduction → Method(s) → Results → Discussion → Conclusion

The other texts in Exercise 3.1 also exhibit predictable stages, or moves: Text 5 is obviously the beginning of a children's story. This type of story, or fairy tale, typically begins with *Once upon a time,* and the next move provides information as to setting and characters. Text 2 we can recognize as a letter of recommendation, which would typically continue with a statement to the effect that the writer highly recommends the candidate, along with an offer of willingness to provide further information about the candidate if needed. We can also recognize Text 4 as a taking part in an exchange involving employment, in this case that of job application; an application letter typically opens with a declaration of the writer's intention (*I am writing to apply for the position advertised ...*) and ends with a declaration of the candidates' willingness or desire to provide more information and attend an interview, along with further contact details. Somewhere in the middle of those two moves, we would expect to find some explication of the candidates most important qualification for the position, as in Text 4.

These staged moves help us recognize genres, and form the basis for our own writing in these recurring situations, thus allowing us to participate in communicative situations in a way which others will readily recognize as targeted toward giving a communicative purpose. In addition to recognizing genres for the different communicative moves they make, we can also recognize them because of the lexicogrammatical choices text producers make in writing or speaking them. In the psychiatric article (Text 6 in Exercise 3.1), the authors use verbs such as *conclude* and *summarize* to report on what others have said about the syndrome; they also use lengthy noun phrases, or nominal groups, with psychiatric and medical terms *aetiologically heterogeneous disorder, desire for a relationship, a fear of rejection.* The last two phrases could be substituted with other lexicogrammatical choices which are less nominalized, such as *These people desire a relationship but they are also afraid of rejection.* However, scientific and medical journals usually use more nominalized forms of writing, a point which we will return to when we focus on the nominal group in this chapter.

Recipes in English, as in Text 1 in Exercise 3.1, usually include a list of ingredients, and then follow a step-by-step procedure, using the imperative. Assembly instructions also use the imperative, such as in Text 3, yet we do not confuse the two genres, as the lexis in recipes obviously relates to food, and to processes such as *mix, stir, beat* and *fold*, while the lexis of instructions relates to processes of assembling, and items such as *bolts* and *nuts*.

There is much debate about genres, especially regarding the explication of the typical features of genres in terms of their moves and lexicogrammatical features, as many genre researchers feel strongly that they cannot be reduced to their component parts. A focus which analyzes only the texts themselves, and not the **discourse community** in which they participate, leaves out the wider, underlying purposes of a given instance of a genre. A discourse community is a group of people with a set of shared goals and purposes for communicating, which leads to a type or types of communication which tend to be replicated in relatively similar ways. For this reason, many studies within genre-based research have broadened to include descriptions of the context in which the genres under analysis are embedded. These studies can include surveys, interviews and questionnaires of those involved in producing the texts, as well as descriptions of the social relationships that exist amongst readers and writers, and of the potential reasons why writers make the choices they do as they write.

At the same time, there are educators who feel that making generic features explicit can help learners in their efforts to be more successful in the discourse communities in which they wish to participate; thus there are generic descriptions available of academic research articles in various fields, dissertations, theses, school writing in various disciplines, written texts for business purposes, etc. All of this work is useful especially for academic and workplace literacy development. For example, John Swales, a University of Michigan linguist whose work on academic and professional genres has been of key importance, reports on work by several researchers on the moves of the personal statement for entry into college or graduate school. The generic structure of these statements consists of five basic rhetorical moves:

> Move 1: Hook (a narrative to grab the reader's attention)
> Move 2: Program (why this particular specialization/location)
> Move 3: Background (evaluation of skills, landmarks of achievement)
> Move 4: Self-promotion (distinctive individual qualities)
> Move 5: Projection (personal professional goals/career trajectory).
> (Swales, no date)

A good number of effective personal statements include these five moves, and knowledge of this generic structure can be helpful to first time applicants to academic programs.

Swales (1990) also argues that we can say that we really know the conventions of a genre when we can provide a parody of it. Indeed, creativity in writing often involves using a genre in a situation in which it is not typically used. For example, Text 6 in Exercise 3.1 is actually not from a psychiatry journal at all, but rather from an appendix of a novel by Ian McEwan, titled *Enduring Love*, in which one of the male characters becomes obsessed with another male character following a tragic incident which involved them both. The appendix includes an article, 'A homoerotic obsession, with religious overtones: a clinical variant of de Clerambault's syndrome', which is purportedly written by Drs Robert Wenn and Antonio Camia, and reprinted from the *British Review of Psychiatry*. When the novel first came out, some critics suggested that McEwan's basing the story on the article did not show much creativity. With time, however, it became known that it was actually the other way around: McEwan based the article on the novel. That is, he had actually written the article himself, as neither the *British Review of Psychiatry* nor the study's authors exist (in fact, you might notice something interesting if you study the letters of the last names of the two fictitious doctors who wrote the report). In addition to literary critics, McEwan also managed to fool at least one psychiatrist into believing that the article was real,[1] and a book review of the novel appeared in the *Psychiatric Bulletin*, which mentioned McEwan's basing the novel on a published case report. McEwan replied with a letter to the *Psychiatric Bulletin* in August of 1999, in which he clarifies: 'Sir, I can confirm that Appendix 1 of *Enduring Love* is fictional … based on the novel that precedes it rather than the other way round. At the end of a story about rationality, I wanted to produce an extreme example of a highly-determined rational prose such as one might find in a psychiatric case study.' It is fascinating to note the ability of a

---

EXERCISE 3.2

Genre analysis
Explain how our knowledge of genre helps us to see the humor in the letter below.
Dear ......,

> Thank you for your letter rejecting my application for employment with your firm.
>
> I have received rejections from an unusually large number of well qualified organizations. With such a varied and promising spectrum of rejections from which to select, it is impossible for me to consider them all. After careful deliberation, then, and because a number of firms have found me more unsuitable, I regret to inform you that I am unable to accept your rejection.
>
> Despite your company's outstanding qualifications and previous experience in rejecting applicants, I find that your rejection does not meet with my requirements at this time. As a result, I will be starting employment with your firm on the first of the month.
>
> Circumstances change and one can never know when new demands for rejection arise. Accordingly, I will keep your letter on file in case my requirements for rejection change.
>
> Please do not regard this letter as a criticism of your qualifications in attempting to refuse me employment. I wish you the best of luck in rejecting future candidates.
>
> Sincerely,
> John Kador

---

1.   See Miller, Laura (1999, Tuesday September 21) Ian McEwan fools British shrinks. Salon. Retrieved on 1 January 2010 from http://www.salon.com/books/log/1999/09/21/mcewan/

creative writer to so effectively emulate the genre of the psychiatric report, as he suggests was his aim.

In the rest of this chapter, we will explore further kinds of patterns that texts tend to follow, focusing on texts which are written; we then turn to systemic functional grammar to help explain the different kinds of lexicogrammatical choices writers make.

3.1.2 Textual patterns

3.1.2.1 Narrative

Given the pervasiveness of narrative in societies around the world, it is not surprising that text and discourse analysts have focused attention on what it is that makes a narrative in both spoken and written modes. William Labov, based on analysis of spoken interview data in which people related significant events from their lives, suggested that narratives tend to follow a fairly fixed, though flexible structure (Labov, 1972, 1981; Labov and Fanshel, 1977; Labov and Waletsky, 1967). (See Figure 3.1.)

Figure 3.1: Narrative Structure

Abstract	What was this about? Summarizes the point or states a general proposition which the narrative will exemplify. (optional element)
Orientation	Who? When? What? Where? Gives details of time, persons, place, situation.
Complication	Than what happened? Gives the main event sequence and shows a crisis, problem, turning point.
Evaluation	So what? Highlights the point, shows listeners how they are to understand the meaning and reveals the teller's attitude by emphasizing parts of the narrative. (not a separate step; it permeates the narrative)
Result	What finally happened? Shows resolution to crisis
Coda	(Optional way of finishing by returning listeners to present)

Martin Cortazzi (1994) further describes the importance of temporality as a condition to consider something a narrative. Temporality for Cortazzi refers to a sequence of events in time, with a beginning point characterized by a sense of balance (which would correspond to the Orientation in Labov's framework), followed by a middle event which causes that sense of balance to falter through some kind of tension (which corresponds to the Complication), and finally some resolution or outcome based on the lost sense of balance. Indeed, what stands out in a narrative is the tension created by the Complication, by an unexpected twist. Wallace Chafe, in his book *Discourse, Consciousness and Time*, suggests: 'A narrative that fails to conflict with expectations is no narrative at all' (Chafe, 1994: 122).

Guenter Plum (1988) provides an in-depth analysis of different types of story-telling genres, based on the work initiated by Labov and carried further by Cortazzi; in essence, Plum, who also did his research on oral texts, divides narrative further into four genre types. The stages for each of these genres are included in Figure 3.2. Note that the symbol ^ indicates 'followed by'; round brackets, or parentheses, around a stage indicates that it is optional.

Figure 3.2: Story-telling genres

Genre	Generic structure		
	Beginning	Middle	End
Narrative	(Abstract) ^ Orientation	^Complication ^ Evaluation ^ Resolution ^	(Coda)
Anecdote	(Abstract) ^ Orientation	^ Remarkable Event ^ Reaction ^	(Coda)
Exemplum	(Abstract) ^ Orientation	^ Incident ^ Interpretation ^	(Coda)
Recount	(Abstract) ^ Orientation	^ Record of Events ^ Reorientation	(Coda)

(Based on Eggins and Slade, 1997: 236)

Note that an anecdote, like a narrative, contains a kind of complication, or twist, which is not followed by a sense of resolution, as is the narrative. Exemplums are told to make a point, while recounts relate events as they are perceived to have unfolded over time, a genre often used in history textbooks. While these researchers have carried out their analyses on oral texts, we can also apply these generic structures to the analysis of written texts.

EXERCISE 3.3

Identify the stages of the following stories. Which story-telling genre does each best fit? Why?

1. **Text 1**
    These were 10–11 year old kids in a class where I taught English, general knowledge and a bit of music. One day, one of the kids asked about AIDS as it came up in conversation. I explained all about AIDS (in Spanish). I was feeling very good about my explanation; I felt like patting myself on the back, as this was the first time I'd explained something like this to children. The children were in complete silence as they listened, as they were really interested, and I felt that they probably also realized that this was a very delicate topic. So there I was, feeling very good about this explanation, when one boy raised his hand and asked 'Excuse me, teacher, but when you sleep with Sonia, the arts teacher, do you use a condom?'

I went bright red.

But after that, it got really interesting because another student challenged the one who had asked the question saying 'Hey, you can't ask a teacher that kind of question'. After that, a debate ensued amongst all the students as to what kind of questions were appropriate for the classroom. I just stood there and watched them, really happy that they were having this kind of debate about their classroom, ultimately, about their education. (Text written in response to an elicitation of a classroom event)

2. **Text 2**

   The Wolf and the Crane (from Aesop's Fables)

   A Wolf who had a bone stuck in his throat hired a Crane, for a large sum, to put her head into his mouth and draw out the bone. When the Crane had extracted the bone and demanded the promised payment, the Wolf, grinning and grinding his teeth, exclaimed: 'Why, you have surely already had a sufficient recompense, in having been permitted to draw out your head in safety from the mouth and jaws of a wolf.'

   In serving the wicked, expect no reward, and be thankful if you escape injury for your pains.

3. **Text 3**

   The Old Man and His Grandson (from Grimm's Fairy Tales)

   There was once a very old man, whose eyes had become dim, his ears dull of hearing, his knees trembled, and when he sat at table he could hardly hold the spoon, and spilt the broth upon the table-cloth or let it run out of his mouth. His son and his son's wife were disgusted at this, so the old grandfather at last had to sit in the corner behind the stove, and they gave him his food in an earthenware bowl, and not even enough of it. And he used to look towards the table with his eyes full of tears. Once, too, his trembling hands could not hold the bowl, and it fell to the ground and broke. The young wife scolded him, but he said nothing and only sighed. Then they brought him a wooden bowl for a few half-pence, out of which he had to eat.

   They were once sitting thus when the little grandson of four years old began to gather together some bits of wood upon the ground. 'What are you doing there?' asked the father. 'I am making a little trough,' answered the child, 'for father and mother to eat out of when I am big.'

   The man and his wife looked at each other for a while, and presently began to cry. Then they took the old grandfather to the table, and henceforth always let him eat with them, and likewise said nothing if he did spill a little of anything.

4. Text 4

Sweet Porridge (Grimm's Fairy Tales)

There was a poor but good little girl who lived alone with her mother, and they no longer had anything to eat. So the child went into the forest, and there an aged woman met her who was aware of her sorrow, and presented her with a little pot, which when she said, 'Cook, little pot, cook,' would cook good, sweet porridge; and when she said, 'Stop, little pot,' it ceased to cook. The girl took the pot home to her mother, and now they were freed from their poverty and hunger, and ate sweet porridge as often as they chose. Once on a time when the girl had gone out, her mother said, 'Cook, little pot, cook.' And it did cook and she ate till she was satisfied, and then she wanted the pot to stop cooking, but did not know the word. So it went on cooking and the porridge rose over the edge, and still it cooked on until the kitchen and whole house were full, and then the next house, and then the whole street, just as if it wanted to satisfy the hunger of the whole world; and there was the greatest distress, but no one knew how to stop it. At last when only one single house remained, the child came home and just said, 'Stop, little pot,' and it stopped and gave up cooking, and whosoever wished to return to the town had to eat his way back.

3.1.2.2 Problem-solution

Michael Hoey, a researcher based at the University of Liverpool, has done a great deal of research into patterns of organization in texts (Hoey, 2001; 1983); these recurring patterns help to explain the interactive nature of texts, as text producers (in both the written and spoken modes) exploit these patterns in order to evoke a response from their readers. One pervasive pattern in our Anglo-phone culture (although other researchers in this area have applied the analysis to texts from other cultures) is that of the Problem-Solution pattern. The pattern basically consists of four moves (Figure 3.3).

Figure 3.3: Problem/solution pattern

Situation	A description of the situation in which the problem takes place (e.g. an example of a specific situation or a description of a general situation)
Problem	An analysis of the problem: e.g. scope, gravity, causes, effects …
Response	An analysis of already existing ways to treat the problem, and/or a novel solution
Evaluation/result	A positive/negative analysis of the response; if negative, then often a better solution is suggested

We can apply this framework of moves to a text which is organized along this pattern, as shown in Figure 3.4.

Figure 3.4: Sample analysis using the problem/solution pattern

Text
So often in my teaching, I find students whose English is communicatively strong, and possibly accurate too, until pen hits paper. Many are badly let down and held back by their spelling. I decided to find out how I could help these learners improve this skill. There is very little EFL material on the subject, so I also researched spelling for native speaker children and adults. The results of that research have led to the following ideas on how to learn spelling, some ways to teach it and some games to revise it. (From Stirling, J. no date. Waht Can Teachers Do to Halp Bor Spillers? Retrieved on January 1, 2010 from http://www.tesol-spain.org/newsletter/stirling.pdf)

Analysis
Situation: *So often in my teaching, I find students whose English is communicatively strong, and possibly accurate too.*
Problem: *Until pen hits paper. Many are badly let down and held back by their spelling.*
Response: *I decided to find out how I could help these learners improve this skill.*
  Further Problem: *There is very little EFL material on the subject,*
    Response: *So I also researched spelling for native speaker children and adults.*
Evaluation/Result: *The results of that research have led to the following ideas on how to learn spelling, some ways to teach it and some games to revise it.* (Note that the evaluation is implied: the response in the form of research is implicitly evaluated as positive, as it has led to ways of dealing with the problem.)

The pattern can occur across whole texts; for example, it can be a powerful way to organize a research paper for a typical first-year university writing course at an American institution, as the writer can focus on the problem itself, analyzing if it really is a problem, or on various responses to the problem, evaluating their effectiveness.[2] It is often used in scholarly and academic journals, as writers argue for their methods or for the validity of their procedures and findings. The pattern can also occur within texts as a mini-pattern, rather than an overall organizational device for the whole text. Finally, the order of moves can be altered, as writers can, for example, begin with an evaluation of a response before explicating the problem; they can leave off steps, and, for example, write only about a problem, offering no response. The canonical S-P-R-E often allows us as readers to fill in the full pattern from our own knowledge of the context, of the situation, and of the pattern itself, which explains the interactive nature of written text: we bring knowledge of patterns of texts to our reading.

2.   See, for example, the award winning first year writing paper by Ella Berven (1995) Cry wolf. Retrieved on January 2, 2010 from http://www.rscc.cc.tn.us/owl&writingcenter/cyberspace/CryWolf.html

EXERCISE 3.4

Apply the Situation-Problem-Response-Evaluation framework to the following texts, following the example in Figure 3.4.

1. **Text 1**

   Question: What Is The Best Type of Cardiovascular Exercise Machine For Losing Fat Weight?

   There are so many cardiovascular exercise machines in the gym that I feel overwhelmed and I'm not sure which one is the best for losing fat weight. Could you please tell me which cardio machine you think provides sometimes the fastest fat loss?

   Answer: In my opinion, the best type of cardiovascular exercise machine for losing fat weight depends on the sort of shape that the bodybuilding trainee is currently at.

   For a bodybuilder who needs to lose over 30 pounds, I rather have them start using a treadmill with no incline and set at a very comfortable speed. As fat weight is dropped and cardiovascular efficiency improves, the speed can be increased in order to make the activity more challenging. Later on, one can also start adding an incline. By the way, using an incline on a treadmill is a great way for the competitive bodybuilder to burn that stubborn body fat in the glutes and hamstrings area.

   For a bodybuilder with less than 30 pounds to lose, or for an advanced bodybuilder, I would rather use a cross trainer elliptical machine, the one where you also get to move the arms. This machine simulates the running motion, but without the impact experienced in the knees and the ankles. Results achieved by this machine are fast since the number of calories burned through the duration of the activity is very significant; much higher than the calories burned in a treadmill.

2. **Text 2**

   Motorcycle Cancer Seat Patent Granted

   MISSISSAUGA, Ontario, Jan. 8, 2008 /PR Newswire/ – The United Kingdom has granted a patent to Canadian inventor Randall Dale Chipkar for his innovative 'electromagnetic shielding motorcycle seat'. The invention is designed to shield motorcycle electromagnetic field radiation from penetrating the rider's vital organs.

   'I am grateful to the UK for sharing my vision and I appreciate their recognition of this serious health concern for motorcyclists. This is a major step in my quest to protect riders worldwide,' Chipkar says.

   'Various types of extremely low frequency (ELF) electromagnetic field (EMF) radiations have been linked to health disorders including cancer. Many motorcycles generate excessive ELF EMF radiation up

through the seat penetrating directly into the rider's groin and torso. The prostate is of major concern as it is one of the closest delicate glands invaded by the radiation. The colon and neighboring organs are also at risk,' adds Chipkar.

ELF EMF radiation at close exposure is unnatural and over time could have devastating biological consequences. Major organizations now agree that ELF EMF magnetic fields are a possible carcinogen. People should not have to gamble with their health because they love riding motorcycles. Consumer safety is priority.

'ELF EMF magnetic fields penetrate through steel and even lead. Only highly processed material can dramatically shield us from these cancer controversial forces. With patent protection, we can now aggressively market innovative internally shielded seats to provide riders with peace of mind,' Chipkar says.

Chipkar adds, 'I am now open to licensing or even selling some of my worldwide patents as long as I am assured shielded seats can reach consumers immediately. Hopefully, this new RiderSaver ™ seat accessory will revolutionize the motorcycle industry to keep riders safer.'

'Let's put "true freedom" back into riding motorcycles!' Chipkar concludes.

3. **Text 3**
    Recipe reviews for: Adrienne's Tom Ka Gai
    'Garlic, ginger, lemon grass, chile peppers, coriander and cumin flavor this Thai-inspired coconut milk soup with chicken and bok choy.'

    I modified this to suit what I had at home. I didn't have peanut oil (used olive oil), left out the ginger, lemon grass, fish sauce and bok choy. I used 2 cans coconut milk, and only 3/4 cup of chicken broth (instead of water) I also skipped the cilantro. I added rice noodles with 10 minutes cooking time left, and I ended up with a wonderful dish of noodles and sauce – which was just excellent! The only thing I would have changed would be to add more broth, since I needed more liquid, but it was excellent the way it was. So maybe it wasn't this recipe in the end but this was what I started from anyway. I think no matter what you do to this it turns out well, so have fun with it!!

3.1.2.3 Related patterns

Hoey (2001) notes other popular patterns of exposition in text which have a similar configuration to that of Problem-Solution. For example, rather than a problem, a text may be focused on a goal, and how that goal might be achieved, and may include an evaluation of the method(s) put forth to do so. Or a text might focus on an opportunity which has presented itself in some way, and include a response to that opportunity (whether it was taken up or not), as well as an evaluation of the response. Another popular pattern within these lines is that of a description of a situation in which a desire is aroused, followed by an explanation of the way in which an attempt was made to fulfill that desire, along with an evaluation of that attempt. A final pattern that parallels these other patterns is that of an indication of a lack of knowledge of something, followed by the means by which that knowledge might be achieved, along with an evaluation of those means. These patterns are summed up in Figure 3.5.

Figure 3.5: Other patterns of text organization

Goal-Achievement	Situation ^ Goal ^ Means of Achievement ^ Evaluation/Result
Opportunity-Taking	Situation ^ Opportunity ^ Taking ^ Evaluation/Result
Desire-Arousal Fulfillment	Situation (Object of Desire) ^ Desire Arousal ^ Attempt at Desire Fulfillment ^ Positive or Negative Result
Gap in Knowledge-Filling	Situation ^ Gap in Knowledge ^ Proposed Filling ^ Evaluation/Result

Hoey (2001:167) shows the relationship between the different patterns through the diagram represented in Figure 3.6.

Figure 3.6: Patterns of text organization summary

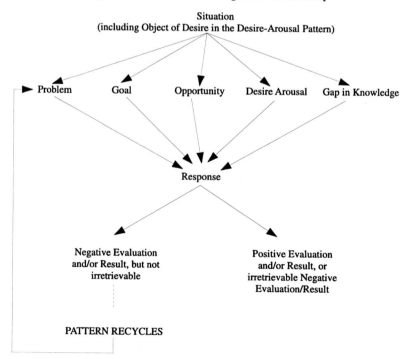

These patterns can occur on their own, as part of a text, and can also co-occur side-by-side or nested inside each other. Hoey (2001) analyzes the tale of *Goldilocks and the Three Bears*, showing that parts of it can be seen as a Problem-Solution pattern: for example, the bears leave the house in order to let the porridge cool down; Goldilocks eats the porridge because she is hungry (hunger is a problem, which is solved by trying two different bowls of porridge which are negatively evaluated as either too hot or too cold, until the final response is judged to be just right); and she uses one of the beds (after two of them are also evaluated negatively) to take care of her problem of tiredness. However, Hoey (2001: 145) quite rightly points out that the middle action of Goldilocks, that is when she sits in a chair, is not in response to any problem at all, but rather she sees the opportunity to sit down and takes it; thus this section of the tale exploits the Opportunity-Taking pattern. In Figure 3.4, the writer includes the line 'There is very little EFL material on the subject, so I also researched spelling for native speaker children and adults', which effectively embeds a Gap in Knowledge-Filling pattern within an overall Problem-Solution pattern. This writer signals that there is indeed a lack of knowledge about a topic when she writes 'there is very little EFL material', and the language teacher readers of the article will then expect the writer to at some point fill in this gap that exists in the collective knowledge. Indeed, as readers, our expectations of the appearance on the scene of the text of a given pattern are often raised based on the types of words writers choose, as they signal these patterns through the lexical choices that they make as they write.

3.1.2.4 Lexical signaling

Patterns in text are often signaled by the word choices we make. These types of word choices are divided into three different categories, which we illustrate here with respect to the Problem-Solution Pattern:

Vocabulary 1 items: subordinators
e.g. *While* I was walking home from work, *because* it started raining, I dashed into the department store. I was able to stay dry.
Note: with subordinators, textual sequencing is flexible. We can also say: I was able to stay dry *by* dashing into the department store *when* it started raining *while* I was walking home.

Vocabulary 2 items: Conjuncts
Last night, I was walking home from work. It started to rain. *Therefore*, I dashed into the department store. *In this way*, I managed to stay dry.
Note: with conjuncts, clause sequencing is not flexible.

Vocabulary 3 items: Lexical signaling

The situation was that I was walking home from work. It started to rain, and it was clear that I was going to take a soaking, as I had no umbrella. I *solved* this *problem* dashing into the department store. This *achieved* the *desired result* of keeping me dry.

or

The *means* whereby I kept dry was by dashing into the department store. The *cause* of my need to keep dry was that it started to rain and I had no umbrella with me. The *circumstance* of my being out when it started raining was that I was walking home from work.

Further signals for the Problem-Solution pattern include such words and phrases as *do about* and *unable* (as in *I didn't know what to do about the rain* or *I was unable to stay dry*). For the Goal-Achievement pattern we might see words and phrases such as *want to, would like to, in order to, aim,* and *objective* (as in *I wanted to stay dry; my goal was not to get wet*). The Opportunity-Taking pattern often simply presents a concept or object as one that has been used for an end, simply because it was available, via adverbial clauses such as *taking advantage of X*; it also employs Vocabulary 3 items such as *opportunity,* or *chance* (e.g. *When it started to rain, I saw that the department store doors were open, so I grabbed the opportunity to stay dry*). The Desire-Arousal Fulfillment pattern uses words that suggest a positive evaluation of an object not possessed (*attractive, helpful*) (e.g. *I saw the welcoming doors of the department store*). The Gap in Knowledge-Filling pattern might use phrases such as *in the absence of (research on, knowledge about), given the lack of, little material about,* etc (as in *I did not know whether or not there was a chance of rain, so I checked the weather online*).

EXERCISE 3.5

Decide which pattern best describes each of the texts below (Problem-Solution, Goal-Achievement, Opportunity-Taking, Desire-Arousal Fulfillment, Gap in Knowledge-Filling). Explain how the text exploits the pattern, and list the signals, along with their type (Vocabulary 1, 2, or 3) which helped you classify the text according to the pattern you chose.

Example text and analysis
If you would like to have a nice vacation in a Branson cabin rental we have some of the nicest vacation rentals and cabins available anywhere.

Enjoying your vacation in Branson Missouri might just be too much fun! (posted on Craigslist, 2009-01-04, 2:20PM CST, Retrieved on January 4, 2009 from http://kansascity.craigslist.org/vac/979994025.html)

This text uses the Desire-Arousal Fulfillment pattern. It first uses a Vocabulary 1 item (the subordinator 'if') to signal a hypothetical situation, including 'a nice vacation in a Branson cabin rental', *which is a Vocabulary 3 item, to signal the object of desire. It provides the response (or means of fulfillment of the desire) through the Vocabulary 3 item* 'nicest vacation rentals and cabins available anywhere'. *It provides a positive evaluation of the response by also choosing Vocabulary 3 item* 'too much fun'.

1. **Text 1**

The path to lean success – WHEN A SPANISH MANUFACTURER UPGRADED ITS PRODUCTION EQUIPMENT IT TOOK THE OPPORTUNITY TO TAKE THE FIRST STEPS ON A LEAN JOURNEY. Serrano, I.; Laca, A.; De Castro, R.

Manufacturing Engineer, *Volume 85, Issue 6, Dec.–Jan. 2006 Page(s): 26–29*

Abstract: Spanish manufacturer of industrial electrical appliances, Fagor Industrial, redesigned its production system to enable lean flows by means of waste reduction. Using the value stream mapping (VSM) technique to analyze and plan the improvement project, Fagor decided to make technological changes to its sheet metal cutting line. The seven Trumpf punching machines were replaced with four new laser technology machines, in addition to the acquisition of the latest generation software. This allowed Fagor to create multi-part programs, guaranteeing good use of sheet metal, which also gives the advantage of working with unitary batches of parts adjusting the production to the demand. This also provided the opportunity of working in kanban supply system, owing to the reduction of format changes in the machines. Furthermore, there is freedom in the design process as the dependency between the set of punches and the geometry of the part is eliminated.

(Retrieved on January 1, 2010 from: http://ieeexplore.ieee.org/xpl/freeabs_all.jsp?tp=&arnumber=4104825&isnumber=4104814)

2. **Text 2**

What's so good about So Good? Well, to be honest, pretty much everything!

That's because since launching twenty years ago, we've done everything we can to provide the healthiest soymilk there is, and the result, well we're proud to say that it's not only New Zealand's most nutritious soymilk, but it's also New Zealand's favourite.

So Good is an easy way to provide your body with healthy nourishment. That's because So Good is made from non-genetically modified soy. It contains high levels of calcium for strong bones, low saturated fats for a healthy heart and absolutely no cholesterol, animal fats or lactose.

Best of all, when you make healthy food choices combined with regular physical activity you make a positive impact on your entire life.

3. **Text 3**

A great deal of research has now established that written texts embody interactions between writers and readers, but few studies have examined the ways that small acts of reformulation and exemplification help contribute to this. Abstraction, theorisation and interpretation need to be woven into a text which makes sense to a particular community of readers, and this invariably involves frequent reworkings and exemplifications as writers assess the processing needs, knowledge and rhetorical expectations of their readers to present and then interpret ideas as they write. Known as code glosses in the metadiscourse literature, these elaborations help to contribute to the creation of coherent, reader-friendly prose while conveying the writer's audience-sensitivity and relationship to the message. Drawing on a large corpus of research articles, I explore how professional academic writers monitor their texts for readers in this way to restate information or provide examples as they construct their arguments. Analysis of the corpus reveals that elaboration is a complex and important rhetorical function in academic writing, and that both its use and meanings vary according to discipline. (Hyland, 2007: 266)

4. **Text 4**

Learn To Type in One Hour – A Giant Leap Forward For Touch Typing

Miracle Type is a fast, simple, effective method for learning to touch type quickly and accurately on your computer. Imagine how much time this could save you!

£11.74 or $19.99

Miracle Type is the answer. Miracle Type is the perfect answer for you if typing on your computer is just taking far too long or if you have given up in frustration after trying to teach yourself to Touch Type with other typing software.

Miracle Type will save you time. Miracle Type is a giant leap forward for Touch Typing. It dramatically reduces the learning time to Just One Hour and will teach you to type faster than any other typing tutor on the market. Guaranteed! (Retrieved on January 4, 2009 from http://www.miracletype.com/)

We are now at the level of lexicogrammar in terms of analyzing how texts work, of explaining the ways in which writers exploit patterns to organize their texts in order to interact with their readers. We turn now to a theory of language which can help us understand further how the linguistic choices we make contribute to meaning-making in interaction, continuing with our focus in this chapter on interaction through the written mode.

3.2   Systemic Functional Linguistics

In this part of the chapter, we introduce concepts of Systemic Functional Linguistics (SFL), a functional account of the lexicogrammar of language (as explained in Chapter 1). There has been a great deal of research put into the theoretical and applied descriptions of language using SFL theory, from the more macro level of genre to the more micro level of groups and phrases. In this section, we begin at the level of groups and phrases, to work up to the makings of a clause, and from there to clause complexes. Then we will be well-equipped to analyze longer stretches of texts by combining analyses of clause complexes with analyses of genre in order to gain insights into why texts are composed in the way that writers (and of course speakers) choose.

Indeed, a key notion within SFL is that of choice: we have choices open to us at all levels, or **ranks**, when we use language to achieve our communicative purposes. SFL posits a **scale of rank**, which exists in the grammar of every language; the rank scale of English (and of other languages) is as follows:

clause
phrase/group
word
morpheme

That is, clauses are made up of phrases/groups, which in turn are made up of words, which in turn are made up of morphemes (see Chapter 4). For our purposes, we will examine the first two ranks, that of phrase/group and that of clause, in terms of what they consist of and how they function in language to contribute to different kinds of meaning. Throughout this section, we will be providing descriptions from what is often called the 'Sydney grammar' of SFL, as there is also a major school of SFL based at the University of Cardiff, under the direction of Professor Robin Fawcett (Fawcett 2008). While there are some differences between the 'Sydney grammar' and the 'Cardiff grammar' (some liken the two versions to different dialects of the same grammar),[3] the versions share the same roots and the same basic concepts.

3.2.1 Groups

3.2.1.1 Nominal group

The nominal group, which is known in formal syntactic theories as the noun phrase, contains a **Head**[4] noun, plus any **Pre-modifiers** and **Post-modifiers**, as illustrated in this example, the Post-modifier contains another nominal group, *black caps*, which consists of a Pre-modifier *black* + a Head noun *caps*:

the two slightly nervous assistant	*professors*	*wearing black caps*
Pre-modifiers	**HEAD**	**Post-modifier**

EXERCISE 3.6

Identify the head nouns of the following and label the Pre-modifiers and Post-modifiers.

1. *various descriptions of the pre-morbid personality*
2. *four new laser technology machines*
3. *results achieved by this machine*
4. *a giant leap forward for Touch Typing*
5. *the cashier who was shown the video footage*

The elements of a nominal group can be further analyzed into their specific functions with respect to the head noun. The internal experiential structure of the nominal group specifies the function of each of the modifiers to the Head, for example as to whether the modifier in question further describes, or provides an indication of the quantity, or qualifies it in some way. Table 3.1 names and explains the different types of functions modifiers can carry out within the nominal group.

---

3.   See the Cardiff grammar website for more information. Retrieved on 20 February 2010 from http://www.cardiff.ac.uk/encap//fontaine/cardiffgrammar/cardiffgrammar.htm

4.   Note that in Systemic Functional Linguistics, the convention is to capitalize the first letter of clause functional elements.

Table 3.1: The experiential structure of nominal groups

Function	Explanation
Thing	The main entity (usually, but not always, coincides with Head)
Deictic	Indicates whether or not some specific subset of the Thing is referred to
Post-deictic	A second deictic element; adds further information for the identification of the Thing
Numerative	Indicates some numerical feature of the Thing: either quantity or order, either exact or inexact
Epithet	Indicates some quality of the Thing, either an objective property, or some expression of the speaker's attitude toward it
Classifier	Indicates a particular subclass of the Thing in question
Qualifier	Further characterizes or specifies the Thing

We can now look at our earlier example and analyze each of the functions of the nominal group:

the	two	slightly nervous	assistant	professors	wearing black caps
Deictic	**Numerative**	**Epithet**	**Classifier**	**Thing**	**Qualifier**
<———— pre-modifiers ————>				Head	post-modifier

The Qualifier in this example contains a further nominal group: *black caps*, consisting of Epithet and Thing.

Deictics point us towards a specific instance or tell us if we are to have in mind a non-specific instance of the main element of the nominal group. In English, we have several resources to signal deixis:

> **Specific:** the, this, that, these, those, my, your, her, his, her, our, their, Anne's, one's, which, what, whose
> **Non-specific:** a(n), all, either, both, each, every, neither, no, some, any

The absence of a Deictic indicates a non-specific nominal group (e.g. Ømoney, Øpeople).

Post-deictics further identify the Thing by making reference to its familiarity, its status in the text, or its similarity/dissimilarity to some other entity already mentioned (e.g. *same, different, other, certain, possible, aforementioned, infamous,* etc.).

Numeratives also limit the scope of reference, in terms of 'how many'. In addition to definite numeratives, such as *one, two, three, first, second, third, next, last, a couple (of), a quarter (of), dozens, hundreds, millions,* etc., there are also indefinite numeratives, such as *many, much, a lot of, several, some, any, a few, a little, few, little, fewer, fewest, less, least, more and most.*

Epithets provide the speaker/writer's take on the Thing; they tell us some quality or modify in some way a characteristic of the Thing. They can be modified by an adverb, as in <u>very</u> happy, <u>slightly</u> awkward.

Classifiers tell us the type of Thing; they provide a subcategorization of the Thing. They cannot by modified by an adverb. They can be realized by adjectives, nouns, or participles: e.g. *urban growth, city growth, living organisms, assistant professors.*

Sometimes the same word can be used as an Epithet or as a Classifier, as in the nominal group *a Spanish history teacher*; in these instances we can use our functional labels to disambiguate the meaning. If *Spanish* is being used as an Epithet, then it is describing some quality or characteristic of the teacher, and is not classifying her; thus, she is Spanish, from Spain. If *Spanish* is being used as a Classifier, then it is subcategorizing the field of history, and *Spanish + history* serve to categorize the teacher; that is, whether or not she is from Spain, she teaches the history of Spain:

a	*Spanish*	*history*	*teacher*
Deictic	Epithet	Classifier	Thing

We see in the above interpretation that *Spanish* modifies *teacher*, and thus it is a teacher of history, who is Spanish.

a	*Spanish*	*history*	*teacher*
Deictic	Classifier	Classifier	Thing

In this interpretation, *Spanish* serves to classify *history*, so here we have a teacher of Spanish history. We can also note here that *history* is a noun, which modifies another noun, *teacher*. Often nouns modifying other nouns indicates an instance of classifying (as in <u>bus</u> station, <u>train</u> station), although other resources, such as adjectives and –*ing* forms can also serve as Classifiers.

Qualifiers come after the Thing, and provide further specification in terms of *which one?* Structurally, they can be composed as:

- finite clauses: *the child who is sitting in the corner* (note here we have a full clause modifying a noun; in these cases, the clause is embedded, or **rankshifted**, given that it is functioning at a rank lower than itself – see Section 3.2.3.2)
- nonfinite clauses: *the child sitting in the corner*, *the book written by Grimes*
- prepositional phrases: the child *in the corner*

EXERCISE 3.7

Label the functions of the elements in the nominal groups (Deictic, Post-deictic, Epithet, Classifier, Thing, Qualifier).
1. *various descriptions of the pre-morbid personality*
2. *four new laser technology machines*
3. *results achieved by this machine*
4. *a giant leap forward for Touch Typing*
5. *the cashier who was shown the video footage*

EXERCISE 3.8

In some languages, such as Spanish, it is more frequent to use a Qualifier in order to classify a Thing, such as *estación del tren* 'station of the train', while English prefers to use nouns as Classifiers, as in *train station*. This ability to use a noun to function in essence as an adjective is often a difficult aspect of the English language for learners to acquire, and thus they use expressions such as

> *acute pain of the lower back*
> *the nerve roots of the spine*
> *experience in the field and laboratory*

While all of these expressions are correct in English, the following are far more frequent:

> *acute lower back pain*
> *the spinal nerve roots*
> *field and laboratory experience*

The writers of the following nominal groups used the less frequent Qualifier to indicate the type of Thing. Their wording is certainly correct, yet in their original contexts, the phrases were not quite apt in expressing the intended meaning. Rewrite the groups, using Classifiers instead of Qualifiers.

1. *a patient's condition of cancer*
2. *an experience of learning*
3. *many serious problems in relation to racial issues*
4. *the area of the brain that was injured*
5. *inconsistent methods in reporting*

EXERCISE 3.9

Epithet or Classifier? Identify the elements of the nominal groups, commenting on any ambiguity arising from labeling an element as a Classifier or as an Epithet. How could you use them differently in sentences? How might you stress the words differently?
1. *dancing girls*
2. *late train*

EXERCISE 3.10

Choose two different text types (for example, a literary text and a science textbook, or a newspaper article and a travel brochure), and select a paragraph from each. Analyze the nominal groups in the paragraphs in terms of their internal functional structure. How are they similar across the two texts? How are they different?

3.2.1.2 Verbal group

The verbal group is an expansion of the verb, just as the nominal group is an expansion of the noun. The verbal group consists of a **Finite**, which lets us know the tense and number (in English), as it is the element in the verbal group that carries the agreement with the Subject of a clause, plus a **Predicator**, which gives us our lexical information, it lets us know what the process taking place is. In the clause, in some verbal groups the Finite (F) and Predicator (P) are fused into one word:

Teething usually	*begins*... F/P
The lower jaws	*become*... F/P
The speaker	*argued*... F/P

In the case of interrogatives and negative declaratives in English, the Finite and Predicator are separate:

Does	*teething usually*	*begin...?*
F		P

The lower jaws	*don't*	*become...*
	F	P

except in the case of the copular verb *to be*:

Is	*there a reason to...?*
F/P	

In fact, in the case of the verb *to be*, many linguists feel that there is no lexical content, and thus no Predicator, so it is often considered as simply Finite, and labeled only as 'F'.

Verbal groups can consist of other elements in addition to the Finite and Predicator. These other elements may indicate **Modality** (possibility/probability) and **Polarity** (yes/no), or function as **Auxiliaries** (in order to create perfect and imperfect aspect, or the passive voice). Modality, through finite modal operators, such as *can, could, may, might, must, shall, should, will, would,* tells us how possible or probable the event is:

Your baby	*will*	*produce*	
	Finite/Modal	Predicator	

no single cause	*can*	*provide*	*the answer*
	Finite/Modal	Predicator	

Note that the Finite becomes fused with the Modal in these cases.

Polarity comes into play in interrogative and negative declarative clauses, as it refers to the positive/negative poles of the Predicator. English is complex in its construal of negative declaratives and interrogative clauses, as polarity is indicated through *not*, yet we have to add a Finite auxiliary operator in the form of the auxiliary verb *do/did* in most verbal groups (unless there is a modal operator present, unless it is the verb *to be*, or unless there is another Auxiliary present):

that defense	*did*	*not*	*get off*	*to a promising start*
	Finite/Aux	Polarity	Predicator	

the symptoms of teething	*do not*	*include*	*bronchitis*
	Finite/Aux/Polarity	Predicator	

it	*doesn't*	*have*	*a monopoly in operating systems*
	Finite/Aux/Polarity	Predicator	

Do	*they*	*sing*	*well?*	*Does*	*he*	*sing*	*well?*
Finite/Aux		Predicator		Finite/Aux		Predicator	

The verbal group also can consist of Auxiliaries, such as the case of *have/ had* when used with the past participle to indicate perfect (completed) aspect (*have* seen, *had* learned), the form of the verb *be* when used with the present participle to indicate imperfect (incomplete) aspect (*are* going, *was* living), and the form of the verb *be* in the case of the passive (*was* given, *is being* airlifted). If there is no other Finite present (such as the verb *do* in the case of negative or interrogative, or one of the Finite Modal Operators), then the Auxiliary contains the Finite:

they	*had*	*learned*	*quite a bit*
	Finite/Aux	Predicator	

the glaciers	*were*	*shrinking back*
	Finite/Aux	Predicator

Linguists	*have*	*been*	*characterized*
	Finite/Aux	Aux	Predicator

Verbal groups can be very complex, containing a number of auxiliaries, such as *She may have been being harassed by her boss.*

may	*have*	*been*	*being*	*harassed*
Finite/Modal	Aux	Aux	Aux	Predicator

It is interesting to note the parallelism between the nominal and verbal groups in terms of how they structure experience in order for a smooth interchange to take place between people: 'Both verbal and nominal group begin with the element that "fixes" the group in relation to the speech exchange; and both end with the element that specifies the representational content' (Halliday and Matthiessen, 2004: 336).

EXERCISE 3.11

One way to spot whether a sentence is active or passive is to note that the passive construction consists of some form of the verb *to be* (either as Finite or as an Auxiliary) followed by the past participle as Predicator. Indicate if the following sentences are active or passive, and analyze their verbal group structures:

E.g. *Was Hamlet written by Shakespeare?*

Passive sentence: *was* = Finite/Aux, *written* = Predicator

1. *A choir was singing yuletide carols.*
2. *Many students brought gifts to the teacher.*
3. *Socks were knitted by thousands of women for the soldiers.*
4. *My car has been stolen three times.*
5. *I had been waiting for three hours when the car was finally brought in.*
6. *The mechanic may have taken it out for a spin.*

EXERCISE 3.12

Analyze the nominal groups in Texts 1 and 2 in terms of their experiential structure. How are they similar? How are they different? Do the same for the verbal groups. *Note*: Do not consider the nominal groups in titles or subtitles, and do not consider the verbal groups which are used in post-modification of nominal groups (for example, in Text 2, do not consider *taken* in the nominal group *length of time taken to erupt*).

1. **Text 1:** Parenting Tips for Your 6 Month Old Baby

   Your baby's first teeth will probably come in easily. She may have slightly inflamed gums, some drooling, and quite a bit of chewing as the first teeth come through. To comfort your baby, rub her gums with your clean finger or give her a cool safe teething ring she can chew.

   *When teething, your baby may have a runny nose or a rash on her face and neck. She also may be fussy. Teething does **not** cause high fever above 101 degrees, vomiting, or diarrhea. If these symptoms occur, call your doctor.*

   After teething, the first tooth is a welcome sight. By the time your child is 2 to 3 years old, all 20 baby teeth should be in.

   (Retrieved on January 1, 2010 from http://www.extension.org/pages/Your_Baby's_First_Tooth_May_be_Causing_Her_Some_Pain)

2. **Text 2:** Eruption of the primary dentition in human infants: a prospective descriptive study.

PURPOSE: This study investigated the clinical process of the emergence phase of eruption of the primary dentition including length of time taken to erupt and the association between soft tissue changes and stages of eruption. METHODS: Twenty-one children aged 6–24 months at commencement of the study were recruited from three suburban daycare centers in Melbourne, Australia. Daily oral examinations of each child were conducted for seven months. RESULTS: One hundred twenty-eight teeth were observed during eruption. Swelling very infrequently accompanied tooth eruption and in all cases was mild. Forty-nine percent of observed teeth demonstrated gingival redness during the emergence stages of eruption, but there was no significant relationship between redness and specific stages of eruption. Mean duration of eruption, from palpable enlargement of the gingival tissue to full eruption, was 2.0 months (range 0.9–4.6 months). The average rate of eruption was 0.7 mm per month. Many of the deciduous teeth appeared to demonstrate an 'oscillating' pattern of eruption, (emerging and then retreating before emerging again). Timing of oscillation was not specific to stage of eruption or tooth type. This was defined as a 'transitional' phase of eruption which appears to be common. (Hulland S A; Lucas J O; Wake M A; Hesketh K D (2000)

Eruption of the primary dentition in human infants: a prospective descriptive study.

Pediatric Dentistry 22(5): 415–421. © 2000 American Academy of Pediatric Dentistry and reprinted with their permission. Retrieved February 24, 2010 from http://www.biomedexperts.com/Abstract.bme/11048313/ Eruption_of_the_primary_dentition_in_human_infants_a_prospective_ descriptive_study

3.2.1.3 Other groups

A **preposition group** consists of a group with a preposition as Head; it may consist solely of a preposition (*in, on, down, under*), or it may be modified, as in *straight up* or *right behind*, where *up* and *behind* are Head of their respective groups. The Head may be a complex preposition, such as *in front of*. A preposition group usually forms part of a **prepositional phrase**, which consists of a preposition group followed by a complement in the form of a nominal group.

A prepositional phrase can function as a Post-modifier/Qualifier, as in *the symptoms of teething*, where *of teething* qualifies *symptoms*. A prepositional phrase can also function as an Adjunct (which we will revisit below), and sometimes ambiguity arises if the function is not clear. We can see this with the sentence: *The man saw the boy with the telescope.* Given that it is not clear who had the telescope, the man (who was perhaps spying from a distance) or the boy (who was carrying it), we can disambiguate the meaning functionally, that is by suggesting that the prepositional phrase functions either as an **Adjunct** (which serves to give us more information related to the clause, a point which we return to below) or as a Qualifier (which functions to give us more information about the nominal group, telling us which boy):

The man	*saw*	*the boy*	*with the telescope.*
nominal group	verbal group	nominal group	prepositional phrase = Adjunct
			(tells us what the man used)

The man	*saw*	*the boy with the telescope.*	
nominal group	verbal group	nominal group with prepositional phrase =	
		Qualifier	
		(tells us which boy)	

An **adjective group**, as its name suggests, has as its head an adjective, which may have pre- and post-modification, as in

(I am)	*slightly*	*nervous*	*about wearing that black cap.*
	Pre-modifier	HEAD	Post-modifier

We are now ready to examine how these groups and phrases work together to create different kinds of meaning through the clause.

3.2.2 Clause metafunctions

Systemic functional linguistics posits three metafunctions of language; that is, through language, we express the **interpersonal**, the **ideational**, and the **textual**. The interpersonal metafunction of language allows us to establish and maintain relationships, to interact with others, and to express our opinions and feelings about propositions, about others, and about the world. The ideational metafunction of language allows us to express our experience, whether that experience be concrete or abstract, real or imaginary, in our minds or out there in the world; it is further divided into two subfunctions: the **experiential**, which 'makes it clear that the underlying function is seen not as the expression of "reality" or "the outer world" but as the expression of patterns of experience; the content given to an utterance by this portion of the language system derives from the shared experience of those participating in the speech situation' (Halliday, 1968: 209), and the

logical subfunction, which allows us to make connections across concepts and events. Through the textual metafunction, we bring the interpersonal and ideational metafunctions into being, as we use language to organize these two metafunctions into ordered or coherent wholes.

We can relate these three metafunctions to different aspects, or systems, of the clause. These systems are known as the **clause as exchange** (which relates to interpersonal meaning), the **clause as representation** (which relates to the ideational function), and the **clause as message**, which relates to the textual metafunction.

3.2.2.1 Clause as exchange

The interpersonal metafunction of language allows us to establish relationships with others through two basic speech functions: giving and demanding. These speech functions of giving and demanding are put into play as a means of providing and eliciting goods and services, on the one hand, and information, on the other hand. We focused to some extent on the elicitation of goods and services in Chapter 2 on the spoken language, with utterances such as 'Would you mind just closing that window for a little bit?', or 'It's cold in here' or 'Shut that window!'. You do not have to respond with actual speech, as you can simply go over and shut the window (or make some gesture to me that indicates what you think of my request for your service!). The exchange of information, on the other hand, does call for a verbal response, as it in essence involves 'tell me something'. By bringing together giving and demanding, on the one hand, and goods/services and information, on the other, we arrive at our four primary speech functions, as shown in Figure 3.7.

Figure 3.7: Primary speech functions

	goods & services	information
giving	offer *Would you like some coffee?*	statement *He is making the coffee.*
demanding	command *Give me some coffee!*	question *What is he making?*

Focusing on the exchange of information, we can construct an imaginary spoken dialogue (but perhaps you have been involved in a similar type):

A: *Mom. John stole my pencil.*
J: *No I didn't.*
A: *Yes you did.*
J: *No I did not.*

A: *Yes you did.*
J: *Did not.*
A: *Did so.*
J: *No I didn't.*
A: *You're a liar.*
J: *No I'm not.*
A: *Yes you are.*
J: *Am not.*
A: *Are so. Look, you're using my pencil.*
J: *This is MY pencil!*
A: *No it isn't.*
J: *It is!*
A: *It is not.*

In this dialogue, very little information is actually being exchanged: just the four bits of information which are underlined *John stole my pencil, you're a liar, you're using my pencil* and *this is MY pencil*; so, in most of the exchanges, it is as if the same information were being tossed back and forth between the two interlocutors using something to stand in for the actual content words. In analyzing just what it is linguistically the rest of the exchanges consist of we are left with (leaving aside the *yes* and *no*):

I didn't/I did not
you did/did so
I'm not/am not
you are/are so
it isn't/it is not/it is

This part of the clause that is being tossed back and forth is known as the **Mood**, and it consists of the **Subject** and the **Finite**. The **Subject** is the element in the clause which is usually realized (expressed) by any type of nominal group and which can be questioned through a tag:

You told me. → *Didn't you?*
There isn't any sugar. → *Is there?*

As we have seen in the section on verbal groups, the Finite is that part of the verbal group which expresses agreement with the Subject. Together, the Subject and Finite form the Mood element of the clause. The order in which the Subject and Finite are configured in a clause tell us how we are to understand the speech exchange, whether it is a statement (declarative), a question (interrogative) or a command (imperative). The configuration options in English are (remember that ^ indicates 'followed by'):

Subject ^ Finite → Declarative clause: *He*   *is*   *here.*
                                          S   **F**

Finite ^ Subject → Yes/No   *Is*   *he*   *here?*   *Who*   *did*   *he*   *call?*
Interrogative clause: **F**   **S**   **F**   **S**

WH-Subject ^ Finite → Wh-Interrogative   *Who*   *is*   *he?*
(where WH is Subject):   **S**   **F**

∅ Finite → Imperative: *Call*   *him*
                         F

Thus the Mood element is that which indicates to our interlocutors the nature of the exchange (e.g. whether it is giving or demanding information). The rest of the clause, which is left off in most of the exchange above in the pencil argument, is known as the **Residue**, which consists of the **Predicator**, as well as possible **Complements** and **Adjuncts**. The Residue, which we see in only four of the exchanges in the pencil argument, gives us the meat of the clause in terms of experiential content.

The Predicator, as we have seen in our discussion of groups earlier in this chapter, is realized by the main verb within the verbal group, and, except in the case of verbs such as *be* and *have*, provides the experiential content of the verbal group. The Predicator is of itself non-finite (although it is often fused in English with the Finite, as in he <u>*makes*</u>); a Predicator without a Finite makes for a non-finite clause, such as those underlined in the following example (non-finite clauses are underlined, their Predicators are in bold):

> these elaborations help <u>to **contribute** to the creation of coherent, reader-friendly prose</u> while <u>**conveying** the writer's audience-sensitivity and relationship to the message</u>

Complements are elements in the clause which could be Subjects, but which are not. They answer the questions 'who(m) or what' related to the Predicator; we can analyze our previous example for a Complement:

> *conveying the writer's audience-sensitivity*: Conveying what?

Complements include what in traditional grammar are known as direct objects and indirect objects, which are both typically, though not always, realized by nominal groups. Further included as complements are those attributes which occur after copular verbs, such as *to be, to seem,* etc., and which are typically realized by Adjectival groups:

He	baked	me	a cake.
S	F/P	C	C

I	am	ecstatically happy.
S	F	C

Adjuncts are peripheral to the clause, and are typically realized by prepositional phrases or adverbial phrases, although they can also be realized by nominal groups and non-finite clauses. Adjuncts provide information which answers questions such as where, why, when, how, what for, etc. The type that answer these kinds of questions are known as **circumstantial Adjuncts** (A^{cir}), and include types of circumstances (Figure 3.8).

Figure 3.8: Types of circumstances

Type	Example
Extent: spatial	*Throughout Europe*
Extent: temporal	*For many years*
Location: spatial	*In parts of the Middle East; at school; behind the shed*
Location: temporal	*in the 1950s; since the beginning of time; yesterday*
Manner	*(by) breaking a few eggs*
	Both individually and collectively
	Unlike the Spartans,
Cause	*As a result of this difficulty,*
	For purposes of protection,
	To do this,
	... thereby placing his fate into her hands...
Contingency	*In spite of the differences in size,*
Accompaniment	*Except in size,*
Matter	*With respect to last point*
Role	*As head of state,*
Angle	*For historians,*

There are two other types of adjuncts: **conjunctive Adjuncts** and **modal Adjuncts**. Conjunctive Adjuncts are those that help connect a clause to a previous clause; examples are included in Figure 3.9.

There are other ways of expressing conjunction, namely the **coordinating conjunctions** *and, but, so, nor* and *or*, which we leave off of Figure 3.9 as they are not Adjuncts. In our analyses, we will label these as 'Conj'.

Figure 3.9: Conjunctive adjuncts

Relation	Examples
ELABORATION: Appositive Clarifying	*that is, in other words, for instance, for example, thus, to illustrate or rather, at least, to be more precise, by the way, incidentally, in any case, anyway, leaving that aside, in particular, more especially, to resume, as I was saying, briefly, to sum up, in conclusion, actually, in fact, as a matter of fact*
EXTENSION: Additive Adversative Varying	*also, moreover, in addition, furthermore* *on the other hand, yet, however, conversely* *instead, apart from that, except for that, (or) else, alternatively*
ENHANCEMENT: Matter Manner Spatio-temporal causal-conditional	*as to that, in that respect, in other respects* *likewise, similarly, in a different way, in the same way/manner* *then, previously, finally, at once, after a while, next time, the next day, meanwhile, at that time, until then, at this moment* *then, therefore, hence, as a result, on account of this, for that purpose in that case, otherwise, if not, yet, still, though*

Adapted from Halliday and Matthiessen (2004): 541–542.

Subordinators, such as *when, while, although* and *until* are other ways of expressing relationships between ideas. They also are not Adjuncts, and in our analysis, we will label them as 'Sub'.

Modal Adjuncts are those that give the speaker/writer's take on the proposition, and are illustrated in Figure 3.10.

Figure 3.10: Modal Adjuncts

Relation	Examples
Probability	*probably, possibly, certainly, perhaps, maybe*
Usuality	*usually, sometimes, often, always, never, seldom, rarely*
Typicality	*occasionally, generally, regularly, for the most part*
Obviousness	*obviously, of course, surely, clearly*
Opinion	*in my opinion, from my point of view, personally, to my mind*
Admission	*frankly, to be honest, to tell you the truth*
Persuasion	*honestly, really, seriously*
Entreaty	*please, kindly*
Presumption	*evidently, apparently, no doubt, presumably*
Desirability	*(un)fortunately, to my delight, luckily, regrettably, hopefully*
Reservation	*at first, tentatively, provisionally, in hindsight*
Validation	*broadly speaking, on the whole, in general, generally speaking*
Evaluation	*understandably, by mistake, foolishly, mistakenly, unwisely*
Prediction	*to my surprise, as expected, amazingly, by chance*

Adapted from Halliday and Matthiessen (2004): 82

We now have a full account of the clause as message: the speech exchange is signaled in the **Subject + Finite**, the **Predicator** tells us the main event, any **Complements** tell us who or what the main event impacts, and any **Adjuncts** provide us with extra information, such as who, what, where, when, how the writer connects the clause with what comes before, and what the writer thinks of the proposition. We can now analyze a set of clauses based on this information. We return to the clauses of a text that we saw earlier in this chapter for analysis.

EXERCISE 3.13

Analyze the clauses below for Subject (S), Finite (F), Predicator, Complements and Adjuncts (A^{cir}, A^{con}, and A^{mod}). Also indicate any Coordinating Conjunction as 'Conj.', and any subordinators (*when, while, although, until*, etc.) as 'Sub'. Indicate the type of realization of each of the elements of the clause structure (the exercise has been started for you, and some clauses have been removed for purposes of this exercise).

There	*was*	*a poor but good little girl who lived alone with her mother*		
Subject	**F**	**C**		
	verbal gr.	nominal gr.		

and		*they*	*no longer*	*had*	*anything to eat.*
(Conj)		**S**	A^{cir}	**F/P**	**C**
coordinating conj.		nominal gr.	adverbial gr.	verbal gr.	nominal gr.

So		*the child*	*went*	*into the forest*
(Conj)		**S**	**F/P**	A^{cir}
coordinating conj.		nominal gr.	verbal gr.	prep phrase

and	*there*	*an aged woman*	*met*	*her*
(Conj)	A^{cir}	**S**	**F/P**	**C**
coordinating conj.	adverbial gr.	nominal gr.	verbal gr.	nominal gr.

and	*presented*	*her*	*with**	*a little pot*
(Conj)	**F/P**	**C**		**C**
coordinating conj.	verbal gr.	nominal gr.		nominal gr.

*for our purposes here, we will take 'with' as forming part of the verbal group

1. *The girl took the pot home to her mother,*
2. *and now they were freed from their poverty and hunger.*
3. *Once on a time when the girl had gone out,*
4. *her mother said,*
5. *"Cook, little pot*, cook."*
   * Some analysts (cf Eggins 1994) label this a Vocative Adjunct; Vocative Adjuncts are usually considered outside of the clause structure.
6. *And it did cook*
7. *and she ate*
8. *till she was satisfied,*
9. *and then she wanted <u>the pot to stop cooking</u>*
   (analyze underlined part as if it were one construction)
10. *but did not know the word.*
11. *So it went on cooking*
12. *and the porridge rose over the edge,*
13. *and there* was the greatest distress.*
    *note: *there* falls into in essence a ord class of its own, *existential there*; it does, however, function as Subject.
14. *At last when only one single house remained,*
15. *the child came home*
16. *and just said, <u>"Stop, little pot,"</u>*
    (analyze underlined part as if it were one construction)
17. *and it stopped.*

We could analyze Exercise 3.13 from the point of view of narrative structure and note that it follows a typical story-telling pattern. We can further note that if we ignore (for the time being) the circumstantial Adjuncts of temporal location (*now, once on a time, at last*) which are typical of narratives as they root the reader/listener in time, the coordinating conjunctions (*and, so, but*) and the subordinators (*when, till*), most of the clauses begin with Subject + Finite, which signals the declarative mood of providing information; the narrator is telling us something (not asking us or commanding us). The exception are the clauses where the pot is commanded to cook, and which are in imperative mood. At any rate, overall, the mood of this story is declarative, that of providing information. But what does that information consist of? In order to model the content in terms of what experience is being represented through the clause, we turn to the clause as representation.

3.2.2.2 Clause as representation

The system of **transitivity** allows a modeling of the representation of experience, of the ways in which language works through clauses to express our views of the world (abstract or concrete, real or imaginary). In Chapter 4, in the section on semantics, we will see an account of thematic roles played by noun phrases in a clause or sentence. SFL has its own set of labels to refer to these roles, as, in this theoretical perspective, the labeling is expanded to account for more aspects of experience. According to SFL, the type of role played by a nominal group with respect to a verbal process depends precisely on the type of process. Thus, the system of transitivity within SFL includes the verbal **processes** which express the event of the clause, the **participants** involved in those processes, and the **circumstances** under which the processes take place. The different types of circumstances which can occur in a clause appear in Figure 3.8 earlier in this chapter. Thus, in this section, we focus first on the different types of processes which clauses serve to express, and then move on to the different types of participants which the processes involve.

Predicators function to express different kinds of processes. *John kicked the ball, John sneezed, John said something funny, John feels sad, John is tall,* and *There is John* are all clauses which involve John in processes; however, *kicking, sneezing, saying, feeling, being* and *existing* express different kinds of processes. The first three are more in line with what

Figure 3.11: Process types

Process	Explanation
Material	active processes, actions: someone/thing is actively doing something, and/or someone/thing is affected by the action expressed in the verb
Behavioral	active processes: typically a conscious being carrying out physiological-psychological behavior
Verbal	active processes with an associated result of verbal expression; process of saying
Mental	active processes, but having no associated overt external action, can be voluntary or involuntary; processes of sensing
Relational	stative process; something (Carrier) is being described as having some attribute, or something is being related to or identified with something else
Existential	stative process; something (existent) is posited as existing

comes to mind when we think of verbs as actions (if we consider 'saying' an action), while the last three construct more of a state of feeling or being. These clauses represent the six different process types that make up the systemic choices open to writers/speakers as they construct experience through language. The process types are explained in Figure 3.11; we now turn to a fuller explanation of each type, along with the types of participants which involve themselves in these processes.

Material clauses and their participants

Material processes are those, which like *kicked*, express some kind of action, as they express doings and happenings. The action can involve/affect different kinds of participants, as demonstrated in the following examples:

John	*kicked the*	*ball.*		
Actor		Goal		

John	*achieved*	*his objectives.*		
Actor		Scope		

John	*gave*	*Mary*	*a ring.*	
Actor		Recipient	Goal	

John	*trampled*	*the field*	*flat*	
Actor		Goal	Resultative Attribute	

John	*built*	*Mary*	*a house*	
Actor		Client	Goal	

John	*built*	*a house*	*for*	*Mary.*
Actor		Goal		Goal

The key	*opened*	*the door.*		
Instrument		Goal		

An **Actor** is a participant which carries out a material process; a **Goal** is a participant which is affected by this same type of process. The **Scope** specifies the range or scope of the process; it differs from the Goal in that we can ask of a Goal 'What was done to X'? but we cannot ask that question of a Scope. Indeed, while *What did John to do the ball? He kicked it* seems to make sense, *What did John do to his objectives? He achieved them* seem rather odd. The Scope often has a close semantic relationship with the verb, and other examples of Scope are *song* in *She sang a song*, *street* in *John crossed the street*, and *bath* in *She took a bath*.

A **Recipient** is the participant that receives something in the performance of the process, while the **Client** is the participant that something is done *for* (so a Client may receive a service, but not a good). A **Resultative Attribute**, usually an adjective, is very similar to **Attribute**, a participant involved in relational processes, which we will turn to shortly. The difference is that a Resultative Attribute comes into the picture as the result of a material process, such as *trampled*. Other examples of Resultative Attributes are *red* in *My face turned <u>red</u>*, and *green* in *They painted the wall <u>green</u>*. An **Instrument** functions almost more as a Circumstance, in that in the example above, *the key* does not really open the door: someone opens the door <u>with a key</u> in normal circumstances. However, the grammar of the clause allows us to express these circumstantial elements as participants in the process, as, for example, *a stone* in *<u>A stone</u> broke the window.*

EXERCISE 3.14

Analyze the clauses (all material) below for the participants involved:
E.g.   The boy inflated the ball with a pump.
        The boy = Actor, the ball = Goal
        (note that in this analysis, *the pump* is part of a prepositional phrase, and is thus *not* a participant in the clause, but rather part of a Circumstance).
1.   Give your baby a cool safe teething ring.
2.   I scheduled appointments for the patients.
3.   The teacher lined the students up.
4.   She carried a basket of food to her grandmother.
5.   The little girl took an automatic out of her basket.
6.   She shot the wolf dead.
7.   Calories are burned throughout the duration of the activity.
8.   The policy was established by UNHCR.

Behavioral clauses and their participants

Behavioral processes are those verbal groups which construct a physiological or psychological behavior, whether it is voluntary or involuntary. They include processes such as *sneeze, laugh, cry,* and *dream,* and their principal participant is a **Behaver**. These verbs are typically intransitive; that is, they do not usually affect another participant, but it is possible that a **Behavior** be included in the construction of the experience. Examples of Behavioral processes and their participants include:

John	_sneezed._	
Behaver		

_I_	_dreamed_	_**a dream.**_
Behaver		Behavior

Behavioral processes are often thought of as an event type somewhere between material and mental processes.

Verbal processes and their participants

Verbal processes are processes of saying. Examples which illustrate the processes and the different participant types are:

John	_said_	_**that he would come.**_	
Sayer		Reported	

John	_said_	_**'I'll come'.**_	
Sayer		Quoted	

John	_asked_	_**me**_	_**if I would go.**_
Sayer		Receiver	Reported

John	_asked_	_**a question.**_	
Sayer		Verbiage	

John	_praised_	_**the organization.**_	
Sayer		Target	

The role of the **Sayer** is clear from the above examples: it is the participant who utters something. That something forms two other participant types, whether it be **Reported** (indirect speech) or **Quoted**, the exact words someone said, enclosed within quotation marks. The **Receiver** is the person spoken to, and the **Verbiage** is an encapsulation of words into a label which packages the words spoken into a type, such as *a question, the truth, the facts*, etc. The **Target** is a tangential participant in a verbal process, and it is that participant which the verbal event is focused on; it does not occur with direct or indirect speech, and includes verbs such as *describe, explain, criticize, flatter* and *blame*.

Mental clauses and their participants

Mental clauses involve processes of our inner states, of sensing, as expressed in verbs such as *know, think, believe, see, smell, want, fear, like,* and *love*. The main participant in a mental process is the **Senser**, the participant who perceives or experiences the inner state or does the sensing. The

Phenomenon is that which is perceived. A Phenomenon can be realized by a nominal group, and it can also be realized by a whole clause:

John	*loves*	***coffee.***
Senser		Phenomenon (nominal group)

John	*loves*	***the fact that his birthday is on Friday this year.***
Senser		Phenomenon (whole clause)

Notice that a Goal in a material process cannot be realized by a clause such as *the fact that* … (It definitely sounds odd to say e.g. *John kicked the fact that* ...) as these kinds of clauses construct abstract phenomena. There is another difference between mental and material processes. When referring to the present moment, mental processes in most varieties of English are usually expressed through the simple present tense: *I like coffee, I know the answer*, and *not *I am liking coffee* or **I am knowing the answer*. To refer to an action in the present moment, in English, material processes (as well as behavioral processes) are usually construed through the present continuous, e.g. *John is kicking the ball*. The present simple, such as *John kicks the ball* is used for habitual actions in the present, repeated actions rather than an action taking place at the moment (e.g. *John always kicks the ball too hard!*).

Relational clauses and their participants

Relational processes are those of being and having. Technically, the verbs used, such as *be* and *have*, are not really processes or events at all. Rather they tie two participants together through states, identities, and possessions, and, thus, unlike the other processes, relational process verbs express no real lexical content. Like mental processes, when talking about the present moment, we tend to use the simple present tense.

John	*is*	***happy.***
Carrier		Attribute

John	*has*	***a tuba.***
Carrier		Attribute

John	*is*	***the boss.***
Identified		Identifier

The boss	*is*	***John.***
Identifier		Identified

Carriers and **Attributes** are participants in **relational attributive processes**. As the name implies, these process assign some Attribute to a Carrier, and include participants linked by verbs such as *be, have, seem,* and *look* (*look* in the sense of *He looks sad*, rather than *He is looking for his book*, which construes a material process). **Identifying processes** are another type of relational process in which the two participants are equal. That is the **Identified** and the **Identifier** refer to the same thing, as in our example above, although the Identifier provides us with some additional role of the Identified.

Existential clauses and their participants

Existential processes simply present something as existing. The most common form of expression for this process type is *there* + a form of the verb *to be*. There is only one participant in Existential clauses, the **Existent**:

There was   __*a book*__   on the table.
                  Existent

__*Many different kinds of people*__   exist in this world.
Existent

__*A woman*__   was in the pool.
Existent

Notice that in this last example, this type of existential clause differs from a relational clause in that there is a circumstantial Adjunct, rather than an Attribute, following the verb *to be*.

Summary of process and participant types

Figure 3.12 sums up the process and participant types.

Figure 3.12: Summary of process and participant types

Process type	Meaning	Participants
Material	'doing'	Actor, Goal, Scope, Recipient, Client, Resultative Attribute
Behavioral	'behaving'	Behaver, Behavior
Mental	'sensing' 'seeing' 'feeling' 'thinking'	Senser, Phenomenon
Verbal	'saying'	Sayer, Quoted, Target, Verbiage, Receiver
Relational	'being' 'attributing' 'identifying'	Carrier, Attribute, Identified, Identifier
Existential	'existing'	Existent

In constructing a text, we draw on these processes, participants and circumstances in varying ways to provide the picture of reality that we wish to provide. There are many different ways of providing information on a similar reality. For example, I can use a material process such as

> *John jumped for joy.*

While this is a metaphorical expression, it is a material process which is used to encode John's happiness, which can also be expressed via a relational process:

> *John was so happy.*

or a mental process:

> *John felt so happy.*

One of the differences suggested in the different encodings is that of perspective: In saying *John jumped for joy*, I imply that I saw a physical response (John leaping about); with *John is so happy*, I seem privy to John's inner state, and with *John felt so happy* to his feelings. These different means of encoding reality allow writers (and speakers) to impose ideological positions on events, as can be seen in the following example:

> *The invasion of Iraq claimed its first significant civilian casualties*
> *Wednesday when a pair of massive explosions rocked a busy Baghdad*
> *marketplace, leaving charred bodies and mangled cars littering the*
> *streets.*
> *At least 15 were killed ....*
> (*The Globe and Mail*, March 26, 2003)

In carrying out a transitivity analysis, the striking aspect of this text is the lack of human actors. *Civilian casualties* are encoded as a Goal, as are *charred bodies*. *At least 15* is also a Goal, as the passive voice leaves out the Actor involved in the process *were killed*. Even more striking is that, through ellipsis, the word *people* is left out, and we have to assume that it is *at least 15 people* who were killed. Thus, the event seems to have happened almost spontaneously, and people are only very tangentially involved.

EXERCISE 3.15[5]

Return to your analysis from Exercise 3.13. First label all of the verbal groups in terms of the process each one represents: material, behavioral, existential, relational, mental or verbal. Then label the Subjects and Complements involved according to the function they represent with respect to the process. Refer to Figure 3.12 for help with processes and participants. Finally, label the circumstantial Adjuncts by referring to Figure 3.8 to help you with the circumstance types. (The exercise has been started for you.)

There	was	a poor but good little girl who lived alone with her mother
Subject	F	C
	verbal gr.	nominal gr.
*	**existential**	**Existent**

*Note that *there* has no role in the experiential structure of the clause; it simply serves as a placeholder for the existent, which comes after the verbal group.

and	they	no longer	had	anything to eat.
(Conj)	S	A^{cir}	F/P	C
coordinating conj.	nominal gr.	adverbial gr.	verbal gr.	nominal gr.
	Carrier	**Circ (Temp)**	**relational**	**Attribute**

So	the child	went	into the forest
(Conj)	S	F/P	A^{cir}
coordinating conj.	nominal gr.	verbal gr.	prep phrase
	Actor	**material**	**Circ (Spatial)**

and	there	an aged woman	met	her
(Conj)	A^{cir}	S	F/P	C
coordinating conj.	adverbial gr.	nominal gr.	verbal gr.	nominal gr.
	Circ (Spatial)	**Actor**	**material**	**Goal**

5.   For more practice with transitivity, visit Ismail Talib's 'Transitivity Quiz'. Retrieved on February 20, 2010 from http://courses.nus.edu.sg/course/ellibst/2102/lct-1920/1920-text.htm

and	presented	her	with*	a little pot
(Conj)	F/P	C		C
coordinating conj.	verbal gr.	nominal gr.		nominal gr.
	material	**Recipient**		**Goal**

*with forms part of the verbal group
(*Note*: leave the following unanalyzed
which when she said, 'Cook, little pot, cook,' would cook good, sweet
porridge; and when she said, 'Stop, little pot,' it ceased to cook.)
1.   The girl took the pot home to her mother,
2.   and now they were freed from their poverty and hunger.
3.   Once on a time when the girl had gone out,
4.   her mother said,
5.   'Cook, little pot, cook.'
6.   And it did cook
7.   and she ate
8.   till she was satisfied,
9.   and then she wanted <u>the pot to stop cooking</u>
     (analyze underlined part as if it were one construction)
10. but did not know the word.
11. So it went on cooking
12. and the porridge rose over the edge,
13. and there* was the greatest distress
     *Note: *there* falls into in essence a word class of its own, *existential*
     there, and it does not have any function (beyond marking the place
     of the Subject) in the transitivity of the clause.
14. At last when only one single house remained,
15. the child came home
16. and just said, <u>"Stop, little pot,"</u>
     (analyze underlined part as if it were one construction)
17. and it stopped.

The story analyzed in Exercise 3.15 contains a good number of material processes, with some verbal processes as well. The little girl's actions save her and her mother from hunger, and her words save the town from 'the greatest distress'. There are some mental processes included, when her mother *wanted* the pot to stop cooking, but *didn't know* the words. Also, no one else in the town *knew how to stop it*. Everyone but the little girl is presented as a Senser who is lacking knowledge; thus, the little girl's knowledge turned into action is what saves the situation. We can compare the girl in this story with female characters in other fairy tales to see if they are constructed as having the same kind of active, knowledgeable role (this type of analysis would support a Critical Discourse Analysis of text; see Chapter 8, *Critical Discourse Analysis*, by Thomas Bloor).

Thus, an analysis of the clause as message provides a way of modeling how language is used to create a picture of the world, whether that world be of an outer 'reality' or an inner consciousness. An analysis of the clause as exchange allows us to model ways in which language creates interaction between interlocutors, between readers and writers. Before turning to an analysis of the clause as message, which allows a modeling of language as a means of organizing experience and interaction, we take some time to analyze in greater depth the nature of clauses and how they can be combined.

3.2.3 Clause complexes and simplexes

3.2.3.1   Parataxis and hypotaxis

In order to carry out an analysis of a text, an understanding of clauses and how they relate to each other is vital. A sentence can consist of a clause simplex (just one clause) or a clause complex (more than one clause). There are basically two ways that clauses are related to each other, **expansion** and **projection**:

> **Expansion** (see Figure 3.9: Conjunctive adjuncts for examples of the types of expansion)
> 1. as elaboration ('i.e.'): one clause elaborates on the meaning of another, via restatement, greater specification, further commentary, exemplification
> 2. as extension ('and', 'or'): one clause extends the meaning of another clause, via addition, exception, provision of an alternative
> 3. as enhancement ('so', 'yet', 'then'): one clause enhances the meaning of another clause, via qualification (e.g. of time, place, manner, etc.)

> **Projection**
> 1. as locution ('says'): one clause projects another, as a locution, as a wording
> 2. as idea ('thinks'): one clause projects another, as an idea, as a meaning

Each of these two overall types of clause relations can be constructed via two syntactic means: **parataxis** and **hypotaxis**. Clauses can be combined as equals, expressing different kinds of meaning. When clauses are related to each other in this way, they are in a **paratactic** relationship. The examples below illustrate the different kinds of meaning achieved through parataxis. (Note that clause boundaries are indicated by //):

> **PARATAXIS (equal clauses; coordination)**
> **Expansion:**
> *Little Red Riding Hood likes to visit her grandmother; // in fact, she's gone to visit her this morning.* [elaboration]

Little Red Riding Hood left early, // and her mother waved goodbye to her. [extension]

Little Red Riding Hood walked slowly, // for she loved looking at all of the plants in the forest. [enhancement]

Projection

She said, // 'I am on my way to my grandmother's house'. [Verbal process: direct speech]

The wolf thought: // 'Obviously, that is the way to go about it.' [Mental process: direct]

HYPOTAXIS (not equal; subordination)

Clauses which are in an unequal relationship to each other constitute a case of hypotaxis. This relationship is what we often call subordination (as in main clause/subordinate clause, or main clause/dependent clause). In this situation, except in the case of non-defining relative clauses, the clause order can usually be reversed.

Expansion:

1. Little Red Riding Hood decided to go to her grandmother's house,// which was on the other side of the forest.[6] [elaboration]

2. Whereas little Red Riding Hood took the long route, / the wolf took a shortcut. [extension]

   The wolf took a shortcut / whereas little Red Riding Hood took the long route.

3. The wolf arrived first // because he took a shortcut. [enhancement]

   Because he took a shortcut, // the wolf arrived first.

Projection

1. She said // that she was on her way to her grandmother's house. [Verbal process: indirect speech]

2. The wolf thought // that it was obviously the best way to go about it. [Mental process: indirect]

In our account of clause complexes up to this point, we have been examining examples of **finite clauses,** that is, clauses which contain a verb in a conjugated form. **Non-finite clauses** are clauses which contain a non-tensed verb (to-infinitives, present participles, past participles) and which also participate in hypotactic clause complexes:

6. *which upset everyone* is an example of a non-defining relative clause; these are clauses which provide more information about a preceding clause, or a part of a clause, but which can be left off of the clause complex with no loss of understanding in terms of who or what is being referred to. Other examples of non-defining relative clauses include: I met the lawyer's wife, *who told me a fascinating story*; John went to London last week, *where he visited my relatives.*

Little Red Riding Hood walked along the path, // singing songs. [elaboration]

The wolf was shot dead in the end, // betrayed by his own naivety. [enhancement]

I don't want // to stay here any longer. [mental process: indirect]

3.2.3.2 Embedded clauses

There is another kind of clause relation which actually does not happen at the clause level, but rather at the group level. This relation is known as **embedding**. Embedded clauses are also known as **rank-shifted** clauses, given that an element is functioning at a rank which is smaller than what it itself is. For example (notice that embedded clauses are enclosed within double brackets [[ ]]):

That's the guy [[who called me last night]].

In this example, we have a nominal group 'the guy who called me last night' in which a finite clause is acting as a Post-modifier; *who called me last night* serves to identify the guy to whom I am referring. This kind of clause is referred to as a **defining relative clause**, as it does more than simply provide more information. The difference between a defining and a non-defining relative clause becomes clear in the following examples:

John likes women, who are intelligent.
John likes women who are intelligent.

The first example is a hypotactic clause complex, in which *who are intelligent* functions as an elaborating clause; it simply provides extra information about women, implying that all women are intelligent and that John likes all women. The second example is a clause simplex including a nominal group (as complement) which contains embedding; thus John likes only a subset of women, the intelligent ones.

In addition to relative clauses, another type of embedding which occurs is that of a noun clause functioning as a Subject or Complement (which is again a case of a larger unit functioning at the rank of a smaller unit, in this case a clause functioning as a noun).

[[What John wanted]]	*was*	*out of his reach.*
S	**F**	**C**

Notice that on the paradigmatic axis, we could substitute a nominal group for *what John wanted*:

<u>*The book*</u>	*was*	*out of his reach.*
S	**F**	**C**

Victory	*was*	*out of his reach.*
S	**F**	**C**

Clauses can also function as Complements:

John	*couldn't*	*achieve*	*[[what he wanted]].*
S	**F**	**P**	**C**

Notice again that we could substitute a noun (e.g. *victory*) for the clause *what he wanted*.

Now that we have an understanding of the various ways in which clauses combine together, we can go on to model ways in which the various combinations and sequencing of groups, phrases and clauses are organized into coherent texts.

3.2.4 Clause as message

3.2.4.1 Theme-Rheme: structure and realization

Halliday writes: 'We may assume that in all languages the clause has the character of a message: it has some form of organization giving it the status of a communicative event' (Halliday, 1994: 37). He further explains that in English this organization is achieved through assigning special status to different parts of the message. For English, what comes first in the clause has special significance, as it is 'the peg on which the message is hung' (Halliday, 1970: 164) or 'the point of departure of the clause as message' (Halliday, 1967: 212). This element which initiates the configuration of the clause as message is known as the **Theme**; as Thomas and Meriel Bloor (2004: 71) describe it, the Theme is 'the idea represented by the constituent at the starting point of the clause', while that which constitutes the rest of the message is called the **Rheme**.

John	*was eating a donut at 6 a.m.*
Theme	Rheme

There are several means of expression for Theme. First of all, there are three main types of Themes: **ideational** (or **topical**) **Theme**, **interpersonal Theme**, and **textual Theme**. You can probably work out what these different types of Themes consist of, and their relationship to the three different metafunctions of language. At any rate, illustrations of these Theme types follow.

The **ideational Theme** is any participant, process or circumstance which appears in first position in the clause. In the declarative mood, the unmarked (or most usual) is the Subject (usually a nominal group) as Theme (in the examples that follow, Themes are underlined):

Subject as Theme: *The average rate of eruption* was *0.7 mm per month*

However, Adjuncts, Complements and Predicators can also appear as Theme; Adjuncts are considered a more marked Theme choice than Subjects, Complements and Predicators are even more marked (in English!):

Adjunct as Theme: *Many years ago* I visited Spain.
Complement as Theme: *Peaches* I love, *canned peaches* I hate.
Predicator as Theme: *Walk away* he did.

It is possible to have more than one nominal group as Theme:

John and Jim were eating donuts at 6 a.m. this morning.

and to have greater complexity in the nominal group via apposition:

Jim, John's older brother, joined him for donuts.

In **yes/no** interrogative clauses, the Theme is the Finite+Subject, while in **WH-**interrogatives (clauses that begin with *who, what, where, when, why,* etc.) the WH word (or question word) is the Theme:

Is it a right?
Who should have that right?

In imperative clauses, the Predicator is the Theme:

Close the door.

There are instances in English when the point of departure of the clause is rather empty of content. This 'emptiness' occurs in cases of existential clauses, such as *There* is no milk, and of extraposed clauses, such as *It* is difficult to avoid stereotyping. In these cases, *there* and *it* can be considered Theme.

In carrying out a Theme analysis, we ordinarily mark the Themes for all independent clauses, and leave off of the analysis the message structure of embedded clauses and hypotactic clauses which do not come first.[7] At the same time clauses themselves can also function as Theme. For example, noun clauses can be thematic, as in:

That language is uniquely human is disputed by many.

7.   Not all analysts agree with this procedure. Some analyze each clause (not only clause complexes) separately for Theme; however, embedded clauses are always left out of the Theme analysis, unless the clause as a whole is the Theme, as in the case of a noun clause functioning as Subject, e.g. What John wants is difficult to know. This is because embedded clauses, as they are rankshifted, function at a level lower than the clause. It is also worth pointing out here that there is some disagreement as to how far into the clause Theme extends, and some systemic functional linguists always include the Subject as part of the Theme.

There is another clause type which functions as Theme, commonly known as a **pseudo-cleft**, which Halliday terms a **thematic equative**, as the clause not only identifies the Theme, but it also equates it with the Rheme:

> _What Mary wanted most_ was to become a doctor.

A final kind of clausal Theme is that of a hypotactic (or dependent) clause as Theme, in the case of the clause complex. Obviously, it is only considered Theme of the clause complex when it is placed *before* the main clause:

> _As fat weight is dropped and cardiovascular efficiency improves,_ the speed can be increased in order to make the activity more challenging

Note that when embedded or hypotactic clauses are *not* first, they form part of the Rheme of the clause complex.

In addition to the ideational Theme, there may be a <u>preceding</u> **Textual** and/or **Interpersonal** Theme. Textual Themes provide information as to the relevance of the clause to the surrounding text, and may be realized by conjunctive Adjuncts and conjunctions:

Conjunctive Adjunct[8]:	_Nevertheless,_	_this kind of teaching_	_could be harmful._
	Textual Theme	Ideational Theme	Rheme
Conjunction:	_but_	_learning_	_should also be enjoyable._
	Textual Theme	Ideational Theme	Rheme

Interpersonal Themes provide the speaker's take on the proposition in terms of possibility or probability, or in some way indicate a speaker's judgment. Interpersonal Themes are realized through modal Adjuncts:

Modal Adjunct[9]:	_Certainly_	_teachers_	_can make it a lot easier_
	Interpersonal Theme	Ideational Theme	Rheme

Note that in the case of conjunctive and modal Adjuncts, they are only considered Theme if they come *before* the ideational Theme. Theme has to do with choice, and we can choose to place these items later in the clause (e.g. *This kind of teaching could be harmful, nevertheless*) where they lose their thematic flavor, and become part of the Rheme.

---

8.   See Figure 3.9 for a listing of conjunctive adjuncts.
9.   See Figure 3.10 for a listing of modal adjuncts.

EXERCISE 3.16

We now return to again to your analysis from Exercise 3.13 and Exercise 3.15. Divide the text into clauses, indicating paratactic and hypotactic clause boundaries (including between sentences) with // and embedding with || ||. Then analyze each of the clause complexes (rather than each of the clauses) for its ideational Theme, which you should label simply as Theme, and for any textual and interpersonal Themes. (The exercise has been started for you.)

There	*was*	*a poor but good little girl [[who lived alone with her mother]]//*		
Subject	F		C	
	verbal gr.		nominal gr.	
	existential		Existent	
Theme	**Rheme**	————————————————>		

and	*they*	*no longer*	*had*	*anything to eat.//*
(Conj)	S	A^{cir}	F/P	C
coordinating conj.	nominal gr.	adverbial gr.	verbal gr.	nominal gr.
	Carrier	**Circ (Temp)**	**relational**	**Attribute**
Textual Theme	**Theme**	**Rheme**	————————>	

So	*the child*	*went*	*into the forest//*
(Conj)	S	F/P	A^{cir}
coordinating conj.	nominal gr.	verbal gr.	prep phrase
	Actor	**material**	**Circ (Spatial)**
Textual Theme	**Theme**	**Rheme**	————————>

and	*there*	*an aged woman*	*met*	*her//*
(Conj)	A^{cir}	S	F/P	C
coordinating conj.	adverbial gr.	nominal gr.	verbal gr.	nominal gr.
	Circ (Spatial)	**Actor**	**material**	**Goal**
	Theme	**Rheme**	————————>	

and	*presented*	*her*	*with**	*a little pot//*
(Conj)	F/P	C		C
coordinating conj.	verbal gr.	nominal gr.		nominal gr.
	material	**Recipient**		**Goal**
	Theme	**Rheme**	————————>	

**with* forms part of the verbal group

(*Note:* leave the following unanalyzed:
which when she said,// 'Cook, little pot, cook, '// would cook good, sweet porridge;// and when she said, //'Stop, little pot, '// it ceased to cook.)

The girl took the pot home to her mother, and now they were freed from their poverty and hunger. Once on a time when the girl had gone out, her mother said, 'Cook, little pot, cook.' And it did cook and she ate till she was satisfied, and then she wanted the pot to stop but did not know the word. So it went on cooking and the porridge rose over the edge, and there was the greatest distress. At last when only one single house remained, the child came home and just said, 'Stop, little pot,' and it stopped.

3.2.4.2 Thematic patterning

We saw in Chapter 2 another type of structure which helps to configure the clause as message, that of Given-New. Given-New is known as **information structure**, and refers to the tension between what the speaker assumes can be taken as known or predictable (Given) and what the speaker assumes is not known, unpredictable, or worthy of special focus (New). Halliday explains that information structure and thematic structure are related, as 'other things being equal, a speaker will choose the Theme from within what is Given and locate the focus, the climax of the New, somewhere within the Rheme' (Halliday, 1994: 299). However, he goes on to point out that they are not the same thing, as 'Theme + Rheme is speaker-oriented, while Given + New is listener-oriented' (ibid), although it is obviously the speaker (or writer) who selects both.

Because Themes are often chosen from something which came before in the text, we can distinguish different types of thematic patterns. Thematic patterning involves connecting clauses and clause complexes together in a way which moves the reader from Given to New. Thematic patterning takes on greater importance in written texts, where the lack of face-to-face contact increases the need for clear connections across clauses and thus across ideas. There are several main types of thematic patterning according to the different sequences of thematic and rhematic choices made throughout the text (Daneš, 1974). In the first one, the **constant pattern**, the same ideational Theme is chosen over several clause complex units. We can see this in the following example (clauses are numbered and Themes are in bold):

*(1) **Urea** is a very important chemical because of its industrial uses and its role on biological processes. (2) **It** is excreted in the urine as the*

chief nitrogen-containing end product of protein metabolism. (3) It is produced on a large scale and used as a fertilizer and raw material in the manufacture of urea-formaldehyde plastics and of drugs. (4) It is usually prepared in laboratories from the reaction between potassium cyanate and ammonium chloride, which is basically a repetition of the Wohler procedure. (from a student lab report)

Urea → it → it → it

In this lab report, a student is describing *urea*, and thus repeats this Theme in all of the main clauses, forming a constant Theme chain.

Another possibility is to pick something from the rest of a clause, i.e. from the Rheme, as the Theme of a subsequent clause. This pattern is called the **linear pattern**, and is illustrated by the following text (Themes are in bold, and referents in the Rheme which subsequently become Themes are underlined):

*(1) **The early feminist movement was** greatly influenced by works like 'On the Vindication of the Rights of Women' (1972) by <u>Mary Wollstonecraft</u>. (2) **She** proposed <u>a feminist agenda whose aims were to expose the exclusion of women from traditionally 'male' spheres like politics, economics, education and religion, to take apart these structures, which denied women their deserved rights and attempt to achieve these rights for them in the male dominated spheres.</u> (3) **These aims** became a main focus for religious women in particular, at the time, in the United States.* (from a student essay)

Figure 3.13

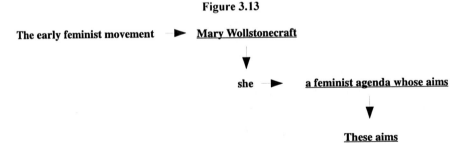

In this text about feminism, the student moves from *the early feminist movement* to *Mary Wollstonecraft*, and the latter then becomes the Theme of the next clause as *she*. Then the writer introduces *the aims of the feminist agenda*, lists those, and then goes on to make *These aims* the Theme of the third clause, and to develop a point about where these aims were important.

Thus, the constant pattern provides more of a static text, which works well with description, classification and often with narration; a repeated Given in Theme position is elaborated on in the Rhemes of each of the clauses with new information about that entity. The linear pattern provides more of a dynamic text, which works well with explanation, as it allows writers to add to points by always moving from a given idea to a new one, from clause to clause. Obviously, texts will combine patterns, depending on the intention of the writer.

There are two more thematic patterns which writers can choose to organize their texts, **derived Theme** and **split Rheme.** Derived Theme texts have to do with hyponymous terms. That is, a more general term is introduced or implied in the text, and subsequent clauses pick up on different specific instances of that term (the main referent in the Rheme of clause 1 is underlined, and its subsequent hyponymous Themes are in bold):

> *(1) During this phase, <u>buildings in Rome</u> reflected the tastes, power, and imperial spoils enjoyed by its dominant aristocratic families ...* **(2) Beautiful homes for the well-to-do, constructed around gracious open patios decorated with fountains and Greek statues,** *were built on the Palatine Hill.* **(3) Delicate temples in the Hellenistic style** *were erected beside the river.* **(4) Warehouses and shops** *expanded to deal with the rising commerce of the empire.* **(5) More ominously, the multi-storied apartment houses of the city's slums,** *expanded to accommodate the thousands of dispossessed farmers ...* (From Willis, F. R. (1981) *Western Civilization: An Urban Perspective.* Volume I. D.C. Heath and Company, p. 160).

Figure 3.14

In this text, *buildings in Rome* is introduced in the Rheme of clause 1, and then is developed via the hyponyms *beautiful homes, delicate temples, warehouses and shops,* and *multi-storied apartment houses.* Thus, these hyponyms of buildings form a derived thematic chain. Note that in clause 5, there is an interpersonal Theme (*more ominously*) preceding the ideational Theme.

Split Rheme involves the introduction of two (or more) participants in the Rheme of one clause which later become thematized in subsequent, separate clauses (the main referents in the Rheme of clause 1 are underlined, and Themes are in bold)

> *(1)* **He** *also enlisted the aid of two able adventurers, <u>Alberoni</u> and <u>Ripperda</u> ... (2)* **Alberoni, the son of an Italian gardener,** *was successively a cook ... (3)* **Ripperda, a Dutch business expert and diplomat,** *ultimately lost the favor ...* (from Brinton, C., J. B. Christopher and R. L. Wolff (1976) *A History of Civilization: 1715 to the Present.* Englewood Cliffs, New Jersey: Prentice-Hall Inc, p. 444)

Figure 3.15

Alberoni and Ripperda

Alberoni   **Ripperda**

EXERCISE 3.17

Read the following texts, in which the clauses are numbered. Determine the Theme of each clause, and trace the thematic patterning of the two texts. Compare the results. For each pair, state which one works better for you as a text, and explain why.

1. Text Pair 1

(1) In a hunting and gathering society, a combination of assertiveness by males and acquiescence by females may have pointed toward social divisions based on gender. (2) A comparative lack of information about the role of women in history may have been one result of such social divisions; (3) a leading theme of historical research in the present generation has been the reconstruction of this role, the restoring of women to history.

(1) In a hunting and gathering society, a combination of assertiveness by males and acquiescence by females may have pointed toward social divisions based on gender. (2) One result of such social divisions has been a comparative lack of information about the role of women in history;(3) the reconstruction of this role, the restoring of women to history, has been a leading theme of historical research in the present generation.

(Adapted from Chambers, M., R. Grew, D. Herlihy, T. K. Rabb, and I. Woloch (1991) *The Western Experience.* Volume I. McGraw Hill, Inc., p. 5.)

2. Text Pair 2

Clove

(1) One of the oldest spices in the world, the clove is the dried, unopened flower bud of a small evergreen tree. (2) Clove forms a major ingredient for a variety of beverages, medicines, cosmetics, perfumery and toiletries. (3) Clove finds extensive application in Indian foods, either powdered or whole. (4) It is a major constituent of garam masala and several kinds of curry powders. (5) Clove is also extensively used in pickles, ketchups, and sweetmeats, toothpastes and mouth-fresheners. (6) It is an important spice used in paan (betel leaf) chewed after meals.

Clove

(1) One of the oldest spices in the world, the clove is the dried, unopened flower bud of a small evergreen tree. (2) A variety of beverages, medicines, cosmetics, perfumery and toiletries all use clove as a major ingredient. (3) Many Indian foods extensively use clove, either powdered or whole. (4) Garam masala and several kinds of curry powder use it as a major constituent. (5) Clove is also extensively used in pickles, ketchups, and sweetmeats, toothpastes and mouth-fresheners. (6) Paan (betel leaf), which is chewed after meals, includes clove as an important spice.

(Adapted from Indichef, available: http://www.indichef.com/spices.asp)

3. Text Pair 3

(1) In Homer, we also see the origin of the Greek ideal of areté, excellence. (2) A passionate desire to assert himself, to demonstrate his worth, to gain the glory that poets would immortalize in their songs, is expressed by the Homeric warrior. (3) Excellence was principally interpreted as bravery and skill in battle in the warrior-aristocrat world of Homer. (4) Homer's portrayal also bears the embryo of a larger conception of human excellence, one that combines thought with action.

(1) In Homer, we also see the origin of the Greek ideal of areté, excellence. (2) The Homeric warrior expresses a passionate desire to assert himself, to demonstrate his worth, to gain the glory that poets would immortalize in their songs. (3) In the warrior-aristocrat world of Homer, excellence was principally interpreted as bravery and skill in battle. (4) Homer's portrayal also bears the embryo of a larger conception of human excellence, one that combines thought with action.

(From Perry, M. (1997) *Western Civilization: A Brief History*. Boston, MA: Houghton Mifflin Company, p. 43.)

EXERCISE 3.18

Divide each of the texts into clauses, identify the Themes of each of the clauses, and determine the main thematic pattern for each of the texts.

1. **Text 1**

   The Themes chosen by the speaker may, for example, refer to place (in this country) *or time* (in the last century); *they may indicate when the speaker is about to express an attitude* (in my opinion) *or give an example* (for example); *a Theme may even begin a rhetorical question* (What are we going to do about the lack of values?).

2. **Text 2**

   The textual within the Theme may have any combination of (i) continuative, (ii) structural and (iii) conjunctive Themes, in that order. (i) CONTINUATIVES are one of a small set of items such as yes, no, well, oh, now, which signal that a new move is beginning: a response in dialogue, or a move to the next point if the same speaker is continuing. (ii) A structural Theme is one of the obligatorily thematic elements listed in Tables 3(4) (conjunctions) and 3(5) (relatives). (iii) A conjunctive Theme is one of the conjunctive Adjuncts set out in Table 3(2). (Halliday, 1984: 54)

3. **Text 3**

   Robert Hooke (1635–1703), one of the first scientists to use a microscope to examine pond water, cork and other things, referred to the cavities he saw in cork as 'cells', Latin for chambers. Mattias Schleiden (in 1838) concluded all plant tissues consisted of cells. Theodore Schwann, in 1839, came to a similar conclusion for animal tissues. Rudolf Virchow, in 1858, combined the two ideas and added that all cells come from pre-existing cells, formulating the Cell Theory. (adapted from *Introduction: The Nature of Science and Biology*, no date. Available: http://www.emc.maricopa.edu/faculty/farabee/BIOBK/BioBookintro.html)

4. **Text 4**

   In 594 B.C., Solon [c. 640–559 B.C.), a traveler and poet with a reputation for wisdom, was elected chief executive. He maintained that the wealthy landowners, through their greed, had disrupted community life and brought Athens to the brink of civil war. Solon initiated a rational approach to the problems of society by de-emphasizing the god's role in human affairs and attributing the city-s ills to the specific behavior of individuals: he sought practical remedies for these ills; and he held that written law should be in harmony with Diké, the principle of justice that underlies the human community. At the same time, he wanted to instill in Athenians of all classes a sense of working for the common good of the city.

   Solon aimed at restoring a sick Athenian society to health by restraining the nobles and improving the lot of the poor.
   (From Perry, M. (1997) *Western Civilization: A Brief History*. Boston, MA: Houghton Mifflin Company, p. 48.)

3.3   Written and spoken language

We have seen in this chapter a number of different lenses which linguists use to analyze written language. We began with analysis of genre and texts, looking at overall patterns and moves which typify certain text types, and moved from there to looking at the make-up of the clause via groups and phrases. We then moved to looking at the lexicogrammatical choices which writers make as they construct their clauses, choices which have to do with setting up the clause: 1. as an exchange (of goods or information); 2. as a representation of the world, whether real or imagined; and 3. as a message which can be unpacked by a reader in order to make sense of the text as a whole. To finish this chapter, we now look at some of the differences between written and spoken language in terms of choices made.

3.3.1 Generic structure

Generic structures exist in all forms of language, whether written or spoken. We are capable of recognizing, for example, when a phone call is nearing completion, given the staged moves that are typical of this communicative event (pre-closing^closing, e.g. 'Well, this must be costing you money'…). Suzanne Eggins and Diana Slade (1997) map out the generic structure of gossip, for example, as following the obligatory moves of Third Person Focus ^ Substantiating Behavior ^ Pejorative Evaluation, along with other optional moves, such as Probe, in which a participant probes for more details. Of course, a major difference with most written genres (although new technologies have made writing, for example via chat, a more immediate interactive event) is that in conversation, the genre is jointly constructed, with the interlocutors having a role to play in the unfolding of the generic structure because of the immediacy of feedback (the head noddings, questions, and back channel devices that we expect from our interlocutors). In most written texts, it is the writers of a text who follow the stages (as we have seen in letters of reference, rejection and application, research articles, etc.) as they alone construct the text, usually without a reader physically present. This is not to say, of course, that writers write in a vacuum; their texts are part of wider interaction, they have a purpose and an audience in mind, and they have generic conventions to help guide their writing.

3.3.2 Clause complexes and groups

One major difference between spoken and written language, or more informal and more formal language, is grammatical complexity. Spoken language is actually quite complex grammatically, in that speakers often bring together strings of clause complexes. So in speaking, for example in a history classroom, a student might say:

> *They didn't use to have watches, so they would look at the sun, and when the sun set, they stopped working and they went home.*

A clause complex analysis shows that there are five finite clauses strung together here in varying relationships, mainly paratactic, but also hypotactic (*when the sun set*). Most of us would classify this as a spoken text, and expect something more condensed for a written version (e.g. *With no watches, they relied on the sunset to know when to stop working and go home*). Indeed, many written texts are worded in a way which we would not say in speaking (unless we are giving a speech or lecture), as the following example from a history textbook shows:

> *The Dark Age saw the migration of Greek tribes from the barren mountainous regions of Greece to more fertile plains, and from the mainland to Aegean islands and the coast of Asia Minor.*

Actually, here we have a clause simplex, as there is only one Subject/Finite combination. What we can see is that spoken language tends to be more intricate in terms of clause complexes, and less lexically dense, while written language tends to be less intricate in terms of clause complexes and more lexically dense. Lexical density refers to the number of content words vs. the number of grammatical words. If we bold the content words in our examples,

> *They didn't use to **have watches**, so they would **look** at the **sun**, and when the **sun set**, they **stopped working** and they **went home**.*

> *The **Dark Age** saw the **migration** of **Greek tribes** from the **barren mountainous regions** of **Greece** to more **fertile plains**, and from the **mainland** to **Aegean islands** and the **coast** of **Asia Minor**.* (From Perry, M. (1997) *Western Civilization: A Brief History*. Boston, MA: Houghton Mifflin Company, p. 48)

we see that the spoken text has 10 (if we include *have*, which is of dubious lexical content) out of 25 content words and the second 17 out of 33. Furthermore, we see far more complexity in the nominal groups of the second text (*migration of Greek tribes, barren mountainous regions of Greece*), with use of Epithets, Classifiers and Qualifiers, while in the first text, all of the nominal groups consist of solely the Head noun. Indeed, one major difference between spoken and written language resides in the complexity of the nominal group in the latter. In fact, highly specialized academic texts tend to be built around nominal groups, with little information conveyed through the verbal groups, as illustrated by the text below, with the nominal groups underlined to illustrate their prevalence in the text:

> <u>Two of the most fundamental nonverbal differences in intercultural communication</u> involve <u>space and time</u>. <u>Chronemics – or the study of meanings, usage, and communication of time –</u> is probably the most discussed and well-researched nonverbal code in the intercultural literature [citations ...] <u>A second nonverbal code that has attracted considerable attention</u> is <u>proxemics, the communication of interpersonal space and distance</u>. (From Anderson, P. (1988) 'Explaining intercultural differences in nonverbal communication'. In L. Samovar and R. Porter (eds) *Intercultural Communication: A Reader*. Wadsworth)

3.3.2.1 Clause as exchange, representation and message

We have already seen differences in the clause as exchange through the pencil argument included earlier in this chapter, where ellipsis of the Residue of the clause takes place (*you did; I did not*). While we may see this in personal letters, it is not a feature of more formal academic English texts. Furthermore, the latter involve mainly the transmission of information, and thus the declarative mood prevails, with some rhetorical questions thrown in to get the reader thinking.

In terms of the clause as representation, one major feature of more formal language (although not unheard of in informal contexts) is that of **grammatical metaphor**. If we look again at our example

> *The Dark Age saw the migration of Greek tribes*

we detect a mental process *saw*. However, the first participant, *the Dark Age* is not at all a usual type of Senser, as ages have no eyes. A more congruent and less metaphorical way of imparting this information is *During the Dark Age, Greek tribes migrated*. Halliday suggests that there is a difference between: 1. more congruent uses of language, where the grammar used is fairly representative of what we might expect: participants (people, places and things) are realized as nominal groups, processes are expressed through the verbal group, qualities and attributes are realized as adjectives, circumstances as adverbs and prepositional phrases, and logical connections as conjunctions; and 2. grammatical metaphor, where the language used does not encode these correspondences, for example when processes (*migrate*) or qualities (*happy*) are encoded through nouns (*migration, happiness*). The following example shows a congruent expression of an event:

> John asked Mary to marry him. So he was happy

John and *Mary* (nouns) encode participants. *Was, asked* and *marry* (verbs) encode processes. *So* (conjunctive) encodes a logical relationship. *Happy* (adjective) encodes a quality. We can express this same event using grammatical metaphor:

> *John's engagement resulted in his happiness.*

John's engagement (noun) encodes a process (note also that *John*, a person, is expressed here as an attribute of *engagement*). *Resulted in* (verb) encodes a logical relationship. *Happiness* (noun) encodes a quality.

Jim Martin provides an explanation for the use of grammatical metaphor in written texts, drawing on the organization of the clause as message:

> The significance of grammatical metaphor is that it is the grammar's most powerful resource for packaging meanings – for grouping them together into Theme and New. Grammatical metaphor re-textures the clause, allowing it to participate in its context in ways appropriate to the organization of texts as text. (Martin, 1993: 242)

That is, grammatical metaphor allows us to be more efficient and effective in packaging up language. Halliday further describes why nominalization became prevalent in written texts, first in scientific writing and then spreading to other genres. In scientific discourse, reports on experiments called for a step by step encoding, in which there was:

> a constant movement from 'this is what we have established so far' to 'this is what follows from it next'. This type of encoding is done most effectively through the single clause, in which each of the steps is transformed into a nominal group, joined by a verb expressing the way in which the second follows from the first. (Halliday, 1993: 81)

Thus, the way in which more formal written texts package information via Theme choice is different from more informal spoken texts. Furthermore, it has been noted that one characteristic of primarily interactional conversational speech is that the interactional aspect is frequently thematized, through, for example, personal pronouns such as *I* and *you* (Brown and Yule, 1983: 143). Finally, we can note differences in the types of textual and interpersonal Themes chosen depending on the register of a text. For example, we have seen in Chapter 2 that *okay* and *right* suggest a topic boundary, *like* can signal reported speech, and *well* signals possible disagreement in spoken language. In written language, we are more likely to use adjuncts such as *in conclusion, to sum up, according to X,* and *on the other hand* to carry out similar functions.

All of the above differences between more informal and more formal uses of language demonstrate that the latter is not somehow superior to the former; rather, they are two different ways of using language to achieve different communicative purposes. At the same time, it is important to point out that not all more formal uses of language are the same. For example, not all academic writing follows the same conventions or makes the same language choices. Ken Hyland, for example, has shown the differences that exist between different fields in academia, including a focus on how academics differ in the way they cite the work of others through differences in reporting verbs; for instance, in philosophy, the most frequent forms in his corpus of research articles were *say, suggest, argue claim, point out, propose, think*, while in biology, the most frequent were *describe, find, report, show, suggest observe* (Hyland, 2000: 27). He also found differences in the number of hedges (words such as *possibly* and *perhaps*, which allow a writer to mitigate the force of commitment to a proposition) and boosters (words such as *clearly* and *obviously*, which allow a writer to increase the force of commitment to a proposition) in different types of academic writing, and in the number of textual markers, which help to guide the reader. Obviously, a history textbook, for example, will be written differently from an article written by an historian for a scholarly journal, given their audiences, while at the same time scholarly articles from different fields will be written differently, given the variances in rhetorical practices.

EXERCISE 3.19

Analyze the following text in terms of: 1. its overall structure (do you perceive any pattern(s) reminiscent of a certain text type or genre?; 2. the SFPCA structure of its clauses; 3. the prevalent process, participant and circumstance types; and 4. the thematic choices, and any discernible thematic patterns.

'Hypnotist' thief hunted in Italy

Police in Italy have issued footage of a man who is suspected of hypnotising supermarket checkout staff to hand over money from their cash registers.

In every case, the last thing staff reportedly remember is the thief leaning over and saying: 'Look into my eyes', before finding the till empty.

In the latest incident captured on CCTV, he targeted a bank at Ancona in northern Italy, then calmly walked out.

A female bank clerk reportedly handed over nearly 800 euros (£630).
The cashier who was shown the video footage has no memory of the incident, according to Italian media, and only realised what had happened when she saw the money missing.
CCTV from the bank showed her apparently being hypnotised by the man, according to the reports.
Story from BBC NEWS:
Retrieved on February 24, 2010 from http://news.bbc.co.uk/go/pr/fr/-/1/hi/world/europe/7309947.stm
Published: 2008/03/22 18:43:02 GMT © BBC MMIX

EXERCISE 3.20

Now tape yourself telling someone about this event, just as you would tell someone about something you have read. Compare the written and spoken versions in terms of 1–4 in Exercise 3.19.

EXERCISE 3.21

Now analyze the following text in terms of 1–4 in Exercise 3.19, and compare the results with those of Exercise 3.19 and Exercise 3.20:

In basic terms, hypnosis refers to an altered psychological state generally characterized by certain physiological attributes (e.g. relaxed muscle tone, reduced blood pressure, slowed breath rate), by an enhanced receptivity to suggestion, and by an increased access to unconscious feelings, ideas and memories (Erickson, 1989). It is not a stereotypical ritual involving pendulums, watches, or crystal balls, nor is it a static, fixed internal state. Rather, it is an interchange or form of communication between two (or more) people that results in the accessing and subsequent utilization of latent or underdeveloped resources. (From Edgette, J. S., 1995, The Handbook of Hypnotic Phenomena in Psychotherapy. Psychology Press, pp. 3–4.)

3.4   Chapter outcomes

After having read this chapter carefully, discussed with others the content, and carried out the exercises, you should assess your ability to:

✓ Define genre.
✓ Define move; analyze texts for moves.
✓ Analyze texts for patterns such as.

- narrative
- anecdote
- exemplum
- recount
- problem-solution
- goal-achievement
- opportunity-taking
- desire-arousal fulfillment
- gap in knowledge-filling

✓ Identify signals of patterns, and classify them as Vocabulary 1, 2 or 3 items.

✓ Analyze nominal groups into pre-modifier, Head and post-modifier.

✓ Further analyze nominal groups into Deictic, Post-deictic, Numerative, Epithet, Classifier, Thing and Qualifier; describe the function of each of these elements.

✓ Explain modality and polarity.

✓ Analyze verbal groups into Auxiliary, Modal Operators, Finite, and Predicator.

✓ Describe the three metafunctions of language (ideational, interpersonal and textual).

✓ List the four primary speech functions (giving goods and services, demanding goods and services, giving information, and demanding information).

✓ Explain what Mood consists of.

✓ Describe the different types of Adjuncts.

✓ Analyze the elements of a clause in terms of Subject, Finite, Predicator, Complement and Adjunct.

✓ Explain the different kinds of verbal processes: material, behavioral, verbal, mental, relational and existential.

✓ Relate different participants to the process types: material: Actor, Goal, Scope, Recipient, Client, Resultative Attribute; behavioral: Behaver, Behavior; verbal: Sayer, Quoted, Target, Verbiage, Receiver; mental: Senser, Phenomenon; relational: Carrier, Attribute, Identified, Identifier; existential: Existent.

✓ Identify whether a sentence consists of a clause simplex or a clause complex.

✓ Identify whether a clause complex consists of expansion or projection.

✓ Identify whether clauses in a complex are related to each other via parataxis or hypotaxis.

✓ Explain and be able to identify embedded, or rank-shifted clauses.
✓ Analyze clause complexes for Theme (including textual, modal and ideational Themes) and Rheme.
✓ Identify the type of thematic patterning (constant Theme, linear Theme, derived Theme or split Rheme) pattern used in a text.
✓ Explain and find instances of grammatical metaphor.
✓ Using the various linguistic tools provided in this chapter, analyze texts for differences in genre and register.

3.5   References and further reading

For further information on Systemic Functional Linguistics, especially its relationship to other functional accounts of language, see Chapter 8, *Functional Linguistics* by Chris Butler.

Bloor, Thomas and Bloor, Meriel (2004) *The Functional Analysis of English. Second Edition*. London: Arnold.
Butt, David, Fahey, Rhondda, Feez, Susan, Spinks, Sue, and Yallop, Colin (2001) *Using Functional Grammar: An Explorer's Guide*. Sydney: Macquarie University, NCELTR.
Chafe, Wallace (1994) *Discourse, Consciousness, and Time: The Flow and Displacement of Conscious Experience in Speaking and Writing*. Chicago, IL: University of Chicago Press.
Cortazzi, Martin (1994) State of the art article: Narrative analysis. *Language Teaching* 27: 156–170.
Daneš, František (1974) Functional sentence perspective and the organization of the text. In F. Daneš (ed.) *Papers on Functional Sentence Perspective* 106–108. Prague: Academia.
Droga, Louise and Humphrey, Sally (2002) *Getting Started with Functional Grammar*. Berry, NSW: Target Texts.
Eggins, Suzanne (1994) *An Introduction to Systemic Functional Linguistics*. London: Pinter.
Fawcett, Robin P. (2008) *Invitation to Systemic Functional Linguistics through the Cardiff Grammar: An Extension and Simplification of Halliday's Systemic Functional Grammar*. London: Equinox.
Halliday, M. A. K. (1970) Language structure and language function. In J. Lyons (ed.) *New Horizons in Linguistics* 140–165. Harmondsworth: Penguin.
Halliday, M. A. K. (1993) Some grammatical problems in scientific English. In M. A. K. Halliday and J. R. Martin (eds) *Writing Science: Literacy and Discursive Power* 69–85. London: The Falmer Press.
Hoey, Michael (2001) *Textual Interaction: An Introduction to Written Discourse Analysis*. London and New York: Routledge.
Hoey, Michael (1983) *On the Surface of Discourse*. London: George Allen and Unwin.

Hyland, Ken (2007) Applying a gloss: Exemplifying and reformulating in academic discourse. *Applied Linguistics,* 28(2): 266–285.

Labov, William (1972) *Language in the Inner City.* Philadelphia, PA: University of Pennsylvania Press.

Labov, William (1981). Speech actions and reactions in personal narrative. In D. Tannen (ed.) *Analysing Discourse: Text and Talk* 212–247. Georgetown University Round Table, Washington, DC: Georgetown University Press.

Labov, William and Fanshel, David (1977) *Therapeutic Discourse: Psychotherapy as Conversation.* New York: Academic Press.

Labov, William and Waletsky, Joshua (1967) Narrative analysis: Oral versions of personal experience. In J. Helm (ed.) *Essays on the Verbal and Visual Arts* 12–44. Seattle, WA: American Ethnological Society.

Martin, James R. (2001) Language, register and genre. In A. Burns and C. Coffin (eds) *Analysing English in a Global Context* 149–166. London: Routledge.

Martin, James R. (1993) Technicality and abstraction: language for the creation of specialized texts. In M. A. K. Halliday and J. R. Martin (eds) *Writing Science: Literacy and Discursive Power* 203–220. London: The Falmer Press.

Martin James R., Matthiessen, Christian M. I. M., and Painter, Claire (1997) *Working with Functional Grammar.* London: Arnold.

O'Donnell, Mick (no date) *Systemic Functional Linguistics* website. Retrieved on January 1, 2010 from http://www.isfla.org/Systemics/index.html

Plum, Guenter (1988) *Text and Contextual Conditioning in Spoken English: A Genre-Based Approach.* Unpublished PhD Thesis, University of Sydney. Retrieved on January 1, 2010 from http://www.ling.mq.edu.au/nlp/network/SysWorld/sflist/gplum_v1.pdf

Swales, John M. (1990) *Genre Analysis: English in Academic and Research Settings.* Cambridge: Cambridge University Press.

Swales, John M. (no date) Worlds of genre—metaphors of genre. Unpublished manuscript. Retrieved on January 1, 2010 from www3.unisul.br/paginas/ensino/pos/linguagem/cd/English/15i.pdf

Thompson, Geoff (1996) *Introducing Functional Grammar.* London: Arnold.

3.6 Some Answers to the Exercises

Exercise 3.1

1. Recipe
2. Letter of recommendation
3. From *Single Shot Instruction Booklet* (2006) Retrieved February 20, 2010 from http://images.ebsco.com/pob/summit/catalog/single_shot.pdf
4. Job application letter
5. Story/fairy tale
6. Purportedly from a journal of psychiatry, but actually from the 'Appendix' in Ian McEwan's *Enduring Love.*

Exercise 3.2

The letter uses the generic structure of a rejection letter for a job application:

Acknowledgment of application
Statement of receipt of large number of applications
Expression of regret
Mention of candidate's positive qualities
Statement of intent to keep CV or resume on file
Closing: wishing the candidate good luck in job search

The letter also uses a lot of the same vocabulary related to job applications/ rejection letters: *outstanding qualifications, previous experience, requirements, employment, regret.*

While the moves and vocabulary are that of a rejection letter for a job application, the writer uses the same slots as a rejection of a rejection.

Exercise 3.3

Answers may vary. For example, Text 1 could be classified as an anecdote: a remarkable event followed by two different reactions. These texts should be used for discussion of how we perceive patterns in text.

Text 1: Narrative

Orientation: *These were 10–11 year old ... this explanation,*
Complication: *When one boy raised his hand and asked 'Excuse me, teacher, but when you sleep with Sonia, the arts teacher, do you use a condom?'*
Result: *I went bright red.*
Evaluation: (implied negative – embarrassment)
Evaluation 2: *Positive Resolution: But after that, it got really interesting ... I just stood there and watched them, really happy that they were having this kind of debate about their classroom, ultimately, about their education.*

Text 2: Exemplum

Orientation: *A Wolf who had a bone stuck in his throat hired a Crane, for a large sum, to put her head into his mouth and draw out the bone.*
Incident: *When the Crane had extracted the bone and demanded the promised payment, the Wolf, grinning and grinding his teeth, exclaimed: 'Why, you have surely already had a sufficient recompense,*

in having been permitted to draw out your head in safety from the mouth and jaws of a wolf.'

Interpretation: *In serving the wicked, expect no reward, and be thankful if you escape injury for your pains.*

Text 3: Narrative

Orientation: *There was once a very old man ... They were once sitting thus*

Complication: *When the little grandson of four years old began to gather ... 'for father and mother to eat out of when I am big.'*

Evaluation: (negative) *The man and his wife looked ... began to cry.*

Resolution: *Then they took the old grandfather to the table ... a little of anything.*

Text 4: This text could be said to contain two different stories fused together. They can be analyzed using the narrative pattern:

Orientation: *There was a poor but good little girl who lived alone with her mother,*

Complication: *and they no longer had anything to eat.*

Evaluation: (implied negative, as not having any food is not a good thing, and then 'sorrow' is mentioned)

Resolution: *So the child went into the forest...it ceased to cook.*

This resolution is evaluated positively: and now they were freed from their poverty and hunger, and ate sweet porridge as often as they chose.

Orientation 2: *Once on a time ... she wanted the pot to stop cooking,*

Complication: *but did not know the word. So it went on cooking ... only one single house remained*

Evaluation: *there was the greatest distress*

Resolution: *the child came home ... had to eat his way back.*

Exercise 3.4

Answers may vary. These texts should be used for discussion of how we perceive patterns in text.

1. **Text 1**

Situation: *There are so many cardiovascular exercise machines in the gym*

Problem: *I feel overwhelmed and I'm not sure which one is the best for losing fat weight.*

Overall Solution: *the best type of cardiovascular exercise machine for losing fat weight depends on the sort of shape that the bodybuilding trainee is currently at.*

Solution 1 (for mini-situation 1): *For a bodybuilder who needs to lose over 30 pounds ...*

Evaluation (positive): *using an incline on a treadmill is a great way ...*

Solution 2 (for mini-situation 2): *For a bodybuilder with less than 30 pounds to lose ...*

Positive Evaluation: *but without the impact experienced .... Results achieved by this ...*

2. **Text 2**

Solution: Canadian inventor Randall Dale Chipkar's *innovative 'electromagnetic shielding motorcycle seat'.*

Evaluation (positive): *The invention is designed to shield motorcycle electromagnetic field radiation from penetrating the rider's vital organs ... a major step in my quest to protect riders worldwide.*

Situation: *'Various types of extremely low frequency (ELF) electromagnetic field (EMF) radiations have been linked to health disorders including cancer ... also at risk, ' ELF EMF radiation at close exposure is unnatural ... possible carcinogen.*

Problem: *'People should not have to gamble with their health because they love riding motorcycles ....' ELF EMF magnetic fields penetrate through steel and even lead.*

Solution: *Only highly processed material can dramatically shield us from these cancer controversial forces.*

(Implied embedded problem: no patent makes the product difficult to market.)

Solution: *patent protection*

Evaluation of patent solution (positive): *... we can now aggressively market innovative internally shielded seats to provide riders with peace of mind*

Evaluation (positive) of both patent and of the motorcycle seat: *'I am now open ...' concludes.*

3. **Text 3**

Recipe reviews for: Adrienne's Tom Ka Gai

Situation: *'Garlic, ginger, lemon grass, chile peppers, coriander and cumin flavor this Thai-inspired coconut milk soup with chicken and bok choy.'*

Solution: *I modified this to suit what I had at home.*
Problem(s):
I didn't have peanut oil
left out the ginger, lemon grass, fish sauce and bok choy.
Solution(s):
(used olive oil),
I used 2 cans coconut milk, and only 3/4 cup of chicken broth (instead of water)
I also skipped the cilantro.
I added rice noodles with 10 minutes cooking time left,
Evaluation (positive): *and I ended up ... excellent!*
Evaluation (negative): *The only thing I would have changed ... I needed more liquid*
Evaluation (positive): *but it was excellent the way it was. ... have fun with it!!*

Exercise 3.5

Answers may vary. These texts should be used for discussion of the ways in which writers signal patterns in text.

1. **Text 1**

   The text uses the Opportunity-Taking pattern. It signals this in the first line, when it uses the Vocabulary 3 item *opportunity*, which is repeated again later in the abstract. Taking the opportunity is evaluated as positive throughout the text.

2. **Text 2**

   Desire-Arousal Fulfillment is signaled in this text through the putting forth of a product which is evaluated with Vocabulary 3 items such as *So Good, healthiest, most nutritious, favourite, easy way to provide your body with healthy nourishment* ... It uses Vocabulary 1 item *because* to indicate why we would desire the product.

3. **Text 3**

   Gap in Knowledge-Fulfillment is signaled through Vocabulary 3 items connected by a Vocabulary 2 item: *A great deal of research ... but few studies* ... The writer indicates his means of filling in the gap in knowledge by using a drawing on a large corpus of research articles.

4. **Text 4**

   This text could be analyzed using the Goal-Achievement pattern. *Touch Typing* is put forth as the goal, and the means to achieve it, *Miracle Type*, is put forth as *the answer,* a Vocabulary 3 item, as are *method for learning* and *the perfect answer*. The text is also a Problem-Solution pattern, the problem signaled through Vocabulary 1 item *if: if typing on your computer is just taking far too long or if you have given up in frustration ...* The solution is evaluated positively: *Miracle Type will save you time ... on the market.* Thus, it is put forth as optimal for achieving the goal.

Exercise 3.6

1. *various*   *descriptions*   *of the pre-morbid personality*
    pre-modifier   **HEAD**   **post-modifier**

2. *four new laser technology machines*
      pre-modifiers   **HEAD**

3. *results*   *achieved by this machine*
    HEAD   **post-modifier**

4. *a giant*   *leap*   *forward for Touch Typing*
    pre-modifiers   **HEAD**   **post-modifiers**

5. *the*   *cashier*   *who was shown the video footage*
    pre-modifier   **HEAD**   **post-modifier**

Exercise 3.7

1. *various*   *descriptions*   *of the pre-morbid personality*
    Numerative   **Thing**   **Qualifier**

2. *four*   *new*   *laser*   *technology*   *machines*
    Numerative   **Epithet**   **Classifier**   **Classifier**   **Thing**

3. *results*   *achieved by this machine*
    Thing   **Qualifier**

4. *a*   *giant*   *leap*   *forward*   *for Touch Typing*
    Deictic   **Epithet Thing**   **Qualifier**   **Qualifier**

5. *the*   *cashier*   *who was shown the video footage*
    Deictic   **Thing**   **Qualifier**

Exercise 3.8

1. a patient's cancer condition
2. a learning experience
3. many serious racial problems
4. the injured area of the brain
5. inconsistent reporting methods

Exercise 3.9

1. *dancing girls* their job may be as dancers, in which case *dancing* is a Classifier (in which case the stress would probably fall on the first syllable of *dancing*), or they may be dancing right now (or they just dance about a lot), in which case the stress would probably fall on *girl* as well as on the first syllable in *dancing*.
2. *late train* the train could be the last one of the day every day, in which case *late* is a Classifier, and would probably be stressed, while if it were a train that was very late, both words would receive stress.

Exercise 3.10

Answers will vary.

Exercise 3.11

Key: Aux = Auxiliary, Modal = Modal operator

1. Active sentence: *was* = Finite/Aux, *singing* = Predicator
2. Active sentence: *brought* = Finite/Predicator
3. Passive sentence: *were* = Finite/Aux, *knitted* = Predicator
4. Passive sentence: *has* = Finite/Aux, *been* = Aux, *stolen* = Predicator.
5. Two clauses: first clause is active: *had* = Finite/Aux, *been* = Aux, *waiting* = Predicator; second clause is passive: *was* = Finite/Aux, *brought* = Predicator.
6. Active sentence: *may* = Finite/Modal, *have* = Aux, *taken* = Predicator

Exercise 3.12 Nominal Groups

Text 1	Text 2
your baby's first teeth	*this study*
she (2 instances)	*the clinical process of the emergence phase of eruption of the primary dentition*
slightly inflamed gums	*length of time taken to erupt*
some drooling	*the association between soft tissue changes and stages of eruption*
quite a bit of chewing	*twenty-one children aged 6–24 months at commencement of the study*
the first teeth	*three suburban daycare centers in Melbourne, Australia*

your baby (2 instances)	*daily oral examinations of each child*
her gums	*seven months.*
your clean finger	*one hundred twenty-eight teeth*
her	*eruption*
a cool safe teething ring she can chew	*swelling*
a runny nose	*tooth eruption*
a rash on her face and neck	*all cases*
teething (2 instances)	*forty-nine percent of observed teeth*
high fever above 101 degrees, vomiting, or diarrhea	*gingival redness*
these symptoms	*between redness and specific stages of eruption*
your doctor	*mean duration of eruption*
the first tooth	*palpable enlargement of the gingival tissue*
a welcome sight	*full eruption*
the time your child is 2 to 3 years old	*2.0 months*
all 20 baby teeth	*range 0.9–4.6 months*
	the average rate of eruption
	0.7 mm per month
	many of the deciduous teeth
	an 'oscillating' pattern of eruption
	timing of oscillation
	stage of eruption
	tooth type
	this
	a 'transitional' phase of eruption which appears to be common

The nominal groups in Text 2 are longer. They use more postmodification, using Qualifiers to build a more abstract world, as in *the clinical process of the emergence phase of eruption of the primary dentition*; in this example, an abstract noun *process* is qualified by another abstract process *phase*, qualified by a nominalized process *eruption*, which is then further qualified by a more concrete process, *primary dentition*, which is quite a technical term compared to *baby's first teeth* in Text 1. Text 2 also uses many more Classifiers, such as *clinical, suburban, daycare, oral, tooth, gingivival,* and *deciduous.* Text 1 only uses *teething* as a Classifier. Text 2 uses nominalizations (verb processes which are turned into nouns), such as *eruption, examinations, enlargement,* and *oscillation.* This nominalization, along with the greater use of Qualifiers and Classifiers, helps to construct a more abstract, scientific text. Text 1 uses pronouns, such as *she, her* and *your*, making the text more personal and overtly interactive with the reader.

Verbal Groups

Text 1	Text 2
will probably come in	*investigated*
may have	*including*
come through	*were recruited*
to comfort	*were conducted*
rub	*were observed*
give	*accompanied*
can chew	*was*
may have	*demonstrated*
may be	*was* (3 instances)
*does **not** cause*	*appeared*
occur	*emerging* (2 instances)
call	*retreating*
is (2 instances)	*was not*
should be in	*was defined*

It is interesting to note the similar number of verbal groups across the two texts, while at the same time Text 2 has more nominal groups, showing the heavily nominalized nature of the scientific text. It is also interesting to note the difference between the two texts in terms of modality: the first text is heavily modalized: *will, can, may* and *should*, while Text 2 has no modal operators. Text 1 also has verbal groups in imperative mood, while Text 1 has none. Text 2 has a number of passive verbal groups, while Text 1 has none. These differences make Text 1 seem more interactive and personal, and Text 2 seem more impersonal and distant. The Predicators are very different, as those of Text 1 are vocabulary that parents probably use frequently, such as *come in, come through, comfort, rub, give, chew,* while those of Text 2 are related to scientific activity, such as *investigated, recruited, conducted, observed* and *defined*.

Exercise 3.13

Key:

S = Subect, **F** = Finite, **P** = Predicator, **C** = Complement, **A**^{cir} = Circumstantial Adjunct

gr. = group

prep = prepositional

Conj = coordinating conjunction (e.g. *and, but, or so*)

Sub = subordinator (e.g. *when, while, although until*)

1) *The girl*	*took*	*the pot*	*home*	*to her mother*
S	**F/P**	**C**	**A**^{cir}	**C**
nominal gr.	verbal gr.	nominal gr.	nominal gr.	prep phrase

2) *and*	*now*	*they*	*were freed*	*from their poverty and hunger.*
(Conj)	**A**^{cir}	**S**	**F P**	**A**^{cir}
coordinating conj.	adverbial gr.	nominal gr.	verbal gr.	prep. phrase

3) *Once on a time*	*when*	*the girl*	*had gone out*
A^{cir}	**(Sub)**	**S**	**F P**
adverbial gr.	subordinator	nominal gr.	verbal gr.

4) *her mother*	*said,*
S	**F/ P**
nominal gr.	verbal gr.

5) *'Cook,*	*little pot,*	*cook.'*
P	**VOCATIVE***	**P**
verbal gr.	nominal gr.	verbal gr.

* Some analysts (cf Eggins 1994) label this a *Vocative Adjunct*, and it is usually considered outside of the clause structure.

6) *And*	*it*	*did cook*
(Conj)	**S**	**F P**
coordinating conj.	nominal gr.	verbal gr.

7) *and*   *she*   *ate*
   (Conj)   S   F/P
   coordinating conj.   nominal gr.   verbal gr.

8) *till*   *she*   *was satisfied*
   (Sub)   S   F   P
   subordinator   nominal gr.   verbal gr.

9) *and*   *then*   *she*   *wanted*   *the pot to stop cooking*
   (Conj)   A^conj   S   F/P   C
   coordinating adverbial nominal   verbal   CLAUSE
   conj.   gr.   gr.   gr.

10) *but*   *did not know*   *the word.*
    (Conj)   F   P   C
    coordinating conj.   verbal gr.   nominal gr.

11) *So*   *it*   *went on cooking*
    (Conj)   S   F/P   P
    coordinating conj.   nominal gr.   verbal gr.

12) *and*   *the porridge* *rose*   *over the edge*
    (Conj)   S   F/P   A^cir
    coordinating conj.   nominal gr.   verbal gr.   Prep prhase

13) *and*   *there*   *was*   *the greatest distress,*
    (Conj)   S   F   C
    coordinating conj. existential 'there' verbal gr. nominal gr.

14) *At last*   *when*   *only one single house*   *remained*
    A^conj   **(Sub)**   S   F/P
    adverbial gr.   subordinator   nominal gr.   verbal gr.

15) *the child*   *came*   *home*
    S   F/P   A^cir
    nominal gr.   verbal gr.   nominal gr.

16) *and*   *just*   *said*   *'Stop, little pot'*
    (Conj)   A^mod   F/P   C
    coordinating conj. adverbial gr. verbal gr. CLAUSE

17) *and*   *it*   *stopped.*
    (Conj)   S   F/P
    coordinating conj.   nominal gr.   verbal gr.

Exercise 3.14

1. *your baby* = Recipient; *a cool safe teething ring* = Goal
2. *I* = Actor; *the patients* = Client
3. *The teacher* = Actor *students* = Goal
4. *She* = Actor; *a basket of food* = Goal *her grandmother* = Recipient
5. *The little girl* = Actor; *an automatic* = Goal
6. *She* = Actor; *the wolf* = Goal; *dead* = Resultative Attribute
7. *Calories* = Goal
8. *The policy* = Goal *UNHCR* = Actor

Exercise 3.15

Key:

S = Subect, **F** = Finite, **P** = Predicator, **C** = Complement, **A**^{cir} = Circumstantial Adjunct

gr. = group

prep = prepositional

Conj = coordinating conjunction (e.g. *and, but, or so*)

Sub = subordinator (e.g. *when, while, although until*)

1.
The girl	took	the pot	home	to her mother
S	F/P	C	A^{cir}	C
nominal gr.	verbal gr.	nominal gr.	nominal gr.	prep phrase
Actor	**material**	**Goal**	**Loc: Spatial**	**Recipient**

2.
and	now	they	were freed	from their poverty and hunger.
(Conj)	A^{cir}	S	F P	A^{cir}
coordinating conj.	adverbial gr.	nominal gr.	verbal gr.	prep. phrase
	Circ (Temp)	**Goal**	**material**	**Extent: Spatial**

3.
Once on a time	when	the girl	had gone out
A^{cir}	(Sub)	S	F P
adverbial gr.	subordinator	nominal gr.	verbal gr.
Circ (Temp)		**Actor**	**material**

4.
her mother	said,
S	F/ P
nominal gr.	verbal gr.
Sayer	**verbal**

5. 'Cook,   little pot,   cook.'
   P   VOCATIVE*   P
   verbal gr.   nominal gr.   verbal gr.
   material   *   **material**

* Some analysts (cf Eggins 1994) label this a *Vocative Adjunct*, and it is usually considered outside of the clause structure, and thus outside of the transitivity of the clause.

6. *And*   *it*   *did cook*
   (Conj)   S   F   P
   coordinating conj.   nominal gr.   verbal gr.
                        Actor   **material**

7. *and*   *she*   *ate*
   (Conj)   S   F/P
   coordinating conj.   nominal gr.   verbal gr.
                        Actor   **material**

8. *till*   *she*   *was satisfied*
   (Sub)   S   F P
   subordinator   nominal gr. verbal gr.
                   Senser   **mental**

9. *and*   *then*   *she*   *wanted*   *the pot to stop cooking*

   (Conj)   A^conj   S   F/P   C
   coordinating   adverbial   nominal   verbal   CLAUSE
   conj.   gr.   gr.   gr.
                                    Senser   **mental**   **Phenomenon**

10. *but*   *did not know*   *the word.*
    (Conj)   F   P   C
    coordinating conj. verbal gr.   nominal gr.
                        mental   **Phenomenon**

11. *So*   *it*   *went on cooking*
    (Conj)   S   F/P   P
    coordinating conj.   nominal gr.   verbal gr.
                        Actor   **material**

12. *and*   *the porridge*   *rose*   *over the edge*
    (Conj)   S   F/P   A^cir
    coordinating conj.   nominal gr.   verbal gr.   Prep prhase
                        Actor   **material**   **Extent: Spatial**

13. | and | there | was | the greatest distress, |
|---|---|---|---|
| (Conj) | S | F | C |
| coordinating conj. | existential 'there' | verbal gr. | nominal gr. |
| | | **existential** | **Existent** |

14. | At last | when | only one single house | remained |
|---|---|---|---|
| A^{conj} | (Sub) | S | F/P |
| adverbial gr. | subordinator | nominal gr. | verbal gr. |
| | | **Existent** | **existential** |

15. | the child | came | home |
|---|---|---|
| S | F/P | A^{cir} |
| nominal gr. | verbal gr. | nominal gr. |
| **Actor** | **material** | **Loc: Spatial** |

16. | and | just | said | 'Stop, little pot' |
|---|---|---|---|
| (Conj) | A^{mod} | F/P | C |
| coordinating conj. | adverbial gr. | verbal gr. | nominal gr. |
| | | **verbal** | **Quoted** |

17. | and | it | stopped. |
|---|---|---|
| (Conj) | S | F/P |
| coordinating conj. | nominal gr. | verbal gr. |
| | **Actor** | **material** |

Exercise 3.16

1. | The girl | took | the pot | home | to her mother// |
|---|---|---|---|---|
| S | F/P | C | A^{cir} | C |
| nominal gr. | verbal gr. | nominal gr. | nominal gr. | prep phrase |
| Actor | material | Goal | Loc: Spatial | Recipient |
| **Theme** | **Rheme** ⟶ | | | |

2. | and | now | they | were freed | from their poverty and hunger.// |
|---|---|---|---|---|
| (Conj) | A^{con} | S | F P | A^{cir} |
| coordinating conj. | adverbial gr. | nominal gr. | verbal gr. | prep. phrase |
| | | Goal | material | Extent: Spatial |
| **Textual Theme** | **Textual Theme** | **Theme** | **Rheme** ⟶ | |

3.

Once on a time	when	the girl	had gone out//	her mother	said,//
A^cir	(Sub)	S	F P	S	F/ P
adverbial gr.	subordinator	nominal gr.	verbal gr.	nominal gr.	verbal gr.
Circ (Temp)		Actor	material	Sayer	verbal
Theme	**Rheme** ------------------------------------>				

4.

"Cook,	little pot,	cook."//
P	VOCATIVE*	P
verbal gr.	nominal gr.	verbal gr.
material	*	material
Theme	**Rheme** --------------->	

*Some analysts (cf Eggins 1994) label this a *Vocative Adjunct*, and it is usually considered outside of the clause structure.

5.

And	it	did cook//
(Conj)	S	F P
coordinating conj.	nominal gr.	verbal gr.
	Actor	material
Textual Theme	**Theme**	**Rheme**

6.

and	she	ate//	till	she	was satisfied//
(Conj)	S	F/P	(Sub)	S	F P
coordinating conj.	nominal gr.	verbal gr.	subordinator	nominal gr.	verbal gr.
	Actor	material		Senser	mental
Textual Theme	**Theme**	**Rheme** ----------------------------------->			

7.

and	then	she	wanted	the pot to stop cooking//
(Conj)	A^conj	S	F/P	C
coordinating conj.	adverbial gr.	nominal gr.	verbal gr.	CLAUSE
		Senser	mental	Phenomenon
Textual Theme	**Textual Theme**	**Theme**	**Rheme** ------------>	

8.

but	*did not know*	*the word.//*
(Conj)	F P	C
coordinating conj.	verbal gr.	nominal gr.
	mental	Phenomenon
Textual Theme	**Theme**	**Rheme**

9.

So	*it*	*went on cooking//*	
(Conj)	S	F/P	P
coordinating conj.	nominal gr.	verbal gr.	
	Actor	material	
Textual Theme	**Theme**	**Rheme**	

10.

and	*the porridge*	*rose*	*over the edge//*
(Conj)	S	F/P	A^{cir}
coordinating conj.	nominal gr.	verbal gr.	Prep prhase
	Actor	material	Extent: Spatial
Textual Theme	**Theme**	**Rheme** ————————>	

11.

and	*there*	*was*	*the greatest distress.//*
(Conj)	S	F	C
coordinating conj.	existential 'there'	verbal gr.	nominal gr.
		existential	Existent
Textual Theme	**Theme**	**Rheme** ————————>	

12.

At last	*when*	*only one single house*	*remained//*	*the child*
A^{conj}	(Sub)	S	F/P	S
adverbial gr.	subordinator	nominal gr.	verbal gr.	nominal gr.
		Existent	existential	Actor
Textual Theme	**Textual Theme**	**Theme**	**Rheme** ————————>	

came	*home//*
F/P	A^{cir}
verbal gr.	nominal gr.
material	Loc: Spatial
————————————————>	

13.

and	*just*	*said//*
(Conj)	A^{mod}	F/P
coordinating conj.	adverbial gr.	verbal gr.
Textual Theme	**Modal Theme**	**Theme**

14. 'Stop,   *little pot'//*

    P   VOCATIVE

    verbal gr.   nominal gr.

    Quoted ————————>

    Theme   **Rheme**

15. *and*   *it*   *stopped.*

    (Conj)   S   F/P

    coordinating conj.   nominal gr.   verbal gr.

                       Actor   material

    Textual Theme   **Theme**   **Rheme**

Exercise 3.17

1. Text Pair 1

Themes

(1) *In a hunting and gathering society*

(2) *A comparative lack of information about the role of women in history*

(3) *a leading theme of historical research in the present generation*

Themes

(1) *In a hunting and gathering society*

(2) *One result of such social divisions*

(3) *the reconstruction of this role, the restoring of women to history*

We can see that in the text on the left, there is new information in Theme position of clauses 2 and 3, while in the second text, a linear Theme pattern is employed, as the Theme in 2 picks up on 'social divisions' from the Rheme in 1, and the Theme in 3 picks up on women's roles from the Rheme in 2. Thus, the text on the right should, in theory, be easier to follow, and was, indeed, the original text.

2. Text Pair 2

Themes

(1) *One of the oldest spices in the world, the clove*

(2) *Clove*

(3) *Clove*

(4) *It*

(5) *Clove*

(6) *It*

Themes

(1) *One of the oldest spices in the world, the clove*

(2) *A variety of beverages, medicines, cosmetics, perfumery and toiletries*

(3) *Many Indian foods*

(4) *Garam masala and several kinds of curry powder*

(5) *Clove*

(6) *Paan (betel leaf)*

The text on the left uses a constant Theme progression pattern, as every clause Theme is a reference to '*clove*'. This pattern is typical of a descriptive text of a single item. The text on the right can throw the reader off into thinking that maybe the writer is changing the topic, especially in clauses 3 and 4 (perhaps to a discussion of Indian food, rather than of the clove), although then in 5 we are back to the clove. Therefore, the text on the left should, in theory, be easier to follow, and, indeed, was the original text.

3. Text Pair 3

Themes	Themes
(1) *In Homer*	(1) *In Homer*
(2) *A passionate desire to assert himself, to demonstrate his worth, to gain the glory that poets would immortalize in their songs*	(2) *The Homeric warrior*
	(3) *In the warrior-aristocrat world of Homer,*
	(4) *Homer's portrayal*
(3) *Excellence*	
(4) *Homer's portrayal*	

The text on the right uses a constant Theme pattern, as all Themes reference Homer. The text on the left contains new information in Theme position in clauses 2 and 3. Also, with respect to where and how information is most optimally placed in the clause, there is principle of **end weight**: in a number of languages, including English, there is a tendency to place lengthier and more informationally packed units at the end of the clause. The principle of end weight also helps explain why we tend to understand more easily sentences such as *It is a shame that the text he wrote is so difficult to understand* rather than *That the text he wrote is so difficult to understand is a shame*. Thus, in theory, the text on the right is easier to process, and was, indeed, the original text.

Exercise 3.18

Textual Themes are in bold, Ideational Themes are underlined:

- **Text 1**
  <u>*The Themes chosen by the speaker*</u> *may, for example, refer to place* (in this country) *or time* (in the last century);// <u>*they*</u> *may indicate* [[*when the speaker is about to express an attitude* (in my opinion) *or give an example* (for example)]];// <u>*a Theme*</u> *may even begin a rhetorical question* (What are we going to do about the lack of values?).

This text follows a constant Theme pattern. All Themes refer to Theme!

- **Text 2**

The textual within the Theme may have any combination of (i) continuative, (ii) structural and (iii) conjunctive Themes, in that order.// (i) CONTINUATIVES are one of a small set of items such as yes, no, well, oh, now, *//which signal [[that a new move is beginning: a response in dialogue, or a move to the next point if the same speaker is continuing]].// (ii) A structural Theme is one of the obligatorily thematic elements [[listed in Tables 3(4) (conjunctions) and 3(5) (relatives)]]. //(iii) A conjunctive Theme is one of the conjunctive Adjuncts [[set out in Table 3(2)]].* (Halliday, 1984: 54)

This text follows a split Rheme pattern, as the Themes of each of the clauses after the first (except for *which* in the third clause, an elaboration of something in the second clause) refer to a point mentioned in the Rheme of the first clause.

- **Text 3**

Robert Hooke (1635–1703), one of the first scientists to use a microscope to examine pond water, cork and other things, referred to the cavities [[he saw in cork]] as 'cells', Latin for chambers. Mattias Schleiden (in 1838) concluded all plant tissues consisted of cells. Theodore Schwann, in 1839, came to a similar conclusion for animal tissues. Rudolf Virchow, in 1858, combined the two ideas and added that all cells come from pre-existing cells, formulating the Cell Theory.

This text follows a derived Theme pattern. The hypernym is not included, but it is easy to supply something to the effect of 'scientists who study cells'.

- **Text 4**

In 594 B.C., Solon [c. 640–559 B.C.), a traveler and poet with a reputation for wisdom, was elected chief executive.// He maintained // that the wealthy landowners, through their greed, had disrupted community life // and brought Athens to the brink of civil war.// Solon initiated a rational approach to the problems of society by de-emphasizing the god's role in human affairs and attributing the city-s ills to the specific behavior of individuals: // he sought practical remedies for these ills; // and he held that written law should be in *harmony with Diké, the principle of justice that underlies the human community.// **At the same time**, he wanted to instill in Athenians of all classes a sense of working for the common good of the city.*

<u>Solon</u> aimed at restoring a sick Athenian society to health by restraining the nobles and improving the lot of the poor.

(From Perry, M. (1997) *Western Civilization: A Brief History*. Boston, MA: Houghton Mifflin Company, p. 48.)

This text follows a constant Theme pattern, as all of the clauses refer to *Solon*, except the first clause, which sets the time frame of this stretch of text.

4 Language and mind

> It seems clear that we must regard linguistic competence – knowledge of
> a language – as an abstract system underlying behavior, a system
> constituted by rules that interact to determine the form and intrinsic
> meaning of a potentially infinite number of sentences. (Noam Chomsky,
> 2006: 62)

The perspectives included in this chapter have been considered (along
with phonetics and phonology in Chapter 2) the mainstay of contemporary
linguistics, especially in North America in the second half of the twentieth
century. In this chapter, we leave aside to some extent considerations of
what we do through language and how it differs depending on its context of
use to look more closely at its structural makeup, and how we might think
of the mental processes which underlie the production of its structures.
We have seen with phonemes (Chapter 2) how our brains tune out certain
information in order to focus on those sounds which contrast, and therefore
provide meaning; for example, we do not notice that the [p] we pronounce
with *pit* is accompanied by a puff of air, while the [p] in *spit* is not. That is,
we hold a mental representation of a given speech sound (phoneme) and
that is what we hear, regardless of its regular variations in pronunciation
(allophones). In this chapter, we examine linguistic theory which attempts
to model the kind of mental knowledge that we hold of how we form words
(**morphology**), of how we form sentences (**syntax**), and how we understand
the meaning of words (**semantics**).

4.1   Morphology: the construction of words

4.1.1 What's in a word?

Let us stop for a moment and consider the notion of **word**. Perhaps you have
clear in your mind that a word is a unit of language that stands on its own
and represents something in our experience. However, the notion of 'word'
is not unproblematic, as dictionary makers know in trying to determine the
inventory of items to include.

EXERCISE 4.1

In the set of sentences below, how many different words are there beginning
with the letter 'b'? List the different dictionary entries that you would
create.

1. The bear attacked him.
2. I can't bear the sight of him.
3. People argue over the right to bear arms.
4. Bare feet are not allowed.
5. She bore up well under the strain.
6. He bears no malice towards those who did him this injustice.
7. I was born at 5 a.m.
8. In the village, there was a woman who bore twins four times.
9. He is such a bore.
10. With bared teeth, he uttered his horrifying threat.

In Exercise 4.1 we have examples of **homonyms** (words which sound the
same but have different meanings, as in *bear, bear,* and *bare,* and *bore* and
bore) and **polysemy** (words with different, but related, senses, such as the
uses of *bear* in numbers 3 and 6, and arguably *born* and *bore* in numbers
7 and 8, *bare* and *bared* in numbers 4 and 10). We also have examples of
a verb inflection in number 6: would you consider *bears* in 'he *bears* him
no malice' to be the same word as *bear* in 'I *bear* him no malice'? Is it an
example of polysemy or is it the same word just inflected differently to
indicate singular or plural? Linguists and lexicographers do not always
agree on these decisions; this lack of consensus has an effect on differences
in head word lists in a dictionary.

So, what is a word? Is it a set of sounds with meaning, which can stand alone?
Is it a set of letters with a space before and a space after? Let's try an exercise
to help us determine just what we mean by 'word' as a linguistic unit.

EXERCISE 4.2

Look at the following list, consider carefully the *meaning* of each item
(you might want to check a dictionary), and determine if it is considered
a word. How are the words different from the other items on the list?

Based on your decisions, can you provide a more precise definition
of the notion of 'word'?

1.	hello	2.	chair
3.	the	4.	friend
5.	friendship	6.	ly
7.	friends	8.	goodbye
9.	ceive	10.	un
11.	gotcha	12.	gonna
13.	coffee cup	14.	cran
15.	blackboard	16.	faked

To complicate the picture further, dictionaries, our repositories of words,
often do include entries for items such as *un-, gonna,* and *gotcha.* Some
people might point out that *gonna* is actually two words, 'going to' and
gotcha is really 'got you'. Then, you might ask, why are *gonna* and *gotcha*
written as one word each? Why is *coffee cup* considered two words, while
blackboard is one? A coffee cup is not a cup of coffee, and in fact we can
drink water or tea out of a coffee cup. The meaning of *coffee cup* is not
equal to the sum of its parts, and thus must really be considered as one
unit. Definitely, the endeavor of defining *word* is not as straightforward as
it seems.

4.1.2 Content words and function words

The word *the* in Exercise 4.2 may have given you pause in considering what
it *means.* It is certainly a different kind of word than is something like *chair,*
or *friend,* entities which you can point to, draw, or describe. To define *the,*
you probably made recourse to what it does in language, to indicate that a
specific something is being referred to. This attempt to define *the* illustrates
the distinction between **content words**, which refer to concepts in the realm
of experience (tangible or abstract, real or imaginary), and **function words**,
which exist to create connections or provide some further specification of
how we are to interpret the content words. Content words consist of nouns,
verbs, adjectives and adverbs, and are an open class of words, as new
content words are being created constantly. Function words are pronouns,
determiners, prepositions and conjunctions, and are a closed class, as they
are fixed, relatively stable, and new ones are not inclined to creep into the
language with any regularity, nor do they tend to be shared out to other
languages, something which frequently happens with content words.

EXERCISE 4.3

Make a list of four or five words which are new to your language. For each word:

1. List its word class: does the word function as an adjective, adverb, noun or verb, or does it belong to more than one class?
2. In what contexts have you heard the word?
3. Look the word up in an etymological dictionary (*Oxford English Dictionary*, or the *Online Etymological Dictionary*, at http://etymonline. com/). Note the origins of the word. How recent is it? How did it enter the language?
4. Google the word. How many hits does it get? Look through some of the hits. Does the way the word is used match your understanding?

EXERCISE 4.4

Invent a function word of your own, a word which you feel that the language could benefit from. How would it be used? What would its function be? How would it fit into the grammar of the sentence?

4.1.3 Morphemes

We can see that the word is not a unit of linguistic meaning that has a clear delineation. However, linguists do agree on the notion of **morpheme**, or the smallest unit of meaning in language. Morphology, which has a long

SINGLE SLICES By Peter Kohlsaat

"They call it a relation "ship" because it so often sinks."

and rich tradition in the study of language, is the area of linguistics which studies morphemes and the ways in which morphemes combine together into larger units of meaning. Morphological knowledge is part of our knowledge of the language(s) we speak, as we have internalized the rules governing how morphemes can combine together. Thus, we know that we combine the derivational morpheme *–ship* at the end (and not at the beginning) of root morphemes such as *friend, scholar,* and *dictator* to create a new meaning indicating a more abstract state or condition of the root.

EXERCISE 4.5

Determine the number of morphemes in each of the words below. Make a list of the morphemes, and consider how you might divide them into categories.

1. dogs
2. unpack
3. carrot
4. behead
5. repackage
6. redness
7. deactivate
8. classroom
9. paper
10. writer's

Exercise 4.5 illustrates that there are several kinds of morphemes, which we can classify according to various parameters. Morphemes can be divided into **free** and **bound** morphemes. Free morphemes are those which can stand alone as words, and bound are those which must be attached to another morpheme. Thus, in Exercise 4.5, we have, for example, the free morphemes *dog, carrot, head, red, class, room, paper,* and *write,* and the bound morphemes *s, er, un, be, de, ate, ness, re,* and *'s.*

Root morphemes are the smallest unit of lexical meaning; they cannot be analyzed into smaller units. Examples of roots include *pack, write,* and *act* from Exercise 3.5. We also have roots such as *ceive* (from *receive, conceive, deceive,* etc.), *rupt* (from *interrupt, disrupt,* etc.), and *huckle* and *boysen,* which both combine with *berry,* none of which can stand alone; thus, they are known as **bound roots.** A **stem** is a root morpheme plus any affixes. For example, to the root *write* we can add the affix *–er* to form *writer.* We can then further add the plural affix *–s* to the stem *writer* to form *writers.*

Affixes are bound morphemes which attach themselves to roots or stems in various different ways:

Prefixes: attach at the beginning of root or stem morphemes; for example, in English *un-, re-, dis-*, etc.

Suffixes: attach at the end of root or stem morphemes; for example, in English *–s, -ness, -ly*, etc.

Infixes: insert in the middle of root or stem morphemes; we do not use infixing in English (some argue that expletives such as un-friggin-believable are examples of infixing, while others argue that they are not, as the inserted item is a lexical word, and not an affix). Other languages do, for example, Bontoc (a language spoken in the Philippines) where the underlined affix is added to the root, e.g. *fikas* (strong) → *fumikas* (to be strong), *kilad* (red) → *kumilad* (to be red).

Circumfixes: attach simultaneously at the beginning and at the end of a bound or stem morpheme; English does not make recourse to this form of affixing (although see Exercise 4.6 for another opinion on circumfixation in English). Be careful: adding a prefix and a suffix at the same time to a word, e.g. *worthy* → *unworthiness*, is NOT an example of circumfixation, as in the case of *unworthiness* each affix changes the word meaning or grammatical form in a different way, and they do not attach simultaneously; in the case of circumfixes, the word is only changed in one way by adding both elements at the same time. German, for example, uses circumfixing: in regular verbs the perfect/passive participle is formed by simultaneously adding a prefix *ge-* and a suffix *–t*. Thus from the root hab ('have') we form *gehabt* ('had').

Transfixes: attach a discontinuous affix to a discontinuous root at more than one position in a word. The Semitic languages use transfixation for almost all word derivation and inflection. For example, in Arabic, the root for *write* is *ktb*, to which the following transfixes can be added:

-a-a-	katab	'he wrote'
-aa-i-	kaatib	'writer'
-i-áa-	kitáab	'books'
-u-u-	kutub	'book'

There are variations on these rule-governed ways of creating new words. For example, Paamese, an Austronesian language, from the Malayo-Polynesian group uses suffix **reduplication** (in this case to amplify the meaning of the original word):

matou 'coconut'   matou-**tou** 'thick coconut milk'
tupas 'smoke'   tupas-**pas** 'smoky'
tiNai 'lean'   tiNai-**Nai** 'lean all over'
sital 'emerge'   sital-**tal** 'emerge in large numbers'

EXERCISE 4.6

Consider the English verbs *enlighten* and *embolden*. Do you think that these verb forms have developed in the language via circumfixation? Provide arguments for your answer.

Finally, we can distinguish between **inflectional** and **derivational** morphemes. Inflectional morphemes do not change the meaning of a word; rather, they change the word because of constraints provided by the syntax of their surrounding phrase or sentence. So I can say *I come* but in my dialect I have to say *he comes*, and not *he come*. Inflectional morphemes provide information on case, gender, person, mood, tense, voice, or aspect. English uses very few inflectional morphemes, only eight in total, which are listed in Table 4.1.

Table 4.1: Inflectional morphemes in English

Morpheme	Function		Examples
Nouns	s	plural	regular: dogs, books
			irregular: feet, phenomena
	's	possessive	John's, the cat's
Adjectives	er	comparative	smaller, cheaper, faster
	est	superlative	smallest, cheapest fastest
Verbs	s	3rd-singular present	walks, eats, screams, closes
	ed	past tense	regular: walked, screamed, closed
			irregular: ate, swam
	en	past participle	regular: cooked, washed
			irregular: chosen, written
	ing	present participle	walking, screaming

It is important to note that these morphemes are considered abstract representations of the surface spoken or written rendering of the word formed by adding them; 'eat' + the past tense morpheme does not equal 'eated', but rather 'ate', as for historical reasons (see Chapter 5) there exist several ways of forming the past tense forms and present participles of verbs in English. Thus, we add the morpheme –*en* to form the past participle in the case of a number of verbs, such as *broken, written, eaten, spoken,* and *chosen.* However, the great majority of our verbs in English no longer form the past participle in this way; rather, they add –*ed,* so we have:

I have written the letter.   *I have broken my promise.*
I have cooked the dinner.   *I have washed the dishes.*

While the -*ed* ending is more frequent, in linguistics -*en* is used to represent the morpheme added to English verbs to form the past participle.

The role of inflectional morphemes is clear: when they are added to a word, they highlight the syntactic relationship of the word to the surrounding words, and are necessary because of our rules of phrase and sentence formation. In Spanish, for example, verb endings provide information as to person, number, and tense:

bebo   = 'eat' + 1st person singular present tense = 'I drink'
bebes   = 'eat' + 2nd person singular present tense = 'you drink'
bebe   = 'eat' + 3rd person singular present tense = 'he/she/it drinks'
bebemos = 'eat' + 1st person plural present tense   = 'we drink'
bebéis   = 'eat' + 2nd person plural present tense   = 'you (plural) drink'
beben   = 'eat' + 3rd person plural present tense   = 'they drink'

In Spanish, the first person singular pronoun is 'yo'. Morphosyntactic rules make it incorrect to combine *yo* with *bebes* (which would result in something like 'I you drink'), and *yo* can only be combined in present tense with 'o', for *yo bebo.* At the same time, it is not necessary or even that frequent to use an overt pronoun in Spanish, given that the information as to who is the agent of the action is included within the morphology of the verb. English, on the other hand, needs to include the overt Subject (either in the form of a noun or pronoun) so that we can know who the agent is, given that we have no inflected verb endings to provide this information except for third person singular present tense; furthermore, in English we know that in the indicative mood, the Subject comes in front of the verb (except for a rare cases of inversion, such as *Had I known*...), knowledge which helps to lessen the ambiguity as to who is carrying out the action of the verb. Spanish includes the referent to the Subject within the verb itself, which also lessens the ambiguity of who is carrying out the action of the verb; thus these two languages use different resources to indicate that information.

Resources for indicating the grammatical role of a given word or phrase in a given utterance differ depending on the language. In English, if we have a sentence such as *The boys call the girls* we know it is the boys who do the calling and the girls who receive the call, and not vice versa, because of the word order: the subject of the action comes before the verb. In Latin, it is the case endings of the noun which tells us who is doing the calling (the nominative case) and who is receiving the call (the accusative case):

pueri	puellas	vocant
'boys'	'girls'	'call'
+nominative plural 'i'	+accusative plural 'as'	3rd person plural
The boys call the girls.		

pueros	puellae	vocant
'boys'	'girls	'call'
+accusative plural 'os'	+nominative plural 'ae'	3rd person plural
The girls call the boys.		

English has lost many of its inflectional morphemes over the centuries (for example, in Old English, nouns and adjectives had morphemes to indicate case), and is now a weakly inflected language, relying more on the order of words to convey grammatical meaning. Other languages, like the Romance languages, have a rich system of verb inflections, but have lost their inflections for case, which they would have inherited from Latin. Spanish makes the case clear in the above sentence type through the use of the particle 'a' (rendered below as 'acc. part' for 'accusative particle') before the accusative case when referring to a human participant as direct object:

Los chicos	llaman	a	las chicas
'the boys'	'call'	acc. part.	'the girls'
The boys call the girls.			

We will leave aside further concerns with syntax, or the arrangement of elements in the clause, for a bit later in this unit and return to our discussion of morphology.

While inflectional morphemes are few in English, the derivational morphemes are many. Also, while an inflectional morpheme does not change the grammatical class or the underlying meaning of a word, a derivational morpheme changes one or the other. Derivational morphemes such as *–ness* and *–ly* change the grammatical class of a word:

friend (noun)	→	friendly (adverb)
friendly (adverb)	→	friendliness (noun)

Certain derivational morphemes limit themselves to certain word classes to form new words. For example, *-ly* attaches to adjectives to form adverbs:

Adjective	Adverb
sad	sadly
happy	happily
quick	quickly
momentary	momentarily

Other derivational morphemes change or add to the meaning of the root or stem, but do not change the grammatical class:

unhappily
impossible
intolerant
mistreat
friend**ship**
blue**ish**

We can create more complex words by adding on more and more morphemes. The way these morphemes attach reflects a hierarchical structure. That is, if we take a word such as *unhappily*, we can illustrate the order of attachment of morphemes via a tree diagram:

The prefix *un-* usually attaches to adjectives (not to adverbs) so to the root *happy* we add *un-* to create the stem *unhappy*, to which we add the suffix *-ly* to get our surface form *unhappily* (our spelling rules of English change the surface written form to *unhappily*). In our morphological hierarchy, derivational morphemes attach before inflectional morphemes; thus, we could represent *befriended* as:

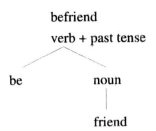

befriend

verb + past tense

be   noun

friend

EXERCISE 4.7

Analyzing the hierarchical structure of words can help disambiguate meaning in a word like *unlockable*. Look at each of the trees below and determine the two different meanings.

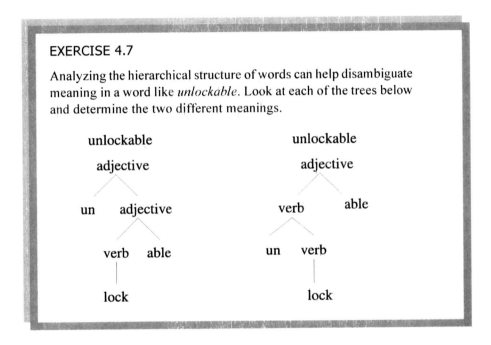

unlockable

adjective

un   adjective

verb   able

lock

unlockable

adjective

verb   able

un   verb

lock

SINGLE SLICES   **by Peter Kohlsaat**

It's not quite a relationship...
it's more of an inclination ship.

K.hlsaat   2·29
© 1996 Los Angeles Times Syndicate

EXERCISE 4.8

Look at the morphemes in Column A, and match them with a morpheme in Column B to create an existing word in English. Make sure you use each morpheme only once, and that you use them all. Which morphemes would you classify as bound roots, and why?

Column A Column B

huckle	ceive
cran	berry
dent	rupt
re	istry
matern	ity
luke	apple
inter	warm

EXERCISE 4.9

Examine the following words from Spanish, and fill in the missing morphemes:

1. debo   'I owe'
2. debes   'you owe'
3. deb___   'he/she/it owes'
4. debemos 'we owe'
5. debéis   'you (plural) owe'
6. deben   'they owe'
7. com___   'I eat'
8. com___   'you eat'
9. come   'he/she/it eats'
10. com___ 'we eat'
11. com___ 'you (plural) eat'
12. com___ 'they eat'

Now, make a list of all of the morphemes which occur. What are their different meanings?

e.g. 'o' = 1st person singular indicative.

EXERCISE 4.10

Draw the morphological trees for the following words (as with *unlockable*, in Exercise 4.7.

1. unbelievable
2. inflexibility
3. uncannily
4. encouragement
5. unfulfilled
6. groovily

4.1.4 Morphophonemics

Morphophonemics, as the name implies, brings together morphology and phonemics. We have sets of morphemes which have the same underlying meaning, but which take on different guises in their surface spoken and written representation. For example, the prefixes *im* and *in* both have the meaning of 'not', as in *impossible* and *inflexible*. Like our examples of [k] and [k°], which are allophones of the same phoneme /k/, we can say that [in] and [im] are **allomorphs** of the same morpheme /in/. This is again because of assimilation rules: it takes more movements of the mouth to move from the alveolar nasal sound [n] to the bilabial [p] than it does from the bilabial nasal [m], thus, *impossible*. Our spelling of the word takes into account this feature of its sounding; this is not the case, however, of *input*, which was formed from the preposition *in* + *put*; most people pronounce it [ɪmpʊt] in natural spoken language, yet it is spelled with the *n*, perhaps to differentiate from the 'not' morpheme *im*.

We see allomorphy in the formation of the plural of nouns in English. Look at this data:

A	B	C	D
clicks [klɪks]	pigs [pɪgz]	flaws [flɔz]	kisses [kɪsəz]
clips [klɪps]	beds [bɛdz]	days [deɪz]	judges [ʤʌʤəz]
plates [pleɪts]	caves [keɪvz]	knees [niz]	sashes [sæʃəz]
myths [mɪθs]	pans [pænz]	plows [plaʊz]	churches [ʧɚ ʧəz]

What we see is that there are different pronunciations of the plural morpheme depending on the surrounding phonetic context. What do the sounds at the end of the words in Column A all have in common? Immediately before the plural ending [s], we have an unvoiced consonant. In Column B, in each case we have a voiced consonant; in Column C, we have words ending in vowels (and vowels are voiced). Because of the articulatory process of assimilation (see Chapter 2), we pronounce the morpheme differently: it is easier to move from a voiced consonant to the voiced sibilant [z], and from an unvoiced consonant to the unvoiced sibilant [s]. So we move from an abstract mental concept of the plural morpheme marker /z/ to its actual realizations [z] and [s]. We take /z/ to be the underlying mental concept because it occurs most frequently (note that the sounding and the spelling are not in sync). Thus, we can map the rule for plural nouns in English as:

noun + /z/ → [s] after an unvoiced consonant

In Column D, we see vowel epenthesis (see Chapter 2), or the addition of a vowel, in the case of [ə] after [ʧ] and [ʃ] and before the plural morpheme. This epenthetic vowel allows us to differentiate the ending of the word in the singular with the ending of the word in the plural. Thus, our complete rule is:

noun + /z/ ⟨ ▼ [s] after unvoiced consonant
▲ [əz] after sibilants

We learn these allomorphic rules as we learn to produce the sounds of our language, just as we learn the exceptions to these rules, or the irregular plural nouns such as *children, feet,* and *oxen.*

EXERCISE 4.11

Write the phonetic transcription for the following words (the first ones in each column have been done for you), and answer the questions which follow.

A	B	C	D
needed [nidəd]	freaked [fɹikt]	hummed [hʌmd]	clawed [klɔd]
wanted	sipped	buzzed	played
blended	kissed	hugged	kneed
fasted	cashed	paved	plowed

1. What regularities to you find in each column? How does each column differ from the other columns?
2. How many allomorphs are there for the past tense morpheme marker in English? What is the underlying morpheme?
3. Explain why the different forms exist using the articulatory processes from Chapter 2.
4. Write the rule for the surface forms of regular past tense verbs in English.

EXERCISE 4.12

Write the phonetic transcription for the following words (the first ones in each column have been done for you), and answer the questions which follow.

A	B	C	D
needs [nidz]	freaks [fɹiks]	kisses [kɪsəz]	claws [klɔz]
hums	sips	buzzes	plays
shuns	putts	cashes	knees
paves	laughs	patches	plows

1. What regularities do you find in each column? How does each column differ from the other columns?
2. How many allomorphs are there for the third person singular present tense morpheme marker in English? What is the underlying morpheme?
3. Explain why the different forms exist using the articulatory processes from Chapter 2.
4. Write the rule for the surface forms of regular third person singular present tense verbs in English.

We have seen in this section on morphology how words are altered to provide new meanings via derivational morphology, and how they are altered to fit into different grammatical contexts via inflectional morphology. When a new word enters a language, it is subject to these processes. Let's take for example the word *taser*, a word which is fairly recent in the English language, and which entered as a noun, according to the *Oxford English Dictionary*, around 1972, from **Tom Swift's** electric *rifle*, from the Tom Swift book series; it now refers to a real weapon which emits an electric shock. Through derivational morphology, it now appears as an adjective, as in '*Tasered* man's last moments', and, through further derivation, the negative of the adjective now exists: 'Mr Massey could have gone on his way -- *untasered* and unarrested -- had he simply signed the ticket'. It also appears as a verb: 'Police officer *tasers* handcuffed woman multiple times', inflected for third person singular; it can also be inflected for past tense: 'Police *tasered* 82-year-old woman'. The verb form also appears as *tase* in 'Don't *tase* me, bro', and *tased*, as in 'Police shot and *tased* a man', demonstrating that this new word is experiencing uncertainty as it becomes part of the language.

4.2   Morphology and syntax

We now have an understanding of how words morph according to meaning and in order to fit effectively into a syntactic string. Indeed, all languages use morphology to convey meaning. Linguists suggest that languages string morphemes together in one of three ways, depending on how they combine morphemes to make meaning, and languages are classified based on the predominating way of doing so:

> In **isolating languages**, morphemes that are separate words are combined; thus words do not change, verbs are not inflected, etc.
>
> In **agglutinating languages**, grammatical morphemes with differing meanings are added on to roots and stems, often resulting in the buildup of long words of many morphemes, each adding an additional and discrete bit of meaning
>
> **Fusional**, or **inflecting**, **languages** morphemes often include more than one aspect of meaning (e.g. in our Spanish examples in Exercise 4.9, the morpheme 'o' provides information as to person, number and tense), or they are difficult to separate out, thus, in essence, making a new word.

English uses all of these ways of making meaning, for example, with verbs:

> Future: Add a separate word, in this case a particle, *will* (*I will call him tomorrow*)
>
> Past tense: Add the suffix -ed (*The police tasered the student*)
>
> Past tense: Make a different word (*see* → *saw; buy* → *bought*)

and with nouns:

> Noun Plurals: Add a separate word: *three <u>head</u> of cattle*
>
> Noun Plurals: Add a suffix –s: *three cows*
>
> Noun Plurals: Make a new word: *child* → *children; foot* → *feet*

EXERCISE 4.13

Turkish is an example of an agglutinating language, and thus what is written as one word in Turkish often needs translating into several words, or a whole clause, in English. Note that the graphic symbol ğ represents the sound [ɣ], a voiced velar fricative, and the graphic symbol ş represents the sound [ʃ] (as in English <u>shoe</u>).

To do this exercise, first of all, look at the following data from Turkish:

gitmek	'go'	
giderim	'go' 1st person singular present	'I go'
gidersin	'go' 2nd person singular present	'you go'
gider	'go' 3rd person singular present	'he/she/it goes'
gideriz	'go' 1st person plural present	'we go'
gidersiniz	'go' 2nd person plural present	'you all go'
giderler	'go' 3rd person plural present	'they go'
gideceğim	'go' 1st person singular future	'I will go'
gideceksin	'go' 2nd person singular future	'you will go'
gidecek	'go' 3rd person singular future	'he/she/it will go'
gideceğiz	'go' 1st person plural future	'we will go'
gideceksiniz	'go' 2nd person plural future	'you all will go'
gidecekler	'go' 3rd person plural future	'they will go'
gidecekmişim	'go' 1st person singular future dubitative	'It is said that I will go'
gidecekmişsin	'go' 2nd person singular future dubitative	'It is said that you will go'
gidecekmiş	'go' 3rd person singular future dubitative	'It is said that he/she/it will go'
gidecekmişiz	'go' 1st person plural future dubitative	'It is said that we will go'
gidecekmişsiniz	'go' 2nd person plural future dubitative	'It is said that you all will go'
gideceklermiş	'go' 3rd person plural future dubitative	'It is said that they will go'

1. List the morphemes for:
    (a) go
    (b) first person singular
    (c) first person plural
    (d) second person singular
    (e) second person plural
    (f) third person singular
    (g) third person plural
    (h) present tense
    (i) future tense
    (j) hearsay
2. Find an example of allomorphy. Explain the rule.

EXERCISE 4.14

Fill in the blanks with the missing morphemes from Turkish. You will need to refer to Exercise 4.13 to help you in this exercise.

bilmek	'know'	
bilirim	'know' 1st person singular present	'I know'
bilir_____	'know' 2nd person singular present	'you know'
bilir	'know' 3rd person singular present	'he/she/it knowes'
bilir_____	'know' 1st person plural present	'we know'
bilir_____	'know' 2nd person plural present	'you all know'
bilir_____	'know' 3rd person plural present	'they know'
bileceğim	'know' 1st person singular future	'I will know'
bil_____	'know' 2nd person singular future	'you will know'
bilecek	'know' 3rd person singular future	'he/she/it will know'
bil_____	'know' 1st person plural future	'we will know'
bil_____	'know' 2nd person plural future	'you all will know'
bilecekler	'know' 3rd person plural future	'they will know'
bilecek____	'know' 1st person singular future dubitative	'It is said that I will know'
bil_____	'know' 2nd person singular future dubitative	'It is said that you will know'
bilecekmiş	'know' 3rd person singular future dubitative	'It is said that he/she/it will know'
bil_____	'know' 1st person plural future dubitative	'It is said that we will know'
bil_____	'know' 2nd person plural future dubitative	'It is said that you all will know'
bileceklermiş	'know' 3rd person plural future dubitative	'It is said that they will know'

EXERCISE 4.15

Fill in the blanks with the missing morphemes from Turkish. You will need to refer to Exercise 4.13 to help you in this exercise. Note that that graphic symbol 'ı' stands for the close back unrounded vowel [ɯ], and that, in Turkish, when the final vowel of the verb is 'a', the endings use the vowel 'ı'.

koşmak	'run'	
koşarrım	'run' 1st person singular present	'I run'
koşarsın	'run' 2nd person singular present	'you run'
koşar	'run' 3rd person singular present	'he/she/it runs'
koşar_	'run' 1st person plural present	'we run'
koşar_	'run' 2nd person plural present	'you all run'
koşarlar	'run' 3rd person plural present	'they run'
koşacağım	'run' 1st person singular future	'I will run'
koşacak_	'run' 2nd person singular future	'you will run'
koşacak	'run' 3rd person singular future	'he/she/it will run'
koşacağız	'run' 1st person plural future	'we will run'

koşsacak_	'run' 2nd person plural future	'you all will run'
koşacaklar	'run' 3rd person plural future	'they will run'
koşacakmışım	'run' 1st person singular future dubitative	'It is said that I will run'
koşacakmışsın	'run' 2nd person singular future dubitative	'It is said that you will run'
koşacakmış	'run' 3rd person singular future dubitative	'It is said that he/she/it will run'
koşacak_	'run' 1st person plural future dubitative	'It is said that we will run'
koş_____	'run' 2nd person plural future dubitative	'It is said that you all will run'
koşacaklarmış	'run' 3rd person plural future dubitative	'It is said that they will run'

4.3   Formal syntax

As we have seen with morphology, languages use different finite resources to create infinite possibilities for meaning. For example, English uses very little inflection to provide information as to person and number through its verbs; thus, we have to have an overt subject, e.g. *I eat spinach*, which in the indicative mood has to be positioned before the verb to indicate that it is indeed the subject (except in rare cases of inversion, such as *Had I eaten more spinach* ...). Thus in English how linguistic elements are ordered in a string is very important; if I say *Eat I spinach* or *Spinach eat I*, people would look at me strangely, perhaps, given their assumption of my adherence to the Cooperative Principle, discussed in Chapter 2, attempting to attribute some meaning to that random string of words. Syntax is the study of how we join elements together in order to form acceptable clauses and sentences in natural languages. We have also seen in Chapter 2 that we often speak in incomplete sentences, as context helps our interlocutors understand our full intent. In Chapter 3, we have used Systemic Functional Linguistic theory to explain why clauses are they way they are in terms of how they are used in a given context. Formal studies of syntax (see Chapter 8, *Formal Linguistics*, by Amaya Mendikoetxea), on the other hand, take as their focus of analysis not the utterance in use, but rather the complete, well-formed utterances that we are capable of recognizing as such. Thus, syntactic studies attempt to explain how we know that the following utterance is acceptable in English:

I eat spinach and broccoli.

and that the following is not:

*I eat spinach and the.
(Note that it is customary to mark unacceptable forms with a *.)

As we delve into formal syntactic theory, you may see resonances with Chapter 4; at the same time, a formal account of grammar differs from a functional one in its motivations and in its analyses, and having an idea of both will equip you with a deep understanding of language structures and functions.

EXERCISE 4.16

Mark each of the following sentences with a • if you decide that it is a well-formed utterance in English, a ✓ if you feel that it is not an acceptable utterance, and ? if you feel that it is questionable. Explain any instances of * and ?.
1. The boy angrily kicked the ball.
2. The boy kicked angrily the ball.
3. John is eager to please.
4. John is easy to please.
5. It is easy to please John.
6. It is eager to please John.
7. He believed that I believed that linguistics is wonderful.
8. Linguistics is wonderful he believed that I believed.

Rather than describe actual language in use, formal theories of syntax strive to explain the rules of language use that we hold in our heads. By 'rules' here, we do not refer to the type of grammar rules that you may have learned in your language classes at school, be it in your first language or in another language, such as rules of comma use, which suggest a right or wrong way of doing things. Rather, theories of syntax set out to *describe* the way natural language works, the way it assembles into well-formed strings of words and phrases. This study of syntax (along with phonetics, phonology, and morphology) is often considered to be the center of what linguistic study should properly consist of. In this chapter, we will not go through all of the theories of syntax available, which are many.[1] We focus on the theoretical perspective linked to Noam Chomsky, transformational generative grammar (TG), after a brief look at its precursor, Phrase Structure Grammar.

4.3.1 Phrase structure grammar

4.3.1.1 Immediate constituent analysis

Immediate constituent analysis (a term introduced by the great American structural linguist Leonard Bloomfield), as its name implies, looks at the constituents which make up linguistic units; we have seen how words can be broken down into morphemes (and morphemes into phonemes). Here we examine how the sentence can be broken down into its structural units, and how those units, e.g. phrases, can be broken down into smaller units, until we reach the smallest constituents (and we can continue breaking down from words to morphemes to phonemes). If we take the sentence *The boy kicked the ball*, and we ask what its immediate constituents are, where might you make an initial division? You might think of two options: either

(a) *the boy kicked   the ball*

or

(b) *the boy   kicked the ball*

There are reasons for choosing the option (b), reasons which have to do the dimensions mentioned in Chapter 1 introduced by Ferdinand de Saussure, the syntagmatic and paradigmatic dimensions. On the syntagmatic dimension, we know that we can add elements *between* our constituents in (b):

> *The boy quickly kicked the ball.*
> *The boy angrily kicked the ball.*

But to do so in (a) seems questionable:

> **The boy kicked quickly the ball.*
> **The boy kicked angrily the ball.*

At the same time, we can include this addition at the end of the [kicked the ball] constituent:

> *The boy kicked the ball quickly.*
> *The boy kicked the ball angrily.*

---

1.   *The Concise Encyclopedia of Syntactic Theories* consists of 494 pages, which provides a sampling of the different theories available at the time of its publication in 1996.

While we have simplified the syntagmatic test here, it does provide evidence to argue for a division of constituents between *boy* and *kicked*. The paradigmatic dimension of language, which focuses on the ability of the same constituent types to be substituted for each other, provides further evidence. If we look at what we can substitute for *kicked*, we know that we have thousands of verbs in English that would do the job, including verbs like *kick* (in this meaning) which are transitive and take an object, and verbs which are intransitive, and do not, e.g. *The boy laughed*. Here the division would be between *the boy* and *laughed* (if not, we would have no division!) and so the paradigmatic dimension also gives us further reason to divide our original sentence between *the boy* and *kicked the ball*.

The other divisions are easier: *the boy* consists of *the* and *boy*, *kicked the ball* consists of *kicked* and *the ball*, which consists of *the* and *ball*. Thus, our immediate constituent analysis renders the following:

[[*the*] [*boy*]] [[*kicked*] [[*the*] [*ball*]]]

4.3.1.2 Phrase structure rules

Of course, now we need to label the constituents that result from our analysis, and describe what they consist of. As in Chapter 3, our labels have a familiar look to them, as they draw on terms that we use when we learn grammar at school. The terms are also similar to those we saw in Chapter 3 in connection with Systemic Functional Linguistics, although there are some differences. For example, our sentence above consists of:

the boy   kicked the ball
noun phrase (NP)   verb phrase (VP)

Thus, **sentence (S)** consists of a noun phrase plus a verb phrase, which we can annotate as:

S → NP VP

We see that the noun phrase in our example consists of:

the   boy
determiner   noun

Yet we know from other noun phrases in English that they can consist of an array of possibilities, involving, in addition to determiners (Det) and nouns (N), adjective (phrase)s (AdjP) and prepositional phrases (PP); or a noun phrase can consist solely of a pronoun (Pro) or proper noun (PN). Thus we can have any of the following:

girl (N)
a girl (Det N)
a tall girl (Det AdjP N)
a tall girl with long hair (Det AdjP N PP)
she (Pro)
Mary (PN)

We can write our noun phrase, or NP, rule as the following (note that parentheses ( ) indicate that the element is optional):

NP → (Det) (AdjP) N or PRO or PN (PP)

The verb phrase (VP) also has an array of possibilities:

John	*angrily*	*kicked*	*the ball*	*against the wall*
NP		VERB PHRASE (VP)		
	ADV	V	NP	PP

Of course the verb phrase (VP) contains the verb (V), and it can also include adverbs, noun phrases, adjective phrases (*John was <u>happy</u>*), and prepositional phrases.

VP → (ADV) V (NP) (AdjP) (PP)

We can specify further rewrite rules (as these rules are called) for each of our constituents, for example:

PP → Preposition NP
AdjP → (Adverb) Adjective (PP)

Now, phrase structure grammars, as linguistic approaches rooted in this theory came to be called, show further the relationships amongst the parts by using tree diagrams:

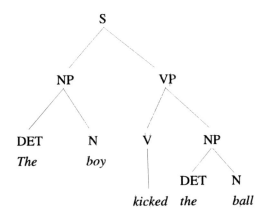

Through this method, thorny problems, such as defining *subject* and *object* become straightforward. Each point on the tree is called a **node**, and each node defines a syntactic category. The NP dominated immediately by the S (Sentence) node is the subject of the sentence. The NP dominated by the VP is an object. Thus, through the theory, subject and object are defined through the role they play in syntax, through syntactic terms, rather than semantic ones.

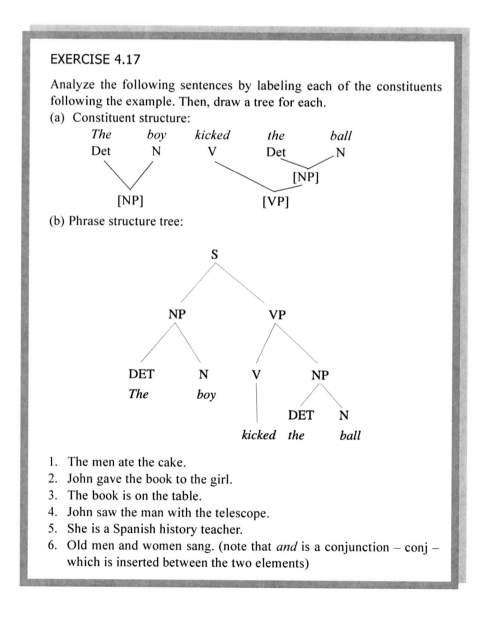

EXERCISE 4.17

Analyze the following sentences by labeling each of the constituents following the example. Then, draw a tree for each.

(a) Constituent structure:

(b) Phrase structure tree:

1. The men ate the cake.
2. John gave the book to the girl.
3. The book is on the table.
4. John saw the man with the telescope.
5. She is a Spanish history teacher.
6. Old men and women sang. (note that *and* is a conjunction – conj – which is inserted between the two elements)

4.3.2 Transformational generative grammar

4.3.2.1 Motivation

There are certain aspects of phrase structure grammar which Noam Chomsky felt did not explain efficiently or effectively certain aspects of syntactic structure. For example, he saw that structuralist explanations could not distinguish between sentences such as *John is eager to please* and *John is easy to please*; in a phrase structure analysis, *eager to please* and *easy to please* would seem to be equivalent constituents; however, while the surface structure is similar, the deep structure reveals a major difference: the implied subject of 'please' in the first is John, and in the second the implied subject of 'please' is anyone else, and 'John' is actually the object. That is, in *John is eager to please*, it is John who does the pleasing, while in *John is easy to please*, it is other people who do the pleasing, and not John. Chomsky also realized that the structuralist attempt to describe any language, such as English or Spanish, was not the same for some elements of linguistic structure, such as phonemes, which are finite in number, and others, such as sentences, which are infinite in number and in length. That is, we create new sentences all the time, and it is theoretically possible (though practically impossible) to create a sentence which goes on infinitely.

EXERCISE 4.18

Take a simple sentence and show how it can be expanded on infinitely, as in the Mother Goose nursery rhyme, *The House that Jack Built*, which begins:
> This is the house that Jack built.

and ends:
> This is the farmer sowing his corn that kept the cock that crowed in the morn that waked the priest all shaven and shorn that married the man all tattered and torn that kissed the maiden all forlorn that milked the cow with the crumpled horn that tossed the dog that worried the cat that killed the rat that ate the malt that lay in the house that Jack built.

Another problem that Chomsky had with phrase structure grammar is that it failed to account for relations between sentences which are similar in meaning, such as active-passive counterparts. That is a sentence like *Shakespeare was written by Hamlet* clearly has a relationship with *Shakespeare wrote Hamlet*, yet this relationship was not captured by phrase structure grammar.

EXERCISE 4.19

For each sentence, state whether it is active or passive voice; then
provide the counterpart (active if the sentence is passive, and passive if
the sentence is active). Try to explain in your own words what happens
in the transformation from active to passive.

    e.g. *Shakespeare wrote Hamlet*. ACTIVE
           PASSIVE = Hamlet was written by Shakespeare

1. Mary baked several cakes.
2. A choir was singing yuletide carols.
3. Many students brought gifts to the teacher.
4. Socks were knitted by thousands of women for the soldiers.
5. My car was stolen.
6. Mistakes were made.

A further difficulty which Chomsky experienced with phrase structure
grammars was that they could not explain the ambiguity which can arise from
the syntactic arrangement of clauses. Indeed, ambiguity can come about in
language for a variety of reasons. For example, in the headline which makes
its rounds on the Internet as purportedly real, *Drunk gets nine months in
violin case*, the ambiguity stems from the lexical item *case*, and the humor
comes about because, instead of 'court case', we are invited to entertain the
thought that a drunk person is sentenced to nine months stuffed into a case
designed for carrying a violin. Ambiguity can also come about because of
the structural configuration of a clause. For instance, in the also purportedly
real headline, *Stolen painting found by tree*, we might be led to believe that
a tree found a painting, rather than that a painting was found near a tree. In
this instance, the ambiguity does not come about solely because *by* can be
interpreted in different ways. It comes about because *tree* can be understood
as the agent in a passive sentence, much like *Shakespeare* in *Hamlet was
written by Shakespeare*.

EXERCISE 4.20

Explain in your own words the ambiguity in the sentences below.
1. I watched a movie with Paul Newman.
2. The man saw the boy with the telescope.
3. John likes her cooking.
4. Old men and women sang.
5. They are fighting dogs.

Chomsky wanted to move beyond these weaknesses of phrase structure grammar, failures to account for structures which look similar on the surface but which are quite different in essence; he also wanted to capture the infinite generating capability of language, to explain syntactic ambiguity, and to account for relations between sentences. Thus, Chomsky revolutionized the work done on language description by the structuralists, and moved linguistics to a new plane of analysis, one which would allow for greater explanation of how syntax works. His early theory was termed transformational generative grammar. Let us look first at the generative part.

4.3.2.2 Generative structure

Before we do that, we need to add something else to our phrase structure rules, an addition that came about as linguists worked with Chomsky's theory. We have seen that each of our categories has a head. For example, the head of a NP is a noun, and the head of a VP is a verb. One question which came up in applying the theory is: what is the head of a sentence? An answer was provided in a later edition of the theory, called *Government and Binding Theory*. The answer was that it is the information as to tense/aspect/modality, which provides the frame for the information in the sentence. Information such as whether the sentence is in present or past tense, whether it contains a modal, such as *can* or *may*, and whether the verb is presented in perfect or continuous aspect (*have worked* and *is working* respectively) is the kind of information gathered up into what is called *Aux*. Thus, we can redraw our example, including this important information:

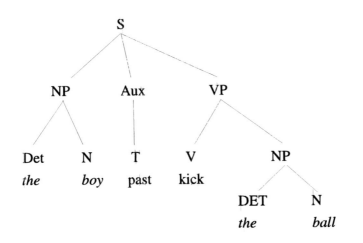

If we take a sentence like *I believe that linguistics is wonderful,* we note that we have a different kind of object, or complement, after the verb. *That linguistics is wonderful* functions here in a way which is similar to a noun, as we can substitute nouns for that phrase:

> I believe that linguistics is wonderful.
> I believe <u>her story</u>.

Indeed, a clause such as *that linguistics is wonderful,* is considered in our traditional grammar books to be a noun clause, as it can function as both subject and object in sentences:

> <u>That linguistics is wonderful</u> is a belief held by many. (Subject)
> I believe <u>that linguistics is wonderful</u>. (Object)

These types of clauses are typically introduced by the complementizer *that,* although we can omit *that* when the clause is the object of the verb, thus *I believe linguistics is wonderful.* To account for noun phrases in a syntactic theory, we need to introduce a new syntactic category, that of the Complementizer Phrase (CP), and our phrase structure trees can exhibit the recursive nature of language by altering the rewrite rule of the verb phrase:

VP → (Adv) V (NP) (PP) (**CP**)
CP → Comp S

So, for a sentence like *I believe that linguistics is wonderful,* we can draw the following tree:

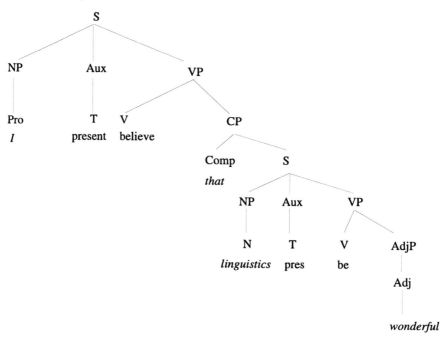

We can see from this sample tree the generative nature of the theory: we can generate any number of sentences from this tree (*I argue that syntax is easy, He claims that I am wrong*, etc.). If we take a sentence like *I believe that John believes that linguistics is wonderful,* we can see how the rewrite rules for the NP would allow us to continue generating more embedded sentences, as we can continue to embed an S in our NPs infinitely, in subject or object position, for *My mother believes that I believe that John believes that linguistics is wonderful.*

EXERCISE 4.21

Draw trees for the following sentences.
1. He thought that she was beautiful.
2. He said that he thought that she was beautiful.
3. That the answer was right was obvious.
4. That she believed that the answer was right was obvious.

4.3.2.3 Transformations

The transformation part of the theory allows us to see relationships between sentences, to disambiguate ambiguity by analyzing the syntax, and to show how sentences with similar surface structures have different deep structures. In order to examine the possibilities of the theory to establish relations between sentences through transformational rules, we turn to **passivization** and **data movement**.

In early transformational generative theory, passive sentences were thought to have the same deep structure as active sentences. Thus, for a sentence such as *John was led by Mary*, we would draw the deep structure tree for its active counterpart *Mary led John*, as:

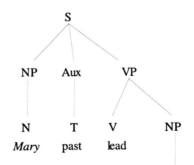

Now we can take the result generated by the deep structure tree '*Mary past lead John*' through our passivization transformation, by which we move the NP <u>dominated by S</u> to the VP, attaching *by* at the front of this NP, thus creating our '*by Mary*' surface structure. We also move the NP <u>dominated by the VP</u> to the spot in front of the VP (or to the spot that we can think of as Subject position). We also add to the Vgrp the morphemes *be* + *en*. So the transformational rule is:

	ACTIVE				→	PASSIVE					
Passivization:	NP¹	Aux	V	NP²	→	NP²	Aux	**be + en**	V	**by**	**NP²**
Passivization:	Mary	past	lead	John	→	**John**	past	**be + en**	lead	**by**	**Mary**

The string then goes through another transformation, in which we attach the affixes to their correct roots (a transformation aptly, though perhaps quirkily, named **affix hopping**):

Affix hopping: John   be + past   lead + en   by Mary

Because we know our rules for word formation from our knowledge of allomorphy, we can easily generate the correct surface form:

John was led by Mary.

There is a further rule related to passivized constructions, that of **by-deletion**, through which, as the name suggests, we delete the 'by phrase'. Thus, if we have a sentence such as *English is spoken here*, where the agent is not present in the surface structure, we include an 'empty' agent in the deep structure (after all, English is spoken by somebody!), symbolized by Δ, and then carry out the transformations as follows:

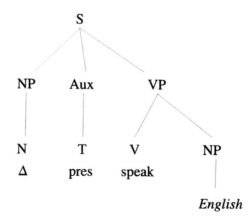

Passivization:	English	pres	be + en	speak	by Δ
Affix hopping:	English	be + pres		speak + en	by Δ
By-deletion:	English	be + pres		speak+en	$\varnothing$
Surface form:	*English is spoken*				

Chomsky did *not* argue that human beings go through this process, either consciously or unconsciously, when we produce language. Rather, he argued that we have internalized these rules, and that these illustrations through syntactic theory represent the underlying linguistic competence that we possess; they are models of human linguistic knowledge.

Another example of pairs of related sentences are those involving direct and indirect objects. We have two very similar structures: *Mary baked a cake for the boys* and *Mary baked the boys a cake*, as English allows this quirky surface structure of putting the indirect object after the verb and before the direct object. In the following tree, note the use of the large triangles to indicate that we are not spelling out every relation for every node on the tree: this is just to save time, especially with syntactic structures which are not under focus for our present purposes.

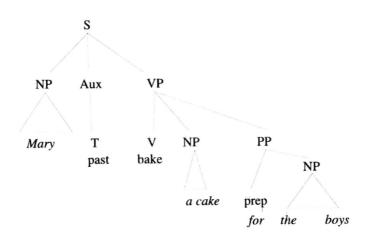

Through a transformation known as **dative movement** we can move the NP out of the PP in the VP, while deleting the preposition:

Dative movement: Mary   baked   the boys   a cake

4.3.2.4 Structural ambiguity

Our underlying linguistic competence also allows us to understand syntactic ambiguity, an understanding which we can illustrate through our deep structure trees. If we take the sentence *The man saw the boy with the telescope*, the surface structure does not make it clear who had the telescope. Did the man see the boy through the telescope, or did the man see the boy who was carrying the telescope? In Chapter 3, we disambiguated this sentence by applying our functional labels. Here, we will use structural means to disambiguate the meaning. Our deep structures, one for each of the two interpretations, make clear the meaning in each case, as there we specify what dominates the prepositional phrase 'with the telescope' – the VP immediately dominates the PP in the tree on the left, which matches the interpretation that it was the man who had the telescope, and the NP within the VP dominates the PP *with the telescope* in the tree on the right, which means that it was the boy who was carrying the telescope:

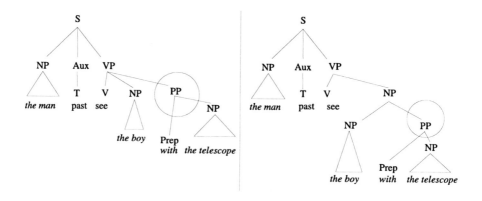

Notice the different placement of the PP in the VP; given that it is dominated immediately by the VP in the diagram on the left, we know that it specifies something about the verb, indicating how the man saw the boy; thus this prepositional phrase is adverbial in nature. In the diagram on the right, the PP is dominated by the NP within the VP, so we know that the PP modifies *the boy*, indicating that the boy was holding the telescope when the man saw him; thus, this prepositional phrase is adjectival in nature.

We can also disambiguate conjoined phrases in which it is not clear whether or not one element of the phrase modifies just one or more than one of other constituents. Let's take, for example, *Old men and women sang*. Who is old? Both the men and the women, or just the men? We have two different deep structure trees (note the added category of *conj*, or conjunction).

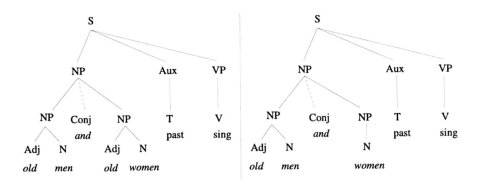

In the tree on the left, we can then carry out a transformation which allows us to eliminate redundant elements in equal conjoined syntactic elements, in order to elide the word *old* before *women;* thus, the scope of the adjective *old* over *women* is present in the surface structure only by implication from the deep structure. In the tree on the right, the deep structure never had *old* as part of the NP involving *women*, and thus *women* are not considered *old* in the surface structure.

4.3.2.5 Different deep structures

We can now look to another problem: sentences which seem to be related because of similar surface structures, but whose syntactic components in the deep structure show that they are actually different. For example, let's look at *She turned up the street* and *She turned up her nose*. In the first, she was walking along, and turned to walk up a particular street, while in the second, we understand that she snubbed someone or something by turning her nose up at them or it. We can see that in the first we have a prepositional phrase 'up the street', while in the second, we have a verb + particle 'turn up'. Our deep structures illustrate this difference:

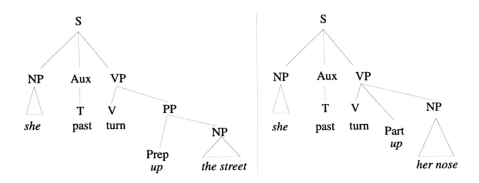

We have a further transformational rule which allows us to shift the particle out of the VGrp to the right-hand side of the NP in the VP:

Particle shift: She turned her nose **up**

Note that we cannot do that with the tree on the left, as there is no particle; it *is* possible to say *She turned the street up*, but that has a different meaning than walking along and turning up to continue walking along a street, and would seem to involve a bulldozer (and would, of course, involve a tree like the one on the right, with 'up' as a particle, forming the phrasal verb *to turn up*, equivalent to *to dig up*).

We have now looked at phrase structure grammar and at transformational generative grammar in order to have an understanding of what our underlying syntactic knowledge consists of in terms of constituents and operations. Chomsky and his followers have continued to refine the theory, as the original TG theory has provoked an immense amount of research on the way syntax operates across languages. An understanding of the early theory is necessary to understand the controversies which have led to later developments. We will not go into those controversies or developments here; if you are interested in matching your own questions about the theory with later developments, you might wish to read further on x-bar theory, government and binding theory, and minimalist theory. The section on *Formal Linguistics*, by Amaya Mendikoetxea, in Chapter 8 will also point you towards different applications and fields of research within this theoretical perspective on language.
Further exercises on syntax

EXERCISE 4.22

There is a condition for which particle shift is obligatory. Do you know what that condition is?

EXERCISE 4.23

Draw the phrase structure trees for the deep structure and carry out any necessary transformations to arrive at the surface structure of the following sentences. In cases of ambiguity, draw both trees.
1. I watched a movie with Paul Newman.
2. You can order soup and salad or French fries. (Note: the Aux contains the modal verb *can*, which you should label *Mod*).
3. Socks were knitted by thousands of women for the soldiers.
4. Mistakes were made.

5. The bottle was broken.
6. Her work was done on time.
7. They are fighting dogs. (Note: for one of the trees, you will need to include both tense (T) and Aspect (A) under Aux. The aspect is *Cont* (for continuous)).
8. They ran up the bill.
9. They ran up the hill.

EXERCISE 4.24

Discuss numbers 5 and 6 in Exercise 4.23. Think about the notion of passive sentences as counterparts of active sentences, keeping in mind the notion of agency, of just who it is that carries out the action.

4.4   Semantics

In Chapter 2, we looked at pragmatics, or the study of meaning in context. The study of **semantics** involves the study of meaning independent of situational context, what we often think of when we talk of meaning, what we tend to search for when we look up a word in a dictionary. Meaning, in this sense, refers to words and set phrases, and to the notions we hold in our minds of these words and phrases, hence the inclusion in this chapter on language and the mind. Work in this field, as we have seen with syntax, tries to model how we as human beings deal with linguistic meaning. Semantics is a very broad and diverse field within linguistics, and here we will only bring in a few of the different approaches to the study of semantics: **semiotics, sense** and **reference, semantic relations among words, componential analysis,** and **thematic roles.**[2] We reviewed semiotics in Chapter 1, in the section on Ferdinand de Saussure, and his notions of signified and signifier. Thus, we turn to the other areas of semantic study in this chapter.

4.4.1 Sense and reference

Semanticists distinguish between **sense** and **reference**. Sense is 'meaning' without reference to the specific real object in the world; thus, if someone utters the word *house*, depending on your cultural background, you might have in mind something like:

---

2.   A further area of semantics looks at how words change in meaning over time, which is dealt with in Chapter 5.

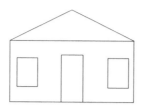

You also might be thinking along the lines of a dwelling which serves as a living quarters for people. That general image or imagining of a concept is a word's **sense**.

Reference, on the other hand, is 'meaning' tied to a specific instance. For example, if someone says *the red house*, you might now have a more specific instance of a house in mind; the same is the case for *the house at end of the block*. Interestingly, *the red house* and *the house at the end of the block* do not have the same meaning in terms of **sense**, but they actually could **refer** to the same house, as in *You know, the red house – the house at the end of the block*. In this case, two different senses of house are actually **coreferential**.

EXERCISE 4.25

Some argue that proper names have only reference and no sense. Do you agree?

It is possible that proper nouns have reference but no sense, like *Spain*. There are also noun phrases that have sense but no reference, like an oft-cited example *The present king of France is bald*.

4.4.2 Semantic relations

Semantics also involves defining the different relations which hold between pairs and sets of words. These relationships include everything from synonymy to antonymy, with other relationships coming into the playing field.

Synonymy: Synonymous words have (more or less) the same meaning. It has been argued by some linguists and language philosophers that no two words have exactly the same meaning, as they may differ in connotation (e.g. *slender, slim, skinny*) or in their typical contexts of use (*buy, purchase*).

Polysemy: A word is considered to be **polysemous** when it has more than one closely related meaning. Thus, *wood* is polysemous, as *wood* can mean 'a piece of a tree' and *wood* can also mean 'a group of trees'. In a dictionary, polysemous words often are listed as one head word, with several different senses listed under that head word; thus, returning to our example words in Exercise 4.1, if we look *bear* up in the dictionary, in this case the *Websters Ninth New Collegiate Dictionary*, we find two separate entries, or head words. One of the entries consists of several related senses, including: 1(a) 'to move while holding up and supporting'; 2(a) 'to give birth to'; and 3(a) 'to support the weight of'. Each of these senses is broken down into several related senses, so 1. also consists of 1(c) 'to hold in the mind'. Polysemy means that there is a relationship between the senses of a word; however, our check in the dictionary show that the other separate head word for bear is not a verb and does not have any relationship to holding; rather it refers to a big shaggy animal. This leads us to our next relation, which is **homonymy**.

Homonymy: Homonymous words, such as *bear/bear*, are words which are pronounced (**homophones**) and possibly spelled the same (**homographs**), but with different meanings, e.g. *to, too, two/ bat* (animal), *bat* (stick), and *bat* (as in 'bat your eyelashes').

Heteronymy: Heteronymous words have the same graphic form, that is they are written the same (i.e. they are homographs) but which have a different phonetic form, that is they are pronounced differently, and they also have different meaning, e.g. *bass/bass* (either a musical instrument or a fish, pronounced [beɪs] and [bæs] respectively, and *read/read*, either the base form or the past/past participles forms of the verb 'to read', pronounced [rid] and [rɛd] respectively.

Hyponymy: Hyponymous relations refer to words whose meanings are specific instances of a more general word; for example, *red, blue,* and *yellow*, are hyponyms of *color*, while *bed, sofa, table* and *chair* are hyponyms of *furniture.*

Antonymy: Antonyms are words that are closely related, that is they have properties in common, such as grammatical class and lexical field, but they oppose each other typically in one aspect of meaning. Antonyms are often divided into three different types. Antonyms are considered **complementary pairs** when the presence of one implies the absence of the other, for example *alive/dead*, and *present/absent*. This complementarity is not the case with some words which we consider to be antonymous, such as *rich/poor* ('I am not rich' does not imply 'I am poor'); these antonyms are called **gradable** antonyms, and include others such as *happy/sad, short/long*. The third type of antonyms refers to **relational opposites**, in which the existence of one implies the existence of its converse, e.g., *buyer/seller, husband/wife*.

Autoantonyms: are homographs which mean the opposite of each other; for example, *to clip* means both 'to cut out' as in 'She clipped the article from the newspaper' and 'to join together', as in 'She clipped the articles together'.

Antiautonyms: Antiautonyms are pairs of words which mean the same thing, although it seems that they should be the 'opposite' of each other, for example *boned* and *deboned* both refer to removing the bones from something.

EXERCISE 4.26

For each of the pairs of antonyms below, decide whether it is a complementary pair, a gradable pair, or a case of relational opposites.
1. odd/even
2. polite/rude
3. short/long
4. pass/fail
5. good/bad
6. moral/immoral
7. asleep/awake
8. mother/daughter
9. black/white
10. winner/loser

EXERCISE 4.27

For each of the categories below, provide four examples. Try to find examples which your classmates won't find!
1. synonymy
2. polysemy
3. homonymy
4. heteronomy
5. hyponymy
6. autoantonyms
7. antiautonyms

EXERCISE 4.28

Note down the synonyms of a classmate(s) from a) in Exercise 4.27. For each decide whether they are exact synonyms, that is, whether they can easily be substituted for each other.

4.4.3 Componential analysis

Given that we have been looking at Noam Chomsky's work in this chapter, we will mention the place held in his early theory by semantics and its relationship with **componential analysis**. It must be stressed that Chomsky privileged the study of syntax over semantics. Like Bloomfield (1933) and other American structuralists before him, Chomsky was more concerned with syntactic structures, and attempted to bleach the study of meaning from the study of syntax. Thus, in his early theory, he separated out the components of syntax, semantics and phonology, and established their interrelationships. Syntax consists of two components: 1. the base component, which is basically the phrase structure rules and their hierarchical relationships, modeled by the deep structure trees; it is the base component which generates the deep structure; and 2. the transformational component, which consists of the transformational rules; it is this component which generates surface structures. Now, deep structures provide the input to the semantic component, which describes their meaning, while surface structures provide the input to the phonological component, which describes their sounds. Meaning is generated both by the syntax, as we have seen through cases of syntactic ambiguity, and also through the words which attach to nodes of the trees. Thus, in addition to the categorial rules, the base component also consists of a **lexicon**, in essence our mental dictionary which contains all of the information (morphosyntactic, phonological and semantic) related to the vocabulary items of a language (e.g. whether a verb is transitive or intransitive, the way in which we form its past participle, how it is pronounced, etc.).

The semantic information contained in the lexicon is represented in terms of what are called **semantic features**, which are arrived at through **componential analysis,** an analysis not invented by Chomsky, but one which he saw as complementary to a generative syntactic analysis. Componential analysis breaks down the lexical item into its smaller semantic components, which are then listed through **feature notation**, which includes the semantic and phonological features as well. For example, the entry for 'boy' specifies that it has the syntactic features [+ Noun], [+ Count], [+ Common] (i.e. it is a noun that can be singular or plural and it is not a proper noun), and it also consists of semantic features, such as [+ Human], which subsumes other semantic features such as [+ Animate]. This use of features draws on previous work in semantics, on what is known as the **conceptual sense** of a word, which denotes its stable semantic features:

| boy | + HUMAN | – ADULT | + MALE |
| girl | + HUMAN | – ADULT | – MALE |

man	+ HUMAN	+ ADULT	+ MALE
woman	+ HUMAN	+ ADULT	− MALE

The categorial rules generate a string of slots (as we see in our trees above at the bottom of each tree, e.g. 'Det N past V') to be filled with items from the lexicon via lexical insertion rules. Each slot has associated with it a set of features which indicate which kind of item can be filled in. By combining these features with those features in the lexicon, (the V in the string 'Det N past V' might specify that it can only occur with an animate noun) the lexical insertion rules (which in effect are transformations) generate such sentences as *The boy laughed*, but not such sentences as *The chalk laughed*:

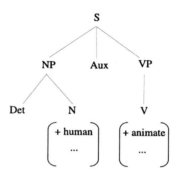

Hence we can explain why certain combinations are considered ungrammatical; as in the case of *The chalk laughed*, for example, there is a mismatch between the specifications in features of the deep structure and an item chosen from the lexicon (*chalk* is − animate and thus −human).

EXERCISE 4.29

For each of the trees below, decide what semantic features the node marked with a ? would have to have in order to generate sentences which make sense. Suggest sample sentences that would be generated, and sentences which would not.

e.g.

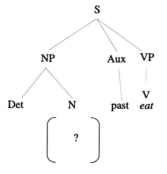

The noun here would have to be + animate (either + human or + animal), to produce *The man ate, the horse ate,* etc. (and not *The chalk ate*).

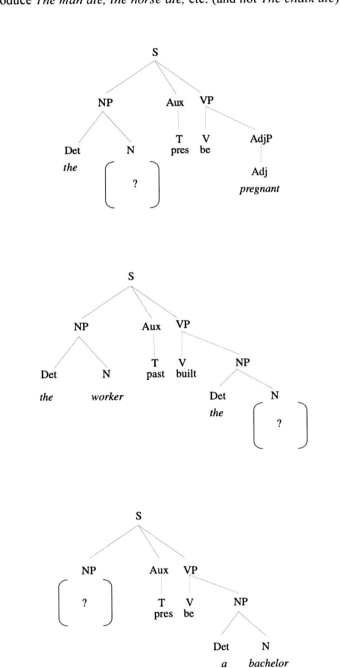

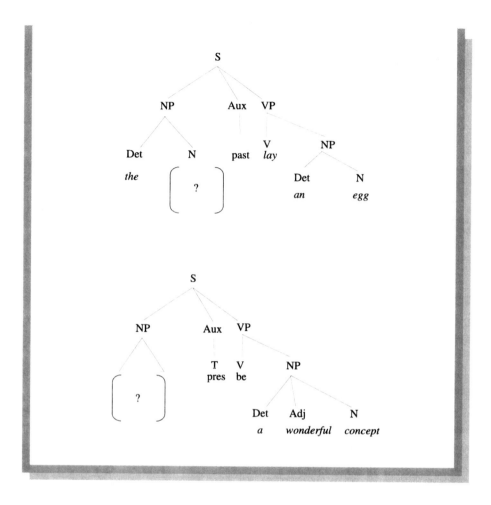

4.4.4 Thematic roles

Thematic roles, or relations, refer to the semantic roles which noun phrases play in relationship to the verb of the clause. Indeed, many linguists assign the verb the central role in the clause, and roles are assigned to participants depending on their relationship to the verb (see for example Section 3.2.2.2 in Chapter 3). For example, in the sentence *The boy kicked the ball*, 'the boy' is the doer of the action, and hence is the **agent**; 'the ball' is the receiver of the action and is changed by it, and hence is the **patient**. While there is not complete agreement on the names of the roles, or on the exact delineation of the roles, a possible list, based on Saeed (2005) is:

agent	deliberately carries out an action	The boy kicked the ball.
experiencer	receives sensory or emotional input	The boy smelled the roses.
theme	receives the action without a change of state, or its location is described	The boy held the ball. The ball is in the yard.
patient	receives the action, resulting in a change of state	The boy inflated the ball.
instrument	something used to perform an action	The boy inflated the ball with a pump.
location	the place where an action occurs	The boy played in the street
goal	what the action is directed towards	The boy kicked the ball towards the goal.
recipient	receives transfer of possession	The boy gave the ball to the man.
time	the time at which an action takes place	The boy played this morning.
beneficiary	receives the benefit of the action	The boy performed for the crowd.

It is important to point out the differences with the participant types we saw in Chapter 3, Section 3.2.2.2, in Systemic Functional Linguistics. There is overlap in terminology (as in all linguistics!), although often the same term is used for a different participant. For example, note that Goal in SFL overlaps with patient here, not with goal. Also, Theme in SFL has quite a different meaning altogether, as it has to do with how information is structured. These differences in terminology may cause understandable frustration; it is best not to get too hung up on terms at early stages, and focus rather on an overall understanding on the ways in which linguists focus on language.

EXERCISE 4.30

In each of the sentences below, identify all of the noun phrases, and indicate their thematic role with relationship to the verb.

E.g. The boy inflated the ball with a pump.

The boy = agent, the ball = patient, the pump = instrument

1. Give your baby a cool safe teething ring.
2. I scheduled appointments for the patients.
3. The teacher lined the students up.
4. She carried a basket of food to her grandmother.
5. The little girl took an automatic out of her basket.
6. She shot the wolf dead.
7. Calories are burned throughout the duration of the activity.
8. The camp was established by UNHCR.

4.5 Chapter outcomes

After having read this chapter carefully, discussed with others the content, and carried out the exercises, you should assess your ability to:

- ✓ Explain why 'word' is a difficult concept to pin down.
- ✓ Explain the difference between content words and function words, using examples.
- ✓ Define morpheme.
- ✓ Explain the different types of morphemes: free, bound, root, stem, derivational, and inflectional, providing examples of each one.
- ✓ Explain affixes, including prefixes, suffixes, infixes, circumfixes, and transfixes, giving examples of each type.
- ✓ Explain reduplication.
- ✓ Analyze the hierarchical structure of the morphological make-up word using a tree diagram.
- ✓ Explain what allomorphs are and give examples.
- ✓ Describe constituents and phrase structure rules; list what each of the following consist of: sentence, noun phrase, verb phrase, prepositional phrase, adjective phrase, complementizer phrase.
- ✓ Draw deep structure trees for simple sentences and for sentences with complementizer phrases in subject or object position.
- ✓ Carry out the following transformations: passivization, dative movement and particle shift.
- ✓ Use deep structure trees to clarify structural ambiguity.
- ✓ Explain the difference between sense and reference.
- ✓ Give examples of semantic relations of: synonymy, polysemy, homonymy, heteronymy, hyponymy, antonymy, autoantonymy, and antiautonymy.
- ✓ Give examples of componential analysis and explain its relationship to syntax.
- ✓ Distinguish between pairs of antonyms in terms of whether they are complementary, gradable, or relational opposites.
- ✓ Explain the concept of thematic roles and apply the labels to noun phrases in sentences.

4.6 References and further reading

Note: For further reading, see Chapter 8, *Formal Linguistics*, by Amaya Mendikoetxea.

Bloomfield, Leonard (1933) *Language*. New York: Henry Holt and Co.

Broderick, John P. (1975) *Modern English Linguistics: A Structural and Transformational Grammar*. Philadelphia, PA: Harper & Row, Publishers. Retrieved February 15, 2010 from http://www.odu.edu/al/jpbroder/modengling.html

Chomsky, Noam (2006) *Language and Mind*. *Third Edition*. Cambridge: Cambridge University Press.

Chomsky, Noam (1986) *Knowledge of Language: Its Nature, Origin, and Use*. Westport, CT: Greenwood Press.

Graffi, Giorgio (2001) *200 Years of Syntax. A Critical Survey. Studies in the History of the Language Sciences 98*. Amsterdam: Benjamins.

Haegeman, Liliane (1994) *Introduction to Government and Binding Theory*. Oxford: Blackwell Publishing.

Lepschy, Giulio C. (1982) *A Survey of Structural Linguistics*. London: Andre Deutsch.

Saeed, John I. 2003) *Semantics. 2nd Edition*. Malden, MA: Blackwell Publishing.

Searle, John (1972) Chomsky's revolution. *The New York Review of Books*. Retrieved on February 21, 2010 from http://www.chomsky.info/onchomsky/19720629.htm.

4.7   Some answers to the exercises

Exercise 4.1

Answers will vary. One possibility:

1. *bear* referring to the animal (number 1)
2. *bear* meaning 'to stand, to support' (numbers 2, 5)
3. *bear* meaning 'to carry, to hold' (number 3 and metaphorically number 6)
4. *bear* meaning 'to give birth to' (numbers 7 and 8)
5. *bore* meaning 'a dull person' (number 9)
6. *bare* meaning 'naked' (numbers 4 and 10)

Exercise 4.2

Answers will vary.

Most probably, you may have considered the following to be words: *hello, chair, the, friend, friendship, friends, goodbye, blackboard, faked*

and the following to be non-words: *ly, ceive, un, gotcha, gonna, cran*

and the following to be two separate words: *coffee cup*

However, these distinctions might seem arbitrary, especially given that *gotcha* and *gonna* are often written as one unit, and sometimes included in dictionaries, and compounds vary from those consisting of one word, such as *blackboard*, to those including a hyphen, such as *absent-minded* or *mother-in-law*, and those which are written as two separate words, such as *fact sheet* or *school day* (but note *schoolwork*, and the *Oxford English Dictionary* lists *schoolday*). Defining the word *word* is not easy!

Exercise 4.3

Answers will vary.

Exercise 4.4

Answers will vary. One possible new function word for English could be a gender neutral pronoun, in order to avoid the awkward *he/she*. Another one is a second person plural pronoun, one which already exists in many varieties of English, in the form of *you guys, y'all,* or *youse*. Another possibility, although perhaps less useful, is another first person plural pronoun; *we* can refer inclusively (*we* meaning all of us present) or exclusively (*we* meaning *us, not you*). Other languages have function words which we do not have in English. For example, Spanish has three sets of demonstratives, *este* means 'this', *ese* means 'that', and *aquel* means 'that one that's even farther away'.

Exercise 4.5

1. dogs = dog + s
2. unpack = un + pack
3. carrot = carrot
4. behead = be + head
5. repackage = re + pack + age (or re + package)
6. redness = red + ness
7. deactivate = de + active + ate (more doubtful de + act + ive+ate
8. classroom = class + room
9. paper = paper
10. writer's = write + er + 's

Possible categorization (answers may differ):

1. *dog, pack, carrot, red, active, class, room, paper* and *write* might all be classed together as recognizable words which can stand on their own.
2. *un, be, de* and *re* as morphemes which are placed at the beginning of a verb and which change its meaning; these might also be included in a broader category involving *ness* and *er* as morphemes which are placed at the end of an adjective or a verb, resulting in a noun
3. *s* and *'s* as morphemes which do not change the meaning or the word class, but change how the word relates to the surrounding words.

Repackage may cause some discussion. The noun *package* comes from *pack + age*, and it seems that the verb *to package* came from the noun *package*. So in essence the morphological analysis is *re + package*.

Deactivate comes from adding *de* to the verb *activate*, which can be further broken down into *active + ate*. Etymological dictionaries do not suggest that *active* can be broken down further into *act + ive*, at least not in English, as the word came through French from Latin (*act-+vus*). It is difficult to know when to stop in doing a morphological analysis in this sense.

Exercise 4.6

Answers may vary. Certainly we can say *lighten*, and we have other verbs which have *en* added as a prefix (*ensnare*). However, *lighten* has quite a different meaning from *enlighten*, which perhaps lends credence to the notion that *en-* and *-en* are added at the same time, and thus constitute a circumfix. However, the *Oxford English Dictionary* suggests that the etymology of the word formation is doubtful, and that perhaps *inlighten* was formed from *inlight*. *Embolden*, however, shows no other explanation than the prefix and suffix attaching simultaneously, and thus could have been created through circumfixation. The prefix *em* is the same as *en*, with the *m* coming into existence through the process of assimilation (see Chapter 2) toward the bilabial *b*, which is why many argue that *en-* + *-en* constitutes a circumfix in the case of these two words.

Exercise 4.7

The diagram on the left shows the hierarchical structure of the word *unlockable* in its meaning 'not able to be locked'; that is the verb *lock* is made into an adjective with the suffix *able*, and then that adjective is negated. In the diagram on the left, we see the hierarchical structure of the word *unlockable* in its meaning 'not able to be unlocked'; that is, the prefix *un* is added to the verb *lock*, creating the verb *unlock*. Then the suffix *-able* is added to the verb *unlock*.

Exercise 4.8

    huckleberry
    cranapple
    dentistry
    economics
    receive
    maternity
    lukewarm
    interrupt

Bound roots: *Huckle, luke* and *cran* function to combine with other words in much the same way as compounds combine. *Huckle* does not occur with any other words (though it is an obsolete word), yet *berry* can be combined with *blue, straw,* and *black,* for example. *Luke* only occurs with *warm* (unless it is a proper name, which is a different case). Thus, *huckle* and *luke* are bound roots. *Cran* can also combine with *berry,* although we never use it on its own, so we could classify it as a bound root. *Re* and *ceive* are interesting, as neither can stand on its on, so which is the root? We have other words such as *deceive, conceive* and *perceive,* based on the Latin root *capere,* so we can classify *ceive* as a bound root. The same is the case for *rupt* (also *corrupt, disrupt, rupture*), *mater,* (*maternal, maternity*) and *dent* (*dental*).

Exercise 4.9

1.	debo	'I owe'
2.	debes	'you owe'
3.	deb<u>e</u>	'he/she/it owes'
4.	debemos	'we owe'
5.	debéis	'you (plural) owe'
6.	deben	'they owe'
7.	com<u>o</u>	'I eat'
8.	com<u>es</u>	'you eat'
9.	come	'he/she/it eats'
10.	com<u>emos</u>	'we eat'
11.	com<u>éis</u>	'you (plural) eat'
12.	com<u>en</u>	'they eat'

'o'   = 1st person singular indicative
'es'   = 2nd person singular indicative
'e'   = 3rd person singular indicative
'emos' = 1st person plural indicative
'eis' = 2nd person plural indicative
'en'   = 3rd person plural indicative

Exercise 4.10

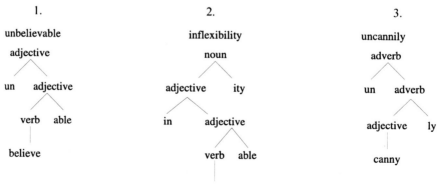

It is possible to break it down further, as according to the *Oxford English Dictionary*, canny was derived from the verb *can*.

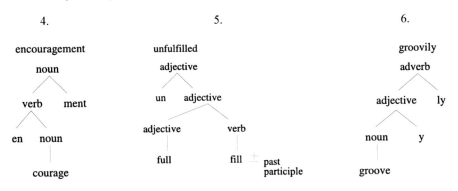

Exercise 4.11

A	B	C	D
needed [nidəd]	freaked [fɹikt]	hummed [hʌmd]	clawed [klɔd]
wanted [wɑntəd]	sipped [sɪpt]	buzzed [bʌzd]	played [pleɪd]
blended [blɛndəd]	kissed [kɪst]	hugged [hʌgd]	kneed [nid]
fasted [fæstəd]	cashed [cæʃt]	paved [peɪvd]	plowed [plaʊd]

1. Column A adds [əd] to verbs which end in alveolar stops. Column B adds [t] to verbs which end in unvoiced consonants. Column C adds [d] to verbs which end in voiced consonants, and Column D adds [d] to verbs which end in vowels.
2. There are three different allomorphs of the past tense morpheme in English. /d/ is probably the underlying form, as it occurs in the greatest number of contexts.
3. Columns C and D use the underlying form, so we only need to explain why Columns A and B are different. For the verbs in Column A, in order to differentiate the present from the past tense pronunciation, we need to insert a sound between the two alveolar consonants, hence the epenthetic ə. In column B, the verbs all end in a voiceless consonant, and thus assimilation explains why the voiceless alveolar plosive is used.
4.

verb + past tense /d/   → [t] after unvoiced consonant

→ [əd] after alveolar plosives

Exercise 4.12

A	B	C	D
needs [nidz]	freaks [fɹiks]	kisses [kɪsəz]	claws [klɔz]
hums [hʌmz]	sips [sɪps]	buzzes [bʌzəz]	plays [pleɪz]
shuns [ʃʌnz]	putts [pʌts]	cashes [cæʃəz]	knees [niz]
paves [peɪvz]	laughs [læfs]	patches [pætʃəz]	plows [plaʊz]

1. Column A adds [əd] to verbs which end in alveolar stops. Column B adds [t] to verbs which end in unvoiced consonants. Column C adds [d] to verbs which end in voiced consonants, and Column D adds [d] to verbs which end in vowels.

2. There are three different allomorphs of the past tense morpheme in English. /d/ is probably the underlying form, as it occurs in the greatest number of contexts.

3. Columns C and D use the underlying form, so we only need to explain why Columns A and B are different. For the verbs in Column A, in order to differentiate the present from the past tense pronunciation, we need to insert a sound between the two alveolar consonants, hence the epenthetic ə. In column B, the verbs all end in a voiceless consonant, and thus assimilation explains why the voiceless alveolar plosive is used.

4.
verb + plural /z/

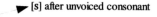

[s] after unvoiced consonant

[əz] after alveolar plosives

Exercise 4.13

1. (a) gitmek
   (b) im
   (c) iz
   (d) sin
   (e) siniz
   (f) Ø
   (g) ler
   (h) er
   (i) ecek
   (j) miş

2. The future tense morpheme *ecek* becomes *eceğ* before a vowel.

Exercise 4.14

bilmek	bilirim
bilir<u>sin</u>	bilir
bili<u>riz</u>	bilir<u>siniz</u>
bilir<u>ler</u>	bilece<u>ğim</u>
bil<u>ece</u>ksin	bilecek
bil<u>ece</u>ğiz	bil<u>ece</u>ksiniz
bilecekler	bilecek<u>mişim</u>
bilec<u>ekmiş</u>sin	bilecekmiş
bil<u>ece</u>kmişiz	bil<u>ece</u>kmişsiniz
bileceklermiş	

Exercise 4.15

koşmak	koşarım
koşarsın	koşar
koşa<u>rız</u>	koşar<u>sınız</u>
koşarlar	koşacağım
koşacak<u>sin</u>	koşacak
koşacağız	koşsacak<u>siniz</u>
koşacaklar	koşacakmışım
koşacakmışsın	koşacakmış
koşacak<u>mışiz</u>	koş<u>acakmış</u>siniz
koşacaklarmış	

Exercise 4.16

Answers may vary.

1. √
2. * or perhaps ? (although *angrily* in this reading might need quite a bit of stress)
3. √
4. √
5. √
6. * or perhaps ? if we could imagine that 'it' refers to an animal
7. √
8. * or perhaps ? if we added quotes '*Linguistics is wonderful,*' *he believed that I believed* (although that still seems odd)

Exercise 4.17

1.

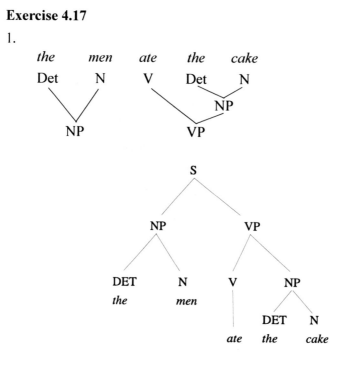

2.

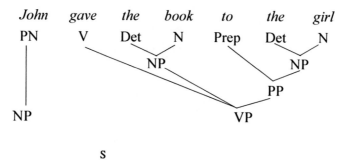

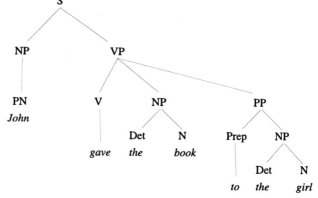

3.

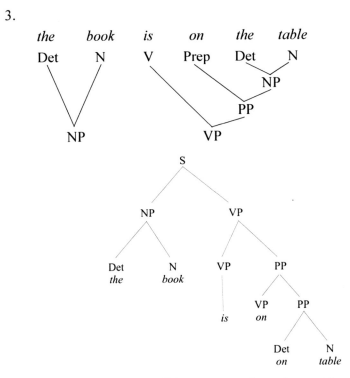

4. There are two possible answers (see the section on 'Structural ambiguity' in Chapter 3)

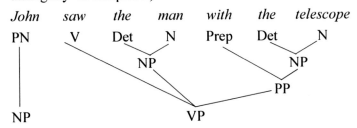

Note: in this tree John, saw the man by using the telescope.

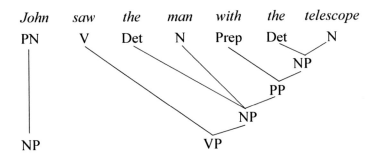

Note: in this tree John, saw the man who was carrying the telescope.

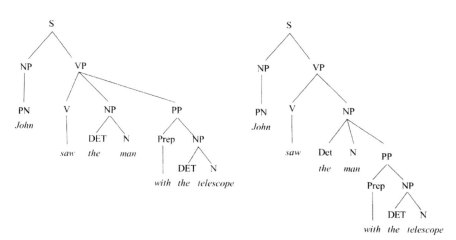

 5.

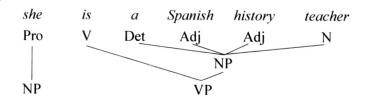

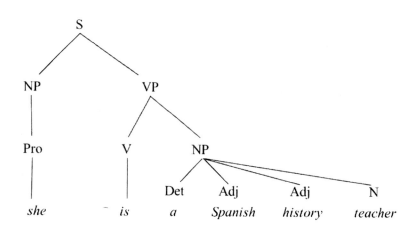

6.

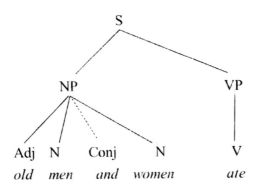

Note that this is the tree for the interpretation that both the men and the women are old. For the interpretation that only the men are old, we would need to have two separate NPs in the sentence NP.

Exercise 4.18

Answers will vary.

Exercise 4.19

1. *Mary baked several cakes.* ACTIVE
   PASSIVE = *Several cakes were baked by Mary.*
2. *A choir was singing yuletide carols.* ACTIVE
   PASSIVE = *Yuletide carols were being sung by a choir.*
3. *Many students brought gifts to the teacher.* ACTIVE
   PASSIVE = *Many gifts were brought to the teacher by the students.*
4. *Socks were knitted by thousands of women for the soldiers.* PASSIVE
   ACTIVE = *Thousands of women knitted socks for the soldiers.*
5. *My car was stolen.* PASSIVE
   ACTIVE = *Someone (?) stole my car.*
6. *Mistakes were made.* PASSIVE
   ACTIVE = *Someone (?) made mistakes.*

Exercise 4.20

1. It is not clear whether I watched a movie with Paul Newman, or if I was with Paul Newman when I saw the movie.
2. It is not clear who had the telescope: the man or the boy.
3. Either John likes the taste of the food she cooks, or he likes to see her cooking in the kitchen.
4. Who is old? Both the men and the women, or just the men?
5. Is someone fighting some dogs, or are the dogs of the fighting type?

Exercise 4.21

1.

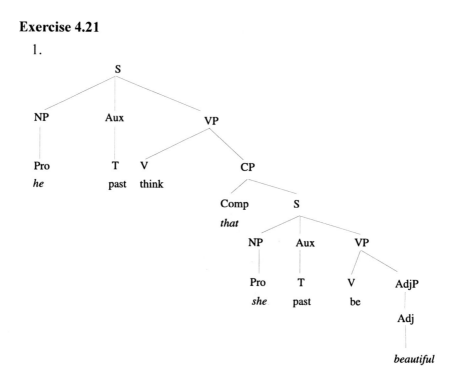

2. He said that he thought that she was beautiful.

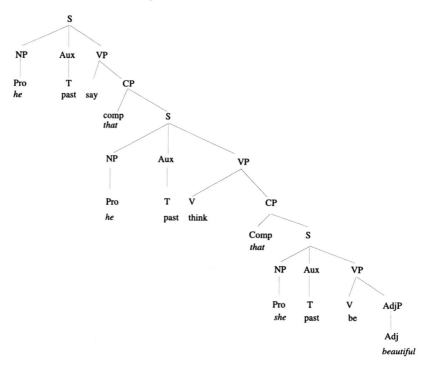

3. That the answer was right was obvious.

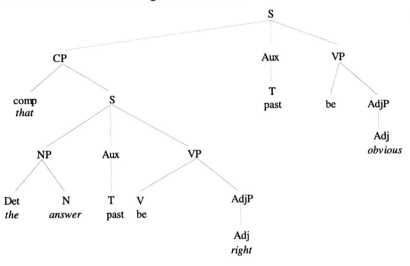

4. That she believed that the answer was right was obvious.

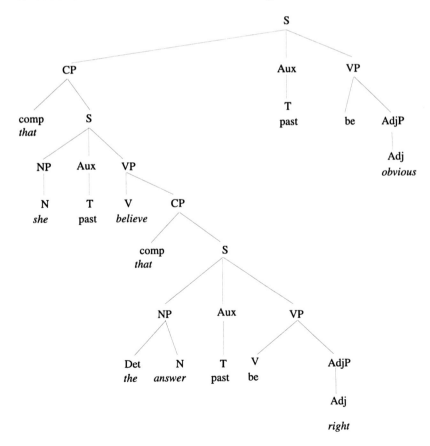

Exercise 4.22

When the NP in the VP is a pronoun. We cannot say, with reference to *his nose* in the case that we see a guy snub a group of people: **He turned up it.* It is obligatory to move the particle after the pronoun for *He turned it up.* The same is the case for other verb + particle combinations, e.g. *They ran up the bill – They ran it up.*

Exercise 4.23

1.

2.

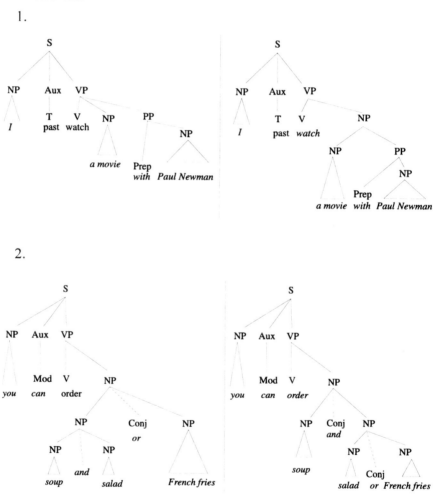

3.

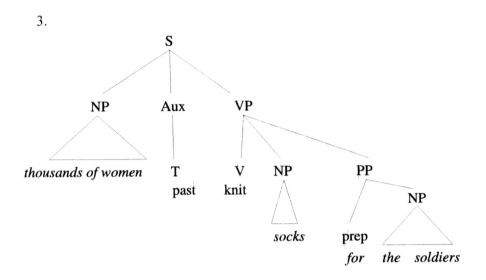

Passivization: socks   past   be + en   knit   by thousands of women
Affix hopping: socks   be + past   knit + en   by thousands of women

4.

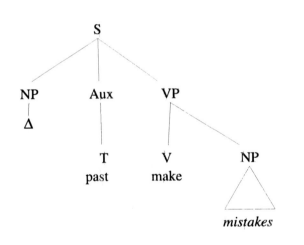

Passivization: mistakes   past   be + en   make   by Δ
Affix hopping: mistakes   be + past   make + en   by Δ
By-deletion: mistakes   be + past   make + en   ∅

5. The bottle was broken.

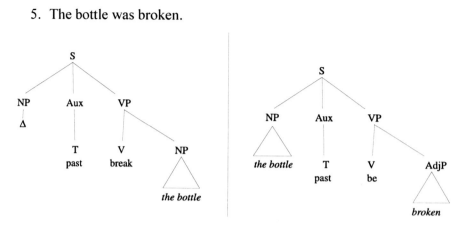

In essence, there are two possible interpretations for this sentence. The first is that we follow the notion that passive sentences have the same deep structure as active sentences and then go through transformations, as with the sentence on the left and the following transformations:

Passivization: the bottle   past   be + en   break   by Δ
Affix hopping: the bottle   be + past   break + en   by Δ
By-deletion: the bottle   be + past   break + en   ∅

However, if we come across a broken bottle and later report on it, we would be focusing on something different if we said *Someone broke the bottle*. In that utterance, we focus on the actions of some unknown person, and we may just wish to focus on the fact that the bottle was broken. Past participles often function as adjectives in English (for example, we can say *the broken bottle*), so the interpretation on the right, with *broken* as an adjective seems to fit more with the meaning. At the same time, Chomsky's focus was not on meaning, but rather on structures and their generative capability.

6. Her work was done on time.

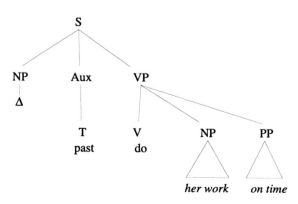

Passivization:	her work	past	be + en	do	by Δ
Affix hopping:	her work	be + past		do + en	by Δ
By-deletion:	her work	be + past		do + en	Ø

It might be tempting to include *by her* in the deep structure, but there is nothing in the surface structure to indicate that she actually did the work – perhaps someone else did it for her!

7.

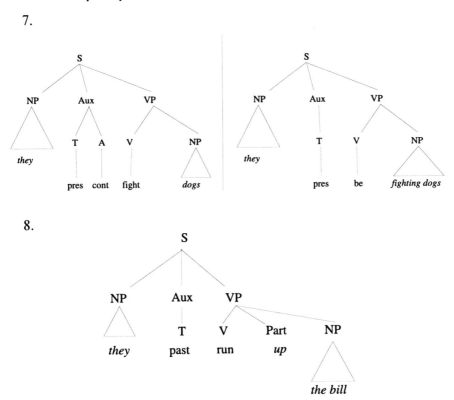

8.

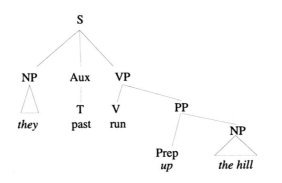

9. They ran up the hill.

Exercise 4.24

See comments above for Exercise 4.23 numbers 5 and 6.

Exercise 4.25

Answers will vary. It is worth pondering, for example, that many names conjure up in our minds a male or female before we even meet the person, which seems to be 'meaning' in terms more of sense than it is of reference.

Exercise 4.26

1. complementary
2. gradable (although a student once suggested that where she comes from, if you are not polite, then you are rude)
3. gradable
4. complementary
5. gradable
6. complementary
7. complementary
8. relational opposites
9. gradable
10. complementary

Exercise 4.27

Answers will vary.

Exercise 4.28

Answers will vary.

Exercise 4.29

Answers will vary. Some possibilities:

1. + feminine + adult + animate; *girl, woman, lady, mare, cow* ... are possible; *boy, man, stone* are not
2. – animate – already existing; *shed, house, platform* ... are possible; *dog, the ocean, the sun* are not
3. + masculine + adult + marriageable; *the man, he, John, that guy* ... are possible; *girl, little boy, the Pope* are not...
4. + oviparous + female + adult *hen, duck, goose* ... are possible; *cow, rooster, chick* are not.
5. + abstract – animate + good; *freedom, equality, justice* ... are possible; *that lamp, the boy, destruction* are not.

Obviously, we play with language, and we can talk about a lamp as a wonderful concept (because of its unique design perhaps). In films, males can become pregnant and we can build all sorts of things for the stage.

Exercise 4.30

1. *your baby* = recipient; *a cool safe teething ring* = patient
2. *I* = agent; *appointments* = patient; *the patients* = beneficiary
3. *the teacher* = agent; *the students* = patient
4. *she* = agent; *a basket of food* = patient; *her grandmother* = beneficiary
5. *the little girl* = agent; *an automatic* = patient; *her basket* = location
6. *she* = agent; *the wolf* = patient (as an adjective, *dead* would not be assigned a thematic role)
7. *calories* = patient; *the duration of the activity* = time
8. *the camp* = patient; *UNHCR* = agent

5 Language change

5.1 Introduction

5.1.1 Development of human language

From the time of our ancient hominid ancestors, on through the era of the first known written language, on through Shakespeare's time, and up until today, the ways in which humans communicate have experienced massive development and change. Steven Mithen, in *The Singing Neanderthals*, suggests that our six-million-year-old hominid ancestors communicated via a repertoire of a relatively restricted set of calls and gestures similar to that of modern apes. This set of calls and gestures was used to manipulate the behavior of others; for example one call might get others to dash up into the trees at the sight of a ground predator approaching, and a different call might get others to dash down in the case of the approach of an air predator. Move up four million years, and changes during that time in social structure, anatomy (including increased bipedalism and brain size), habitat and foraging practices brought about an enhanced system of communication which was more complex than that of modern apes in terms of varieties of calls, musicality, and gestures. While this communication system provided more complexity in type and number of communicative acts, brought about because of a greater number of types of predators and need for cooperation, along with greater needs for expressing and eliciting both social commitment and emotion, it was still not language as we know it today. Early hominid language was holistic, in that a communicative act basically had one representation. Modern language is compositional, in that a communicative act can be expressed by putting together a variety of linguistic and non-linguistic components in numerous different ways, drawing on speech sounds, morphology and syntax, as well as contextual cues, gesture and facial expressions, to get across a meaning which can very well refer to something that is not in the realm of our immediate experience, something which early hominid communication probably could not do.

At some point between two million years ago and at least a hundred thousand years ago, our early hominid system of communication developed into language, complete with signs created from arbitrary strings of speech sounds to become separate words with conventionalized meanings. At some point, syntax became necessary to put those words into longer regularly ordered strings which could combine together in finite ways to convey an infinite number of meanings. How and at what rate this might have happened is the basis for on-going debate amongst researchers and theorists of human language origins.[1] At the same time, a study of how language may have developed has only in recent years become of interest to linguists perhaps largely due to the interest in how language develops in children (a topic for Chapter 7).

Of course, we can only conjecture about the origins of language based on archeological findings in the form of tools, cave paintings, skeletal remains, etc. That is indeed the case until language began to be written down. The evidence from the first written records of language from the Sumerians, which date back to around 5000 BC, provide hints to the fact that at least 7000 years ago modern-style syntax existed, and that the people of the time were able to use their language to communicate a vast array of individual and societal needs. Sumerian writing systems changed over the next few thousand years from a pictorial representational system to one which moved towards capturing the spoken language in writing.

5.1.2   Tracing language change

The main focus of this chapter is on how and why human language as we know it today changes. Indeed, there is a major difference between the changes which occurred in the communicative behavior of our hominid ancestors and the kinds of changes which occur since human language developed, as experienced in Sumerian writing systems. Talmy Givón and Bertram Malle explain that the pre-language behavior was adaptive in that it increased the chances for survival and reproduction of those who were successful in changing their communicative repertoire. On the other hand, '[l]inguistic change, which began in the post-language communicative era of hominid evolution, however, is by and large tied to society and culture. It has nothing to do with life expectancy, reproductive success, genetic mutation or natural selection' (88).

So, on the one hand we have an adaptive process which took millions of years, in which early hominid communication changed from pre-language behavior to complex language complete with signs and syntax. On the other hand, we have human language as we know it via all of the languages spoken around the world, all of which change constantly and relatively rapidly. We know this from our own experience throughout our lives, as well as from research through historical linguistics (see Chapter 8, *Historic Linguistics*, by Michael Cummings). We know that languages such as Spanish, Italian,

---

1.   cf. Bickerton (1992), Carstairs-McCarthy (1999), Givón and Malle (2002), Burling (2005), Laks (2008), to mention only a few, and Christiansen and Kirby (2003) for a summary of work on language evolution.

Catalan, Portuguese, Romanian and French are direct descendents from Latin, itself part of a family of languages known as Italic, which is itself part of a larger family of languages known as **Indo-European**. Other Indo-European language families in addition to Italic are Armenian, Balkan, Balto-Slavic, Celtic, Germanic, Hellenic, and Indo-Iranian; and to these various families belong modern languages such as English, Hindi, Urdu, Bengali and Russian. Other world language families include Finno-Ugric (with languages such as Hungarian, Finnish, and Estonian), Sino-Tibetan (including Chinese languages), and Afro-Asiatic (including Hebrew and Arabic), to mention just a few. Of course there is controversy as to where exactly to draw lines around major families and their sub-families, especially as scholars move back further in time. Also, there are isolated languages which seem to belong to no family, as is the case with the Basque language, spoken in the Basque region of Spain and in parts of southern France.

Linguists have long been involved in tracing languages back through time in search of common ancestors using the **comparative method**. This method involves examining cognates across languages, looking for regularities in the sound structure that point to past similarities. Of course, all languages are affected by surrounding languages, and words are assimilated from one language to another, as in English *patio* and *canyon* taken from Spanish. We could not then say that these two languages come from a common ancestor because they share these words. Rather, with the comparative method, linguists document how a language branch of a language family regularly substituted one sound for another, for example [f] for [p], as in the case of English *father* and German *fater*, yet Latin *pater*, and Greek *patir* (a regular change noted in Grimm's Law, which we revisit in Section 5.2.4.1). Basque, of course, shares a number of words with the Romance languages, because of centuries of proximity. However, the application of the comparative method shows that it is not related directly to the Indo-European languages; scholars classify it as a pre-Indo-European language, and there are several hypotheses as to what other languages, modern or ancient, it might be related to. Robert Trask argues that it is not related to any language, except possibly an ancient language called Aquitanian. His book, *The History of Basque*, contains detailed descriptions of the Basque language and culture. He draws on linguistic evidence, such as the absence of word initial [p], [t], [d] or [r], and the complete absence of [m] in the Basque language as it would have been spoken over 2000 years ago, to show that the presence of these sounds, either word initially or at all, in modern Basque is due to proximity to other known languages, and not to ancestry.

The similarities which have been discovered among the languages which have been classified via the comparative method as Indo-European have prompted linguists to reconstruct a common ancestor, known as **Proto-Indo-European (PIE)**. For example, the word for *mother* (in English) has its counterparts *māter* (Latin), *mētēr* (Greek), and *mātár* (Sanskrit), while *$*mèh_a tēr^2$* is the most agreed upon form in reconstructed PIE. Of course, we cannot know what language our homo sapiens ancestors spoke; the reconstruction is conjecture based on commonalities amongst the Indo-European languages for which we have lasting records, as well as on regularities in language change. Furthermore, the reconstruction is based on basic vocabulary of frequent use, such as kinship terms like *mother* and names of features in our environment, such as *water* and *fire*. These basic words are also the words which tend not to change throughout time.[3]

EXERCISE 5.1

Look at the following words from PIE. Try to guess their meaning.
1. *bhréh_ater
2. *dhuĝ(h_a)tēr
3. *swésōr
4. *wodr
5. *h_ékwos
6. *tréyes
7. *swékuros (note: knowledge of Spanish might help for this one!)
8. *ph_atar

Interestingly, at present, there is a Proto-Indo-European revival movement which argues for the use of a reconstructed version of PIE, a common language for all without any one group being a dominate speaker, in the European Union. While the success of this endeavor remains to be seen, official and unofficial bodies which call for and mandate language policy have always been purveyors of linguistic survival and change in one way or another.

---

2. It is common to mark reconstructed PIE words with an asterisk.
3. While different words referring for example to father certainly exist and vary over time, age, gender, and geographical location (*Pop, Pops, Pa, Papa, Dad, Dads, Daddy, old man*) the standard kinship term does not pass out of fashion, and is indeed similar to the Old English term *fœder*. Likewise, the Old English word for *water* is *wæter*; and the most commonly attested PIE word for it is *$*wodr$*.

5.1.3   Loss of world languages

At the same time that there now exists this movement to revive an ancient language, languages are dying at a rapid rate. Researchers on the world's languages estimate that there are somewhere around 7000 languages (more if the world's sign languages are included in the count), a high percentage of which will no longer be spoken by the end of this decade. According to *Ethnologue: Languages of the World* (Gordon 2005), it is likely that hundreds of currently existing languages will not be passed on to the next generation. Indeed, the *Ethnologue* lists 516 languages which are right now on the verge of extinction. For example, in Cameroon, in 1986, there was only one 70-year-old native speaker of Bikya left. Once a language dies, the culture it has represented for generations is lost as well. Thus one highly pressing task of linguists is to record these languages, especially those with no written tradition that would leave a lasting record of their existence. Documenting endangered languages allows for preservation of their speech sounds, morphology, syntax, stories, myths, songs and poems. Organizations such as SIL (http://www.sil.org/) devote a wealth of resources to this end,[4] resources which are vital in keeping alive ways of expression and meaning which are a testimony to the diversity and richness of human language, thought, culture and history. Joshua Fishman suggests a comprehensive set of steps to apply in order to reverse the loss of a language, moving from encouraging acquisition of the language (by adults in cases where the only speakers are left are the elderly), prompting the use of the spoken language in informal settings as well as in neighborhood institutions (where it could be used exclusively), and promoting literacy in the language. Once these steps have been achieved, its use in compulsory education, the workplace, local government services and mass media, and finally in higher education and the government can be encouraged.

At the same time, Fishman stresses that a top down approach, or one which begins by promoting language use at these broader institutional levels only, may not be successful in bringing the language back to life. Necessary for revival is the use of the language by people for everyday communicative purposes. Perhaps on a parallel note, when governing bodies mandate a language policy which forbids the use of a given language, as was the case of Basque, Catalan, Galician, and other languages in Spain during the Franco dictatorship era, often speakers will treasure their language, while speaking it only in small circles of families and friends. Once an oppressive policy is lifted, these languages have groups of speakers who are then especially

---

4.   Crystal (2002) provides a list of organizations dedicated to dying languages.

keen on seeing their language come back to life and can promote its use at all of Fishman's levels. Indeed, language revival in Spain after Franco's death during the past 35 years has been momentous, with national languages, as they are called, holding co-official status with Castilian-Spanish (or *castellano*) in the various autonomous regions of Spain.

Even after no native speakers of a language have been around for some time using and living the language, successful attempts at revival have taken place. For example, Kaurna, a South Australian Aboriginal language, which had been extinct – or sleeping, a metaphor preferred by many over that of death – for over 80 years, has been revived and seems to be on its way to survival. Fortunately, German missionaries in the mid-nineteenth century dedicated their time to carefully documenting the language, noting down its pronoun system, verb inflections, noun affixes, vocabulary, and so on. The Australian colonial government subsequently banned all use of the Aboriginal languages, and even forbade the missionaries from preaching in Kaurna, and it is estimated that its last native speaker died shortly before 1930. Its revival began in 1990 at a songwriters' workshop, followed by the learning of songs by both children and adults. There are now courses at all levels of education, books and websites dedicated to its promulgation. David Crystal (2002) points out that not all of the original functions and vocabulary of revived languages such as Kaurna can be restored; however, the revival of the language allows for a revival of a culture and a way of thought, and, at the same time, new vocabulary and functions will be created in the language, just as with all living languages.

> **EXERCISE 5.2**
>
> Choose one of the near extinct languages listed at http://www.ethnologue.com/nearly_extinct.asp. Find out everything you can about the language. Do you think it would be possible to revive the language? Why or why not? Describe what will be lost in addition to the language itself if it is not possible.

5.1.4 Language degeneration ... or change?

In the case of languages which are in no danger of becoming extinct, there are many speakers who fear the loss of what are currently accepted ways of speaking. Some countries have official bodies whose job it is to dictate what is and what is not acceptable in language use. For example, in Spain, for *email*, the *Real Academia Española* provides only *correo electrónico* (electronic mail), thus not giving legitimate status to the ubiquitous *mail*, as in *envíame un mail* ('send me an email'). In addition to official bodies, people around the world write irate letters to the editors of newspapers and blogs on the internet decrying lack of 'proper' language use. It seems that many are afraid of slipping standards which could lead to future chaos in communication. However, language change is as unstoppable as the tides, as even the *Real Academia* has had to acknowledge every time it publishes a new edition of its dictionary. Now included in that dictionary are words taken from English such as *internet* and *leasing*. People adapt language to suit their needs for ease of and precision in communication, as well as to identify themselves with a particular group. In this chapter, we look at the ways in which languages change and identify some reasons for the changes.

EXERCISE 5.3

List your own pet peeves as far as language use is concerned (e.g. the substitution of *less* for *fewer*) for your own language. If you have none, list those that you know other people have. Why do you think people find these uses bothersome? What effect do these changes in ways of using language have on communication?

5.2   The ways in which languages change

5.2.1   A very brief history of English

We can see some of the changes that have happened in English over the past 1500 years by looking at a short passage from the Bible in Figure 5.1,[5] which we will refer to as we make our way through a brief history of the English language, and as we comment on the ways in which languages change.

English is by origin a West Germanic language, a member of the Frisian family, other members of which are spoken today in parts of the Netherlands and Germany. Sometime after 400 AD, around the time the Roman occupation ended, German invaders brought the Anglo-Frisian dialect to the mainly Celtic-populated Britain, where it began to spread and dominate. In the following years, Germanic tribes (Angles, Saxons and Jutes) continued to force their way throughout Britain, pushing the Celts into areas of Scotland, Wales and Cornwall. The dialects spoken by

---

5.   Indeed, given that the Bible has been written in so many languages, it provides an excellent source of comparison across languages throughout time. To see (and compare) many different versions of the Bible in English: http://etext.library.cornell.edu/cgi-bin/etext/bie-idx?type=compare

Figure 5.1: The Gospel of Matthew 13: 3–4

1. he spæc to heom fele on bispellen cweðende. Soðlice ut-eode se sæwere hys sæd to *he spoke to them much on parables saying: Truly out went the sower his seed* sawenne & a þa he seow. sume hye feollen wið weig. & fugeles comen & æten þa. *to sow & then when he sowed, some they fell towards the path & fowls came & ate them.* (West Saxon I Bible *c.* 990)

2. And he spac to hem many thingis in parablis, and seide, Lo! he that sowith, summe seedis felden bisidis the weie, and briddis of the eir camen, and eeten hem. (The Wyclif Bible, 1395)

3. And hee spake many things vnto them in parables, saying, Behold, a sower went foorth to sow. And when he sowed, some seedes fell by the wayes side, and the foules came, and deuoured them vp. (King James Version 1611)

4. And he spake many things to them in parables, saying, Behold a sower went forth to sow. And while he sowed, some seeds fell by the wayside, and the birds came and devoured them. (Wesley's New Testament, 1755)

5. And he told them many things in parables, saying: 'Listen! A sower went out to sow. And as he sowed, some seeds fell on the path, and the birds came and ate them up.' (The New Oxford Annotated Bible, 1991)

the invaders formed what is known as Old English, and example of which we see in number 1, in Figure 5.1.

In 1066, the Norman conquest initiated major changes in the English language. The Anglo-Norman rule lasted for 300 years, and brought with it French vocabulary and syntax, as the language of the court and of the upper classes was French. The resulting language is what is now referred to as Middle English. We can see an example of the effect on vocabulary between Old English and Middle English by looking at the word for 'parable' in 1 and 2 in Figure 5.1: *bispell* is an Anglo-Saxon word, and *parabilis*, from the Anglo-Norman and Old French *parable* (previously from the Latin *parabola*, meaning 'comparison'), came to replace it. During this time, English was imbued with both Latin and French vocabulary, and furthermore underwent a loss in its system of inflections. Then, in the late thirteenth century, English was restored as the official language of all of the classes and of the courts. Up until this time, English was mainly a spoken language (thus the difficulty of scholars who work on Old English, as manuscripts vary widely in spelling). However, from this time on, English continued to develop in both its written and spoken varieties in its modern form (and we will come back to some other changes throughout this chapter).

Thus, the passages in Figure 5.1 attest to changes in the English language over time, for example, in the lexis, or vocabulary. The Old English word for *parable* was replaced by a Norman word. *Fugeles* became *briddis*, and then *foules* and then *birds* (note the wavering between *fowl* and *bird* as a lexical choice through the passages); *wayes side* has become *wayside*. These examples of changes in words to express a similar meaning brings us to our first section on language change, that of lexical change.

5.2.2 Lexical growth and loss

By far, the most noticeable change we see happening over and over in all human language is that of lexis. Changes include shifts of meaning for already existing words, which we will look at in the next section on semantic change. In this section, we begin with the ways in which new words enter our languages.

We have seen in Chapter 4 that new words may be added to a language by adding derivational morphemes to roots and stems. For example, nouns morph into verbs, as with *television* into *televise*, even in the case of proper nouns, so *Google* becomes *to google*. A good number of nouns which turn into verbs do not change their base form, as with *google*; other examples include *respect, shop, impact* (which some people object to) and, more recently, *prank* (as in *I was pranked*). This process of changing the word class without changing the word form is known as **conversion**. Further examples include the conversion of *pretty* as an adjective, as in *pretty girl*, to *pretty* as an adverb, as in *I'm feeling pretty awful*, as well as *bad* moving from an adjective to a noun, as in *Sorry, my bad*. In addition to additions via derivations and conversion, new words enter into language as **compounds, blends, back-formations, acronyms, clippings, eponyms,** and **loanwords**.

We use **compounding**, or the joining together of more than one free morpheme, to create new adjectives, adverbs, nouns and verbs, by combining these word classes in different ways, to come up with, for example, *bittersweet, breakfast, blackboard, scarecrow, user-friendly*, and so on. With compounds, the whole is not always equal to the sum of the parts, as we know, for example, with compounds like *skyscraper* and *deadline*. Sometimes the two words fuse into one graphic word, as with the just-mentioned examples; others use a hyphen, such as *merry-go-round, well-being*, and *on-site*; and there are others which are written as two separate words, such as *green light, small talk*, and *high school*. There are some compounds which different people write in different ways, such as *lifestyle, baby-sitter*, or *tea cup*.

EXERCISE 5.4

Say the following words to some people, asking them to write them down. Then, check a few dictionaries. Is there agreement on how they are written?

1. *healthcare*
2. *teacup*
3. *grownup*
4. *manmade*
5. *passerby*
6. *lifestyle*
7. *babysitter*
8. *onsite*
9. *trashcan*
10. *tryout*
11. *loanword*
12. *email*

This variation in the spelling of compounds attests to the changing nature of language. Many of these words enter the repertoire of expressions in a language as two separate words, and with time they become hyphenated or move to becoming spelled as one word. New compounds enter the language frequently, for example, from technological advances, such as *pen drive, flash drive, videotape,* and *whiteboard.*

Most languages use compounding to create new words, and they do so by combining different word classes in various ways. For example, languages use noun-verb combinations, in which the verb is combined with its object, such as *breakfast* and *spoilsport* in English. Other languages also combine nouns and verbs, often using variations of the verb inflection. In Spanish, for instance, the word for *corkscrew* is *sacacorchos*, from the verb *sacar* (to remove) in the third person singular indicative form, along with the plural for *cork*, or *corchos*. Another example in Spanish is *salvavidas*, from the verb *salvar* (to save) and *vidas* (lives), or lifesaver.

EXERCISE 5.5

Look at the following nouns and verbs from Spanish, and then create compound words for the English translations given.

Verbs	Nouns
1. cascar (to crack)	1. nuez ('nut')
2. parar ('to stop')	2. rayo ('bolt of lightening')
3. rascar ('to scrape')	3. cielo ('sky')
4. romper ('to break')	4. cabeza ('head')
5. parar ('to stop')	5. choque ('crash')
6. abrir ('to open')	6. lata ('can' or 'tin')
7. quitar ('to remove')	7. nieve ('snow')
8. lavar ('to wash')	8. plato ('dish')

Example

1. 'nutcracker' = cascanueces (note how the 'z' changes to a 'c' to follow Spanish spelling rules)
2. 'lightning rod' = pararrayos (note the change in spelling: in Spanish: when the trilled 'r' sound happens at the beginning of a word, such as is the case with *rayo*, it is represented by the grapheme 'r'; however, when it occurs between two vowels within a word, it is represented by the grapheme 'rr').

3. 'skyscraper' =
4. 'brainteaser' =
5. 'bumper' =
6. 'can opener' =
7. 'snow plow' =
8. 'dishwasher' =

Another way of creating new words is through **blending**, which involves taking a part of one word and joining it to a part of another word to come up with a word which blends the meaning of both, such as *smog, brunch, broast* and *motel*. The resulting words are known as *blends* or *portmanteau words*. **Back-formations** are lexemes that we might assume to have existed <u>before</u> the lexeme from which they were formed existed, which actually is not the case; so, for example, *televise* was created, or back-formed, from *television* (and not the other way around) and *resurrect* from *resurrection*. **Clipping** happens when we use parts of words for wholes; examples include *pub* for *public house*, *gas* for *gasoline*, *gym* for *gymnasium*, and, more recently, *vic* for *victim*, and *perp* for *perpetrator*. **Acronyms** are formed by taking the first letter from each word in a phrase, such as *taser* (as we saw in Chapter 4), *scuba*, from 'self-contained underwater breathing apparatus', and *pin* as in Personal Identification Number. With time, we usually forget that these words are formed from other words, hence the redundancy when we ask someone to provide a 'pin number' rather than simply a PIN. **Eponyms** are words formed from real or fictitious names, such as *Kleenex* (a brand of facial tissues, and the word often used to refer to all tissues no matter which brand), *sandwich* (from the Earl of Sandwich, who purportedly asked for his meat between two pieces of bread so that he could continue playing cards), or *rollerblade* (which was a proprietary brand name but is now used to refer to all roller skates with in-line wheels). Other recent eponyms include words such as *Bluetooth*, the capital *B* indicating a proprietary name. However, it has now morphed into a verb, so we can ask questions such as 'Can you bluetooth it?'. The same is the case for *google*, which is now a verb as well, and is further undergoing further derivations via words such as *misgoogle*.

Loanwords are words which, rather than being lent or borrowed, are absorbed into the language from other languages, such as in English *canyon, patio, fiancé,* and *anchovy* (which is thought to have been adapted originally from Basque, and then into the Romance languages of Italian, Portuguese and Spanish, before coming into English).[6]

6.   The World Loanword Database (WOLD), edited by Martin Haspelmath and Uri Tadmor, for the Max Planck Digital Library, Munich (2009).is available for searching at at http://wold.livingsources.org/.

EXERCISE 5.6

Classify the following words in terms of the process by which they entered the language. You might want to use an etymological dictionary.

1. apartheid
2. bulldoze
3. diplomat
4. fax
5. homepage
6. emoticon
7. jacuzzi
8. ketchup
9. kindergarten
10. lab
11. memo
12. newsgroup
13. radar
14. vaseline

SINGLE SLICES   **by Peter Kohlsaat**

Alec... I'm looking for intimacy.

Yeah, I know... I'm looking for outimacy.

K.hlsaat   8-27

© 1997 Los Angeles Times Syndicate

As we add new words and phrases to our languages, we also lose some along the way.[7] Rather than actually being lost, they become obsolete, as they are they are no longer useful (as perhaps the concept they refer to is no longer part of our lives) or no longer in fashion. At the same time, words which have been included in written documents are never completely lost. Thus, in reading we can come across words such as *trunk-hose*,[8] in *Tristram Shandy* p. 583), which we would probably want to look up in a dictionary:

> **trunk hose** – puffed breeches of the 16th and 17th centuries usually worn over hose
>
> breeches, knee breeches, knee pants, knickerbockers, knickers – trousers ending above the knee

Based on WordNet 3.0, Farlex clipart collection. © 2003–2008 Princeton University, Farlex Inc.

Given that we no longer wear these 'loose-fitting breeches', we do not have a use for the word, unless we are reading the novel, in which case the endnotes are necessary for a definition. (We might wonder if 250 years from the present time a mention of *tank top* in a novel written in early twenty-first-century North America will warrant a footnote.) We no longer have much use for the words *phonograph* or *gramophone*, the US and British words respectively for a wind-up record player, as our technology for listening to recorded music has changed considerably. *Walkman* is on its way to becoming archaic, if it is not so already, as we now have *mp3* players.

7. In order to help save lost words in English, visit http://www.savethewords.org/
8. Defined as 'Loose-fitting breeches of the previous century, sometimes stuffed with wool, as opposed to the tighter breeches of the eighteenth century, which could not be stuffed'. In Sterne, L. *The Life and Opinions of Tristam Shandy, Gentleman.* New, M. and New, J. (eds). Penguin Classics, p. 583.

EXERCISE 5.7

Look at the following letter written by Catherine of Aragon to Henry VIII. Pick out expressions that are unfamiliar to you and look them up in a dictionary. For each expression, suggest why it is not in common use any longer. Rewrite the letter as a modern divorced wife (obviously quite wealthy!) to her husband.

1535

My Lord and Dear Husband,

I commend me unto you. The hour of my death draweth fast on, and my case being such, the tender love I owe you forceth me, with a few words, to put you in remembrance of the health and safeguard of your soul, which you ought to prefer before all worldly matters, and before the care and tendering of your own body, for the which you have cast me into many miseries and yourself into many cares.

For my part I do pardon you all, yea, I do wish and devoutly pray God that He will also pardon you.

For the rest I commend unto you Mary, our daughter, beseeching you to be a good father unto her, as I heretofore desired. I entreat you also, on behalf of my maids, to give them marriage-portions, which is not much, they being but three. For all my other servants, I solicit a year's pay more than their due, lest they should be unprovided for.

Lastly, do I vow, that mine eyes desire you above all things.

EXERCISE 5.8

Make a list of words which are in current use but which you think might not last too long (such as *walkman*). Explain why you think the word might not last.

Many words simply fall out of fashion, not because the concept they refer to is no longer in existence or useful to us, but because people like to mark a difference with their language as much as they do with their clothing and hairstyles. While people have mocked others they find lacking in social savvy for ages, whether that person is called a *nerd* or a *square* will depend mainly on the decade, or perhaps on the age of the speaker. This lively, colloquial use of language is referred to as **slang**, which is not usually acceptable in more formal registers of language use. At the same time, what is slang in one era may not last for very long; for example, in nineteenth-century novels, we can find the word *nevy* to refer to someone's nephew, yet that colloquial form is not part of our language now. On the other hand, today's slang could become acceptable with time. To some people, the use of 'kids' to refer to 'children' is reprehensible, and a few generations grew up hearing the reprimand: *kids are baby goats*. However, nowadays more and more people refer to 'their kids', and *kids* has indeed become acceptable in many registers (witness the number of book titles about children using the word *kid*). The *Oxford English Dictionary* lists the word *absolutely* in its use as a substitution for the word *yes* as colloquial, yet it is acceptable today in a wide variety of situations, including more formal interviews and debates.

EXERCISE 5.9

Make a list of words used by your generation the meanings of which were expressed by different words in previous generations, e.g. *he's handsome> he's hot/good-looking; they're courting> they're dating/ going out; dungarees> jeans*. How are the senses of these synonyms across time different?

EXERCISE 5.10

Make a list of slang words used by your generation. How do older generations express the same meanings? Which, if any, of the words on your list might become more acceptable and widespread in its usage with time?

This discussion of changes in words we use to express similar meanings leads directly into differences in language use across generations, a topic which we take up again in the next chapter on language variation. It also leads into the fact that meanings of words change over time; semantic change is thus a further way for new meanings to be taken up through the words we use.

5.2.3   Semantic change

In addition to adding new lexical items to our languages and losing others, we also change existing words and phrases through meaning shifts. The example we just saw in the previous section, *square*, is an example of this type of change. The *Oxford English Dictionary* explains that 'square' meaning 'someone who is not socially "with it"' originated in the United States within the jazz movement in the 1950s. Before that, when referring to people, it meant someone who was morally upright. So, in essence, it took on a rather negative connotation; perhaps we can think that someone who is morally upright in yesterday's world is old-fashioned and not 'with it' in a more contemporary world. Indeed, words and expressions slip from positive to negative connotations, and sometimes back again. Words also take on more meanings or become more precise in what they refer to. Linguists involved in the study of semantic change have devised a number of classification systems to describe the type of change, in terms of cause, consequence and nature of the change. Consequences of semantic change include **specialization, generalization, pejoration** and **amelioration**.

Specialization results in a new meaning of a word which is subordinate to the older meaning. Specialization, also called restriction, limitation, or narrowing, occurs when a word becomes, as the terms suggest, more specialized, limited, restricted or narrow in the meanings it stands for. For example, the word *meat* used to refer to *food* in general, and then became restricted to the flesh of an animal. The word *skyline* has become more limited in that it used to refer to any horizon, and it now conjures up perhaps mainly urban profiles. *Deer*, according to the *Oxford English Dictionary*, once meant *beast*, or any four-legged animal (as opposed to birds and fish) and now refers solely to a ruminant quadruped of the Cervidæ family. *Fowl*, or *fugel*, as we see in Figure 5.1, used to mean *bird* in general, and now is restricted to specific types of birds, such as game birds, poultry and water birds.

Generalization occurs when the meaning of a word extends beyond an older meaning so that it becomes superordinate to the older term. It is also called extension, expansion or broadening. *Holiday* is a good example of this phenomenon, as it initially meant a day of religious celebration (a compound from *holy day*), and then expanded to mean any day in which people did not have to work (and of course in the past the only days in which people did not have to work were religious festivals). In Spanish, the word *caballero* initially referred to someone who rode a horse and then extended to mean any gentleman. *Navigate* used to be limited to finding one's way about the seas, and now its meaning has generalized to include finding one's way about skies, the streets, the World Wide Web, etc. Another sea term that has expanded its field of application is *surf*, as we can now surf the Internet. Generalization is called by some **semantic bleaching**, especially in instances where the word has been bleached of all specific meaning. This is the case with words such as *thing*, which began its semantic life in Old English, from Old Frisian, with reference to 'a meeting, or the matter or business considered by it', according to the *Oxford English Dictionary*, and now refers to any item in general.

The example of *square* in the previous section taking on negative evaluative meaning is an example of semantic **pejoration**. Other examples of words that have undergone pejoration include *awful* (which used to mean 'awe-full', something inspiring awe), *silly* (which once meant happy or prosperous) and *hussy*, which comes from *housewife*. This last example leads to a rankling observation: words referring to women seem to undergo greater pejoration than those which refer to men. Examples include *wench*, which went from referring to a girl, to a girl of rustic background, to a woman of bad reputation. *Spinster* is seen as pejorative in referring to a single woman as it conjures up images of a woman who is unattractive. Not so with the male counterpart *bachelor*, whose much more positive connotation led to the coining of *bachelorette*. Other examples include *wizard/witch, master/mistress,* and *sir/madam.*

Amelioration is the opposite, as it refers to instances in which words take on a more positive evaluation. Many young people today use *wicked* to mean, not something evil, but rather something good. The word *nice* once meant 'stupid' or 'foolish' (from the Latin *nescius,* or 'ignorant'), a meaning which is now obsolete for *nice* in English. In certain contexts, it seems that *nice* may be on the verge of going in a negative direction and becoming pejorative, as phrases such as *He is such a nice guy* suggests that he is not outstanding in any way, as in addition to amelioration, the meaning of *nice* has generalized so extensively, it has become so semantically bleached that it no longer seems a compliment in certain situations.

We can also trace semantic change across related languages via false friends, or words which seem to be cognates, but which are not. Once, in Italy, I was quite surprised to see the word *morbidissimo* on the bottle of shower gel, and thought twice before using it. In English, we connect the adjective *morbid* with something that is deadly or gruesome. The context of the shower gel bottle, however, suggested a much more positive connotation, and, indeed, I then discovered that *morbido* in Italian means *soft*. At some point, the Latin word *morbus* for *disease* (*morbidus* meant *diseased)* ameliorated into a positive adjective in Italian, with *morboso* taking up the work of the more deadly meaning.

Thus, as a consequence of language change, words generalize, specialize, pejorate and ameliorate. Two of the vehicles by which words and expressions change are **metaphor** and **metonymy**. **Metaphor** refers to an extension of the meaning of a word to concepts which have similar properties in some way. For example, the word *crane*, a large bird with long legs, came to be used to refer to machinery with long extensions, such as that used for buildings. *Mouse*, a rodent, is the word used for the device used to work with computers. We can sometimes see similar metaphorical extensions at work across languages. For example, in English, the word *grasp*, in its physical sense, used to refer to holding on to something or taking hold of something, also came to include the cognitive meaning of *to understand*. In Spanish, the verbs *pillar* (to catch) and *captar* (to capture) are used in the same way to refer to comprehension. Eve Sweetser (1991) provides further examples across languages of this same conceptual metaphorical transfer. *Head* in English refers to more than just the body part which contains our brain. We also use it to refer to people who are in roles of responsibility and authority, such as *head of the family* (in Spanish, also *cabeza de familia*). Conceptual metaphor, a theory put forth extensively by George Lakoff and Mark Johnson in the book *Metaphors We Live By*, suggests that there is a connection between certain metaphorical transfers and human neurological mappings, given the similarity across languages in these transfers. This work is taken up further in the field of cognitive linguistics (see Chapter 8, *Cognitive Linguistics*, by Dirk Geeraerts).

We can also see examples of word use which draw on metaphor for shifting their meanings in which the new meaning did not take hold. For example, the word *refrigerator* according to the *Oxford English Dictionary*, entered the language sometime during the early sixteenth century with the meaning 'that which refrigerates or cools'. In nineteenth-century novels, *refrigerator* was used to refer to people who are cool, as in unflappable, or even cold. We can see this meaning in Charles Dickens' *Bleak House* 'He moves among the company, a magnificent <u>refrigerator</u>', and in Mary Elizabeth Braddon's *Lady Audley's Secret* 'he's a dear, good-hearted, stupid creature, and twenty times better than that peripatetic, patent <u>refrigerator</u>, Mr Robert Audley'.

Change based on **metonymy** occurs when a word takes on a meaning close to its original meaning in space or time. This includes part-whole relationships, as has happened with the word *bar*, which is associated with the legal profession (via the barrier that existed in court around the judge's seat), and which is also associated with a place in which one can have an alcoholic drink (from the wooden counter in public houses and inns). Further examples include *the crown* to refer to the monarchy, *hand* to refer to *help* (as in 'give me a hand with this'), and *brass* to refer to the military.

Another way in which word meaning shifts is via **taboo** and **euphemism**. Taboo words are those which are deemed unacceptable in certain contexts; the list of taboo words, also known as swear words, shifts over time. In English, words referring to religious concepts were taboo, such as *zounds* (for 'by God's wounds'). Now the most often used taboo words are words which refer to bodily functions; that is, taboo in some social contexts, as in others, they are quite ubiquitous and accepted. Often we look for a neutral term to express a stigmatized concept, a concept whose mention is taboo or socially unacceptable for whatever reason (for example, political correctness platform often suggests which words and phrases are taboo). An example is the infamous *collateral damage* to refer to unintended victims in armed combat. Another example *to drink*, as in 'he had too much to drink last night', which everyone knows refers to alcohol; in this sense, this sense of the word *drink* has undergone a specialization. Rather than saying someone is unemployed, the more accepted phrase is now *between jobs*. Of course, with time, the euphemism can come to be seen as negative as the original term it sought to replace, thus suffering pejoration, as is clearly the case with *collateral damage*.

EXERCISE 5.11

Look at the following words and phrases. Identify an older meaning and a newer meaning. Explain the ways in which the meaning has changed. You might want to use an etymological dictionary.

1. cool
2. liberal
3. cookie
4. memory
5. partner
6. to share
7. The head has cold feet.
8. Washington phoned the chair.

Add 3 or 4 words and phrases of your own to the list.

5.2.4 Sound change

5.2.4.1 Individual sounds

Just as languages change lexically, they also change phonologically. Indeed, a major change in the English language, which occurred between 1200 and 1600, with special alacrity in the first half of the fifteenth century, and which is one of the markers of difference between Middle and Modern English, is known as the **Great Vowel Shift.**[9] Before the shift, the major vowels were

---

9.   For more in-depth information, including recordings of the changes, see http://facweb. furman.edu/~mmenzer/gvs/

pronounced as they are now in modern languages such as Spanish and Italian [aː] [eː] [iː] [oː] [uː]. These long vowel sounds (and other vowels as well, such as [ɛ] and [ɔ]) shifted upwards in terms of the height of the tongue during their articulation. Figure 5.2 shows the original vowel sound and its modern counterpart after the shift.

Figure 5.2: Vowel sounds before and after the GVS

Middle English sound	Modern English sound	e.g.	Middle English pronunciation	Modern English pronunciation
[aː]	[eɪ]	name	[namə]	[neɪm]
[ɛ]	[iː]	beak	[bɛk]	[biːk]
[eː]	[iː]	geese	[geːs]	[giːs]
[iː]	[aj]	mice	[miːs]	[majs]
[ɔ]	[ou]	stone	[stɔnə]	[stoun]
[oː]	[uː]	goose	[goːs]	[guːs]
[uː]	[aw]	mouse	[muːs]	[maws]

While the chart shows the initial and final stages of the shift, it was a shift in that the sounds moved up slowly over the centuries. What happens during the time of these shifts is that there are variations both within and across individuals and groups in terms of their use of the feature undergoing change, until the changed form becomes the prevalent one, and the older form falls out of use. Many writings on the history of the English language suggest that first the high vowels [iː] and [uː] shifted slowly into the dipthongs [aj] and [aw]. This left space available for other vowel sounds to shift as well, and thus [eː] took up the space left by [iː], as did [ɛ], although this sound first changed into [eː] along the way; [oː] moved into the space left by [uː]. Those shifts then left space for further shifts, and thus over time a major change in pronunciation of vowel sounds occurred in the English language. Our language still shows traces of the original pronunciation in the spelling of words. For example, words like *break* and *heaven* kept the original sound-grapheme correspondence of *ea* → [ɛ], while in other words, such as *sea* and *mead*, the pronunciation shifted from [ɛ] to [iː].

According to some researchers, currently in North America a similar phenomenon is occurring in what is known as the **Northern Cities Vowel Shift**. William Labov (in Siegel 2006) notes that the shift started to be noticed in the 1950s in cities such as Chicago, Detroit, Cleveland, Buffalo, and Rochester. As Labov notes in an article in *The New Yorker*, 'The "eah" sound, which you hear in "happened" – heahppened – is a young, very invasive sound that is rapidly changing a number of other sounds around it' (Seabrook 2005). Indeed, the first change documented in this shift is the raising, tensing and lengthening of [æ] in words like *cat* towards a dipthong which varies regionally in its pronunciation, but can be represented as [eə] or [eæ], thus *cat* becomes [keət] or [keæt]. Then, this shift left a space for the low back vowel [ɑ], as in *cot* or *hop* to move more toward the front of the mouth towards [a] (as in *spa* as it is pronounced by speakers from New England, Australia and New Zealand) or even [æ]. Then the mid-back vowel [ɔ], as pronounced in *caught* by speakers who have not shifted their vowel pronunciation, moved down towards [ɑ]; this means that for speakers who have shifted, *caught* may sound like *cot* to speakers who have not shifted. Finally, [ʌ], as in *but*, has shifted back towards [ɔ], making that word sound similar to the *caught* of the speakers who have not shifted.

EXERCISE 5.12

Go to the following website to hear the Northern Cities Vowel Shift: http://www.cambridge.org/resources/0521612357/3263_Ch.%209%20 Exercise%203-%20NorhernCitiesShift.ppt. How does the pronunciation compare to your own pronunciation of the vowel sounds?

It is interesting to compare the versatility of English vowel sounds with vowels in other languages, such as Spanish. The sound-spelling correspondence in languages such as Italian and Spanish for the five vowel sounds [a:] [e:] [i:] [o:] [u:] has remained constant for centuries; indeed, for speakers of these languages, there is a direct correspondence between the phonetic symbol and the graphic symbol for the sound in their alphabet. This observation in no way suggests that Spanish speech sounds have not changed over time; however, the change occurs far more frequently with the ways in which consonants are pronounced (or not). For example, a major difference amongst dialects of Spanish is the pronunciation of the graphic symbols *c* and *z*. In what is known as *castellano* (Castilian Spanish), *c* in front of [e] and [i], and *z* in front of [e], [i] and [a] are pronounced as [θ] (the first sound in *think*). Thus, *zapato* ('shoe') is pronounced [θapato], and *cerveza* ('beer') is pronounced [θerβeθa]. However, in other parts of the Spanish speaking world, the sibilants are pronounced differently (a point which we will return to in Chapter 6 on language variation), demonstrating how phonological change evolves differently across dialects and languages.

Scholars working on developing Proto-Indo-European during the eighteenth and nineteenth centuries stumbled upon another clear example of consonant change over time. We can see this by looking at regular correspondences in cognates in Indo-European Languages. Figure 5.3 illustrates some of the changes by comparing Latin, Sanskrit with German, Old English and modern English.

Figure 5.3: Some Indo-European cognates

Sanskrit	Latin	German	Old English	English
podos	pedis	Fuss	fot	foot
piska	piscis	Fisch	fisc	fish
bhrātā	frater	Bruder	broþor	brother
no cognate	geli	kalt	ceald	cold
śun	canis	Hund	hund	hound
trata	tertius	thritto	þridda	third
dasan	decem	zehn	tien	ten

Jacob Grimm gathered together the regularities in the differences in cognates across languages and summarized them in what is now known as Grimm's law. Grimm's law shows that the changes occurred as part of a chain shift, like the vowel shifts we reviewed earlier. It specifies that:

1. voiceless stops, such as ([p], [t], [k]) became voiceless fricatives ([f], [θ], [h])
2. voiced stops ([b], [d], [g]) became voiceless stops ([p] [t], [k])
3. voiced aspirated stops ([bʰ], [dʰ], [gʰ] became voiced fricatives and then, in most of the Germanic languages, they became voiced stops.

Thus, sometime during the first millennium BC, the Germanic branch of Proto-Indo-European underwent a series of sound changes, changes whose effects we see in today's modern English.

5.2.4.2 Sound change at word level

The ways in which we pronounce and spell words changes over time in a variety of ways, some of which are explained by the articulatory processes we saw in Chapter 2. The most common process which results in change is that of **assimilation**, in which a sound becomes more like a surrounding sound to make it easier to articulate. Thus we find the examples of sound change in words in different languages, such as in Spanish, *senda* (meaning 'path') changed from the earlier form *semda*. **Epenthesis** occurs when a sound is added; an example of consonant epenthesis can be seen in the origins of the word *thunder*, which in Old English was *þoner* and sometime during middle English became *þonder*. **Deletion**, or elision occurred with the *n* in *an* to become the article *a* in front of words beginning with consonants. **Dissimilation** refers to the process by which one sound becomes less like another in the environment For example, the word *pilgrim* derives ultimately from the Latin *peregrines*, via the Anglo-Norman *pilegrin*; the [l] sound came about through the process of dissimilation: the first [r] in the word moved to [l] to become less like the later [r]. Another example of the [l] dissimilation is the word *marble*, from the Anglo-Norman *marbre* (direct from Old French).

We know from numbers 2 and 4 (Figure 5.1) that sometime between the years 1395 and 1755 the word for *bird* underwent **metathesis**, by which a sequence of sounds changes in order, as the word was originally *brid*. Indeed, the transposition of a vowel sound and *r* is by far the most frequent metathetic change in English; another example is *horse*, which was *hros*. However, there are other kinds of metathetic changes, such as *wasp* from *wæps* and *hasp* from *hæpse*.

EXERCISE 5.13

Look at the following examples of language change. Identify the process undergone in each example.
1. Old English *spinel* → modern English → *spindle*
2. Latin *schola* → Spanish → *escuela*
3. Latin *octo* → Italian → *otto*
4. Proto-Slavic *berza* → Serbo-Croation *breza* ('birch')
5. Latin *arborem* → Spanish *arbol*
6. Old English *Ænglaland* → modern English *England*

5.2.5 Morphological change

From the West Saxon passage included in Figure 5.4, we see with the word cweðende ('saying') that the present participle was formed by adding –*ende*. However, Old English was much more complex in its verb morphology than that simple correspondence would suggest. OE verbs had different declensions depending on the type of verb class they fell into. For example, *cweðan* (the infinitive form) was considered a **strong verb**; strong verbs contrast with **weak verbs** in that the latter add endings for purposes of inflection for gender, number, etc. (as in English *talk – talked*), while strong verbs inflect via changes in the sounds within the word (as in English *think – thought*). The forms of *cweðan* in the present indicative are shown in Figure 5.4.

Figure 5.4: *cweðan* present indicative

cweðe	1st person singular
cwyst	2nd person singular
cweð	3rd person singular
cwæðað	1st/2nd/3rd person plural

Weak verbs simply added the endings shown in Figure 5.5 onto the stem of the verb, such as for the present indicative.

Figure 5.5: Weak verb endings present indicative

-e	1st person singular
-est	2nd person singular
-eþ	3rd person singular
-aþ	1st/2nd/3rd person plural

So, for example, the verb *tellan* (to tell) in the present indicative takes the forms shown in Figure 5.6.

Figure 5.6: *Tellan* present indicative

telle	1st person singular ('I tell')
tellest	2nd person singular ('you tell")
telleþ	3rd person singular ('he/she/it tells')
telleþ	1st/2nd/3rd person plural ('we/you/they tell')

The above only tells a very small part of the complete verb inflection story in Old English, as verbs took different endings depending on mood (indicative, subjunctive and imperative) and tense, in addition to person. Modern English is much simpler, having, for example, only the –s on the third person singular present tense form, and no differences for mood (so 'you talk' 'do you talk?' and 'Talk!' all use the same form). It is interesting to note also that most of our irregular verbs (e.g. *teach/taught, write/wrote*) have developed from Old English strong verbs. Verbs which have entered the language since that time have a strong tendency to take on the weak form version of simply adding endings, rather than the strong form version of changing the sounds within. Even some verbs which were strong have become weak, a process known as **analogical leveling**; for example, the Old English verb *helpan* was a strong verb (e.g. its third person singular past tense form was *healp*). Modern English *help* has become a weak verb, and we now form the past tense form by adding –*ed*. Interestingly, the opposite phenomenon, known as **analogical extension** has also occurred, with verbs such as *dig*, which moved from the weak verb category to the strong. At the same time, the most frequent verbs in English are irregular in their past tense forms (*be, go, do, become, see,* etc.), and linguists suggest that their frequency may help them retain their irregularity in form.

EXERCISE 5.14

Look again at the Old English bible passage from Figure 5.1, reproduced here for the sake of convenience. Underline the verbs, and comment on any regularities and differences you see in the forms.

he spæc to heom fele on bispellen cweðende. Soðlice ut-eode se sæwere hys sæd to sawenne & a þa he seow. sume hye feollen wið weig. & fugeles comen & æten þa.

Furthermore, Old English had a complex case system for its nouns and adjectives, which would take different forms depending on their function in the clause. So, for example, in Figure 5.1, text 1, *bispellen*[10] is in the plural dative case, as it is functioning as the object of a preposition. The singular dative is *bispelle*, the nominative and accusative cases in both singular and plural is *bispell,* while the genitive case also distinguishes between singular and plural, *bispelles* and *bispella* respectively. In modern English, we use the same form whether the noun is functioning as a subject, object, possessive, etc., and we only distinguish between singular and plural forms, so we have only two different forms of the noun to deal with. This loss of the case system had a major effect on the syntax of English, as we will see in the next section.

5.2.6   Syntactic change

Syntactic change involves a modification of the way morphemes are strung together in significant ways in the clause, to indicate information such as relationships between participants and mood choices (interrogative, indicative, subjunctive, and imperative). In Old English, it has been said that the syntactic order of words in the clause was more variable than in Modern English. However, scholars have shown that it was not completely free (as might be suggested by the proliferation of nominal case endings). The loss of the case endings is noted as coming about at the same time as word order was becoming more fixed. It does seem that Old English used

---

10. In many texts, spelled *bispellum.*

a double system, both word order and case endings, to convey syntactic meaning, and thus the case system was somewhat redundant, which may explain its loss. At the same time, there were differences in OE word order when compared with Modern English, as for example:

> *ut-eode se sæwere hys sæd to sawenne*
> out-went the sower his seed to sow

where in Modern English, we would be more likely to say:

> *the sower went out to sow his seed*

as Old English often favored a word order (among others) which placed the infinitive at the end of the clause.

Another major change which has occurred over time in English is the addition of the auxiliary *do* for interrogative and negative declarative forms of the clause. In previous times, interrogative mood was realized by inversion of the subject and the verb, and negation by addition of a particle *no* or *not*. Shakespeare shows that the various ways of realizing these moods co-existed during the time of Middle English. The following lines are all uttered by the Duke of Gloucester, in Richard III:

> 1a. *Brother, good day; what means this armed guard/That waits upon your grace?*
> 1b. *Why dost thou spit at me?*
> 2a. *Say that I slew them not.*
> 2b. *I did not kill your husband.*

In the first set, we see the Wh-interrogative both without and with the auxiliary *do* (*what means* ... and *why dost thou* ...); in the second set, we see the negative also both without and with the auxiliary (*I slew them not* and *I did not kill*), all occurring within the same text.

With time, except for with modal auxiliaries and the verb *to be*, *do* became a necessary auxiliary to form questions and negations.

EXERCISE 5.15

Compare the two versions (Old English and modern) of The Lord's Prayer. Make lists of translations of words. Note that the pronunciation of ð and þ is like 'th' in modern English. Comment on any regularities and differences in forms. List any questions that your analysis suggests. Remember that this is not a test of how well you know Old English, but rather of your knowledge of morphosyntax and language change.

Fæder ure þu þe eart on heofonum	Our Father in heaven,
si þin nama gehalgod	Hallowed be your name
to becume þin rice	Your kingdom come
gewurþe þin willa	Your will be done
on eorðan swa swa on heofonum	On earth as it is in heaven.
urne gedæghwamlican hlaf syle us to dæg	Give us this day our daily bread
and forgyf us ure gyltas	And forgive us our trespasses
swa swa we forgyfað urum gyltendum	As we forgive those who trespass against us
and ne gelæd þu us on costnunge	Lead us not into temptation,
ac alys us of yfele soþlice.	And deliver us from evil, Amen.

5.2.7   Changes in text and discourse

EXERCISE 5.16

Can you recognize the text type?
> Pur faire holsom drynk of ale, Recipe sauge, auence, rose maryn, tyme, chopped right smal, and put þis and a newe leyd hennes ey in a bage and hange it in þe barell. Item, clowys, maces, and spikenard grounden and put in a bagge and hangen in þe barell. And nota þat þe ey of þe henne shal kepe þe ale fro sourynge. Par Sibill Boys. (Retrieved February 15, 2010 from http://ling.lll.hawaii.edu/faculty/stampe/Oral-Lit/English/paston-letters.html)

Perhaps you could recognize the text in Exercise 5.15 as a recipe. It contains certain generic features of recipes, such as lexical items related to food as the ingredients, and the clauses are mainly in imperative mood. Figure 5.7 contains a recipe from a website which provides translations of medieval recipes, along with a modern version:

Figure 5.7: Recipe

Crispels
PERIOD: England, 14th century | SOURCE: Forme of Cury | CLASS: Authentic
DESCRIPTION: Round pastries basted in honey

ORIGINAL RECEIPT:
171. Crispels. Take and make a foile of gode past as thynne as paper; kerue it out wyt a saucer & frye it in oile; oþer in grece; and þe remnaunt, take hony clarified and flamme þerwith. Alye hem vp and serue hem forth.
- Hieatt, Constance B. and Sharon Butler. Curye on Inglish: English Culinary Manuscripts of the Fourteenth-Century (Including the Forme of Cury). New York: for The Early English Text Society by the Oxford University Press, 1985.

GODE COOKERY TRANSLATION:
Crispels. Take and make a sheet of good pastry as thin as paper; carve it out with a saucer & fry it in oil; or in grease; and to finish them, take clarified honey and baste there-with. Do them up and serve them forth.

INGREDIENTS:
Pastry dough
Olive oil
Honey

DIRECTIONS:
Roll out the pastry as thin as possible; cut into circles. Fry the pastry in a little olive oil until lightly brown & crisp. Drain well. Place the honey in a saucepan and slowly bring to a boil, skimming off any scum that rises. Brush the pastries with the hot honey and serve forth!

Retrieved February 15, 2010 from http://www.godecookery.com/mtrans/mtrans38.htm

It is interesting to note the change from the word *receipt*, which was the widely used word to refer to a procedural cooking text up until fairly recently, a further example of lexical change. At the same time, the genre of recipes has remained fairly stable in its lexical and mood choices; however, modern version of recipes in English usually begin with a list of separate ingredients, as the *Gode Cookery* exemplifies.

The shape that texts take have changed over time, due to advances in technology and the desire to make a text more appealing to contemporary audiences. Nineteenth-century newspapers contained more tightly-packed articles, with longer paragraphs, while twenty-first-century print newspapers contain shorter paragraphs and far more images. This is also the case for textbooks. All types of correspondence have experienced change in shape over time, for example love letters, job applications, and notes passed between students in school. The functions of these genres remain fairly stable; what changes over time are features such as layout, organization, paragraph length, and lexis. Witness the increase in use of abbreviations to fit the small screen of mobile phones, as well as the limited budget of users who wish to keep the number of keystrokes to a minimum. Emails to some should resemble written letters, and thus contain headings ('Dear John') and a signature, while to others they should incorporate all of the advantages of rapid correspondence, including no heading, no capital letters, minimum punctuation, and no signature, as the email address often gives that information away.

It is more difficult to study the way conversation changes over time, as tape recorders are a fairly recent invention, and even with recording technology, it is not easy to capture naturally occurring conversation. Still, we do recognize changes in, for example, formality across age, class, and occupation, as exemplified by the current massive reduction of the formal *usted* in Spanish in the urban centers of Spain, in favor of the more familiar *tú* in direct address. Note that in English, we gave up the more familiar singular second person form *thou*[11] for the more formal *you*, which was at one time actually the plural objective form. Given that this meant using the same form for both second person singular and plural, different regional varieties of English had coined their own forms, such as *youse, y'all,* and *you guys,* for informal conversation. Conversational discourse markers also change over time; for example, *like* is now ubiquitous in conversation in English across the globe, while *innit,* as a general tag question used to indicate that the speaker knows that the listener also knows, thus creating solidarity, is now becoming more and more frequent in British English.

EXERCISE 5.17

Think of a genre or text type which you write differently from a previous generation. What are the features that are similar? What has changed? If you can, get older and newer samples to exemplify the changes.

EXERCISE 5.18

Find an example of a page from a newspaper or a textbook from the nineteenth century (check on the Internet). Compare samples with modern versions. What features are similar? What has changed?

---

11. Note that the plural form for second person was *ye*; the other forms of *thou* included *thee* in the objective form, *thy/thine* in the possessive.

5.3   Why languages change

There is no one clear reason why languages change as extensively as they do; there are several explanations which cover various aspects of change, in the case of sound change we have seen that ease of articulation, mentioned in Section 5.2.4.2, has historically been a motivator. With respect to sound change, it is important to mention the impact that the written language has had on language change. If we look once again at the gospel passage in Figure 5.1, we might notice that we can understand fairly easily something written in the early fifteenth century. However, a text written in Old English of the twelfth century is impenetrable without some close study of the language. The printing press has allowed the written language to become fairly stable in terms of alphabets and spelling. However, we know from our own experience of dialects around us that the spoken language continues to change, and, of course, we also experience lexical change, especially additions to the lexicon of our languages.

Indeed, a major reason why languages change is because the needs of the users change. A clear example of this behavior is in any technical field, where new terms are coined or existing terms taken on and given a more specific meaning, such as *Theme* in functional linguistics (see Chapter 3), *double jeopardy* in law, and *population* in experimental research. Our needs of expression expand as new inventions and ways of being and doing come into the culture, and they contract where certain practices no longer are carried out the way they were. As our world expands, we come into contact with items that we did not previously meet. In many places in the world now, we can buy produce from far-flung places, thus making words such as *kiwi, guava, mango,* and *jalapeño,* entries in dictionaries around the world. During the time of the early settlers in American, new words were added at a rapid rate, words often borrowed from Native American languages, as the settlers did not arrive with words for previously unknown phenomena, such as *raccoon, tomahawk,* or *woodchuck* (words obviously adapted to English phonology and spelling). Indeed, one major site for change in language is when we have close contact with other languages and dialects (the study of which is called *contact linguistics*). Global media, much of which is in English (with international news programs, such as CNN and BBC, along with vast number of on-line newspapers, website and bloggers on the Internet) provides a major means of contact which extends beyond traditional dialect and language boundaries.

Also, over time social practices change, and we often want new words and expressions to reflect that change, to mark that it is something different from before. For example, the words *courtship* and *dating* refer to similar kinds of activity, yet the first word sounds old-fashioned. *Courtship* conjures up images of a man seeking the attention of a woman, by (usually publicly) taking her out, giving her tokens of affection (such as flowers and candy), and ultimately asking (probably her father) for her hand in marriage. *Dating* (which came into the American language with this meaning sometime in the early twentieth century) brings with it a different social-cultural practice, usually with greater intimacy and privacy for a couple, who do not necessarily have in mind marriage as a final goal. Younger generations often come up with new words in order to reflect that the concept they are referring to is different from that of past generations. Indeed, many wish to hold on to a word like *courtship* because they long for a past world which they view as nobler and simpler, in the hope, perhaps, that applying the word will change the social practice. Sometimes changes in social practices call for new words to express those practices. Witness, for example, the difficulty of finding a word to refer to people who are in a longer term intimate relationship but who are not married. *Partner? Significant other?*

Indeed, new words related to new social practices continue to be added to the language at a fairly good clip. There are websites which provide new words being added daily; for example, for English, there is http://www.wordspy.com, which includes recent entries such as *wedsite* (a web page where people post information about their wedding) and *prebituary* (an obituary drafted prior to a person's death) at the time of writing this textbook. Also at the time of writing, during the economic crisis of the last part of the first decade of the twenty-first century, the word *staycation* was heard, as in 'this summer, whether you are going on a vacation or a staycation …', given the shortage of money for what can be considered unnecessary expenditures, hence the need to stay home on vacation time (and, one hopes, a **nonce** word, one that is coined for a particular need or purpose, and one that will not need to stay around in the language). These changes in social practices call for new means of expressions.

Furthermore, individuals experience language change throughout their lives, especially if they are highly mobile, but also if they communicate with a wide variety of individuals. Often, young people use language differently than their parents, in the same way that they dress differently and listen to different music, in order to create an identity which sets them apart from their parents' generation. Here we are entering the realm of language variation, the topic of Chapter 6.

5.4   Chapter outcomes

After having read this chapter carefully, discussed with others the content, and carried out the exercises, you should assess your ability to:

- ✓ Explain the comparative method and its role in helping linguists reconstruct past languages.
- ✓ Discuss loss of languages and suggest what is needed in order to avoid it.
- ✓ Explain the different types of lexical growth, and give examples of each (derivations, conversions, compounds, back-formations, acronyms, clippings, eponyms and loanwords).
- ✓ Explain the different types of semantic change and give examples of each (specialization, generalization, pejoration and amelioration).
- ✓ Explain how metaphor and metonymy are an important vehicle for semantic change.
- ✓ Give examples of the ways in which the sounds of languages have changed.
- ✓ Explain the processes of sound change (assimilation, epenthesis, deletion, dissimilation, metathesis).
- ✓ Give examples of morphological and syntactic changes.
- ✓ Give examples of the ways in which texts and genres have changed.
- ✓ Provide reasons for language growth, loss and change.

5.5   References and further reading

Also see Chapter 8, *Historical Linguistics* by Michael Cummings

Bickerton, Derek (1992) *Language and Species*. Chicago, IL: University of Chicago Press.

Burling, Robbins (2005) *The Talking Ape*. Oxford: Oxford University Press.

Carstairs-McCarthy, Andrew (1999) *The Origins of Complex Language*. Oxford: Oxford University Press.

Christiansen, Morten H. and Kirby, Simon (2003) Language evolution: consensus and controversies. *TRENDS in Cognitive Sciences* 7(7): 300–307. Retrieved on February 15, 2010 from http://www3.isrl.illinois.edu/~junwang4/langev/localcopy/pdf/christiansen03trends.pdf

Crystal, David (2002) *Language Death*. Cambridge: Cambridge University Press.

Fishman, Joshua A. (1991) *Reversing Language Shift: Theory and Practice of Assistance to Threatened Languages*. Clevedon: Multilingual Matters.

Fishman, Joshua A. (ed.) (2001) *Can Threatened Languages Be Saved? Reversing Language Shift, Revisited: A 21st Century Perspective*. Clevedon: Multilingual Matters.

Geeraerts, Dirk (1997) *Diachronic Prototype Semantics: A Contribution to Historical Lexicology*. Oxford: Oxford University Press.

Givón, Talmy and Malle, Bertram (2002) *The Evolution of Language out of Pre-Language.*

Gordon, Raymond G., Jr. (ed.), (2005) *Ethnologue: Languages of the World, Fifteenth edition.* Dallas, Tex.: SIL International. Retrieved February, 15 2010 from http://www.ethnologue.com/

Labov, William, Ash, Sharon and Boberb, Charles (2006) *The Atlas of North American English: Phonetics, Phonology, and Sound Change: a Multimedia Reference Tool.* Berlin and New York: Walter de Gruyter.

Laks, Bernard (2008) *Origin and Evolution of Language: Approaches, Models, Paradigms.* London: Equinox Publishing.

Mallory, J.P. and Adams, Douglas Q. (2006). *The Oxford Introduction to Proto-Indo-European and the Proto-Indo-European World.* Oxford: Oxford University Press.

Mazeroff, Geoffrey Porter, Hayden, and Menzer, Melinda J. (2000) *The Great Vowel Shift.* Retrieved February, 15, 2010 from http://facweb.furman.edu/~mmenzer/gvs/.

Mitchell, Bruce (1965) *A Guide to Old English.* Oxford: Blackwell.

Mithen, Steven (2005) *The Singing Neanderthals: The Origins of Music, Language, Mind and Body.* London: Weidenfeld & Nicholson.

Seabrook, John (2005, November 14) *Talking the Tawk. The New Yorker.* Retrieved February 15, 2010 from http://www.newyorker.com/archive/2005/11/14/051114ta_talk_seabrook

Siegel, Robert (2006, February 16) American accent undergoing Great Vowel Shift (interview with William Labov). Retrieved February 15, 2010 from http://www.npr.org/templates/story/story.php?storyId=5220090

Sweetser, Eve (1991) *From Etymology to Pragmatics: Metaphorical and Cultural Aspects of Semantic Structure.* Cambridge: Cambridge University Press.

Trask, Robert Lawrence (1997) *The History of Basque.* London and New York: Routledge.

For more information on Indo-European languages, visit: The University of Texas/Austin website: http://www.utexas.edu/cola/centers/lrc/

5.6   Some answers to the exercises

Exercise 5.1

1. brother
2. daughter
3. sister
4. water
5. horse
6. three
7. father-in-law
8. father

Exercise 5.2

Answers will vary in terms of choice of language. In discussion what needs to be done to maintain the language, you should discuss the feasibility of Fishman's comprehensive guidelines: 1. encouraging acquisition of the language (by adults in cases where the only speakers are left are the elderly); 2. prompting the use of the spoken language in informal settings as well as in neighborhood institutions (where it could be used exclusively); and 3. promoting literacy in the language.

Exercise 5.3

Answers will vary.

Exercise 5.4

Answers will vary, as different dictionaries suggest differences in spelling with or without hyphen, and some suggest that both ways are acceptable.

Exercise 5.5

3. parachoques
4. abrelatas
5. quitanieves
6. lavaplatos

Exercise 5.6

1. loanword from Afrikaans
2. back formation from *bulldozer*
3. loanword from French *diplomate*, a back-formation from *diplomatique*
4. clipping from *facsimile*
5. compound
6. blend of *emotion* and *icon*
7. eponym
8. loanword from Malay
9. loanword from German
10. clipping from *laboratory*
11. clipping from *memorandum*
12. compound
13. acronym (kind of) from <u>ra</u>dio <u>d</u>etection <u>an</u>d <u>r</u>anging
14. eponym

Exercise 5.7

Answers may vary. Words and expressions that might seem unfamiliar in the context include *commend, draweth fast on, tendering, beseeching, heretofore, entreat* and *marriage-portions*.

A possible rewrite from a divorced wife:

Dear X,

How are you doing? Given that I don't have much time left, the love I have felt for you inspires me to remind you to take care of yourself and your mental well-being, which you should put first before all material things, even above your obsession with your body, which caused me ... and you ... a lot of problems.

I forgive you, and I hope that God forgives you too.

About the others, please take care of Mary, our daughter, and be a good father to her, something I've always wanted. I also ask that you help the 3 long-term house staff find new positions, and give a decent severance pay to the rest of the help.

Finally, just to let you know, I have always loved you above all else.

Exercise 5.8

Answers will vary.

Exercise 5.9

Answers will vary.

Exercise 5.10

Answers will vary.

Exercise 5.11

Answers will vary. Some suggestions for discussion:

1. *Cool* started out referring to temperature, and then extended to mean something that is hip or fashionable. Along the way, it extended to referring to sums of money (e.g. 'a cool Thousand' – 1721); perhaps a metaphorical transfer
2. *Liberal* was originally used to refer to the study of arts and sciences (which were 'worthy of a free man' *Oxford English Dictionary*); its meaning has extended in many directions; for example, now in the United States, it is used to refer to those whose political beliefs include government action to promote social change and equality. It can be used by those whose views are more conservative to refer in a disparaging

way (pejoration) to those they see as throwing around government money, perhaps even wastefully.

3. *Cookie*, a word borrowed from the Dutch *koekje* 'little cake', has been used in the United States to refer to a flat, sweet type of food, such as *chocolate chip cookie*. It is now used in computing to refer to a packet of data, perhaps from metaphorical transfer.

4. *Memory* is another term which has transferred via metaphor to the realm of computing, from the human act of remembering to the capacity of a machine to store data.

5. *Partner* moved from meaning a person who has a joint share in something, or who is party to something (*Oxford English Dictionary*) and for a time if someone referred to someone else as his/her *partner*, we might have thought 'business', yet now the predominate understanding might be more specialized now to 'relationship', unless *business partner* is specified. Many people express unhappiness with the term 'partner' to refer to someone in a romantic relationship, as they feel it takes on connotations of 'business'. It is interesting the difficulty society has with finding a term that people are happy with.

6. The meaning of *share* generalized from referring specifically to dividing something up in portions and sharing them out to having something in common with others (suffering, for example) or giving them something which you have and they do not (e.g. *share your story*).

7. *The head has cold feet.* Metaphorical transfer (so an extension of meaning) allows us to understand that the *head* refers to the top person in an organization, and *cold feet* is an lexical phrase we use to refer to feeling afraid or timid before striking out into new territory (and the etymology on that expression is not at all clear: by all accounts, it seems to be probably metonymy at work).

8. *Washington phoned the chair*: Metonymic transfer allows us to understand that *Washington* refers to the United States government, and that *chair* refers to the head of a board of trustees, or a university program, etc.

Added words and phrases will vary.

Exercise 5.12

Answers will vary.

Exercise 5.13

1. Consonant epenthesis
2. Vowel epenthesis

3. Consonant deletion
4. Metathesis
5. Dissimilation (the second [r] changed)
6. Vowel deletion

Exercise 5.14

he <u>spæc</u> to heom fele on bispellen <u>cweðende</u>. Soðlice ut-eode se sæwere
hys sæd <u>to sawenne</u> & a þa he <u>seow</u>. sume hye <u>feollen</u> wið weig. &
fugeles <u>comen</u> & <u>æten</u> þa.

Exercise 5.15

Answers will vary. The following are only some suggestions of what we
could say about Old English from the text, and without having studied it
in greater depth.

1. *Fæder* = *Father* (very close to modern English, but with a change in
   the first vowel and the alveolar plosive for the interdental fricative,
   which is explained by Grimm's law.
2. There are two different ways to say 'our' *ure/urne* (*ure Fæder, urne
   gedæghwamlican, ure gyltas*) although it is not clear from so little data
   what the difference might be.
3. It is also interesting to compare *urum gyltendum* with *ure gyltas. Gyltas*
   and *gyltendum* are obvious related (and maybe to the word guilt?),
   probably two forms of the same word, as we know that Old English
   had case endings. Perhaps *urum gyltendum* refers to our guilts that are
   done to us?
4. 'On' and 'in' seem to be expressed by the same pronoun, *on*.
5. *heofonum* is obviously 'heaven', and it seems to have the same ending
   as 'gyltendum'. What kind of meaning could this ending express?
6. *nama* is 'name'. We know from Figure 5.2 that the first vowel sound
   was more like the vowel in 'spa', and that the last vowel sound was
   pronounced.

7. *gehalgod* must be 'hallowed'. This reminds me of what we saw in
   Chapter 4 on the German circumfix ge- -t to form the past participle.
   I wonder if the initial *ge* in *gehalgod* is the same thing? The other
   participle 'done' must be *gewurþe* and it also has the initial *ge*. Might
   be worth checking!
8. *rice* must be kingdom, so the word has been replaced by a later
   word.
9. *willa* is very close to 'will' of today.
10. *eorðan* is similar to 'earth'. I wonder if *an* is some kind of inflectional
    ending.

11. *us* is the same!
12. *to dæg* is very close to 'today'. Did *to* mean 'this'?
13. *and* has not changed (typical for function words!)
14. *forgyf* is very close to 'forgive'. There are two different forms: *forgyf* is the imperative, and *we forgyfað* is first person plural indicative, as in Figure 5.5, with perhaps and alternative spelling for the inflection *að*.
15. *gelæd* for 'lead'. There is the initial *ge* again – maybe it is some kind of suffix, but in this case the translation is into the imperative, and not into the participle.
16. *costnunge* for 'temptation'. 'Temptation' is obviously a Latin word, so it came into the language after the Normans arrived in England.
17. *alys* must mean 'deliver'. There are a number of verbs which are in imperative mood in the modern text: give, forgive, lead, deliver. It is difficult to work out the translation for 'give', but the other verbs are *forgyf, gelæd* and *alys*. Difficult to see any pattern there!
18. *yfele* is 'evil'. Again a consonant sound which has become voiced, the same as *forgyf*. Perhaps after *y* (which must be a vowel sound) for some reason?

There are some bits of language which are difficult to explain without having ever studied Old English and without looking the words and phrases up in an OE grammar, such as:

1. þu þe
2. si (perhaps 'be')
3. gewurþe (perhaps 'be done')
4. to becume (come?)
5. swa swa
6. gedæghwamlican (could be 'daily bread')
7. hlaf syle
8. þu
9. ne (might mean 'not')
10. soþlice
11. ac

Exercise 5.16

A recipe

Exercise 5.17

Answers will vary.

Exercise 5.18

Answers will vary.

6 Language variation

6.1 Synchronic variation, sociolinguistics, and speech communities

Language varies across time (as we saw in Chapter 5), a phenomenon called **diachronic variation. Synchronic variation**, on the other hand, refers to the variation in language at a given moment in time, the variation that would be discernible if we took a still photograph of language at a certain point. This variation can be attributed to a variety of social factors, such as geographical location, socio-economic background, ethno-cultural background, level of education, gender, and age, as well as situational and contextual factors, who is speaking to whom about what and where. Of course, diachronic and synchronic variation are inextricably linked, as the synchronic variation of a given period leads to the language change we see from a vantage point in the future. For example, what are now called the Romance languages started out as dialects of Latin. When Old English (as it is called now) was in its early formation, based on the diffusion of Old Frisian during the Anglo-Saxon invasion of what is now England (see Chapter 5), and its contact with the languages spoken there at the time, many different dialectal varieties were in existence simultaneously. Over time, communicative forces led toward some semblance of standardization, consolidated by the growth of English as the language of the court and of government starting in the thirteenth century. Of course, English today is not at all a uniform language, as we know by the different ways of speaking the language found around the globe.

Indeed, linguists such as David Crystal (cf Crystal 2003, 2004) have researched the position of English today in the world, highlighting its various forms, such as American, British and Australian English, and including what have been called at some point 'new Englishes', or varieties of English which came into existence in countries such as India, Singapore, Ghana and Nigeria, once they had achieved their independence. In these countries, English was the language of the colonizers, and so it was viewed negatively by many. At the same time, it seemed less politically controversial at the time of independence to continue using English as a national language, the language used for government during colonial times, than it was to choose one ethnic language over another. At the same time, these countries have adapted English in their own ways to create their own identity; the Nigerian novelist Chinua Achebe writes: 'I feel that English will be able to carry the weight of my African experience. But it will have to be a new English, still in full communion with its ancestral home but altered to suit its new African surroundings' (1976: 84). Crystal predicts that these varieties may become nearly mutually unintelligible with other varieties of English in spoken form with time, just as some varieties of English within the borders of the UK are perhaps to American speakers, and varieties of American English to speakers in the UK. At the same time, Crystal suggests that there will most likely continue to exist a standardized written form, such as that of books and the internet, so that an English speaker could pick up a newspaper from anywhere around the globe and, aside from some specific local references, be able to follow it. We see in the notion of standard, on the one hand, and variety, on the other, the forces of communication and identity, pushing toward common understandings while pulling away toward identifiable differences, a strong force in creating language variety.

Thus, distance from other speakers and geographical borders serve to create spaces for dialects to develop, and perhaps grow into different languages. In addition to geography, social factors indeed often drive language variation. For example, the Great Vowel Shift (see Chapter 5) may have been motivated by a desire for a prestige dialect following the loss of French as the prestige language. This explanation does not mean that people consciously decided to pronounce their vowels differently, but rather little by little a change in pronunciation caught on, with one change leading to another across several vowels. While this change in the way people pronounced the vowels did lead ultimately to a change in the English language, not all variation turns into a change in the wider language. Variations co-exist, and with time a feature of a variation may spread and be adopted by the majority of speakers of a language, leading to a change which is discernible as such at a later date. The Northern Cities Vowel Shift (Chapter 5) is an example of variation which is spreading from urban center to urban center, especially around the Great Lakes, in the United States. At the same time, the shift is not noticeable in the pronunciation of the majority of African American speakers in these urban centers, and, of course, it still remains to be seen just how far the shift will spread.

Sociolinguistics is the branch of linguistics which analyzes the effects of society on the different forms of language use (see Chapter 8, *Sociolinguistics*, by Jeffrey Reaser). We saw in Chapters 2 and 3 that language varies according to situation; that is, if, for instance, there is a distance and a difference in power or status between people (e.g. teacher/ student) the language used in an email exchange between them will most likely show differences in linguistic features from that of an email exchange between people who are on equal footing (e.g. friends or colleagues), and it will also be different than the language used in face-to-face conversations. Languages show variety at all levels: in their genres, text types, lexico-grammar and phonology, and this variation is easily witnessed when we move across social registers and geographical locations, encountering different **speech communities** along the way.

Speech communities are defined by the language they use, as their language use forms their boundaries. A speech community, as Alessandro Duranti (1997: 82) suggests, is 'the product of the communicative activities engaged in by a given group of people'. Speech communities exist at very broad and more open to very narrow and more closed levels. Thus, we can speak of the speech community of English, American English, north-Eastern US English, and New York English. Groups which use technical jargon may form a speech community, such as the community of systemic functional linguists, or groups which use particular forms of slang, such as gangs or fans of particular types of music like hip hop, or those with any kind of 'in-language'. Sometimes families form their own particular speech community, as they use words and expressions which outsiders to the family might not always understand. A speech community is not identifiable exclusively based on spoken language. Communities on the internet use the written language to interact, as do specialists in any given field in the academic journals they use to communicate their research. These communities that we choose to belong to are usually referred to as **discourse communities** (see Chapter 3), and the term speech community is usually reserved for the communities

EXERCISE 6.1

Make a list of the speech/discourse communities that you consider yourself a part of. What features of language use define the community?

EXERCISE 6.2

Make a list of any expressions that you use with your family that perhaps you avoid outside of that sphere. Include expressions used to refer to other family members (e.g. how do you refer to your parents' parents?), to food, illness, bodily functions, particular family practices, etc.

EXERCISE 6.3

Think back over your own use of language throughout your life. How has it changed?

which we are born into or in which we live our daily lives. Throughout our lives, we may belong to several speech communities synchronically and diachronically, as we move in and out of different communities, interacting with other members. Indeed, each of us has our own individual way of using language, known as our **idiolect**, which is shaped by our multiple and varied interactions in our different speech communities, and which changes as we age.

6.2   Dialect and vernacular

A variety of language used in a social or geographical speech community is called a **dialect**, while accent is a lay term which refers only to phonological differences. A dialect is a variety of a particular language which is in theory mutually intelligible to speakers of that language. However, the distinction between a dialect and a language is not so clear cut. There are cases in which varieties of the same language are not easily understood by all of its speakers. For example, Arabic speakers from the Middle East often cannot understand Arabic speakers from North Africa (although the latter can often understand the former, because of exposure to television in Egyptian Arabic, which is, for the most part, intelligible to a wide variety of Arabic speakers). On the other hand, there are sets or pairs of what are considered separate languages which are mutually intelligible, such as Gallego, spoken in Galicia, the northwestern region of Spain, and Portuguese. It is often contentious to define a variety as being an example of a dialect of a particular language, rather than as a language in its own right, as there are political implications. Indeed, as there is no clear set of linguistic criteria to distinguish the two, a variety is often defined as a dialect rather than as a language because of factors such as lack of a written form (with no corresponding press or literary tradition), lack of nationhood for the people who speak the dialect, or lack of prestige.

   A **standard dialect** is a variety which speakers of a language assume is the norm. It is debatable about whether or not a standard really exists outside of the collective minds of the speakers. Language purists believe they do exist, and they usually equate it with the elite, with the language used, for example, in higher education circles. Indeed, in schools in most countries, one of the goals is to teach a standard form, one which is deemed useful for purposes of education and work places, and one which constitutes the widely accepted written form of the language. The term **vernacular** is often used to refer to what are perceived to be non-standard dialects or languages in a country. It can be used to refer to different aspects of language use; for example, it can refer to a language or dialect which does not have a literary written tradition, or to the language or dialect which is learned in the home but not used in formal settings such as school or government. Unfortunately, in these settings, dialects which do not match closely the idealized standard version are often thought of as somehow rudimentary or indications of a lower level of intelligence at worst, or an impediment to academic success at best.[1] In Chapter 1, I stressed the very important point that any language or dialect is equal to the task of embodying the communicative needs of its speech community, as all languages and dialects can draw on resources through the flexibility of their lexicogrammar. Therefore, whether a variety is termed 'standard' or 'vernacular', they are equal in their status as varieties of a language in the eyes of the linguist.

Children who grow up in homes where the standard is dominant, homes in which children are read to and families converse on a range of topics in the standard dialect of the educational system, will be more likely to feel more comfortable when learning the variety in their first language classes in school. Children who grow up in homes where a vernacular is the dominant language may find their way of speaking stigmatized at school, where they are told that their grammar is 'incorrect'. Given the relationship between our way of speaking and our identity, the possible implications for issues of self-esteem and alienation are clear. There are real individual and societal losses in stigmatizing any community's way of using language. In Chapter 8, Jeffrey Reaser highlights the role of dialects in creating identity and community. It is most probably the case that those who are comfortable in the standard dialect of a speech community will be more successful in the workings of that community. At the same time, rather than attempting to suppress dialects, with an accompanying loss of identity and diversity, educational systems can embrace dialect diversity, while including a focus on which ways of speaking and writing will allow people to achieve what they wish to achieve through their use of language in different situations. In this sense, and from the perspective of linguistics – which sets out to *describe* language – it is more profitable to speak of *appropriateness* of dialects to given communities and situations, rather than of correctness or inherent quality.

1. However, as Jeffrey Reasner (Chapter 8 of this book) so aptly points out 'It is important to note that no study has effectively demonstrated that any language or dialect in and of itself constitutes a barrier to academic success. Instead, it is the schools' and teachers' treatment of students and their language varieties that is the ultimate source of language-related academic failure.'

> **EXERCISE 6.4**
>
> When you speak with your family, what dialectal variation do you speak? What kinds of social judgments are made about your dialect? Do you agree with those judgments?

6.3 Diglossia

Situations in which there is a difference between the home/community-based variety and the official language variety of a country are referred to as **diglossia**. Charles Ferguson (1959) used the term to refer to specific situations in which two varieties of the same language exist: one variety, that which is used for official purposes, he termed the 'high' variety (H), and the one which is used for more informal purposes the 'low' variety (L). The two varieties are used for separate functions, with little overlap between the uses of one and the other. H is used for education, politics and government, and L is the language spoken at home and in casual conversations in the community; children are brought up speaking L, but H must be learned in a more formal setting. H has a long-standing literary tradition, while L does not. An example of diglossia is Arabic; classical Arabic is the high variety, as it is the written standard in all Arabic-speaking countries, with the local dialect in each case forming the low variety.

Joshua Fishman uses the term **extended diglossia** for other types of situations in which there are two varieties, which may be two separate languages, such as French and English in medieval England. A more modern example of this phenomenon is Vèneto, or Vènet, a language spoken in Veneto, one of Italy's 20 regions. It is not a dialect of Italian, although it is referred to as a dialect by Italians outside of the region; indeed, according to *Ethnologue*, Vèneto and Italian belong to different sub-branches of the Italo-Western branch of the Romance languages: Venetian is a member of the Gallo-Romance group, which also includes French, while Italian is a member of the Italo-Dalmatian group. The grammar of Vèneto is different in many ways from that of Italian, and interestingly it actually has a number of dialects of its own, within the Veneto region as well as in Brazil, Croatia and Mexico. In Italy, and within its own region, it was until fairly recently viewed as the low variety, with Italian being the high, and thus is an example of extended diglossia.

However, as with many other languages in Europe, attitudes are changing toward vernaculars; what have been considered low varieties now have their own written grammars, bills and laws to help ensure their status, along with their promulgation in more and more contexts, and groups of middle class speakers who are proud of them and promote their use. In addition to Vèneto, in Europe there are a number of other examples of what in the past would have been considered low varieties achieving status, such as Galician in Spain, Welsh in Wales, Gaelic in Scotland, and Irish in Ireland.

This is not the case with all diglossic situations, as in many cases low varieties are stigmatized. Sociolinguists now also use the term diglossia to refer to situations in which a community has a high and a low variety, even when the high variety is used by some speakers in their everyday lives, as is the situation in Jamaica with Jamaican Standard English (H) and Jamaican Creole (L) In many of these cases, attitudes toward H are more positive, while L is regarded as less than H. These attitudes are perpetuated by the uses of the varieties, as the high variety has a well-established literary tradition, and is associated with the written language and with education, while the low variety is often regulated to cartoon characters or the speech of certain characters, usually sinister, comic or cute, in novels or films. Thus, L is seen as divergent, and H as the norm, and the attitudes toward the language are often extended to the speakers themselves.

Diglossia often involves its speakers in **code-switching**, as they move from one variety to another, given the situation, and it is much more likely that those who speak the low variety will be bilingual or bidialectal than those who grow up in homes where the high variety is spoken.

Project work: Choose one of the following contexts and find out about the existing diglossic situation. Write a paragraph explaining the situation, using the terms *high* and *low variety*, and explain the attitudes existing toward each. Explain when one or the other variety tends to be used, and also any other factors (other languages involved in the situation, for example – a phenomenon sometimes called **triglossia, quadriglossia** or even **polyglossia**).

1. Switzerland: Swiss German and Standard German
2. Haiti: French and Haitian Creole
3. Singapore: Singapore Standard English and Singlish
4. Greece: Katharevousa and Dimotiki (until 1976)
5. Tanzania: English and Swahili
6. Hong Kong: English and Hong Kong Cantonese

7. Morocco: Classical Arabic and Moroccan Arabic
8. Zaire: French, Kikongo, Tshiluba, Lingala and Kiswahili
9. Papua New Guinea: English, Tok Pisin and Hiri Motu
10. Cape Verde: Portuguese and Cape Verdean Creole

6.4   Pidgins and Creoles

We have seen in the previous section that Jamaican Creole is considered a low variety, and, indeed, even its own speakers view it as a corrupt or in some way incomplete form of language. In order to understand why this view is not one any linguist would hold, it is important to have an understanding of **pidgins** and **creoles**. A pidgin is often a hybrid of two languages – although one may predominate – and comes into existence in an area where at least two different language groups come into contact and have specific communicative needs. Indeed, known pidgins from earlier times, such as a Mediterranean pidgin called *Sabir*,[2] emerged amongst sailors and traders, so that they could carry out their business. Other pidgins arose in plantations where slaves from other regions were forcibly brought in, such as in the Caribbean and the South Pacific. In these cases, it is usually the language of the dominating power which provides much of the vocabulary for the pidgin.

As happens in labeling many kinds of linguistic phenomena, linguists do not always agree on what constitutes a pidgin. However, there is some general agreement; in terms of its lexicogrammar, a pidgin has relatively few lexical items, and those that are adopted tend to lend themselves to ease of pronunciation. Its grammatical rules undergo simplification from the input languages; pidgin verb systems usually do not demonstrate number, tense, voice, and mood (indicative, imperative, subjunctive, etc.). Furthermore, a main characteristic of pidgins which distinguishes them from creoles/ languages is that no one grows up speaking a pidgin at home; that is, a pidgin is not learned as a native language.

In some cases, people from the different communities may marry and have children, and continue to use the pidgin as their common way of understanding each other. Thus, their children are brought up speaking the pidgin, and these children develop it more fully, in which case the pidgin becomes creolized, and a new language comes into existence. Creoles are pidgins which have become or are well on their way fully developed

2.   This Mediterranean pidgin, spoken between the ninth and eleventh centuries, was also called Lingua Franca, and is considered to provide the origin for that term itself. To see sample texts, go to http://www.uwm.edu/~corre/franca/edition3/texts.html

languages; their vocabulary and grammar are more varied and complex. They are as complete as any other human language (and note that language change is indicative of the fact that languages are always developing to meet the needs of their communities), and are used in a wide range of communicative situations, such as newspapers and television, not just for purposes of bridging a communicative gap between people who speak different languages. An example of a pidgin which has become creolized, and is now an official language of Papua New Guinea, is Tok Pisin. The difference between pidgins and creoles is thus one of degree, rather than of absolutes. Their names do not always help to determine whether they are indeed considered as one or the other.

Project work: Look up information on the following. Determine the origins of each, and make notes on each in terms of whether it can be classified as a pidgin or a creole. Provide rationale for your decision in each case.

1. Nigerian Pidgin
2. Krio (Sierra Leone)
3. Hawaiian Pidgin English[3]
4. Papiamentu (Netherlands Antilles)
5. Broome Pearling Lugger Pidgin (Australia)
6. Fanagolo (South Africa)

6.5   Sociolect

Dialects are examples of regional variations in language use. Another perspective on variation taken up by sociolinguistics focuses on the social groups that we form part of. Our socio-cultural and economic background, gender, age and occupation all have an effect on the shape of the language we use, and work together in varying ways to form our **sociolect**. Providing descriptions of the differences in language use across some of these factors, for example socio-economic class, gender and age, has spawned quite a bit of controversy, perhaps not surprisingly. There is a danger in describing the way a certain group of people use language, be it a group of people who are classified as belonging to the upper middle class due to a set of social factors, such as their residence, income, and level of education, or be it women or men in general, and then suggesting that all people who are

3.   The Hawai'i Creole English website, created by Jeff Seigel and Ermile Hargrove, explains some of the syntactic rules of this language. Try the exercises! (http://www2. hawaii.edu/~gavinm/hcegrammar.htm).

classified as a member of group use the same features of language. In some ways, that claim would be something like saying that 'all members of the middle class' or 'all men' wear the same kinds of clothes. Obviously, it is hard to separate out the different factors, as a woman who works as a police officer will probably show differences in her language use from a woman who works as a corporate lawyer when they are on the job. At the same time, they might be close friends, and when they meet up outside of work with other friends, their way of speaking would show great similarities. Our ways of using language are influenced by all of these social factors, as well as by other factors (such as disability, personality and mood, and whether or not we are first or second language speakers of the language).

However, probably most of us make judgments about people's socio-economic class, gender, age and occupation based on the language they use, and the work of sociolinguists is to describe the perceived differences in actual language use, and perhaps to go beyond to attempt to explain why they occur and what effects they may have. In this section, we look at some of the history of the kind of research that has been carried out in sociolinguistics, focusing on English (although a wealth of studies has been carried out on other languages, including sign languages, along the same lines).

6.5.1 Language variation based on socio-cultural and economic background

It is an over-generalization to equate a linguistic variable, such as the pronunciation of [n] or [ŋ] at the end of words like *talking* and *laughing*, or absence or presence of *ain't* in someone's speech, with one socially defined group; however, linguistic variables do seem to have a social status of their own, in a way similar to types of cars, ways of dress, or leisure activities. People make judgments about a person's socio-cultural background when they overhear someone using these linguistic features (or not) in conversation. In standard Castilian Spanish, for example, upon hearing someone use the definite article (*el* or *la*) in front of a proper first name (*la Charo, la Pili*), the hearer would probably make the assumption that the speaker is from a rural or working-class environment. Unfortunately, often these judgments go beyond simply locating a speaker in a socio-cultural position, but also entail further judgments as to a person's intelligence or personality (e.g. as aggressive or deferential), serving to further stereotypical biases. In order to better understand why people hold these judgments, both in terms of the existence of actual differences and in terms of dispelling judgmental and stereotypical myths, social class has held a central place in sociolinguistic research.

William Labov's (1966a; 1966b) now famous study of rhoticity (among other variables) in a department store in New York City provided early inspiration for a vast number of studies based on quantitative analyses of the presence or absence of variables across speakers from different backgrounds pronouncing words or phrases which contain the analyzed variables in different contexts. It is important to note here that the linguistic variable type of study is also used in the study of dialects, or difference in language use across geographical lines, as well as in studies which correlated speakers' socio-economic background with the absence or presence of the variable. In his 1966 study, Labov set out to study rhoticity (see Chapter 2), which refers to the pronunciation of postvocalic [ɹ], both when followed by a consonant and when word final; at the time of Labov's study, there was variation within New York City as to whether the [ɹ] was pronounced or not; thus, for example, *fourth* could be pronounced [fɔθ] or [fɔɹθ]. At that time, a rhoticized accent was held to be more prestigious than a non-rhoticized accent. To collect his data, Labov went to three different department stores in New York City which were determined to differ on the socio-economic scale based, in part, on the prices in each of the stores: one with relatively high prices (Saks'), one with relatively low prices (Macy's), and one in the middle (Klein's). On each of the floors in each of the stores, he asked where an item located on the fourth floor (e.g. ladies' coats or shoes) could be found, in order to elicit *fourth floor*. Upon receiving that first answer, he asked each of his informants to repeat, in order to elicit a more careful response.

Overall (and greatly simplifying the results), in the most prestigious of the stores, he found the greatest number of [ɹ] inclusions, and in the least prestigious, the smallest number, suggesting a correlation between socio-economic class and the pronunciation of the [ɹ]. Interestingly, at the store considered to be in the middle range, he found a significant change in pronunciation in terms of the number of [ɹ] inclusions in the careful speech as compared to casual speech. At the same time, Labov found a complex set of correlations amongst different variables in the population under study, such as age, ethnic background and gender of the participants. Thus, while socio-economic class has a role to play in whether or not a linguistic feature will be part of a person's linguistic repertoire or not, it is only one factor amongst other factors.

Peter Trudgill (1971) investigated language variation in Norwich, UK, analyzing speech of 60 individuals, from a random sample of people from a variety of socio-economic backgrounds, who were divided, based on a number of factors, such as income, education, occupation, father's occupation, type and location of residential dwelling, into the following categories: middle middle class, lower middle class, upper working class, middle working class and lower working class. Various tasks were used to elicit speech which was then examined for 16 variables, including +/– [h] in phrases like 'happy home', and the pronunciation of [n] or [ŋ] at the end of words such as *walking* and *laughing*. He used a range of techniques to elicit the variables in different styles of speaking: casual, formal, reading a passage, and reading a word list. His results showed clear differences in the frequency of the variables; for example there was greater use of [ŋ] the 'lower' the class on the socio-economic scale, and also greater use the more casual the speech. At the same time, studying the range of responses across the continuum from more careful to more casual speech allowed Trudgill to see that the purveyors of language change are the middle- and upper-working classes. That is, language change does not come from those in the most powerful socio-economic positions in society, nor from those in the most marginalized positions, as both of those positions are relatively isolated. Rather, it comes from those who perhaps are most mobile in that their occupations bring them into contact with others from a broader range of socio-cultural backgrounds, a finding which is echoed by Penelope Eckert (1988: 184).

> Lower-middle-class speakers show a far greater stylistic range than those above or below them on the socioeconomic hierarchy, and in doing so they regularly show more conservative speech in formal style than upper-middle-class speakers and sometimes show more innovative speech in casual style than work working-class speakers.

James Milroy and Lesley Milroy (1985) studied language use in Belfast, in three different communities. They measured the density of the social network in each of the communities; a social network with a higher density is one in which community participants all know each other's personal contacts and one with a lower density is one which is more open, and where participants do not know all of the personal contacts of the rest of the people in the community, indicating greater social mobility. The community with the highest social network density showed the greatest use of vernacular features, especially amongst the men. In addition to the density of the social network, the participants' patterns of participation in the labor market impacted on whether they conformed more to the local vernacular or incorporated features of speech from the wider community. David Sankoff and Suzanne LaBerge (1978) conceptualized the 'linguistic market' index, which measures the extent to which an individual's life requires them to use the form of language which holds the most cachet in a given community (which is often considered to be the standard). A criticism which has been leveled at much of sociolinguistic research, especially in the early days, was the implicit suggestion that people aspire to the standard, or to a norm, such as the way the middle class speak or the way men speak (see next section). However, marketplaces, as we know, are more complex than that, and the value of commodities changes in different situations. For example, Walt Wolfram and Natalie Schilling-Estes (1998) write about the community of Ocracoke Island, an island off of North Carolina in the US, where college-educated businessmen who operate in the standard dialect on the mainland, when on the island, speak the vernacular. They suggest that in small, close-knit communities, the correlation between differences in language use and differences in socio-economic status may not be anywhere near as significant as that existing in large urban communities. In the case of Ocracoke, the commodity of identity attached to the vernacular dialect outstrips that of the commodity of standard 'correctness'. Thus, we can see that language is not neutral, as in different contexts different configurations of language are awarded a different status based on multiple factors including, in large part, power and identity.

Around the same time research by Labov and Trudgill, the British sociologist Basil Bernstein theorized the differences between two broadly different uses of language, which he called 'restricted code' and 'elaborated code'. Restricted code is a way of using language which assumes a great deal of shared knowledge among speakers. Bernstein (1971) suggested that examples on the far end of restricted codes include those instances of language use which are fully predictable, such as religious rituals, formulaic exchanges such as greetings and introductions, and exchanges which are regulated by protocol. Outside of these instances of predictable language use, exchanges which are difficult to understand by an outsider suggest a restricted code is being used, as it is more economical in its use of language, and tends to rely on shared contextual information. Close-knit groups use restricted code, as do families and circles of friends (see Chapter 2, for example, on the use of vague language among young people) or people with shared interests. While it is rich in meaning to those involved, it relies on a more restricted set of linguistic forms, and more on shared understanding, to convey that meaning. Elaborated code, on the other hand, is more explicit, and thus uses a wider variety of expressions from the lexicogrammar. Elaborated code is thus more apt for conveying abstract and non-localized meaning. While everyone speaks using a restricted code at some point in their lives, the elaborated code is not the dominant code in the working class.

Bernstein came under intense criticism: some critics suggested that Bernstein in essence was arguing that it is the fault of the working classes for their position in society because of the way they speak. However, what Bernstein was actually arguing, and which he made painstakingly clear in subsequent publications, was that society and education needed a theoretical framework which would reveal the way language is used in pedagogy, and that the hidden biases toward ways of using language should be made visible. Subsequently, work within Bernstein's theory focused on the differences in language rather than as a dichotomy (either restricted or elaborated code) but rather as a continua – either more context dependent or more context independent. Research by linguists such as Ruqaiya Hasan and Carmel Cloran (Hasan 2001; Cloran 1994) analyzed the language of working class and middle class mothers interacting with their children. They found in data that they gathered between 1983 and 1986 that the middle class interactions showed greater relative frequency of rhetorical units such as generalizations of the type 'everything dies one day', which call for a more context independent use of language, the type of language in which school meanings are often expressed.

Hasan and Cloran's work in language variation is different from that of linguists in the tradition of Labov; in the Labovian tradition, there is a focus on the sociolinguistic variable, such as phonological variables, as seen in the New York study, or morphosyntactic variables, such as the use of active vs. passive constructions, and these variables are correlated with socio-economic groups. While work in this tradition has been tremendously fruitful in helping to remove unhelpful notions of inherit correctness in ways of speaking, and in deepening understandings of the complexity of social factors which are connected to variety in language use, criticism has been leveled against these types of studies for treating language as if it were a guise; that is, the underlying premise seems to be that meanings are fixed and stable, and that different groups of people simply express the same meanings in different ways (Hasan 2009). However, if we take a functional view of language (see Chapter 3), then we notice that language choices construct meaning beyond mere truth-conditions, as the ideational, the interpersonal and the textual are jointly expressed in linguistic interaction. Hasan draws on her corpus of mothers and children interacting to explain semantic variation; we can imagine a feature of the context of situation in mother-child interaction which occurs frequently: the action of commanding. The mother can choose to express that content as an exhortative as in *listen, you behave yourself and just cut it out please* or consultative in *can you get me a tissue please?* (Hasan 2009: 195). In this research, semantic variation was found to a statistically significant degree when mothers of the two identifiably different social classes interacted with their children, as well as when mother's were talking to girls vs. when they were talking to boys, which leads to the topic for the next section.

6.5.2 Language variation based on gender

The analysis of language use along gender lines received its major impetus from Robin Lakoff (1975), who put forth a list of ways in which women's language differs from that of men. She argued (based on her own observation and intuition) that women use more hedging (*It's sort of hot in here, I kind of disagree, I guess so*) and tag questions (*It's warm today, isn't it? She can come along, can't she?*); they apologize more, and use more 'empty' adjectives like *cute, wonderful,* and *fantastic*. Thus, Lakoff argued, women's language choices put them forth as lacking in power and authority and as seeking approval. She also suggested that little girls are socialized into language use, often scolded for not talking as nice little girls should, as an explanation for their speech patterns which carry on throughout their lives.

EXERCISE 6.5

Look at the following dialogue. Do you think W is male or female? What do you base your answer on?

Lawyer: *And you saw, you observed what?*

W. *Well, after I heard – I can't really, I can't definitely state whether the brakes or the lights came first, but I rotated my head slightly to the right, and looked directly behind Mr Z, and I saw reflections of lights, and uh, very very instantaneously after that I heard a very loud explosion – from my standpoint of view it would have been an implosion because everything was forced outward like this, like a grenade thrown into the room. And, uh, it was terrifically loud.*

Question for discussion: Robin Lakoff wrote *Language and Woman's Place* in 1975, almost 30 years ago. Ruqaiya Hasan and Carmel Cloran's data was collected in the early 1980s, in Sydney. Do you think that the way boys and girls are brought up in your society is different? Are different ways of speaking for boys and girls promoted? Do parents and teachers interact differently with children, depending on whether they are boys or girls? What kind of evidence could you use to support a response?

Lakoff's initial claims of the typical linguistic features of women's language unleashed a furor. Many sociolinguists set out to provide empirical evidence for Lakoff's assumptions, by collecting data (both men and women's speech) to analyze for Lakoff's list of features. The findings of these studies were not conclusive, which caused linguists to reappraise Lakoff's claims. Indeed, Lakoff's arguments received intense criticism; like Bernstein, Lakoff was criticized for seeming to blame women for their position in society because they use the language they use. Deborah Cameron (1985) suggested that Lakoff took for granted that women were in need of approval and thus interpreted tag questions and other features which she perceived as typical of women's speech as constitutive of this need. However, in one study, where men came out with greater numbers of tag questions, attempts were made to explain the difference by suggesting that there are types of question tags which are forceful (*stop doing that, will you?*) and types which are more tentative (*that's ok, isn't it?*); no attempt was made to explain that the men in this particular study were seeking approval because at the time of this research the stereotype was that men did not seek approval. Cameron highlights that there is a danger in taking the linguistic form as an example of the phenomenon which the researcher believes exists, as there is no one set form-function relationship between a linguistic item and its use.

William O'Barr and Bowman Atkins (1980), in their study of language in a courtroom, challenge Lakoff's assumption that the features which she suggests are typical of female speech are due to gender. Rather, they argue that these features are present in females and males who are in a position of powerlessness. Janet Holmes (1990) characterized Lakoff's list as a functional one; that is Lakoff identified linguistic features which function to express epistemic modality, which is the degree of certainty that we have about a proposition, as well as the speaker's affective stance toward the person(s) with whom they are interacting. Holmes also highlighted the necessity of taking intonation into account, as the illocutionary force (see Chapter 2) can vary greatly depending on how it is uttered. She analyzed a corpus of male and female speech, and found that the differences were not in frequency of use, but rather in ways the features were used by women, which included positive politeness strategies (see Chapter 2), suggesting that the women in her study used language in order to be facilitative and collaborative conversationalists.

Thus, Lakoff's initial claims also led sociolinguists to keep in mind that there is no set form-function relationship in language use, as we have just seen with tag questions. What may be labeled as 'aggressive' in one context may not be labeled so in another. Sociolinguists now enlist informants who can independently indicate whether or not they think a speaker is being more or less deferential than another speaker, rather than assume that the presence of a feature or set of features suggests so. The presence of numerous tag questions in the speech of, for instance, a doctor in a hospital may indicate displays of concern for her patients, and thus she may be thought of as an effective and competent professional (Cameron 1992). It is not very productive in sociolinguistics to talk of 'women's language' but rather of how women use language in specific interactions. Cameron (1992: 24) suggests that the questions sociolinguists need to seek answers to are 'questions about how language is being used, by real people in real situations, to construct gender and gender relations'.

EXERCISE 6.6

What differences, if any, do you note between the way males and females, for example your father and mother, sisters and brothers, and male and female friends, use language?

EXERCISE 6.7

Robin Lakoff's research is from nearly 30 years ago. Do you think that women's ways of speaking have changed in these 30 years? Have the ways in which girls and boys are socialized into language changed?

EXERCISE 6.8

William Atkins and Bowman O'Barr (1980), in their study of language in a courtroom, challenge Lakoff's assumption that the features which she suggests are typical of female speech are due to gender. Rather, they argue that these features are present in females and males who are in a position of powerlessness. From your own observations, would you side more with Lakoff or with Atkins and O'Barr?

6.5.3   Language variation based on age

The language we use changes over our lifetime, and thus we notice major differences in language use across ages. Nikolas Coupland has said as recently as 2001 (p. 185) that, while sociolinguistics has made outstanding contributions to gender research, providing 'one of the cornerstones of modern feminist scholarship', '[a]ge is sociolinguistics' underdeveloped social dimension'. At the same time, perhaps to your parents' dismay (and their parents before them), adolescence is a particularly ripe time for language development, as adolescents have a desire to mark themselves as different from their parents' generation. Similarly to clothes and hairstyles, language is their way of creating a different identity, and often parents remark that they cannot understand their teen-aged children. Young people use more slang and what are considered taboo words by their parents. They vary their pronunciation as well as their intonation patterns. In the UK, the word 'teenglish' has been coined to refer to the particular way teens have of speaking English. In a 2005 BBC article, titled 'A lexicon of teen speak', parents are asked if they can understand 'Crump! You're safa. Wanna cotch down my yard?', which a teen would understand to mean 'Wow! You are the coolest person. Do you want to hang out at my place?'. The article goes on to give a glossary of teenspeak of that time. A comparable glossary from Australia was also made available from an educational group in Queensland in 2006, in order to help parents understand their children.[4] In 1996, Connie Elbe published *Slang & Sociability: In-Group Language among College Students*, based on 20 years of study of students at the University of North Carolina at Chapel Hill. In 2009, Lucy Tobin, also in the UK, published *Pimp your Vocab*, which is a guide for parents and educators on teen language. The ever-growing on-line *Urban Dictionary*[5] is further evidence of the creativity of young people in their language use, through which they strive to create their identity as a separate group, defying the authority of their parents' generation.

William Labov, in his 1963 Master's thesis which was published in *Word* in that same year, was one of the first sociolinguists to write on the connection between age-based language variation and language change. His research on Martha's Vineyard, an island off the coast of Cape Cod, in New England in the US, analyzed the pronunciation of the dipthongs in words such as *night* and *about*. While many American speakers pronounce

4.   See http://education.qld.gov.au/publication/schoolsandparents/2006/issue2_teenspeak. html

5.   www.urbandictionary.com

these dipthongs as [aɪ] and [aʊ] respectively, he noticed that some social groups on the island used a more centralized vowel sound for the nucleus [a] to produce something more like [əɪ] and [əʊ], so that *night* sounds like *noit* and *about* like *a-boat*. Labov found that younger speakers did this with greater frequency than older speakers. Penelope Eckert (1988) affirms that there is a relatively high degree of phonological innovation during adolescence. Her study of different adolescent groups in several schools around the Detroit area in the United States shows that adolescent identity and speech patterns are inextricably linked. For example, Eckert examined the speech of two groups: 1. 'jocks', who she describes as embracing not only sports, but also as being more conformist to American society in general, as they demonstrate 'an acceptance of the school and its institutions as an all-encompassing social context and an unflagging enthusiasm and energy for working within those institutions' (Eckert 1998: 189); and 2. 'burnouts', early 1970s slang for someone burned out on drugs; the term burnout in the context of Eckert's study does not refer to someone who necessarily takes drugs, but it does refer to someone who expresses an attitude of rebellion against institutional culture. She examined the speech of adolescents at different schools in the Detroit area, focusing on the variable [ʌ], as in *bus*. The burnouts were more likely to have shifted their pronunciation of the vowel sound in a word like *bus* toward [ɔ], making that word sound similar to *boss*. This shift is part of what Labov calls the Northern Cities Vowel Shift (see Chapter 5), a shift happening in urban centers such as Detroit, and thus Eckert makes the point that the less conformist adolescents were more influenced by Detroit urban speech patterns. Eckert argues that this provides evidence for the notion that phonological change tends to move outward from urban centers as well as upward through socioeconomic groups, from less well off groups to more well-off ones. Eckert also writes about the 'in-between' groups of students, who identify with neither the jocks or the burn-outs; in her study, this group demonstrates the vowel shift to some extent, and thus they provide a mechanism of change for the jocks. The jocks group also show tendencies toward accepting the change, as they strive to differentiate themselves ultimately from their parents. This research by sociolinguists such as Labov and Eckert provides a fascinating window onto language change in process, highlighting the role age-based variation plays in promoting that change.

EXERCISE 6.9

Consult a 'teenglish' slang glossary or dictionary. Make a list of 10 words along with their definitions. Compare your list with that of your classmates. Do they know/use the words you chose? Does your teacher?

6.5.4   Language variation based on occupation/activity

Occupations and other specialized activities often use language which is specific to that endeavor, known as **jargon**. The linguistic world of a hairdresser is different from that of a football coach, stamp collector or nuclear physicist. To talk of feathering, spritzing, streaking, and layering conjures up images of a beauty salon, while bombing, blitzing, defensive holding, controlling the clock, and line of scrimmage put us on the American football field. Technical and field specific terms are not always easily understood by those who are not familiar with the context and the activity.

Peter Galison (1997) writes on the ways in which people from the same language (namely English) but from different specialties within a specific field, such as theorists and experimenters in nuclear physics, have distinct jargons. Thus, they compromise on a trade language in order to work together, creating pidgins and creoles, just as people who speak different languages do. In language teaching, the proliferation of field-specific courses (such as English for Specific Purpose, or ESP, courses in business, law, healthcare, tourism, etc.) is acknowledgment of the need for learning the language of a field, and not just the language in general, in order to be able to operate in that field. At the same time, there is much debate about whether or not language teachers can teach people the concepts from a field that they are not active members of, as, of course, knowing how to use a word or phrase means understanding the concept it refers to. In some cases, we may find a one-to-one correspondence between a specialized term and a lay term. However, a simple equivalence does not always hold, and can be misleading. For example, one dictionary on medical terms suggests that *hyperemesis gravidarum* is equivalent to *morning sickness*. However hyperemesis gravidarum is actually a rare form of morning sickness, one which involves severe nausea and vomiting during pregnancy, which may even involve hospitalization. While very many women experience some form of morning sickness during pregnancy, few experience hyperemesis gravidarum.

EXERCISE 6.10

Match the specialized term in Column A with its lay counterpart in Column B.

Column A

1. *acer freemanii* _____
2. enuresis _____
3. hypermetropia _____
4. *narcissus* sp. _____
5. *nicotiana langsdorfii* _____
6. patella _____
7. pyrexia _____
8. rhinotillexomania _____
9. rhytidoplasty _____
10. singultus _____

Column B

a) bed-wetting
b) daffodil
c) face lift
d) farsightedness
e) fever
f) hiccups
g) kneecap
h) maple tree
i) nose-picking
j) tobacco plant

© United Features Syndicate. Reprinted with permission

There are myriads of specialized terms which do not have an easily understood counterpart. At the same time, these terms may look familiar, as they are words or sets of words which we use in more familiar contexts. For example, in nuclear science the term *decay branching* is defined as 'The nuclide decay rate by a particular decay mode' (*Glossary of Nuclear Science Terms*). To someone who knows nothing about nuclear science, the definition is as opaque as the phrase itself, in spite of the fact that both *decay* and *branching* provide no mystery on their own. In Chapter 3, we have seen the word *Theme* used in a specialized way within functional linguistics, as the point of departure of a message as encoded in a clause. These are examples of words and phrases which look familiar, yet take on a different meaning within a specialized context.

© United Features Syndicate. Reprinted with permission

Often, jargon is viewed negatively by those who are not a part of the speech community in which the words and expressions are used, as the specialized lexis often excludes those who are not part of the activity, and many find it pretentious and obfuscatory. In the business and political worlds especially, this kind of jargon is referred to as **buzzwords**, which seems to carry the connotation that the life of these words is fleeting, as they buzz around and are used to impress others; thus when they become more frequently used, they lose their intrigue and cachet. Some examples of terms which have negative connotations, further leading to a negative view of jargon, include: from human resource activity *dehire* and *rightsizing* to refer to firing people and from the political world *negative economic growth* and *period of economic adjustment* to refer to a recession.

6.6   Register

Dialects and sociolects are varieties of language based on personal characteristics, such as region where a person comes from, social class, gender, age and occupation, which all work together to create language variation within society and within individuals, as they move from one speech community to another. Thus, dialect and sociolect refer to language variation based on the users of the language. **Register**, on the other hand, refers to variation based on the social context in which language is being used: who is using language with whom, about what, and using which particular medium or mode, as explained more fully in Chapter 3. Researchers who analyze texts (including transcripts of recordings) from various social situations, such as emails, doctor-patient consultations, academic articles, and textbooks, for register differences have concluded that there is a broad cline of registers, moving from the informal, such as conversation between peers, to the highly formal, such as government and legal documents, which are written at a distance from their readers. This is not to say that spoken language is always more informal, and written language always more formal, as we know from speeches, which can be quite formal in terms of their lexicogrammar, and from emails and computer-mediated chat, which can be quite informal.

Obviously, the words 'formal' and 'informal' refer to the social occasion, yet we also use these terms to refer to the language itself. Research has been done on the linguistic manifestations of 'formal' and 'informal' language, and what is clear is that the differences are not absolute; rather, they can be arranged along a cline, with clusters of linguistic features creating a more spoken, or informal, register at one end, with a more written, or formal, register at the other end. One feature of more formal registers is lexical density, which refers to the number of content words (nouns, verbs, adjectives and adverbs) per total words of a text. Let's look at the following example from a history textbook:

> This _new_ _edition_ thus _incorporates_ much _new_ _research_ that has _modified_ _views_ _held_ _only_ a _few_ _years_ _ago_, _particularly_ in the _greater_ _awareness_ of _women's_ _roles_, of the _lives_ of _ordinary_ _people_, of the _lasting_ _structural_ _arrangements_ by which _society_ is _organized_, of _social_ _conflicts_ often _ignored_ and _subtle_ _changes_ _easily_ _overlooked_.[6]

The content words (underlined in the example) total 32 out of the 52 words used, for a lexical density of 61%, which indicates a rather dense text, typical of textbooks. Another way of conveying the same information in a less dense way is through the following doctored version of the same text:

> This _new_ _edition_ thus _incorporates_ much _new_ _research_ that has _caused_ _people_ to _change_ the _views_ which they _held_ only a _few_ _years_ _ago_. _Particularly_, _research_ has _made_ us _more_ _aware_ of how _women_ _acted_ and what they _did_, how _ordinary_ _people_ _lived_, and how _people_ _organize_ _society_ through _structures_ that they _arrange_ and _maintain_. _Research_ has also _made_ us _more_ _aware_ that there were _conflicts_ in _society_ which we often _ignored_, and also that _changes_ _took_ _place_ which _weren't_ very _obvious_, and thus we often _easily_ _overlooked_ them.

This second version uses 90 words to convey the same information as the previous version. It has 45 content words for a lexical density of 50%. The decrease in lexical density comes about through an unpacking of the dense nominal groups of Text 1; that is Text 1 uses complex nominal groups (see Section 3.2.1.1), with pre- and post-modification, while Text 2 uses

6.   From Chambers, Mortimer, Raymond Grew, David Herlihy, Theodore K. Rabb and Isser Woloch (1991) *The Western Experience*. McGraw Hill, Inc.

less complex nominal groups (only post-modification is used) and more clauses (and thus more verbs) to make it clearer through the language who did what:

Text 1 (more nominal)	Text 2 (more verbal)
greater awareness of women's roles	*more aware of how women acted and what they did*
the lives of ordinary people,	*how ordinary people lived*
the lasting structural arrangements by which society is organized,	*how people organize society through structures that they arrange and maintain*
social conflicts often ignored	*conflicts in society which we often ignored*
subtle changes easily overlooked	*changes which weren't very obvious and thus we often easily overlooked them*

The reduction in the complexity of the nominal group also brings with it an increase in the number of clauses. In essence, Text 1 consists of one sentence, which basically consists of one clause: *This new edition thus incorporates much new research.* The rest of the sentence, *that has ... overlooked* is a rankshifted[7] clause functioning to modify the word *research.* Text 2 consists of a greater number of rankshifted and non-rankshifted clauses. To sum up, as the information gleaned from these two examples demonstrates, more formal texts tend to have a higher lexical density, denser nominal groups, and usually a reduction in the number of clauses. Less formal texts tend to have a lower lexical density, simpler nominal groups, and usually a greater number and complexity of clauses. The register brings about these differences: often written academic texts convey greater abstraction of concepts, and downplay actors, hence the greater amount of complex nominal groups and the use of passive voice. An admonition often given to student writers is to avoid the passive voice and use active verbs because that advice is thought to lead to clearer writing. However, it can create a register which is at odds with a need to create an academic text with chains of reasoning which may call for greater abstraction.

---

7.   As explained in Chapter 3, a rankshifted clause is one that acts at a rank lower than itself, e.g. a modifying, or adjective, clause acts to modify a noun, and thus is rankshifted. Non-rankshifted clauses are clauses which operate at the level of parataxis or hypotaxis, as main and subordinate clauses.

A particular kind of register research in the field of sociolinguistics has been inspired by Doug Biber (cf. 1988), an American linguist who applies the tools of corpus and computational linguistics (see Chapter 8, *Computational Linguistics*, by Mick O'Donnell and *Corpus Linguistics* by Michaela Mahlberg) to large amounts of texts from a number of different registers in what is called multi-dimensional analysis. Researchers use computer programs to search the texts for a range of linguistic features, including first and second person pronouns, nominalization, -*that* relative clauses, past tense verbs, use of hedging devices, word length, and speech act verbs. The goal is to then analyze how features cluster together in the different registers, and thus to determine dimensions of functional variation. Biber discovered five sets of features which co-occurred with great frequency across the texts. For example, one set included third-person pronouns, 'public' verbs (reporting verbs such as *claim, assert, admit, tell, say, declare*), simple past tense verbs, and perfect aspect verbs; Biber concluded that this set indicated the functional variety of <u>narrative</u> (Dimension 2). From the five sets, Biber arrived at five dimensions of functional variation along which texts will range:

1. Informational vs. Involved production
2. Narrative vs. Non-narrative concerns
3. Elaborated vs. Situation-dependent reference
4. Overt expression of persuasion
5. Abstract vs. Non-abstract information

Different genres or types of texts are arranged differently with respect to each of these dimensions. For example, fiction texts are high on the 'Narrative concerns' end of the Dimension 2, while official documents are at the opposite end. In Dimension 1, informational production involves linguistic features such as nouns, attributive adjectives and prepositional phrases (which indicate complex nominal groups) and longer words, while involved production, on the other hand, relies on, for example, private verbs (verbs that express mental states such as *think, feel, believe*), contractions, present tense verbs, first and second person pronouns, demonstrative pronouns, WH questions, modals of possibility, emphatics (*a lot, such a ...*) and clause final prepositions. While academic texts are on the 'informational' end of Dimension 1, face-to-face conversation and personal letters are high on the 'involved production' end. In Dimension 3, on the elaborated reference end we find relative clauses which begin with a preposition (*of which ..., about whom ...*) and nominalization, while at the situation-dependent reference we find adverbials of time and place which refer to the discourse situation. Government documents and legal texts are found on the elaborated end of Dimension 3. Dimension 4 includes clusters of features such as suasive verbs (*propose, argue*), modals of necessity (*ought to, should, must*), and conditional clauses (*if ..., unless ...*), the presence of which indicates overt expression of persuasion, and the absence of which suggests, of course, no overt persuasion. Texts types which contain clusters of features in Dimension 4 include editorials and political speeches. Dimension 5 includes passive constructions, which are the main markers of the abstract end of the dimension, along with conjuncts (*however, therefore*) and adverbial subordinators (*since, although, while*).

Different text types will score higher or lower in each of the dimensions, depending on the presence or absence of the linguistic features. For example, Biber (1988) points out that spontaneous speeches are on the more involved end of Dimension 1 and the non-abstract end of Dimension 5; they are not high in the features of persuasion (Dimension 4), while they have a moderate amount of features of narrative (Dimension 2), and an intermediate score on Dimension 3, which means they use both types of reference, elaborated and situation-dependent. The kind of work inspired by Biber shows clearly that we create different registers based on the ways in which we bring together a range of linguistic resources. In his 1995 book, *Dimensions of Register Variation: A Cross-linguistic Comparison*, Biber shows how register variation exists in other languages, and predicts that there are some cross-linguistic universals in this type of variation.

EXERCISE 6.11

Analyze the following text for features from Biber's 5 dimensions.

No person shall be held to answer for a capital, or otherwise infamous crime, unless on presentment or indictment of a Grand Jury, except in cases arising in the land or naval forces, or in the Militia, when in actual service in time of War or public danger; nor shall any person be subject for the same offense to be twice put in jeopardy of life or limb; nor shall be compelled in any criminal case to be a witness against himself, nor be deprived of life, liberty, or property, without due process of law; nor shall private property be taken for public use, without just compensation. (Fifth Amendment, United States Constitution)

6.7   Speech accommodation

Speech accommodation leads us to position ourselves with respect to other speakers through **convergence** and **divergence**, as it refers to the process by which speakers change the way they speak according to the person they are talking to. Speakers **converge** (adopt similar styles of speaking) when they wish to reduce the social distance between one another. Speakers **diverge** (speak differently from the way others are speaking) when they wish to emphasize their distinctiveness or increase their social distance.

In order to be successful in different situations and activities, we often need to take on the style of speech or writing of the community. Surfers will speak differently to their surfing buddies than they might giving a talk to a roomful of strangers. Students will write their papers in a different register than they do their emails to their friends. When language users do not converge in these situations, or when they do not know how to do so appropriately, often they are not successful in their interactions. This calls for a fluidity in our ability to adapt our language. When we move to a new location, we may converge to the dialect of the area, and revert to our 'native' dialect when we call friends and family from back home. At the same time, we may hang on to our way of speaking as a part of our identity. Kirk Hazen (2004) writes on accommodation within families: parents accommodate to each other, children to their parents, and often when they have teens, parents to their children, which often is the cause of huge cringe factor in the latter, and which may cause them to diverge further from their parents' norm.

EXERCISE 6.12

Do you find that you accommodate your speech/writing when speaking/ writing to others? Provide specific examples. Also, provide examples of when you might purposely diverge from others' way of speaking or writing.

6.8   Lexical variation

In this section, we look at the different ways in which words and expressions vary across speech communities.

EXERCISE 6.10

What do you call the following items?

1

2

3

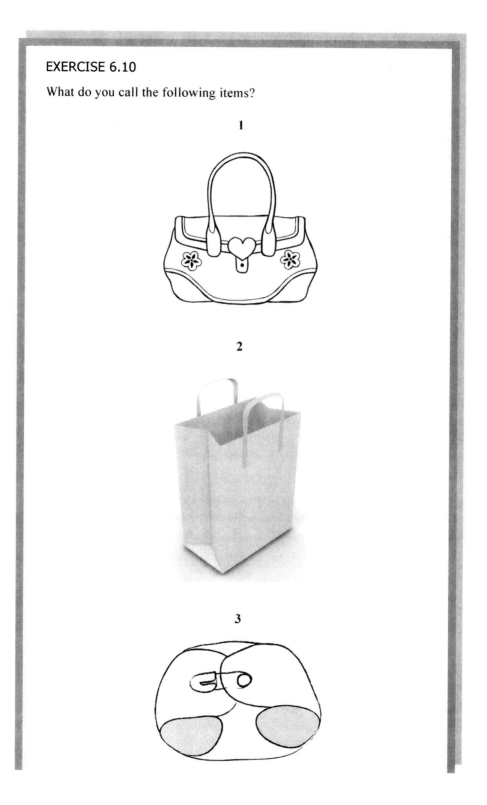

4

5

6

7

8

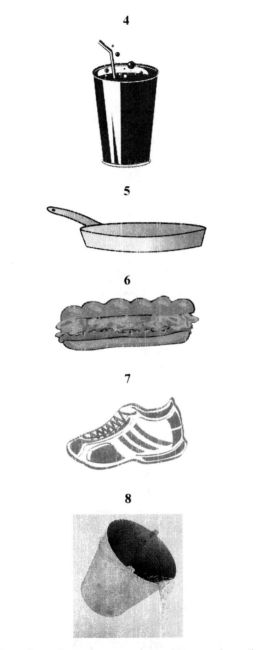

Make a list of words and expressions that you have heard which are different from those you would use for the above items. Make a separate list of words and expressions which you use, and which you know are different from those others use.

As we move across social and geographical communities within a wider speech community, we find differences in words and expressions used to refer to the same or similar items and phenomena. Lexical variation based on geographical location exists in all languages, and not only includes different names for essentially identical meanings or referents, as in *lift* and *elevator*, or *pop* and *soda*, but also the same word might be used to refer to distinct meanings. For example, in Spain, a *tortilla* refers to an omelet made of egg, potato and onion, while in Latin America, it refers to a corn or wheat flour flat cake. Lexical variation also exists in signing, as chronicled by Edgar and Susan Shroyer, in their book *Signs across America*, which illustrates different signs for lists of words such as *about, apple* and *banana*, across various regions of the United States. Sometimes, lack of knowledge of word meanings in a different dialect of the same language can cause embarrassment. A Spanish student, after years of study of British English, went to the US to do a year of high school; there, she once asked in a loud voice in a math class 'Does anyone have a rubber?' For her, a *rubber* referred to an eraser, something to use to erase (or *rub out* in British English) marks written with a pencil. She had no idea that in American English a *rubber* refers to a condom!

In addition to regional lexical variation, we vary the words we use depending on the register, on who is talking to whom, about what, and in what mode – a textbook, a letter, a conversation, a sermon, an online chat, etc. Words which are considered synonymous, such as *purchase* and *buy*, often have the same denotational meaning (see Chapter 4); however, they often serve to create different registers. *I bought a new car* and *I purchased a new automobile* conjure up different images of who is speaking to whom and in what situation. Note how these different choices also situate speakers with respect to their interlocutors in interaction, and are judged as appropriate within a context of situation.

Lexical variation comes about in all of the ways explained in Chapter 5 on lexical change. For example, the word 'rents' is a clipping of the word 'parents', while also a play on the word 'rent', as it refers to the fact that teens usually live rent free with their parents. 'Phat' in essence is an example of a loan word from another dialect, as younger speakers of more standard American English adopted it from African American dialects. Acronyms proliferate, especially in SMS and on-line chat, such as *lol, ttyl,* and *OMG*. Lexical variation is lexical change in process, although only time will tell which variants will become more lasting members of the dialect and the wider language.

EXERCISE 6.14

Benjamin Franklin, in the *Pennsylvania Gazette*, in 1736, listed over 200 words for 'drunk', including a few we might recognize today, such as *booz'd, intoxicated*, and *stew'd*, and many others which we wouldn't, such as *cherry merry, wamble crop'd, half way to concord, fuddled, as dizzy as a goose, got the glanders, hammerish, moon-ey'd, pungey*, and *raddled*. Make a list of words that you use to refer to someone who is drunk. Ask others from another generation and/or another geographical location for their list and compare the lists.

6.9   Sound variation

The sounds of our languages can vary across speakers in terms of word stress, intonation and phonology. With word stress, for example, an English speaker from North America says 'CONtroversy', while a speaker from the UK says 'conTROVersy'. Differences can exist in word stress in closer proximity as well. For example, where would you place the word stress for *guitar*? In many parts of the US, especially in the south, the stress is placed on the first syllable, while in other places it is on the second. Intonation may vary as well, as there are differences in the uses of rising and following intonation, as well as in word and syllable length and speed. Variation in phonology is perhaps the most prominent way we have of recognizing the regional identity of speakers of different variants of the same language. Articulatory processes help (see Chapter 5) explain only in part why this dialectal variation takes place. For example, **assimilation**, or the process whereby sounds are affected by adjacent sounds to the extent that they take on some of their articulatory features, explains why some speakers of English say *inneresting*, while **deletion** explains why others say *intresting*.

EXERCISE 6.15

Using the International Phonetic Alphabet (see Chapter 2), transcribe your pronunciation of the following words. If you know of other ways of pronouncing the words, transcribe that as well. For words of more than one syllable, include an indication of word stress, by placing ` before the syllable that receives the most stress.

1. *caught*
2. *cot*
3. *pen*
4. *pin*
5. *ride*
6. *bet*
7. *bit*
8. *interesting*
9. *laboratory*
10. *guitar*

Much of the phonological variation in English occurs with the pronunciation of vowels, in patterns of change which may be motivated by a number of factors, including desire for identity and difference, or aspirations of belonging to a group which speaks another variety, as has been suggested as a motivation for the Great Vowel Shift. In Chapter 5, we saw the Northern Cities Vowel Shift, a demonstration of the way in which vowel sounds are pronounced differently in different parts of the United States. Further differences include what is known as the *pin-pen* merger, which is one of the characteristics of Southern English in the United States, and which involves the sounding of /ɛ/ as closer to /ɪ/ before nasal consonants [n], [m] and [ŋ].

While English shows perhaps more differences in vowel sounds amongst its varieties, Spanish shows more differences in consonant sounds. If we take the two words *casa* ('house') and *caza* ('hunt') we find the following regional variants in pronunciation:

[kasa] [kaθa]: distinct, in which the graphemes *z* and *c* (before *e* and *i*) are pronounced as [θ], and *s* are pronounced as [s]; this variant is called *distinction*, and is found in northern and central Spain.

[kaθa] [kaθa]: same pronunciation, in which the graphemes *z*, *c* (before *e* and *i*) and *s* are all pronounced as [θ]; this variant is known as *ceceo* [θeθeo], and is found in parts of southern Spain.

[kasa] [kasa]: same pronunciation, in which the graphemes *z*, *c* (before *e* and *i*) and *s* are all pronounced as [s] (known as *seseo* [seseo]), and is found in most of Latin America as well as in parts of mainland Spain and the Canary Islands.

Within peninsular Spain, many people consider *distinción* to be the standard, and award it more prestige, while the *ceceo* is often thought of as an indication of backwardness. Indeed, around the world, the ways in which varieties of a language are pronounced attract social judgments, and people often have rather fixed, sometimes positive or negative, reactions when they hear them. These language attitudes are often exploited in television programs and films, such as in *Shrek*[8] where the actor Eddie Murphy speaks in AAVE (African American Vernacular English) in his role as the Donkey, which he uses to take on a comic personality. Similarly, in Spain, a number of years ago *La vuelta al mundo de Willy Fog*, a cartoon version of *Around the World in 80 Days*, included a mouse, Tico, who traveled everywhere with Willy Fog. Tico spoke in an Andalusian accent, also in a way which was designed to achieve a comic effect. At the time, there were some voices of protest on the part of people from Andalucia, who saw it as a belittlement of their way of speaking. In her article titled 'Teaching children how to discriminate: What we learn from the Big Bad Wolf', Rosina Lippi-Green (1997) includes more examples how children can learn negative prejudices through these kinds of practices in film and television.

David Crystal (2007) writes on negative attitudes toward the regional Birmingham accent in the UK. He comments on 'Brummy', as this dialect is called: 'It isn't just that people have said it's ugly. They've gone further, and said that it makes the speakers sound lazy, bolshy, and stupid' (2007: 72). He goes on to make the important point that there is no relationship between the way a language or dialect sounds and the intelligence or willingness to work hard of its speakers. Furthermore, the sounds of the dialects of a language lose any social prestige or stigma when heard by people who do not speak the language or are not from the country. Crystal played tapes of the Birmingham accent to foreigners who did not speak English and they said that they found it pleasant to listen to because of its melodious and musical nature. Thus, language attitudes are socially motivated, as there is nothing inherent in the speech quality or physical acoustic properties which would provide a basis for the kinds of judgments about and attitudes toward language varieties which people hold and express.

8. For an in-depth study of language variation in Shrek, and what the choices in dialectal variants reveal about language attitudes, visit http://diggy.ruc.dk/bitstream/1800/2254/1/ Final%20version%20-%20digital%20bib.pdf , a final BA project.

Register plays an important role in the ways in which we pronounce language. For example, we tend to enunciate more in a formal speech than in an informal conversation with friends. Research also suggests that women enunciate more toward the standard than men; for example, men are more likely to produce reduced forms such as *gonna* than women. Furthermore, there is intonational variation across gender and across age groups, as, for example, there is a trend amongst teenage girls in certain social contexts in the United States to end a declarative on a rising tone, thus sounding more as if they are asking a question than issuing a statement; this feature of their speech is used toward achieving in-group solidarity, and thus may be used solely in certain situations, such as conversation amongst friends. Here we see register, gender and age combining to explain a variation in how language sounds.

6.10 Morphosyntactic variation

EXERCISE 6.16

Look at the following pairs of sentences. Which are you more likely to say? Do you think that either one of the pair is more acceptable than the other, or are both equally acceptable?

1a. *If he had kept his mouth shut, he'd be more popular now.*
1b. *If he would have kept his mouth shut, he'd be more popular now.*
2a. *If he were smart, he'd shut up and listen.*
2b. *If he was smart, he'd shut up and listen.*
3a. *He has proven that he has poor judgment.*
3b. *He has proved that he has poor judgment.*
4a. *Somebody left their notebook on the desk.*
4b. *Somebody left his/her notebook on the desk.*
5a. *Today there are fewer people than yesterday.*
5b. *Today there are less people than yesterday.*
6a. *He dived into the water.*
6b. *He dove into the water.*
7a. *John and I went to the movies last night.*
7b. *Me and John went to the movies last night.*
8a. *He don't like getting up so early.*
8b. *He doesn't like getting up so early.*

The appropriateness of each of the choices in Exercise 6.16 will depend where they are uttered. I grew up in the Midwest of the United States, convinced that in a counterfactual statement about the past, both clauses take the conditional perfect 'would have', as in 1b. When I started teaching English, I discovered that this choice was 'wrong', and that the past perfect 'had had' was the 'correct' choice for this construction. However, that choice is not the most appropriate for a good number of people (as evidenced by a search on Google for 'if I would have'). For set 2a and 2b, it seems pedantic now to insist on 'if I were', except in the most formal of registers. The sets in 3 and 6 are both acceptable, perhaps one more so than another depending on where you are from. The sets in 4 and 5 are disputable, with some people wishing to hold on to the singular pronoun reference in 4b, and others wishing to avoid the unwieldy situation of including both gendered pronouns, and thus opting for 4a. If you are 16 years old and chatting to your friends about what you did the previous evening, 7a might seem odd, as might 8b in the same kind of context. Thus, like other types of variation, morphosyntactic variation is also affected by social factors.

We have seen in Section 6.8 that variation exists with lexical, or content, words; variation also exists in function, or grammatical, words. For example, in English, we have no formal pronoun to refer to second person plural, so some people use a form such as *you all, y'all, you guys, you lot, youse, yous, yous guys, yunz, you'uns, yinz,* or *yiz'all,* depending on the country and region they are from. The Spanish language sees variation in the second person singular form *vos,* widely used in several parts of Latin America, such as in Argentina and Uruguay, as compared with *tú,* the form used in Spain and in other parts of Latin America.

As with other linguistic features of variation, there are features from dialects, especially those on the lower end of the socio-economic scale, which are viewed as incorrect versions of a more standard dialect. However, dialects *are* dialects, and all are equally rule-governed, although those rules vary across dialects. African American Vernacular English (AAVE), for example, is a form of English with several syntactic rules which are different from SAE (Standard American English). AAVE uses negative concord, such as 'He don't know nothin'', as do other dialects of English, such as Cockney, in England ('He didn't know nothin'') and hosts of other languages, such as Spanish ('Él no sabe nada'). As in other languages and dialects, AAVE uses the double negative consistently, and thus it is a regular grammatical feature of the dialect. Another regular feature is that of the habitual *be.* In AAVE, if an action or state is repeated, or is more or less a permanent condition, the verb *be* is used in its simple form, such as *John be happy* (John is always happy) and *John be late* (John is habitually late). If the action or state occurs at the present time, no copular verb is used, such as *John happy* (John is happy right now) and *John late* (John is late today). The lack of a copular verb in the present tense is a regular syntactic feature of many languages, such as Arabic and Russian. It is also often a feature of standard varieties of English in informal, conversational contexts, such as 'Where you at?' There are other regular morphosyntactic features of the AAVE dialect, just as there are of other dialects of English.

Walt Wolfram (2004) reports on a morphological difference from Standard American English (SAE) dialects of the south-east of the United States: a number of verbs which are irregular (or 'strong', see Chapter 5) in SAE show leveling, as in '*Everybody knowed him*' and '*He drinked the soda*' (Wolfram 2004: 82). Thus these dialects demonstrate a phenomenon which has been occurring for centuries in English: a greater tendency toward the weak verbs, or those whose past tense is formed by adding *–ed* to the stem. At the same time, some of the varieties have retained the irregular past tense *holp* (from *help*), while other varieties, including SAE and British dialects, leveled *help* into a weak verb centuries ago. The point is that language variation is neutral: there is no right or wrong way to go about it.

6.11 Chapter outcomes

After having read this chapter carefully, discussed with others the content, and carried out the exercises, you should assess your ability to:

✓ Explain the difference between diachronic and synchronic variation, and discuss the relationship between the two.
✓ Explain the scope of sociolinguistics.
✓ Define speech community and compare to discourse community.
✓ Explain idiolect.
✓ Define dialect and explain why it is a difficult concept to distinguish from language.
✓ Explain the notion of 'standard' and 'vernacular' dialects.
✓ Differentiate the notion of 'appropriateness' from 'correctness'.
✓ Explain diglossia.
✓ Explain pidgin and creole.
✓ Explain sociolect.
✓ Describe the type of study which involves the sociolinguistic variable (as, for example, in work by Labov and Trudgill); explain what those studies can show, as well as any drawbacks.

✓ Discuss the complexity of factors involved in language variation (include notions of context, identity, and meaning).
✓ Explain lexical density.
✓ Explain the concept of speech accommodation (convergence and divergence).

6.12 References and further readings

See also Chapter 8, *Sociolinguistics* by Jeffrey Reaser

Achebe, Chinua (1976) *Morning Yet on Creation Day: Essays.* Garden City: Doubleday Anchor.

A lexicon of teenspeak. (2005, June 10) *BBC News.* Retrieved on February 15, 2010 from http://news.bbc.co.uk/2/hi/uk_news/magazine/4074004.stm

Bernstein, Basil (1971) *Class, Codes and Control* (Volume 1). London: Routledge & Kegan Paul.

Biber, Douglas (1995) *Dimensions of Register Variation: A Cross-linguistic Comparison.* Cambridge: Cambridge University Press.

Biber, Douglas (1988) *Variation Across Speech and Writing.* Cambridge: Cambridge University Press.

Cameron, Deborah (1992) Not gender difference but the difference gender makes: the politics of explaining sex differences in language. *International Journal of the Sociology of Language* 94(1): 13–26.

Cloran, Carmel (1994) *Rhetorical Units and Decontextualisation: An Enquiry into Some Relations of Context, Meaning and Grammar. Monographs in Systemic Linguistics, No. 6.* Nottingham: Department of English Studies, University of Nottingham.

Coupland, Nikolas (2001) Age in social and sociolinguistic theory. In N. Coupland, S. Sarangi, and C. Candlin (eds) *Sociolinguistics and Social Theory* 185–211. London: Longman

Crystal, David (2003) *English as a Global Language.* Cambridge: Cambridge University Press.

Crystal, David (2004) The past, present and future of World English. In A. Gardt and Bernd Hüppauf (eds) *Globalization and the Future of German* 27–46. Berlin: Mouton de Gruyter. Retrieved on February 15, 2010 from http://www.davidcrystal.com/DC_articles/English9.pdf

Crystal, David (2007) *By Hook or By Crook: A Journey in Search of English.* London: HarperCollins Publishers.

Duranti, Alessandro (1997) *Linguistic Anthropology.* Cambridge: Cambridge University Press.

Eckert, Penelope (1988) Sound change and adolescent social structure. *Language in Society* 17: 183–207.

Ferguson, Charles A. (1959) Diglossia. *Word* 15: 325–340.

Fishman, Joshua (1967) Bilingualism with and without diglossia; diglossia with and without bilingualism. *Journal of Social Issues* 23: 29–38.

Franklin, Benjamin (no date) *The Writings of Benjamin Franklin: Philadelphia, 1726–1757.* Available: http://www.historycarper.com/resources/twobf2/pg36-37.htm

Galison, Peter (1997) *Image & Logic: A Material Culture of Microphysics*. Chicago, IL: University of Chicago Press.

Grey, Clive (no date) Towards an overview of work on gender and language variation. Available: http://faculty.ed.umuc.edu/~jmatthew/articles/overview.html#SOCIO%20 WORK

Glossary of Nuclear Science Terms. Retrieved on February 15, 2010 from http://ie.lbl. gov/education/glossary/glossaryf.htm

Hasan, Ruqaiya (2001) Ontogenesis of decontextualised language. In A. Morais, I. Neves, B. Davies and H. Daniels (eds) *Towards a Sociology of Pedagogy. The Contribution of Basil Bernstein to Research* 47–79. London: Peter Lang.

Hasan, Ruqaiya (2009) *Semantic Variation: Meaning in Society and in Sociolinguistics*. London: Equinox.

Hazen, Kirk (2004) The family. In J. K. Chambers, P. Trudgill, and N. Schilling-Estes (eds) *The Handbook of Language Variation and Change. Blackwell Handbooks in Linguistics* 503–524. Malden, MA and Oxford, UK: Blackwell.

Holmes, Janet (1990) Hedges and boosters in women's and men's speech. *Language and Communication* 10(3): 185–205.

Labov, William (1963) The social motivation of a sound change. *Word*, 19: 273–309.

Labov, William (1966a) *The Social Stratification of English in New York City*. Washington, DC: Center for Applied Linguistics.

Labov, William (1966b) The linguistic variable as a structural unit. *Washington Linguistics Review* 3: 4–22. Retrieved on February 15, 2010 from http://www.eric.ed.gov/ ERICDocs/data/ericdocs2sql/content_storage_01/0000019b/80/33/c5/73.pdf

Lakoff, Robin (1975) *Language and Woman's Place*. New York: Harper Row.

Lippi-Green, Rosina (1997) Teaching children how to discriminate: What we learn from the Big Bad Wolf. In R. Lippi-Green (ed.) *English with an Accent* 79–103. London: Routledge.

Milroy, James and Milroy, Lesley (1985) Linguistic change, social network and speaker innovation. *Journal of Linguistics* 21: 339–384.

O'Barr, William M. and Atkins, Bowman K. (1980) 'Women's language' or 'powerless language'? In S. McConnell-Ginet, R. Barker and N. Furman (eds) *Women and Language in Literature and Society* 93–110. New York: Praeger.

Sankoff, David and Laberge, Suzanne (1978) The linguistic market and the statistical explanation of variability. In D. Sankoff (ed.) *Linguistic Variation: Models and Methods* 239–250. New York: Academic Press.

Stockwell, Peter (2007) *Sociolinguistics: A Resource Book for Students*. London and New York: Routledge.

Trudgill, Peter J. (1971). The social differentiation of English in Norwich. Edinburgh University: Unpublished Ph.D. Thesis.

Trudgill, Peter J. (1972) Sex, covert prestige and linguistic change in the urban British English of Norwich. *Language in Society*, 1(2): 179–195.

Wolfram, Walt (2004) The grammar of rural and ethnic varieties in the Southeast. In B. Kortmann and E. Schneider (eds) *Handbook of Varieties of English* 74–94. Berlin: Mouton de Gruyter. Retrieved on February 15, 2010 from http://www.ncsu.edu/ linguistics/docs/pdfs/walt/PDF-Rural_Southeast.pdf

Wolfram, Walt and Schilling-Estes, Natalie (1998) *American English: Dialects and Variation*. Malden, MA: Blackwell.

For examples of language variation, see the clips at the Linguistic Society of America website: http://www.uga.edu/lsava/Topics/Language%20Variation/Language%20 Variation.html

6.13 Some answers to exercises

Exercise 6.1

Answers will vary. An example:

> I consider myself to be a member of what has been termed the 'ex-native speaker' community in Madrid, Spain. My way of using language has been shaped by first having been born and raised in the mid-west of the United States, and then living in Spain and working in English language teaching in Madrid. My pronunciation definitely places me from the United States, although English language teaching has altered my enunciation of words and phrases. In terms of vocabulary, I do not know the current slang of my native country or region, and I often use a mix of American, British and Spanish words when speaking English. I am also part of the Systemic Functional Linguistic discourse community (see Chapter 3), and am comfortable reading articles and books in the field which refer to concepts such as Theme, Rheme, grammatical metaphor, clause as exchange, representation and message, etc.

Exercise 6.2

Answers will vary. An example:

In my family in the US, when I was growing up, my siblings and cousins always referred to our grandmothers as *Nana* plus their last names, so *Nana McCabe* and *Nana Lascara*. We only grew up with one grandfather, who was known as Gramps. Given that my mother is from southern Virginia, she grew up pronouncing the word *aunt* as [ɔnt], a pronunciation which she carried with her to Rockford, Illinois, after she married my father. So during our childhood, my brothers, sister and I always addressed our aunts in Virginia as [ɔnt] and our aunts in Illinois as [ænt].

Exercise 6.3

Answers will vary, and will probably include a combination of information from answers to Exercises 6.1 and 6.2.

Exercise 6.4

Answers will vary. An example:

> With my family in Madrid, when we speak in Spanish we speak what is considered standard *castellano* (Castilian Spanish), a variety which is probably considered neutral by many (the variety used by newscasters on TV and radio), but which is hardly neutral in its advantageous position in society.

Exercise 6.5

According to O'Barr and Atkins (1980), W is a man.

Exercise 6.6

Answers will vary. An example:

   I have noticed that the Spanish men I know in general use more taboo language than the females in mixed company, but also I notice that younger women use more of what has been considered taboo language than do older women. I have noticed that more of my female students from the United States seem to use rising intonation (so it can sound like they are asking a question) than my male students. Neither of these generalizations have been empirically tested, so they are only based on my perception!

Exercise 6.7

Answers will vary. You might consider whether parents and teachers speak differently to their male and female children, the kinds of games children play, and whether or not there are differences in topics that children are told they should not speak about.

Exercise 6.8

Answers will vary. You can ultimately argue that it boils down to individuals, that there are males in positions of powerlessness who do not resort to using the features which Lakoff suggests are typical of female speech, and that there are females who do not do so either, meaning that neither Lakoff or Atkins and O'Barr are right, or at least have the evidence to make the generalization. The kind of large scale study needed to empirically test the hypothesis one way or the other is difficult to carry out.

Exercise 6.9

Answers will vary

Exercise 6.10

   1. maple tree
   2. bed-wetting
   3. farsightedness
   4. daffodil
   5. tobacco plant
   6. kneecap
   7. fever
   8. nose-picking
   9. face lift
   10. hiccups

Exercise 6.11

The text is high on the informational end of Dimension 1, as there are no personal pronouns, contractions, or private verbs, and there are complex nominal groups with lots of prepositions and attributive adjectives. There are no reporting verbs or verbs in the past tense, so it is low on Dimension 2, the narrative dimension. With respect to Dimension 3, Elaborated/situated reference, the text does not refer to any specific time or place (*time of War and public danger* can refer to many different possible times), and it uses nominalizations (*presentment, indictment*) to push it more toward the elaborated end. The text does contain some interesting features of Dimension 4: an 'unless' clause, as well as *shall* which expresses a high degree of certainty as well as some degree of obligation (as in 'Thou shalt not kill'). As for Dimension 5, it contains a number of passive constructions as well as subordinators (*unless, except, when*) which places it high on the abstract end. In sum, the text is informational and persuasive, yet abstract and removed from everyday experience.

Exercise 6.12

Answers will vary. An example:

I tend to speak more quickly when I am with people from my own country, from the US. When I am with British speakers, I vary my lexical choice. While I do not use words like 'lift' or 'nappy', I do use 'queue up' and other turns of phrase. I also codeswitch quite a bit with both friends and family between Spanish and English. I do not converge in terms of my pronunciation, mainly because I am not very good at imitating other patterns of phonology and intonation. I rarely diverge from other's ways of speaking.

Exercise 6.13

Answers will vary, and may include:
1. purse, handbag, pocketbook, bag
2. bag, sack
3. diaper, nappy
4. soda, pop, sodapop, coke, soft drink
5. frying pan, fry pan, skillet
6. hoagie, submarine sandwich
7. tennis shoe, running shoe, gym shoe
8. pail, bucket

Exercise 6.14

Answers will vary, and may include: *hammered, pissed, wasted, decimated.* For more, see the BBC news article '141 words for "drunk"' (March 20, 2002) Retrieved on February 21, 2010 from http://news.bbc.co.uk/2/hi/uk_news/1883481.stm

Exercise 6.15

1. [kɔt] [kɑt]
2. [kɑt]
3. [pɛn] [pɪn]
4. [pɪn]
5. [ɹaɪd] [ɹad]
6. [bɛt]
7. [bɪt]
8. [ɪnəɹstiŋ] [ɪntɹəstiŋ]
9. [ˈlæbɹətoɹi] [ləˈboɹətɹi]
10. [gɪˈtɑɹ] (note that ´ indicates stress) [ˈgɪtɑɹ]

Exercise 6.16

Answers will vary. See paragraph directly following the exercise in the chapter for further comment.

7 Language, Biology and Learning

The relationship between language and the brain is an area of major interest to many linguists. There is much debate about whether or not humans have an innate faculty for language or whether it is more a matter of humans having a powerful and complex brain which responds effectively to the linguistic data it encounters. As evidence for what the relationship between the brain and language entails, brought into the discussion are research on the brain itself, on language development, and on animal communication, areas that we will delve into in this chapter.

7.1   The brain and language

An intriguing question is that of where language is located in the brain.[1] The human brain, like that of other large mammals, contains a cerebral cortex, which is the outer layer of the cerebrum. The cerebral cortex is a vital site for key abilities, such as memory, attention, thought, and consciousness, and, of course, language. The cerebral cortex is divided into two halves called the cerebral hemispheres, which are connected by the corpus callosum, a thick band of millions of nerve fibers. The right hemisphere controls functions on the left side of the body, and the left hemisphere those on the right side. Each hemisphere is divided into four lobes: frontal, parietal, occipital, and temporal. These divisions are marked by the gyri (or ridges) and sulci (or fissures) that characterize our brains. Each of the lobes is responsible for different functions:

Figure 7.1: Cerebral cortex

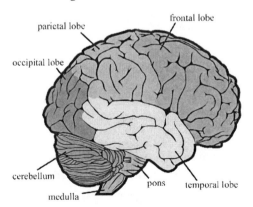

1.   For a complete overview of the brain and language, see a website designed by Bruno Dubuc *The Brain from Top to Bottom*, at http://thebrain.mcgill.ca/flash/index_d.html (choose the desired level, and click on 'From thought to language').

Figure 7.2: Cerebral cortex: superior view

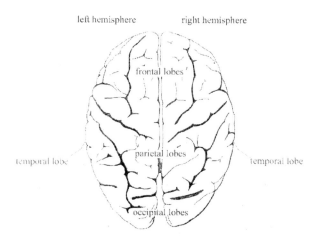

the frontal lobe for reasoning, problem-solving and emotions; the parietal lobe sensory processing related to touch, temperature and pain, as well as visuo-spatial processing; the temporal lobe for processing of sound and smell, as well as memory; and the occipital lobe for visual processing.

We have not yet mentioned where language is located in the brain. Indeed, if we have some kind of innate language faculty, which Noam Chomsky (1965) hypothesized might be thought of as a *language acquisition device*, we would expect some region of the brain to have a more notable relationship with language. The science of **neurolinguistics** studies the neural mechanisms in the brain that are related to the acquisition and use of language, and neurolinguists are interested in what happens in the brain as we learn, comprehend and produce language. The field has its origins in studies from the nineteenth century of patients who suffered some form of brain damage called **aphasia**, a neurological term used to refer to a language disorder caused by brain lesions which have been brought about for any number of reasons, such as strokes, tumors, infections, and traumas like accidents and gunshot wounds.

On April 11, 1861, at the general infirmary of Bicêtre where he worked, Paul Broca, a Parisian neurologist, met Leborgne, a patient who had been admitted because of a gangrenous leg. Leborgne displayed excellent language comprehension; however, his speech production was severely impaired. In fact, he would only repeat the syllable 'tan' to anything he was asked, which he accompanied with gestures in order to express himself. Later that year, Leborgne died, and Broca performed an autopsy, discovering brain damage in the left hemisphere, at the junction of frontal, parietal, and temporal lobes. A few months later, Broca encountered a second patient, Lelong, an

84-year-old man who had suffered a stroke. He could only say five words, 'oui' ('yes'), 'non' ('no'), 'tois' (by which he meant 'trois' – three – which he said for all numbers) 'toujours' ('always') and 'Lelo' (to refer to himself). An autopsy revealed damage in a similar area of Lelong's brain. Thus Broca confirmed that language production belongs to the left side of the brain, as damage to this front part of the left hemisphere (now known as **Broca's area**) resulted in loss of speech. Not all patients of expressive aphasia, or Broca's aphasia, lose speech completely, but they speak haltingly and with great effort, as exemplified by this exchange:

> *Examiner:* What brought you to the hospital?
> *Patient:* Yeah ... Wednesday, ... Paul and dad ... Hospital ... yeah ... doctors, two ... an' teeth. (Goodglass 1993: 81)

Some years later, Carl Wernicke, a German neurologist, studied patients who had difficulty understanding what was said to them. They spoke fluently, not with the halting speech of Broca's aphasics, but with normal flow and intonation, yet their speech was full of nonsense words. As the cause of this type of speech, Wernicke identified lesions in the left rear parietal/temporal lobe, an area now known as **Wernicke's area**. This type of aphasia is known as Wernicke's aphasia (or receptive aphasia or sensory aphasia). A patient diagnosed with Wernicke's aphasia constructed the following in telling a story about a picture:

> Well this is .... mother is away here working her work out o'here to get her better, but when she's looking, the two boys looking in other part. One their small tile into her time here. She's working another time because she's getting, too. (Cookie theft picture description, in Martin *et al.* 2007: 434, from Carroll 1999)

Figure 7.3: Broca's and Wernicke's areas

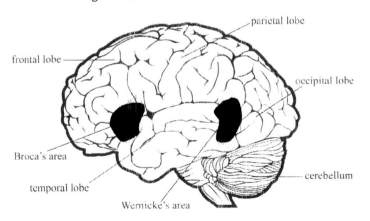

Figure 7.2 shows the parts of the brain which correspond to Broca's and Wernicke's areas. Based on the research by Broca and Wernicke, it was thought for some time that Broca's area was related to speech production, and that Wernicke's area was the seat of speech comprehension. Since that time, vast amounts of research on aphasia[2] have modified these views. For example, Broca's aphasics tend to speak in **agrammatic** forms; that is they have problems planning and producing syntactically correct sentences.[3] **Agrammatism** can present itself in a variety of ways. Speech production may be telegraphic, with many function words left out. Aphasics may leave off verb endings, or use only infinitives, with no inflected verbs in their sentences. Obviously, the language of the aphasic will have an effect on the type of agrammatism. In Chapter 4, we saw that the Semitic languages inflect via transfixes, and an Arabic aphasic may have difficulty using the correct tense marker, e.g. they may confuse 'katab' (he wrote) for 'ktub' (he writes). Patients with damage to Broca's area who are hard of hearing and who use sign language show problems in coordination of signs (while bimanual non-linguistic tasks may not be problematic, providing more evidence for the relationship between Broca's area and language). Broca's, or non-fluent, aphasics also can lose the ability to understand thematic roles (Chapter 4), or the relationship between participants and processes (Chapter 3). So they may have difficulty understanding who did what to whom, especially in the case of passive sentences ('The girl was chased by the boy') or cleft sentences ('It was the girl who chased the boy'). Thus, over the years, a revised version of aphasia damage came to be accepted, which is that damage to Broca's area results in syntactic difficulty, while damage to Wernicke's area results in loss of the ability to use and understand lexis meaningfully.

Broca's area is found in the left hemisphere of most right-handed people, and this area is larger than the corresponding area in the right hemisphere. Some left-handed people with damage to the corresponding area in the right hemisphere suffer the same types of aphasia as their right-handed counterparts, suggesting that their Broca's area develops in the right side of the brain. It is also worth pointing out that lesions in Broca's area are accompanied by weakening, and in some cases paralysis, on the opposite side of the body. Thus, Broca's aphasics have great difficulty with writing, if they can write at all, and their writing shows the same agrammatisim as

2. For a history of the study of aphasia, see Ahlsén (2006). For an overview of neurolinguistics, see Ingram (2007).
3. Dr. Aniruddh Patel, whose research focuses particularly on music and the brain, has discovered that Broca's aphasics also show difficulty in processing the syntax of music. See http://vesicle.nsi.edu/users/patel/Patel_2003_Nature_Neuroscience.pdf

their speech. Wernicke's aphasics, on the other hand, can write, although their written production is much like their spoken production: fluid, but full of nonsense words.

Much of the research done on aphasics up until fairly recently was clinical; patients were studied for their symptoms and responses to treatment, and autopsies were used to reveal the parts of the brain affected. Advances in medicine have broadened the opportunities to study the brain and its functions. For example, in the Wada test, sodium amobarbital is used to anesthetize the side of the brain under study (and the opposite side of the body in correspondence). The procedure is named after a Canadian neurosurgeon, Juhn Atsushi Wada, who invented it in order to test which side of the brain in epileptic patients was dominant for language and memory functions, in order to avoid disturbing these functions during surgery. During the test, patients are asked to read words, identify objects, pictures, numbers and shapes, and answer questions about what they see. If the patient has difficulty in or cannot respond to the questions, then we can assume that the side of the brain which has been put to sleep is that which is dominant for those functions. Through Wada testing, researchers have been able to ascertain that indeed a vast majority of right-handed people and a good portion of left-handed people have their major language functions in the left hemisphere. Physiologists label this hemisphere the categorical hemisphere (Ganong 2005: 273), as it is dominant for categorization and symbolization, as well as verbal memory and rational thought. The other hemisphere is called the representational hemisphere, and it is more concerned with visuospatial relationships, musical ability, and memory for shapes, as well as with insights and imagination.

Brain imaging techniques, such as positron emission tomography (PET), functional transcranial Doppler sonography (fTCD), functional magnetic resonance imaging (fMRI), and Near-Infrared Spectroscopy (NIRS), offer fascinating opportunities to study what happens in the brain when we use language in healthy subjects as well as in patients. Using these imaging techniques, researchers have been able to determine which portions of the brain are most active during various language tasks. For example, research by Laura-Ann Petitto and her team at University of Toronto Scarborough,[4] using Near-Infrared Spectroscopy (NIRS), demonstrate that 3-month-old babies show activity in Broca's area in the left hemisphere when hearing linguistic sounds, but not when exposed to non-linguistic stimuli, such as a flashing black and white checkerboard image.

---

4.   See http://www.utsc.utoronto.ca/~petitto/lab/projects1.html

At the same time, findings emerging from these imaging techniques indicate that the classical view of Broca's and Wernicke's areas is too simple and contained to convey the richness of activity in various parts of the brain, as well as the variety amongst individuals as to which parts of the brain show activity.[5] This is not to say that Broca's and Wernicke's areas are not vital for language production and comprehension, as they obviously are, but rather to point out that much more of the brain than initially thought is involved in language. In 2003, a group of researchers (Dronkers *et al.* 2007) published an article based on the results of MRI scanning of Leborgne and Lelong's brains (which Broca had carefully preserved). The scans show that the lesions suffered by these two men extended significantly into medial regions of the brain, including the superior longitudinal fasciculus, which is a pair of long bundles of neurons that connect the front and the back of the cerebrum. Other research has shown that also involved in language are subcortical structures, or structures which are located deeply below the cerebral cortex, such as the basal ganglia, which are involved in many functions, including cognitive processes and the planning and programming of voluntary movement. Philip Lieberman (2009) highlights the importance of the basal ganglia in aphasia, which never occurs unless there is damage to the ganglia and connecting neural matter.

Lieberman (2009) also writes on fascinating research into the FOXP2 gene, a gene closely related to the basal ganglia and to language. The FOXP2 gene produces a protein which helps to regulate other genes, and which is vital for the development of the brain, lungs and intestines. While it is not the only gene involved in everything that needs to develop in our bodies and our brains for language to exist in a fully functional way, it certainly plays an important role. It was discovered during investigation of a family (called the 'KE family') in England. Early research showed that half of the members of this four-generational family had difficulty with morphosyntactic features relating to number, gender and tense, leading to early speculations that they lacked some kind of grammar gene. However, Faraneh Vargha-Khadem and her team of researchers (1995) pointed out that the difficulties these family members have go beyond these features into other aspects of grammar, and further include highly defective articulation of speech sounds, as well as difficulty with lip/tongue movements such as swallowing, blowing,

---

5.   For a fascinating glimpse into the brain at work, see a video of Dr George Ojemann, Department of Neurological Surgery at the University of Washington School of Medicine, doing neurosurgery on an awake patient under local anesthesia, during which he maps the patients' cortical organization for language. Note: the video is not for the squeamish! http://www.youtube.com/watch?v=EeP14mM2UU8

and sucking (e.g. eating an ice cream cone). MRI and PET scans revealed a reduction in the size of the caudate nucleus, a part of the basal ganglia which is important for motor coordination and for processing information to send to other areas of the brain. In the affected family members, Broca's area was also smaller, and highly activated when doing speech tasks. Then, in 2001, genetic researchers (Lai *et al.* 2001) announced the discovery in all of the affected family members of a mutation of FOXP2.

Wada's test and brain imaging techniques have also contributed to a greater understanding of the role of both hemispheres in language comprehension and production. While the left hemisphere is thought of as the dominant one in terms of language, especially syntax and semantics, the right hemisphere certainly has a role to play. Neuropsychologists Kirsten Taylor and Marianne Regard (2003) display results from experiments which show that the right half of our brain is key in understanding metaphor and deciphering pictographic symbols, and also plays an important role in other semantic functions. A group of researchers at Ghent University, led by Dr Guy Vingerhoets (American Psychological Association, 2003), used fTCD to measure blood-flow velocity on participants who were asked to focus either on the content of what was said or on the emotions as they listened to a set of sentences. The research team found that, when participants were asked to focus on *what* was said, blood-flow velocity went up significantly on the left side of the brain. When participants paid greater attention to *how* something was said, i.e. to whether the tone of voice was happy, angry, sad, etc., velocity also went up significantly on the right side of the brain. Of course, blood-flow velocity remained high on the left side in these instances, as the left side of the brain is needed to process the meaning, and, according to the researchers, to be able to provide a word for the emotion. Studies of patients who have lesions in the right hemisphere lend further support for the role of that side of the brain in providing contextual, metaphorical and emotional meaning to language. Furthermore, in studies of Mandarin speakers, cognitive neuroscientist Sophie Scott and her research team[6] found that the right temporal lobe was activated when hearing words spoken in Mandarin, something that did not happen in the same way for speakers of English when hearing words spoken in English. This difference may be due to the importance of focusing on pitch in a tone language such as Mandarin.

Other evidence for the relationship between the brain and language has come from children who have had a hemispherectomy, a procedure which is recommended in cases of severe seizures and other brain disorders. In this procedure, one of the hemispheres of the cerebral cortex is removed, leaving

6.   See 'Chinese "takes more brainpower"' at http://news.bbc.co.uk/2/hi/health/3025796.stm

in place the basal ganglia, thalamus and brain stem. While this surgery has a life-long effect on the ability to move the limbs on the opposite side of the body of the hemisphere that is removed, case after case show that other functions, such as memory and language, can be taken over by the intact hemisphere, and, indeed, some of those functions may have already been taken over by the healthy hemisphere before surgery. There is the case of a boy, Alex, who at the age of eight and a half years had his left hemisphere removed. Up until the time of surgery, he had not developed speech, could only understand single words and simple commands, and his attempts to communicate were through gestures. However, after having the surgery, his language development improved drastically, and 'by age 10, could converse with copious and appropriate speech' (Rémillard and Cohen 2006: 194), including a number of long words. However, Alex, like other patients with an isolated right hemisphere, still has problems with some areas of comprehension related to more complex syntactic structures, suggesting the dominance of the left hemisphere for syntax. At the same time, the plasticity of the brain allows the right hemisphere to develop language fluency. Indeed, some of these children have gone on to graduate from college and lead the kinds of successful lives which call on complex uses of language.

What we can glean from the above discussion is that perhaps, rather than suggesting that the brain *has* a language organ, the brain has the ability to *be* a language organ. The size of our brains and the number and speed of neural connections allows for intricacy and complexity of motor movements as well as for categorical perception and greater working memory, which are key bases for language use and production, as well as for the development of language. We turn now to how language develops from before infancy and beyond.

7.2   First language acquisition

7.2.1   Child language development

EXERCISE 7.1

Make a list of the kinds of things you said as a small child; you might want to ask those involved in your upbringing what they remember.

EXERCISE 7.2

If you have been involved in the upbringing of a child from birth, make a list of aspects of his or her language development that you have observed.

Researchers on infant language, based on observational data from a great number of language environments, agree on the path followed by most babies who show normal development. In terms of the language input that they receive, babies are surrounded by language, even before they are born. From inside the womb, they are sensitive to the melodies of the voices they hear. As newborns, their interaction with their caregivers involves the latter using what is known as **child-directed speech**, features of which include high pitch, exaggerated intonation, repetition, short phrases, and a sing-song rhythm. It is difficult to know how babies perceive the language that is directed at them, but studies show that from a very early age they can distinguish familiar voices and are sensitive to the emotional cues expressed via the intonation contours of the streams of sound they hear.

Furthermore, babies are capable of **categorical perception**; that is, from sets of phenomena which are actually characterized by continuous flow, such as changing emotions expressed on a person's face or a stream of speech sounds, babies can perceive distinctions in discrete categories. This ability to perceive via categories is tested through a variety of methods, such as HASP (or High Amplitude Sucking Method), in which babies are observed to suck harder when they hear a novel sound,[7] or the Head Turn Preference Procedure,[8] where head turning indicates attention to a familiar phenomenon. Testing shows that babies can distinguish between voiced and voiceless sounds as early as between 1 and 4 months of age. They also can distinguish vowels that are phonemic in the language in which they are raised from the age of 4–6 months, with phonemic consonant recognition coming somewhat later. In fact, by 10–12 months babies have discovered the complete, finite set of sounds of the language(s) they are surrounded by, and can no longer distinguish speech sounds that are not phonemic in their language(s), something they do at younger ages.[9] Indeed, at 4 months, with exposure to sign language, babies are capable of discriminating non-sounded linguistic units, an ability which they are not capable of at 14 months if they have not had exposure to signs. As early as 7 months, babies can recognize words such as *dog* within sentences.

In terms of their linguistic production, new research suggests that babies cry in melodic patterns which are affected by the first language environment. A group in Germany, led by Birgit Mampe (2009), taped 30 French and 30 German babies crying, and analyzed their cries for melody contours. They

---

7.   See http://psych.rice.edu/mmtbn/language/sPerception/infantsucking_h.html
8.   See http://psych.rice.edu/mmtbn/language/sPerception/infantHeadturn_h.html
9.   See http://www.utsc.utoronto.ca/~petitto/LLD2006.pdf

discovered that the French babies produced cries with a rising melody contour, while the German babies produced cries with a falling melody contour. In addition to cries, babies also produce grunts, coos and sighs during their first months, which are taken as bases for interaction by their caregivers. Then, **babbling** begins at around 5–6 months, lasting for some 6–8 months. A fascinating aspect of babbling is that the sounds are made not to indicate some need; rather, babies seem to find pleasure in babbling for the sake of it. Furthermore, many caregivers respond to babbling as if it were initiation of a social exchange in their interactions with their babies, so they respond by verbalizing to the baby, leading the baby to babble more in response. Indeed, the sounds of babbling are 'language-like'; they tend to be open syllables, or consonants followed by vowels, with no ending consonant. Also, baby babble takes on prosodic features of the surrounding language in terms of intonation, stress and pitch. Studies show that babbling is also influenced by the surrounding language. That is, a baby raised in a French-speaking environment and a baby raised in an English-speaking environment will babble using a number of similar sounds, yet at the same time, and especially over time, there are sounds which distinguish one babbler from the other. With some degree of regularity, adults can recognize the first language environment when listening to tapes of babbling babies. At the same time, the early stages of babbling involve producing sounds which are not always part of the surrounding language environment, an ability which babies lose in the later stages of babbling. Caregiver interaction plays a role in this process of discovering the sounds of one's language. In English, during the babbling stage, people invariably hear the baby saying 'goo-goo ga-ga', while similar sounds will cause Spanish caregivers to assume that the baby is saying 'ajo' (which means 'garlic'). In each case, the caregivers will repeat the sounds as *they* hear them back to the baby, thus reinforcing the learning of the sounds the caregivers impose upon the babble. Also in these later stages, around 8–12 months, babies who are deaf stop babbling vocally. However, manual babbling occurs in babies who are exposed to sign language, whether deaf or hearing.

Sometime during the babbling stage, the **one-word stage** sets in. This stage begins in the latter part of the first year or early in the second year. Single words are used to express feelings and demands, and often the words are phonetically different from the word used between adults of the language, such as, in English, *binkie* (for 'blanket'), or *shooshie* (for 'cookie'). Furthermore, small children will regularize, for example, irregular plurals, such as *foots* for *feet*. The number and range of words used and meanings expressed by children in the one-word stage are relatively limited, mainly to who and what inhabit the world of the child, including words relating to people, clothing, food, toys, animals, vehicles and sounds.

During the **two-word stage**, which begins at some point during the second year, usually around 18 months, children begin to put words together in semantically and syntactically coherent strings, although without inflections for number, person or tense, such as *more milk, me go* or *allgone doggie*. Children at this stage tend not to use function words (see Section 4.1.2); thus their language is referred to as 'telegraphic speech'. One line of research amongst linguists who study child language development involves outlining the range of semantic functions expressed by children at the different stages of development, in terms of thematic roles (Chapter 3; Chapter 4); Roberta Golinkoff and Kathryn Hirsh-Pasek (2000: 151) provide a typology of meanings expressed (when context is taken into account), such as 'possessor+possessed' (e.g. *mommy sock*), agent + action (e.g. *car go*), and object + location (e.g. *sweater chair*), expanding slightly on a typology first put forth by Roger Brown (1973).

Then, sometime after the two-word stage has set in, the language of children explodes into developing at a rapid rate. Initially, children continue using telegraphic speech, leaving out function words, as with the two-word stage. (*Nini want that; Cathy build house*). From about the age of 2 onwards, children use an increasingly varied array of syntactic structures. Data from children speaking in English (Peccei 2006: 20–26) demonstrate developmental pathways through acquisition of, amongst other structures, plural –*s*, past tense markers, verb phrase complexity, noun phrase complexity, interrogative structures, and so on. Cross-linguistic research shows differences in age and order of mastery of different syntactic structures, yet, at the same time, whatever the language, by around the age of 5, children have pretty well mastered the syntax of their language. Of course, language development does not stop there; nor, indeed, does it ever stop, as human language development is a life-long process.

Furthermore, child language development does not involve simply an inventory of phonemes, syntactic structures and vocabulary.[9] Discourse development also occurs, as children learn to engage in increasingly appropriate pragmatic uses of language, as well as in how to take turns in conversation (including signaling cues for transition relevant places, see Section 2.5.2), uses which are, of course, culturally bound. Indeed,

9.   See Jean Stillwell Peccei (2006) for a full account of the 'what' of child language development. Peccei also includes a range of activities for investigating child language development.

much interaction with caregivers in English-speaking countries involves the latter telling children when to say 'please' and 'thank you', to 'ask nicely', not to interrupt, and to wait their turn. As early as the age of 2, toddlers can infer communicative intent; for example, if they hear an adult use an excited tone of voice in a given context, they can infer that a new word must refer to an object that has appeared in the context while the adult was away (Johnston 2005). In addition to the spoken language, most cultures in the present developed and developing world, literacy is an important aspect of language development; caregivers will often read to their children, and schools devote many hours a week to the task of promoting increasing ability to the reading and writing of increasingly complex texts throughout the schooling years.

7.2.2 Critical period hypothesis

Is there an age after which it is difficult to learn language if it has not yet been learned? The **critical period hypothesis**, promoted by Eric Lenneberg (1967), suggests that there is an optimal period of time for language acquisition to occur, especially in terms of grammatical structures. It is thought that the age after which acquisition becomes well nigh impossible, in the case of no or highly limited exposure to language, is around puberty. This hypothesis is difficult to test, principally for the obvious reason that it is not ethical to experiment with children, and it is not common to find a child who has not been exposed to language. A famous case is that of Genie (not her real name), a child who was raised in California to parents who locked her in a room from about the age of a year and a half. She was beaten by her father if she tried to speak, and, finally, at the age of 13 her mother left her husband, taking Genie with her. At that time, Genie had a vocabulary of around 20 words. She then went through a succession of foster care situations, and was the subject of research by linguists and psychologists, during which time she was taught spoken and sign language. While Genie advanced quite well with respect to expanding her repertoire of vocabulary, Susan Curtiss, who did her PhD research on Genie, concluded that Genie had great difficulty with syntax. Curtiss stresses that Genie did learn some morphosyntactic regularities of English, such as she knew to attach –*ing* to verbs and not nouns. However, Genie would say things like 'Applesauce buy store' (for 'Buy applesauce at the store') and 'Man motorcycle have' (for 'The man has a motorcycle') (Curtiss 1988: 83). At the same time, she did not learn to use pragmatic aspects of discourse, such as greetings, discourse markers, or vocatives. Given that Genie's case is not one solely of isolation from language, but also of emotional abuse and neglect, it is difficult to use her case as an example of a critical period for language development.[10]

Hemispherectomies in children and adolescents provide evidence that, during the developmental years (in one case, a 16-year-old girl), the brain has the plasticity to allow the right hemisphere (in the case of right-handed children) to take over the functions usually attributed to the left hemisphere, as remarkable language recovery has occurred in a number of these cases; however, in the case of adult hemispherectomy, aphasia always occurs. This difference in the ability of language development to take place suggests that there is a period after which language development becomes more difficult, especially with respect to syntactic structures; the reason may be because the brain loses plasticity in adulthood.

7.2.3   Theoretical perspectives on child language development

One theory of child language acquisition which has dominated much of the research in the field and which has been greatly influenced by the work and thinking of Noam Chomsky is that we are born with an underlying faculty which allows for the acquisition of basic grammatical relations and categories. Chomsky calls this faculty the **Language Acquisition Device** (LAD). Some call this the **innateness hypothesis**,[11] and it is based on the assumption that the grammar we end up acquiring goes far beyond the actual language that we are surrounded by, i.e. children are exposed to an impoverished stimulus, and out of that they acquire a sophisticated set of syntactic and morphological rules. Thus, the brain must have some kind of predisposition (or 'hardwiring' as it is sometimes called) for the acquisition of human language, some kind of innate grammatical knowledge. A correlation of this theoretical stance is that there must be a number of basic properties shared by all human languages, a notion which is captured in the Chomskyan tradition through the concept of Universal Grammar (see Chapter 8, *Formal Linguistics*, by Amaya Mendikoetxea). Those who support this theoretical stance are interested mainly in how children acquire (the terms 'acquisition' and 'acquire' are preferred over 'learning' and 'learn') syntactic structures. They argue that children do not acquire the fully-fledged syntactic system of

---

10. See Jones, Peter E. (no date) Contradictions and unanswered questions in the Genie case: a fresh look at the linguistic evidence. Available: http://www.feralchildren.com/en/pager.php?df=jones1995 for a critique of Curtiss' work with Genie.
11. Chomsky (2000) states that the innateness hypothesis is *not* his; in fact, he cannot imagine what it might refer to. He does argue for the LAD, or some 'Faculty of Language' (FL), an innate mental ability for language.

the language by imitation or reinforcement;[12] nor do they acquire it through carefully structured input from their caregivers who work at correcting errors in the children's output. The language environments in which children are exposed to language vary widely, and yet children ultimately acquire the syntactic system of the language(s) of their community. Furthermore, if children learned by imitation or reinforcement, then what they would be acquiring is a set of forms, rather than a set of grammatical rules; however, it is clear that children internalize their own rules along the way before internalizing those of the adult language system. Children produce words and forms which they have not heard adults say, forms such as *goed* and *feets,* and continue to produce them even after attempts at correction. In sum, the rapid rate at which children acquire a highly complex system of communication from the rather less than complete and representative language they hear suggests that humans are born with some kind of innate language faculty.

However, there is opposition to this view of language acquisition. Some researchers argue that there is no such thing as 'poverty of the stimulus'. Dwight Atkinson (2002) summarizes research that suggests that children experience between 12,000 and 15,000 hours of intensive contact with their caregivers over their early years. Also, some disagree with the very existence of the LAD. Research by, for example, Jenny Saffran, at the Infant Learning Laboratory at the University of Wisconsin-Madison,[13] suggests that the human brain has powerful statistical learning mechanisms that make language learning possible. That is, the brain has the potential to detect patterns in experiential data of all types, linguistic and non-linguistic, and to remember and learn from those patterns. Saffran and colleagues (1996) point out that all organisms, in order to survive, must be able to extract information quickly from their environments during their development. Some species have evolved complex neural mechanisms which allow them to develop adaptive behaviors regardless of the environment; that is, they have evolved mechanisms which are independent of the learning environment, as is the case with bat echolocation. Children obviously needs environmental input to develop language, as children who are not exposed to language, such as Genie, fail to develop it; thus human language

12.   Note that Chomsky's early work on language was a reaction to behaviorist approaches, which suggested that children were born as blank slates, and that language was, in essence, a learned set of behaviors.

13.   See http://www.waisman.wisc.edu/infantlearning/publications.htm for a full list of publications, most of which are available online.

is experience-dependent. Language acquisition research influenced by the Chomskyan tradition has downplayed (though not denied) that aspect of how we acquire language, and has given more importance to the presence of a language faculty, or language acquisition device, which would count as an experience-independent mechanism for language learning. Both theoretical perspectives acknowledge the need for both experience-independent and experience-dependent mechanisms, in other words, nature and nurture, in human language development; at the same time, the difference is more than simply the degree to which more importance is placed on one or another, as the Chomskyan tradition posits a language faculty as part of the human genetic endowment, while the statistical learning theorists suggest that part of the human genetic endowment is actually that humans are whizzes at finding statistical regularities in data such as language.

Saffron and her colleagues support their statistical learning theory with a number of studies, such as that of word segmentation, an aspect of language that must be learned; that is, babies are not born knowing that *pretty* and *baby* are words, while *tyba* is not. They suggest that there are certain statistical probabilities in languages with respect to phonotactics, or the possibilities for combining phonemes, as well as for combining syllables, and that children are exposed to these over and over through child-directed speech.[14] Basing experiments on babies' penchant for focusing on novel phenomena, Saffron played recordings of strings of nonsense syllables, combined into 'words' in regular ways, to babies, and then played recordings of 'words' and 'non-words' from the strings. The 8-month-old babies demonstrated longer listening times for the non-words, or part-words. In sum, the babies heard as novel the non-words, or part-words, but not those that fit the pattern of the 'words', suggesting that they had 'learned' to recognize patterns for the 'words' in the strings. Saffran further argues that this kind of learning based on recognition of units via statistical coherence takes place over other units of human action sequences, such as sequences of tones or visual patterns.

The theoretical stance on language development of Saffran and colleagues brings to mind that of researchers in corpus linguistics (see Chapter 8, *Corpus Linguistics*, by Michaela Mahlburg). Gordon Tucker (2007: 240) argues: 'A very basic fact of language is that speakers are constantly confronted with expressions that they have encountered, either fully or in part, in their

---

14. For example, the probability that *pre* is followed by *ty* is roughly 80% in speech to young infants: however, given that *ty* is word final, and can thus be followed by any number of syllables starting another word, the probability that *ty* is followed by ba, as in pretty baby is roughly 0.03% in speech to young infants.

previous linguistic experience'. While Tucker, like Saffran, is not arguing for language learning as a set of behaviors, he similarly argues that there are probabilities in our language use which set up expectations for what will follow what, what will occur after a certain word or set of words. Michael Hoey's (2005; no date) theoretical view of language development is that of **lexical priming**, which suggests that 'Every word is primed for use in discourse as a result of the cumulative effects of an individual's encounters with the word' (Hoey 2005: 13). That is, lexical priming refers to the expectation that we come to have of certain words and phrases to be used in company with other words (**collocation**), and in certain grammatical environments (**colligation**); furthermore, words have certain semantic and pragmatic associations. As we hear words and phrases (or 'chunks') used over and over, we come to form hypotheses about the ways we can use them, hypotheses which can bear out in our use of the words or not. You might hear the term *bachelor pad* but not *spinster pad*, for instance, as the first set of words are collocates, but the second are not. These more probabilistic views of language do not deny its creativity, but rather suggest that it is somewhat constrained by patterns of use, patterns which the human brain is adept at storing and drawing on for further use.

SINGLE SLICES   by Peter Kohlsaat

M. A. K. Halliday has influenced a great amount of research into child language development from a broader perspective than that of a focus on sounds, structures and words, or solely on the development of phonology and lexico-grammar. This research, based on systemic functional linguistic theory (see Chapter 3), focuses on how children, through social interaction, learn language, including its communicative functions. Thus, the developmental picture looks different than that sketched out in Section 7.2.1 in terms of *what* develops. Halliday (1975/2004) suggests that babies first operate on a two-level system of meaning; that is, one expression form is connected with one meaning, with no intervening system of morphology, syntax or vocabulary. At the same time, these **protolinguistic** signs are not combined together to create further meanings; rather, their functional meaning holds constant,[15] and they express meanings connected to basic needs or emotions. Several communicative functions can be gleaned from how babies use them, such as the instrumental function (*I want* – achieving goods and services), the regulatory (*do as I tell you* – to control the behavior of others), the interactional (maintain contact with others), and the personal (to express individuality and self-awareness). Thus, for Halliday (1975/2003: 33) 'the child has a linguistic system before he has any words or structure at all', as, by linguistic system, he includes functions as well as morphology, syntax and vocabulary.

Usually between 16 to 18 months, babies start the transition toward a three-level system, consisting of sounds which are words which have meanings. Claire Painter (2009), who has researched child language development within this theoretical perspective, explains that the broader metafunctions of language (see Chapter 3) emerge initially through intonation: that is, a child might use the same word to refer to the same thing (the ideational function) using different intonation patterns to signal a different interpersonal meaning (e.g. a statement or a demand). That is, young children begin to differentiate the ideational and interpersonal meaning via intonation, perhaps using a rising/level tone (see Chapter 2) to express 'I want' or a falling tone for 'I notice'. For example, *shooshie* might mean 'I want a cookie' or 'give me that cookie' or 'there's a cookie' or 'Mommy, take a bite of this cookie'. Children continue to develop the language system, as they grow in their ability to dialog with those who surround them, expressing mood choices (see Figure 1.1 in Chapter 1) and transitivity (see Chapter 3) initially via protostructures ('Daddy no', 'me go'), and ultimately developing the full system of the language(s) which they are surrounded by.

15. This lack of ability to combine meanings in novel ways is a major difference with adult language.

7.2.4   Bilingual language development

EXERCISE 7.3

Before reading this section, review Section 7.2 and consider how the information included there might apply to a child brought up with more than one language.

What happens in the case of a child who is brought up in an environment where more than one language is spoken? This situation is the case for most of the world's population. Studies on newborns suggest that babies are born with a preference for the language they heard spoken while still in the womb, and babies born to mothers who spoke two languages show equal preference for the two languages (Werker *et al.*, 2009). In terms of their brain development, according to William Ganong (2005: 274), fMRI reveals that children who learn two languages early in life use the same portion of Broca's area in linguistic tasks in both languages, while individuals who learn a second language as adults used an adjacent but separate portion of Broca's area from that of their first language for tasks in the second language. Also, a review of research on bilingual language development by Fred Genesee and Elena Nicoladis (2006) leads to the conclusion that there are certain aspects of language development which seem to hold constant whether children are brought up in a monolingual or bilingual environment, such as the onset of babbling, first words, and rate of vocabulary growth. Peter Bodycott (1993) shows the same systematic development of protolinguistic functions as those outlined by Halliday (see Section 7.2.3) in a bilingual child, and Genesee and Nicoladis (2006) also summarize findings that show that in terms of pragmatic abilities, bilingual children develop in similar ways to monolingual children.

At the same time, there are some differences. For example, in terms of recognition of phonemic vs. phonetic distinctions, as mentioned in Section 7.2.1, monolingual children stop recognizing phonetic distinctions which are not phonemic roughly by the end of their first year; however, the bilingual child takes longer (Genesee and Nicoladis, 2006). Genesee and Nicoladis also report that 11-month-old bilingual children did not distinguish between words and non-words in a head-turn study in which monolingual babies did. Janet Werker (2009) and her colleagues provide results of tests showing that bilingual babies take longer to distinguish between similar sounding words, which may be because bilinguals need to work out the phonetic inventories of two languages; some sound differences may be phonemic in one language and not in the other, resulting in a more complex learning environment.

Furthermore, the bilingual child exhibits code-mixing and transfer effects from one language to another. For example, Elisa, brought up by an English-speaking mother and a Spanish-speaking father, during her language development would at times mix the two in terms of phonology and syntax. For example, at the one-word stage, her protolinguistic sign for 'I want water' was [awatə], which sounded like a combination of 'agua' and 'water', thus ensuring that whichever caregiver was attending to her would respond to her need. When she was 6 years old, after being out in the sun, she looked in the mirror and pronounced 'I have my nose red', thus effectively using Spanish syntax (*Tengo la nariz roja*) but with English words. Diana, brought up in the same circumstances, would ask 'Can I touch the piano?', for 'Can I play the piano?', thus transferring a lexical item directly from the Spanish '¿Puedo tocar el piano?'

However, while there may be some initial delays in certain aspects of language development, these delays are not significant in their ultimate development. Even with respect to their early development, research by Laura Petitto and colleagues[16] and by Werker and her colleagues (2009) strongly suggests that bilingual children work out the systems of the languages they grow up with from the time they begin their development, whether it is across two spoken language or across two different modalities (i.e. signed and spoken language). In addition to providing the benefits of the ability to converse in more than one language and to understand the world through two linguistic and cultural perspectives, bilinguals also get a boost to the brain, as those who are brought up with another language (with a learning onset before the age of 5) have an altered brain structure, with increased gray matter.[17]

7.3   Second language development

EXERCISE 7.4

What experience have you had learning a second language? What do you think is the best way to learn another language?

---

16. See http://www.utsc.utoronto.ca/~petitto/LLD2006.pdf
17. Mechelli *et al.* (2004).

There is a great deal of controversy over the extent of our ability to learn another language after the initial childhood period of language development. Indeed, one controversial question is whether or not a critical period exists for second language learning. Michael Long (2005) argues that only by starting out as young children can people attain native-like proficiency levels, with different ages for different domains of language. For example, he suggests that a 'native-like' accent is impossible if first exposure to the language does not occur before the age of 12 (even the age of 6 for many people). The same is the case for lexical and collocational abilities: individuals who start learning a language after their mid-teens (again, for some people, after the age of six) will have persistent errors in the use of lexical items in terms of collocation and semantic extension. Finally, effective learning of syntax and morphology ends in the mid-teens.

At the same time, there is evidence that older learners are actually more effective than younger learners at certain aspects of second language development. Jasone Cenoz provides results from research in the Basque country which show that students who started learning English in the sixth grade of primary school at the age of 11 (16 years old at the time of the study) did better on a battery of tests than did students who had had the same number of hours of instruction but had started learning English in the third grade, at the age of 8 (13 years old at the time of the study). Cenoz suggests that this difference can be attributed to the greater cognitive maturity of the older students. Thus, one point of controversy is actually what we mean when we talk about learning another language. Often adults can achieve a very high level of literacy in another language, for example literary scholars or scientists from other language backgrounds who must write in English.

As with other aspects of language development, another key point of controversy is whether or not differences in ability to achieve is due more to nature or to nurture. Long suggests that older learners *cannot* achieve in ways that younger learners can, which would seem to provide support for a biological, or experience-independent, cause, such as a critical period. Much of the research in the field of second language acquisition (SLA) aligns itself with this more cognitive stance, in line with Chomsky's view of first language acquisition. Also as with first language acquisition, researchers in SLA look for common patterns in acquisition of various language structures in terms of phonology, morphology and syntax.

On the other hand, there are those who are more interested in researching other aspects of language learning which are more related to social interaction and environment. For example, in order to explain differences in attainment, some point to motivation and amount of contact with the new language between older and younger learners (e.g. Marinova-Todd *et al.* 2000), which are more experience-dependent factors. Older learners have a language through which they are accustomed to interacting and communicating, and thus the motivation to learn another language can be low. Furthermore, their interactions with and through the second language may be limited to a few hours a week in a classroom. Dwight Atkinson (2002) finds the SLA focus very limiting, as it is centered on what happens in the head and not on what happens in the world. It focuses on structural correctness as a measure for language achievement, ignoring the social interactional nature of language. He suggests that we should conceive of second language learning as both social and cognitive, which would mean that the enterprise of second language learning would need to include discourse and pragmatic concerns, as well as structural ones. In this sense, we can think of users of a second language who retain their first language accent when speaking the second language, and have errors in vocabulary and morpho-syntax, yet who are highly successful in their communicative uses of the second language. Our use of language also helps mark our identity, and thus not every second language learner sets their goals at 'native-like' fluency and accuracy.

7.4   Animals and language

> **EXERCISE 7.5**
>
> How would you define human language in a way which distinguishes it from all other forms of animal communication? That is, what defining traits separate human language from other forms of animal communication?

Conversations on human language, what it is and how human biology is configured to learn and produce it, often lead to comparisons with animal communication. The debate about whether or not animals have 'language' or could learn language is as lively as the rest of the debates about language, biology and learning. Once again, those debates rest in large measure on defining what language is, as for many language is what makes us humans different (for some, superior) to other species. There certainly are interesting parallels between human and animal communication in terms of aspects of language (dialects, functions, syntax) and in terms of brain configurations. There are obvious differences as well, in terms of how and what can be communicated.

7.4.1   Bees and dialects

David Crystal (2007) reports on research by Karl von Frisch into bee communication. Bees communicate to other bees in their hives by carrying out a series of movements, which von Frisch calls bee 'dancing'. When a bee discovers a food source, it returns to the hive and does a dance. If the food source is relatively close by, the bee does a round dance, circling alternately left and right. If the food source is farther away, the bee does a waggle dance, which involves moving in a straight line for a short distance, wagging its body from side to side; it then returns to the starting point via a semi-circular path and repeats the straight line movement, this time returning via a semi-circular path in the opposite direction. The pace of the dance indicates the proximity of the source: the farther away the source is, the fewer cycles per minute. The direction of the source is indicated by the direction of the line in which the bee waggles in relationship to the position of the sun. Von Frisch then carried out experiments with Austrian honeybees and Italian honeybees. There were differences between the two bee groups in terms of the shape of the dance; while the Austrian honeybees only danced in a circle, Italian bees did so only for short distances, using a 'sickle-shaped' dance for intermediate distances. Like the Austrian bees, the Italians did the waggle dance for longer distances; however, their tempo was slower than the Austrians. Because of this difference, when Austrian bees were put into the same hive as Italian bees, they misjudged the distance of the food source as indicated by the Italian bee dance, and looked for it farther away than it actually was. This misunderstanding across bee cultures led Von Frisch to suggest that bees have different dialects, influenced by their environment perhaps because of the size of the swarm and the coldness of the climate. This difference amongst bees suggests that their dance is not entirely innate, and also points towards the possibility of pattern recognition as necessary for learning how to communicate in other species.

7.4.2   Starlings and recursion

EXERCISE 7.6

Is the sentence 'People people cheat cheat' a syntactically acceptable sentence?

Research done at the University of Chicago and the University of California San Diego (Gentner *et al.* 2006) suggests that the species of bird *Sturnus vulgaris*, or the common European starling, uses recursion, a feature of human language, in fact, for Chomsky, **the** defining feature of human language, 'the only uniquely human component of the faculty of language' (Hauser *et al.* 2002: 1569). Recursion is the ability for one element of language to recur within an element of the same type; for example, at the level of the clause, we can embed clauses within clauses within clauses *ad infinitum*, such as 'This is the boy who loves the girl that bought the book that was written by the man that loves the girl that …'. We can also embed nominal groups within nominal groups, as in 'A room with a view of the church in the square'. The researchers recorded a single male starling's 'rattles' and 'warbles, and then combined them into 16 artificial songs, all of which followed one of two patterns. One of the patterns followed a 'finite-state' rule, which adds sounds only to the beginning or the end of a string. For example, the simple song '1 rattle + 1 warble' (or *ab*) could have added to it another rattle+warble (*abAB*). The other pattern followed a 'context-free' rule, which allows for sounds to be inserted into the middle of a string, so a rattle+warble could be inserted into the middle of *ab* for *aABb*. The researchers taught 11 adult birds to distinguish between the two sets. After thousands of trials, most of the starling subjects learned to distinguish the patterns; they had not simply memorized different patterns, as they could distinguish between the two types even in the case of entirely new sequences of rattles+warbles. The birds even treated differently 'ungrammatical' strings, or sequences which did not follow either set of established rules. Thus, the researchers argue that the birds learned a set of rules, and could apply those rules to new situations, showing that other animals share the ability for pattern recognition with humans. Also, they argue that the ability to classify sequences based on recursion is not uniquely human.

Recursion as the defining trait of human language also received a blow from Daniel Everett, a linguist who has worked the Pirahã people in Brazil, and who demonstrates that their language does not feature recursion. At the same time, the starlings in Gentner *et al.*'s research could have relied on counting sequences, rather than on detecting a recursive meaningful pattern. Even for humans, this kind of recursion is difficult to process, as, for example, in the phrase 'people people cheat cheat' (or 'people that people cheat also cheat'). These objections to Gentner *et al*'s research come from Ray Jackendoff, Mark Liberman, Geoffrey Pullum, and Barbara Scholz in a letter to the *Linguist List*,[18] a letter which they had written to *Nature*, where

18. http://www.linguistlist.org/issues/17/17-1528.html

Gentner *et al.*'s study was published, but which *Nature* declined to publish. Jackendoff *et al.* argue that what is unique to human language, rather than solely recursion is 'a very large learned vocabulary consisting of long-term memory associations between meanings and structured pronunciations plus varied phrasal syntax'. For others who research the ability for apes to learn human language, however, even that definition is too restrictive.

7.4.3   Apes and human language

Much of the debate about human language vs. animal communication centers on the genetic make-up and communicative abilities of primates. There have been a number of researchers who have focused their studies of language on chimpanzees and bonobos, given their common ancestry and closeness of DNA structure. Humans, chimps and bonobos descended from a single ancestor species some 6 or 7 million years ago, and the DNA match between these apes and humans is between 98% and 99%. Obviously, the differences are important, as evidenced by human achievements in art, literature, science, to mention only a few areas, as well as by differences in susceptibility to diseases such as AIDS and Alzheimer's. At the same time, there are similarities and differences in our brain structure and genetic make-up.

We saw earlier in this chapter that part of human language learning includes the ability to recognize patterns and the ability of perceive categories. Apes also can detect relational similarities amongst objects and can distinguish categories. Tests on apes have shown the ability to distinguish between consonant sounds, for example. William Ganong (2005: 273) points out that the brain of apes is similar to that of humans in terms of the presence of specialization of the hemispheres, with one, usually the left, showing specialization for categorical perception; this similarity in brain functional organization between humans and apes suggests that categorical perception existed before the emergence of human language. William Hopkins, a primate neuroanatomist at Emory University in Atlanta, has led research which shows that in bonobos, gorillas and chimpanzees, the left and right hemispheres of the brain show the same asymmetry as human brains do in the area corresponding to Broca's area; that is, this area in the left hemisphere of these animals is larger than the corresponding area on the right. Hopkins and his team (Hopkins *et al.*, 2008) further showed that this area is activated in chimps when they are involved in communicating through gestures, suggesting that the neurological substrates underlying language production in the human brain may have been present in the common ancestor of humans and chimpanzees. At the same time, the size and trajectory of the arcuate fasciculus, which connects various areas in the brain related to language, in humans differs from that of apes, meaning that there are more network fibers which play a role the language abilities of humans.

Furthermore, the FOXP2 gene, mentioned in Section 7.1 exists in other vertebrates as well as in humans, although the differences in the gene across species means that inserting the human version into mice causes a change in their brains in terms of synaptic plasticity; that is, the mice brains showed increased activity in connections between nerve cells with the human FOXP2 version of the gene (Lieberman, 2009). Another major difference between animals and humans is the human vocal apparatus; even if we transplanted a human brain into an ape, the ape would not be able to speak because of the positioning of their larynx, which is higher than that of humans. Thus, the human pharynx is longer than that of apes; also humans have a more flexible tongue. These differences mean that humans can produce a wide variety of vowels and consonants, which apes cannot. The position of the human larynx also means that we have the unfortunate ability to choke on our food, which leads Lieberman (2009: 802) to point out that, during our evolution 'a human tongue would be worse than useless unless the hominid in question also had cortico-basal ganglia circuits capable of executing the rapid, complex motor gestures that are necessary to produce articulate speech'. It is also worth noting the incredible trade-off that an increase in the ability to produce different kinds of sounds into more complex and meaningful strings gave us if it came with the price of accidental choking.

Because of the similarities between apes and humans, it is not surprising that apes have been a focal point of research into the ability of animals to learn language. Early experiments with chimps involved using behavior modification techniques in teaching chimps sign language. In these experiments, chimps such as Washoe and Nim Chimpsky were taught signs from American Sign Language over and over, and when they produced a sign similar to the target, they were rewarded. Much of this research was later used as a basis to deny that apes had the ability to produce anything even resembling human language, as chimps were thought to simply produce the signs they had been taught upon the presence of certain stimuli, as might be expected with behavioral modification. Indeed, an important understanding here is that of indexical vs. symbolic signs. Indexical signs connect one sign with one meaning, such as is the case in the protolinguistic signs of babies (see Section 7.2.1). So, for example, vervet monkeys will make a certain type of call if an eagle is sighted and another type of call if a leopard is approaching. For each there is one call equal to one meaning (Benson *et al*. 2005), and the initial understanding of chimp capabilities with language were seen to be limited to this type of sign indexicality. Human language goes beyond the indexical to the symbolic, in that it is a system, comprised of a set of symbols and a set of rules (or grammar – our morphosyntax) which governs the way in which these symbols are combined; the symbols of human languages can be combined in creative ways to convey new information. There are many researchers who argue that humans are the only species who communicate symbolically.

However, monkey calls are shown to exhibit more complexity than simple indexicality. For example, Diana monkeys and Campbell's monkeys also each produce eagle alarm calls, and Diana monkeys actually respond to Campbell's monkey calls by producing their own eagle alarm calls – they cannot reproduce the Campbell's calls, but they can interpret them to then issue their own calls. Furthermore, the Campbell's monkeys also produce what are known as 'boom' calls, which signal that a predator is near, but not yet close enough for danger. The Diana monkeys interpret this as well, and issue reduced alarm calls, unless, of course, the boom call is followed by an alarm call. Benson *et al.* connect these different ways of responding to the different metafunctions of language (see Chapter 3). In other words, the monkeys are using their communication system ideationally (by representing different kinds of experience), interpersonally (by initiating, sustaining or responding), and textually (by constructing salience through signaling new information through boom or alarm calls, or by moving from given to new information through boom^alarm calls). The system is limited to a fixed and small number of calls; however, Benson *et al.* suggest that a strong candidate for an evolutionary prerequisite to human language is the ability to differentiate between indexical signs, and then to combine them in different ways.

Work with bonobos also points to another important prerequisite to human language, which is that of social interaction. Apes are extremely social animals, as, of course, are humans. Thus contexts in cases where apes, especially bonobos, have been brought up interacting with humans show different outcomes than simple learning of indexical signs, produced upon demand. The work led by Susan Savage-Rumbaugh at the Language Research Center at Georgia State University as well as at the Great Ape Trust housed at Iowa State University has shown some extraordinary strides in communication between bonobos and humans, and has convinced even some highly skeptical scientists.[19] The bonobos at the center, such as Kanzi

19. For a fascinating explanation of Dr Stuart Shankar's experience in moving from skepticism to support for Savage-Rumbaugh's work, the podcast at http://www.podfeed.net/episode/ BSP-7+Bonobos+with+Dr.+Stuart+Shanker/1914323 is well worth listening to.

and Panbanisha, understand more complex syntax, and have combined language using a lexigram board, with gestures, facial expressions and gaze, in ways which allow them to create novel meanings. Benson *et al.* report on one conversation, involving a good deal of pronominal reference, including reference to Kanzi who is in another room, in which Panbanisha is able to interpret what is happening, showing that she is able to rely on clues in the discourse itself, and not just those available in the immediate context. Social interaction, as we saw at the beginning of Chapter 5, was vital for the survival of our ancestors, and for the development of language. Claire Painter writes about the 'interpersonal first' factor in the development of language in babies, and perhaps this factor plays a role as well in an increase in the ability of the bonobos to interact in more meaningful ways with their caregivers.

The debates included in this section and this chapter show a central question in linguistics: what is language? For some, it is defined mainly by its structural properties, its phonology, morphology and syntax, while for others, language is defined also by its communicative and interactional properties, by its functions. The differences in defining the object of study, language, lead to a wide variety of approaches for linguists to take when examining language, when describing it and when putting those descriptions to use in further analysis. These different approaches are taken up in Chapter 8.

7.5   Chapter outcomes

After having read this chapter carefully, discussed with others the content, and carried out the exercises, you should assess your ability to:

- ✓ Briefly define neurolinguistics.
- ✓ Explain the importance of aphasia to neurolinguistics.
- ✓ Explain the significance of Broca's and Wernicke's research to an understanding of the relationship between the brain and language.
- ✓ Give examples of the kind of agrammatism associated with lesions to Broca's area.
- ✓ Explain the broad differences in functions of the left and right hemispheres of the cerebral cortex.
- ✓ Describe the features of child-direct speech.
- ✓ Explain categorical perception and its relationship to language development.
- ✓ Describe each of the phases of child language development (babbling, first-word stage, two-word stage, telegraphic speech), including typical duration and age of onset.

✓ Explain what develops in child language development (phonologically, morphosyntactically, lexically, semantically/pragmatically).

✓ Discuss the critical period hypothesis.

✓ Compare and contrast in broad terms different theoretical perspectives on child language development: Chomsky's genetic endowment position, the statistical learning position, and lexical priming.

✓ Compare and contrast in broad terms an approach to language development which focuses on formal development (of phonology and lexico-grammar) of language to one which focuses on functional development of language.

✓ Compare and contrast language development in monolingual children with that of development in bilingual (or multilingual) children.

✓ Discuss some of the issues involved in the debates about whether younger or older learners are better at learning a second language.

✓ List some of the similarities and differences between humans and animals with respect to aspects of language (dialects, pattern recognition, recursion, indexicality).

7.6   References and further reading

Ahlsén, Elisabeth (2006) *Introduction to Neurolinguistics.* Amsterdam: John Benjamins.

American Psychological Association (2003, January 13) Our emotional brains: both sides process the language of feelings, with the left side labeling the 'what' and the right side processing the 'how'. *ScienceDaily.* Retrieved on February 12, 2010 from http://www.sciencedaily.com/releases/2003/01/030113072823.htm

Atkinson, Dwight (2002) Toward a sociocognitive approach to second language acquisition. *The Modern Language Journal,* 86(4): 525–545.

Benson, James D., Greaves, William S., Savage-Rumbaugh, Susan, Taglialatela, Jared P. and Thibault, Paul J. (2005) The evolutionary dimension: the thin end of the wedge – grammar and discourse in the evolution of language. In J. Benson and W. Greaves (eds) *Functional Dimensions of Ape-Human Discourse* 76–99. London and Oakville, CT: Equinox.

Bodycott, Peter (1993) Monitoring protolinguistic development in a bilingual context. *Asia Pacific Journal of Education,* 13(1): 35–49.

Brown, Roger (1973) *A First Language: The Early Stages.* Cambridge, MA: Harvard University Press.

Caplan, David (1987) *Neurolinguistics and Linguistic Aphasiology: An Introduction.* Cambridge: Cambridge University Press.

Carroll, David (1999). *The Psychology of Language, 3rd Edition.* Pacific Grove, CA.: Brooks-Cole.

Chomsky, Noam (1965) *Aspects of the Theory of Syntax.* Cambridge, MA: The MIT Press.

Chomsky, Noam (2000) *New Horizons in the Study of Language and Mind.* Cambridge: Cambridge University Press

Curtiss, Susan (1988) Abnormal language acquisition and grammar: Evidence for the modularity of language. In L. M. Hyman and C. N. Li *Language, Speech, and Mind: Studies in Honour of Victoria A. Fromkin* 81–102. London and New York: Routledge.

Crystal, David (2007) *By Hook or By Crook: A Journey in Search of English.* London: HarperCollinsPublishers.

Dronkers, Nina F., Plaisant, Odile, Iba-Zizen, Marie Thérèse and Cabanis, Emmanuel A. (2007) Paul Broca's historic cases: high resolution MR imaging of the brains of Leborgne and Lelong. *Brain* 130(5): 1432–1441. Retrieved on February 12, 2010 from http://brain.oxfordjournals.org/cgi/reprint/awm042v1?ck=nck

Everett, Daniel (2005) Cultural constraints on grammar and cognition in Pirahã. *Current Anthropology* 46(4): 621–646. Retrieved on February 12, 2010 from http://www.eva. mpg.de/psycho/pdf/Publications_2005_PDF/Commentary_on_D.Everett_05.pdf

Foster-Cohen, Susan H. (1999) *An Introduction to Child Language Development.* Upper Saddle River, NJ: Pearson Education.

Ganong, Wiliam F. (2005) *Review of Medical Physiology.* New York: McGraw Hill Professional.

Genesee, Fred and Nicoladis, Elena (2006). Bilingual acquisition. In E. Hoff and M. Shatz (eds), *Handbook of Language Development* 324–342. Oxford: Blackwell. Retrieved on February 12, 2010 from http://www.psych.mcgill.ca/perpg/fac/genesee/ HDBK%20BFLA%20FINAL.pdf

Gentner, Timothy Q., Fenn, Kimberly M., Margoliash, Daniel and Nusbaum, Howard C. (2006) Recursive syntactic pattern learning by songbirds. *Nature* 440(27): 1204–1207.

Golinkoff, Roberta M. and Hirsch-Pasek, Kathryn (2000) *How Babies Talk: The Magic and Mystery of Language in the First Three Years of Life.* New York: Plume Publishers.

Goodglass, Harold (1993) *Understanding Aphasia.* San Diego, CA: Academic Press.

Halliday, M. A. K. and Webster, Jonathan (2004) *The Language of Early Childhood.* London: Continuum.

Hauser, Marc D., Chomsky, Noam and Fitch, W. Tecumseh (2002) The faculty of language: what is it, who has it, and how did it evolve? *Science*, 298(5598): 1569–1579.

Hoey, Michael (no date) Lexical priming and the properties of text. Retrieved on February 12, 2010 from http://www.monabaker.com/tsresources/Lexical PrimingandthePropertiesofText.htm

Hoey, Michael (2005) *Lexical Priming: A New Theory of Words and Language.* London: Routledge.

Hopkins, William D., Taglialatela, Jared P., Megeurditchian, Adrien, Nir, Talia., Schenker, Natalie M. and Sherwood, Chet C. (2008) Gray matter assymetries in chimpanzees as revealed by voxel-based morphology. *NeuroImage*, 42: 491–497.

Ingram, John C. L. (2007) *Neurolinguistics: An Introduction to Spoken Language Processing and its Disorders.* Cambridge: Cambridge University Press.

Johnston, Judith (2005) Factors that influence language development. *Encyclopedia on Early Childhood Development*. Montreal, Quebec: Centre of Excellence for Early Childhood Development. Retrieved on February 12, 2010 from http://www.enfant-encyclopedie.com/Pages/PDF/JohnstonANGxp.pdf

Lai Cecilia S., Fisher Simon E., Hurst Jane A., Vargha-Khadem, Faraneh and Monaco, Anthony P. (2001) A forkhead-domain gene is mutated in a severe speech and language disorder. *Nature* 413(6855): 519–523.

Lamb, Michael E., Bornstein, Marc H. and Teti, Douglas M. (2002) *Development in Infancy: An Introduction*. Mahwah, NJ: Lawrence Erlbaum Associates.

Lenneberg, Eric (1967) *Biological Foundations of Language*. New York: John Wiley & Sons, Inc.

Lieberman, Philip (2009, May 29) FOXP2 and human cognition. *Cell*, 137(5): 800–802. Retrieved on February 12, 2010 from http://people.psych.cornell.edu/~jec7/pcd%20pubs/liebermanFOXP2.pdf

Long, Michael (2005) Problems with supposed counter-evidence to the Critical Period Hypothesis. *IRAL* 43(4): 287–317.

Mampe, Birgit, Friederici, Angela D., Christophe, Anne and Wermke, Kathleen (2009) Newborns' cry melody is shaped by their native language. *Current Biology*, 19(23): 1994–1997.

Martin, G. Neil, Carlson, Neil R. and Buskist, William (2007) *Psychology*. Harlow: Pearson Education.

Marinova-Todd, Stefka H., Marshall, D. Bradford and Snow, Catherine E. (2000) Three misconceptions about age and L2 learning. *TESOL Quarterly*, 34(1): 9–34.

Mechelli, Andrea, Crinion, Jenny T., Noppeney, Uta, O'Doherty John, Ashburner, John, Frackowiak, Richard S. and Price, Cathy J. (2004) Neurolinguistics: Structural plasticity in the bilingual brain. *Nature* 431: 757.

Painter, Claire (2009) Language development. In M. A. K. Halliday and J. Webster (eds) *Continuum Companion to Systemic Functional Linguistics* 87–103. London, Continuum.

Painter, Claire (2004) The 'interpersonal first' principle in child language development. In G. Williams and A. Lukin (eds) *The Development of Language: Functional Perspectives on Species and Individuals* 137–157. London and New York.

Peccei, Jean S. (2006) *Child Language: A Resource Book for Students*. London and New York: Routledge.

Rémillard, Stephen and Cohen, Henri (2006) Sturge–Weber–Dimitri syndrome and language. In K. Brown (ed.), *Encyclopedia of Language and Linguistics*, 2nd edition. Oxford: Elsevier. Retrieved on February 12, 2010 from http://www.psycho.univ-paris5.fr/IMG/pdf/Remillard.pdf

Saffran, Jenny R. (2003) Statistical language learning: mechanisms and constraints. *Current Directions in Psychological Science*, 12(4): 110–114. Retrieved on February 12, 2010 from http://www.waisman.wisc.edu/infantlearning/publications/saffrancurrentdir.pdf

Saffran, Jenny R., Aslin, Richard N. and Newport, Elissa L. (1996). Statistical learning by 8-month-old infants. *Science*, 274(5294): 1926–1928.

Taylor, Kirsten I. and Regard, Marianne (2003) Language in the right cerebral hemisphere: contributions from reading studies. *News in Physiological Sciences*, 18(6): 257–261.

Tucker, Gordon (2007) Exposure, expectations and probabilities: implications for language learning. In A. McCabe, M. O'Donnell, M. and R. Whittaker (eds) *Advances in Language and Education* 242–253. London: Continuum.

Vargha-Khadem, Faraneh, Watkins, Kate, Alcock, Katie, Fletcher, Paul and Passingham, Richard (1995) Praxic and nonverbal cognitive deficits in a large family with a genetically transmitted speech and language disorder. *Proceedings of the National Academy of Sciences of the United States of America*, 92(3): 930–933. Retrieved on February 12, 2010 from http://www.pnas.org/content/92/3/930.full.pdf+html

Werker, Janet F., Byers-Heinlein, Krista, and Fennell, Christopher T. (2009) Bilingual beginnings to learning words. *Phil. Trans R. Soc. B*, 364(1536): 3649–3663. Retrieved on February 12, 2010 from http://rstb.royalsocietypublishing.org/content/364/1536/3649.full

8 Fields of Linguistics

It is unlikely that any one account of language will be appropriate for all purposes. A theory is a means of action, and there are many very different kinds of action one may want to take involving language. (M. A. K. Halliday 1994: xxix)

8.1 Clinical Linguistics

David Crystal, Honorary Professor of Linguistics at the University of Bangor

I can't think of a more rewarding field of applied language studies than the clinical and remedial domain. Linguistic communication is what makes us fully human, shaping our thoughts, fostering our personal relationships, and identifying our communities. It is, accordingly, the most savage of handicaps when someone fails to develop normal abilities in speaking, listening, reading, or writing, or loses these abilities after a lifetime of relying upon them. And those who work with children and adults to alleviate the isolation and frustration caused by speech and language deprivation are, in my view, the nobility in the therapeutic professions.

Clinical linguistics plays its part in this noble enterprise: the application of the linguistic sciences to the study of language disability in all its forms. The term isn't restricted to medical conditions. Language disability has a wide variety of causes, only some of which are demonstrably medical. We are just as likely to encounter a person with a serious linguistic difficulty in a school classroom, a pre-school playgroup, a young adult training centre, or a home for the aged. The professionals who are involved in the care and treatment of language-handicapped people also illustrate a wide range of backgrounds: they include speech and language pathologists/therapists, school-teachers, educational and clinical psychologists, pediatricians, and social workers. A young child with a language disability may attend a hospital clinic in the morning, receiving help from a speech and language clinician, then go to school in the afternoon and receive further help from a teacher. Clinical linguistics, as a branch of applied linguistics, was devised without reference to the social contexts in which intervention takes place, being focused specifically on the nature of the impaired linguistic system within the individual.

The history of language pathology, and the identification of linguistic symptoms, has been a reflection of the history of ideas in linguistics. Impressionistic phonetic observations of the utterances of aphasic individuals were first made by neurologists in the late nineteenth century (see Chapter 7). By the mid-twentieth century these had been superseded by more systematic transcriptions, especially when a cadre of phonetically trained speech and language professionals came into being. By the 1950s phonetic descriptions were being routinely supplemented by phonological analyses. From the late 1950s, tests of language disability began to take into account basic morphological contrasts; and in the 1960s the first serious attempts at sentence classification began to be made. Sophisticated syntactic accounts of disability emerged during the 1970s, and since then there have been sporadic yet insightful applications of notions from semantics and pragmatics.

The chief aim of clinical linguistics is to provide the clinician or remedial teacher with increasing levels of insight and confidence in arriving at linguistic decisions, and it does this in several ways. It clarifies areas of (especially terminological) confusion found in the traditional classification of disability. It provides ways of describing and analysing the linguistic behaviour of patients, and of the clinicians and others who interact with them. It provides a classification of patient linguistic behaviours, as part of the process of differential diagnosis, and devises more sophisticated schemes of assessment. And, most important of all, it formulates hypotheses for the remediation of abnormal linguistic behaviour, and follows them through as therapy or teaching steadily proceeds.

Clinical linguistics has been operating along these lines since the late 1960s. There are now several introductory books on the subject, a growing number of case studies, a major journal (*Clinical Linguistics and Phonetics*), and a professional association (the International Clinical Linguistics and Phonetics Association). However, although all areas of linguistic structure and use have received some investigation, certain areas are still much neglected. Semantics has received the least attention, and I hope, as the subject progresses, we will see far more studies of this domain, and especially of the huge mountain of vocabulary, which so many find difficult to climb.

Readings

Ball, Martin, Perkins, Michael, Müller, Nicole and Howard, Sara (eds) (2008) *The Handbook of Clinical Linguistics*. Oxford: Blackwell.
Crystal, David (1981/9) *Clinical Linguistics.* Vienna: Springer-Verlag/London: Whurr.

8.2   Cognitive Linguistics

Dirk Geeraerts, Chair, Theoretical Linguistics, University of Leuven, Belgium

If you are fascinated by how words and expressions categorize the world; if you are intrigued by how linguistic utterances build up meaning and construe a certain perspective on reality; if you are enthralled by how metaphorical patterns and other cognitive models pervade our use of language – then Cognitive Linguistics will be your thing. In the landscape of current theoretical linguistics, it is the approach that most explicitly and systematically focuses on meaning, in the broadest possible sense of 'meaning'. As it says in the Editorial Statement of the very first issue of the journal *Cognitive Linguistics*, published in 1990, this theoretical framework sees language 'as an instrument for organizing, processing, and conveying information' – as something primarily semantic, in other words.

Now, it may seem self-evident to you that a 'cognitive' approach to language primarily addresses matters of meaning, but if you are familiar with generative grammar and the many theories that were inspired by Chomskyan linguistics (see Chapter 4), you will know that this is a theory that thinks of language primarily in formal terms: as a collection of formal, syntactic structures and rules, or constraints on such structures and rules. And generative grammar is definitely also a 'cognitive' conception of language, one that attributes a mental status to the language. So we have to be careful with the term *cognitive* in *Cognitive Linguistics*. It not only signals that language is a psychologically real phenomenon, but also that the processing and storage of information is a crucial design feature of language. Linguistics is not just about knowledge of the language (that's the focus of generative grammar), but language itself is a form of knowledge – and it has to be analyzed accordingly, with an emphasis on meaning.

At the same time, Cognitive Linguistics is not the only linguistic approach focusing on meaning: Functional Linguistics goes in the same direction, and further, formal semantics is clearly a semantically oriented approach as well. It lies beyond the scope of this short introduction to provide a systematic comparison with these other semantic approaches, but you will certainly be interested in what is particular about the way in which Cognitive Linguistics deals with meaning. Each of the following characteristics says something specific about the way Cognitive Linguistics thinks about meaning.

1. *Linguistic meaning is about creating perspectives.* Meaning is not just an objective reflection of the outside world; it is a way of shaping

that world. You might say that it construes the world in a particular way, that it embodies a perspective onto the world. The easiest way to understand the point is to think of spatial perspectives showing up in linguistic expressions, and the way in which the same objective situation can be construed linguistically in different ways. Think of a situation in which you are standing in your back garden and you want to express where you left your bicycle. You could then both say *It's behind the house* and *It's in front of the house*. These would seem to be contradictory statements, except that they embody different perspectives. In the first expression, the perspective is determined by the way you look: the object that is situated in the direction of your gaze is in front of you, but if there is an obstacle along that direction, the thing is behind that obstacle. In the second expression, however, the point of view is that of the house: a house has a canonical direction, with a front that is similar to the face of a person. The way a house is facing, then, is determined by its front, and the second expression takes the point of view of the house rather than the speaker, as if the house were a person looking in a certain direction.

2. *Linguistic meaning is dynamic and flexible.* Meanings change, and there is a good reason for that: meaning has to do with shaping our world, but we have to deal with a changing world. New experiences and changes in our environment require that we adapt our semantic categories to transformations of the circumstances, and that we leave room for nuances and slightly deviant cases. For a theory of language, this means that we cannot just think of language as a more or less rigid and stable structure – a tendency that is quite outspoken in twentieth century linguistics. If meaning is the hallmark of linguistic structure, then we should think of those structures as flexible.

3. *Linguistic meaning is encyclopedic in nature.* The meaning we construct in and through the language is not a separate and independent module of the mind, but it reflects our overall experience as human beings. Linguistic meaning is not separate from other forms of knowledge of the world that we have, and in that sense it is encyclopedic and non-autonomous: it involves knowledge of the world that is integrated with our other cognitive capacities. There are at least two main aspects to this broader experiential grounding of linguistic meaning. First, we are embodied beings, not pure minds. Our physical nature influences our experience of the world, and this experience is reflected in the language we use. The *behind/in front of* example again provides a clear and simple illustration: the perspectives we use to conceptualize the

scene derive from the fact that our bodies and our gaze have a natural orientation, an orientation that defines what is in front of us and that we can project onto other entities, like houses. Second, however, we are not just biological entities: we also have a cultural and social identity, and our language may reveal that identity, i.e. languages may embody the historical and cultural experience of groups of speakers (and individuals).

Taken together, these features carve out a broad domain of investigation, rather than a systematic and unified theory. Within that domain, a central position is occupied by topics like categorization, polysemy, metaphor, metonymy, cognitive models, image schemas, radial networks, conceptual integration, constructions and frames, language and thought, language and culture, language in the context of actual use. Perhaps there might be something of interest for you too?

Readings

Evans, Vyvyan and Green, Melanie (2006) *Cognitive Linguistics. An Introduction.* Mahwah, NJ: Lawrence Erlbaum Associates.

Geeraerts, Dirk (ed.) (2006) *Cognitive Linguistics: Basic Readings.* Berlin/New York: Mouton de Gruyter.

Geeraerts, Dirk and Cuyckens, Hubert (eds) (2007) *The Oxford Handbook of Cognitive Linguistics.* New York: Oxford University Press.

Kristiansen, Gitte, Achard, Michel, Dirven, René and Ruiz de Mendoza Ibáñez, Francisco J. (eds) (2006) *Cognitive Linguistics: Current Applications and Future Perspectives.* Berlin/New York: Mouton de Gruyter.

Taylor, John R. (2003) *Linguistic Categorization.* Oxford: Oxford University Press.

Ungerer, Friedrich and Schmid, Hans-Jörg (2006) *An Introduction to Cognitive Linguistics.* Harlow: Pearson Longman.

8.3 Computational Linguistics

Mick O'Donnell, Universidad Autónoma de Madrid

Computational Linguistics involves the use of computers for the modeling and processing of human language. In part, computational linguistics can include linguists exploring the nature of language by modeling it on a computer (writing grammars, preparing lexicons, etc.). More often, however, computational linguistics is application-oriented, with the goal to produce computer programs which can understand or produce human language. Common applications involve speech processing (speech synthesis, speech recognition, human-computer dialogue systems), and text processing (parsing of text to syntactic or semantic levels, generation of text from a database, document classification). Applications which can be applied to both text and speech include information extraction (extracting key information from text or speech) and machine translation.

In the more traditional systems, linguists provide the computer with knowledge of language (lexicons, grammars, dialogue models, etc.), and computer scientists write computer programs which can use this knowledge to process text or speech. In more recent work, computational linguists try to derive this knowledge of language directly from speech or text corpora (statistical modeling; see Corpus Linguistics, this chapter). For instance, to derive a model of how to translate English to Spanish, the system is fed a large set of English texts and their translations in Spanish, and the system identifies the different ways in which each English word or phrase can be translated.

Computational linguistics is usually a group effort, because different skills are required. A typical team will include linguists with knowledge of language, computer scientists with understanding of programming, and computational linguists to bridge between the two. There are however some tools which linguists can use without being able to program. For instance, the Stanford Parser Grammatical Relation Browser (Bou 2009) provides a simple interface to view the syntactic parses of your own texts.

For a quick overview of computational linguistics see the Wikipedia entry (http://en.wikipedia.org/wiki/Computational_linguistics). For a good introduction to computational linguistics, see Jurafsky and Martin (2008). For the basic algorithms of statistical language processing, see Manning and Schütze (1999).

Readings

Bou, Bernard (2009) *Stanford Parser Grammatical Relation Browser*. Retrieved on 4 January 2010 from http://grammarbrowser.sourceforge.net/

Jurafsky, Daniel, and Martin, James H. (2008) *Speech and Language Processing: An Introduction to Natural Language Processing, Computational Linguistics, and Speech Recognition. Second Edition*. Upper Saddle River, NJ: Prentice-Hall.

Manning, Christopher D. and Schütze, Hinrich (1999) *Foundations of Statistical Natural Language Processing*. Cambridge, MA: MIT Press.

8.4   Contrastive Linguistics

Jorge Arús Hita, Universidad Complutense de Madrid

Contrastive Linguistics involves the study or description of linguistic phenomena in usually two (although sometimes more) languages, either for typological contrast or to gain insights applicable to other fields of language studies/linguistics such as Second Language Teaching and Translation Studies, or linguistic theory in general. If the goal of the contrast has to do with diachronic aspects, for example to establish relationships between languages, then we are then no longer in the realm of Contrastive Linguistics but in that of Comparative Linguistics, a linguistic field in its own right.

Languages can be contrasted at different levels, i.e. phonological, word, group, clause or discourse. The unit or units of study will depend on the theoretical approach within which the contrast is undertaken. From a functional point of view, for instance, different aspects of their interpersonal, experiential or textual systems may be contrasted.

In its narrowest sense, Contrastive Linguistics caters for Second Language Teaching by pointing out those areas in which linguistic transfer from the L1 to the L2 is likely to happen and/or why it happens. In a wider sense, whole languages may be described following the same theoretical framework (as in Caffarel *et al.* 2004), and those descriptions be made available for other – or the same – linguists to carry out their contrastive analysis based on those descriptions. On occasions, the contrastive analysis of one language is modeled on the description of another, which allows for a better comparison. This is called 'Transfer Comparison', the method employed by Lavid *et al.* (2010) in the contrastive description of Spanish and English.

The evolution of Contrastive Linguistics has gone hand in hand with that of general linguistic theory. This means that, to a great extent, contrastive studies rely nowadays on the exploitation of linguistic corpora from which they obtain their data. Corpus Linguistics and Contrastive Linguistics are therefore two fields with a high degree of interdependency, as attested by the existence of bibliography (e.g. the volume edited by Granger *et al.* 2003) and academic courses devoted to this dual field, as well as the growing number of parallel and comparable corpora.

There is extensive bibliography related with Contrastive Linguistics. Among the books that had an impact in the earliest times of the discipline – always in connection with Second Language Teaching, its reason for being in its early days, mainly in the United States – two stand out: Fries (1945) and Lado (1957). Numerous works have been devoted to the field since. A good reference to get an overview of the different possibilities existing within Contrastive Linguistics is Fisiak (1980), compiler of a number of other well-known volumes on Contrastive Linguistics. More recent theoretical references, besides those cited above, include Botley *et al.* (2000), Altenberg and Granger (2002) and Willems *et al.* (2004). The number of applied works is so vast and concerns such a variety of languages that an attempt to provide a representative bibliography here would be futile.

The opportunities that the field of Contrastive Linguistics opens to the researcher are wide-ranged. The great number of existing languages allows multiple contrastive combinations. From an applied perspective, fields such as the above-mentioned Second Language Teaching and Translation Studies, along with linguistic theory in general, are always in need of new insights that help them meet new challenges. Many of those insights are provided by research in Contrastive Linguistics.

Readings

Altenberg, Bengt and Granger, Sylviane (eds) (2002) *Lexis in Contrast*. Amsterdam: Benjamins.

Botley, Simon P., McEnery, Anthony M. and Wilson, Andrew (eds) (2000) *Multilingual Corpora in Teaching and Research*. Amsterdam: Rodopi.

Caffarel, Alice, Martin, James. R. and Matthiessen, Christian M. I. M. (2004) *Language Typology: A Functional* Perspective. Amsterdam: Benjamins.

Fisiak, Jacek (ed.) (1980) *Theoretical Issues in Contrastive Linguistics*. Amsterdam: John Benjamins.

Granger, Sylviane, Lerot, Jacques and Petch-Tyson, Stephanie (eds) (2003) *Corpus-based Approaches to Contrastive Linguistics and Translation Studies*. Amsterdam and New York: Rodopi.

Fries, Charles (1945) *Teaching and Learning English as a Foreign Language*. Ann Arbor, MI: University of Michigan Press.

Lado, Robert (1957) *Linguistics across Cultures: Applied Linguistics for Language Teachers*. Ann Arbor, MI: University of Michigan Press.

Lavid, Julia, Arús, Jorge and Zamorano, Juan Rafael (2010) *Systemic Functional Grammar of Spanish: A Contrastive Study with English*. London: Continuum.

Willems, Dominique, Defrancq, Bart, Colleman, Timothy and Noel, Dirk (2004) *Contrastive Analysis in Language: Identifying Linguistic Units of Comparison*. Houndmills: Palgrave Macmillan.

8.5 Corpus Linguistics

Michaela Mahlberg, University of Nottingham

Corpus linguistics is a relatively recent field of linguistics, its development being closely linked to developments in computing. Corpus linguistics investigates language on the basis of electronically stored samples of naturally occurring language. When such samples are collected and stored in a principled way in order to address linguistic questions, we talk about a 'corpus'. Corpora can contain written language, e.g. from newspapers, textbooks, novels, leaflets, essays written by language learners, etc. as well as transcriptions of spoken language, e.g. from conversations, classroom discourse, interviews, TV-shows. Recent developments also include the compilation of video corpora and sign language corpora. Additionally, other electronic collections of texts that were not specifically designed as a corpus (e.g. archives or the web) can still form the basis for corpus linguistic studies.

The empirical basis of corpus linguistics has two main implications for the questions the linguist aims to investigate. First, by using natural data, corpus linguistics emphasizes the social dimension of language. The texts in a corpus are texts that are used by people to interact. In contrast to made-up examples, they are linked to real communicative situations. So corpus linguistics can contribute to the investigation of what people do with language and how they view the world. Second, corpus data is stored electronically in a format that allows further processing with computer tools. The data can be searched and displayed in a number of ways, and the computer makes it possible to easily count words. Thus a key feature of corpus linguistics is the quantitative investigation of linguistic phenomena. A researcher may be interested, for instance, in the frequency of modal verbs over time, or in differences in the use of hedges by men and women.

A basic but important aspect of the quantitative investigation of corpus data is the observation of repetitions. Repeated patterns of words provide information on the different meanings of words. Below is a concordance for the word *hand*. A concordance is a display format that shows a search word, here *hand*, with a specified amount of text around it. By sorting the words around the search word, e.g. in alphabetical order according to the first word of the right of the search word, we begin to discover patterns. Lines 16 to 19, for instance, show that *hand* is repeatedly found together with *luggage*, or lines 24 to 26 illustrate the pattern *hand over.* Such 'collocations', i.e. repeated co-occurrences of words within a given span, show that meanings of words are associated with the patterns they are found in.

A concordance, such as the one for *hand*, highlights the 'co-text' of a word: the words on its left and right. The KWIC format, i.e. 'key word in context' format of a concordance, thus focuses on the similarities between words across a number of texts: when you study the concordance of *hand* you will not normally read all 30 texts from which the 30 concordance lines are taken. The patterns in a concordance are also better visible the more data you have, which is one reason why, especially for lexicography, large general corpora containing several hundred millions words are needed. However, corpus linguists have also become more and more interested in looking at the relationship between words and the texts these words come

1	expected that Henry's sleight of	hand	during the France-Ireland play-off
2	January 20, 2010 A big	hand	for the little lady Miles
3	as Diego Maradona gets another	'hand	from God' Gabriele Marcotti,
4	Prisoners found drinking anti-swine flu	hand	gel to get drunk
5	Home Health Health News Alcoholic	hand	gels removed from hospitals after
6	Wasps' Lemi says sorry as	hand	gesture makes waves By Chris
7	people can only communicate with	hand	gestures, they speak a kind
8	Topics How about that? Bionic	hand	gives car accident student new
9	Python film prop for a	hand	grenade. By Matthew Moore
10	Magic gives Paul Nicholls strong	hand	in Champion Chase with Ascot
11	shows it has the upper	hand	in relations with Britain Recent
12	Obama: The Democrats strengthen their	hand	in the Senate Democrats
13	after racing with an injured	hand	in today's slalom in Austria.
14	British 'have gained the upper hand'	in fight for Afghanistan's Kajaki
15	football party gets out of	hand	It was always going to
16	Home Travel Columnists Travel advice:	hand	luggage restrictions Airline
17	Airlines' limit on liquid in	hand	luggage to be lifted Ban
18	News Virgin Atlantic calls for	hand	luggage review after airliner terror
19	December 26, 2009 US introduces	hand	luggage restrictions after alleged bomb
20	MPs' expenses MPs' expenses: police	hand	more files of evidence to
21	1, 2009 Barack Obama extends	hand	of friendship to Muslim world
22	Barton offers no apology but	hand	of friendship to Alan Shearer
23	Immigration and asylum Michael Palin's	hand	of friendship gives asylum seekers
24	Judge urges Charity Commission to	hand	over George Galloway papers Dominic
25	Should you	hand	over pocket money to children
26	Media Group Lord Heseltine to	hand	over running of Haymarket to
27	The filthy business of	hand	sanitisation Research reveals a US
28	wants a flu jab and	hand	sanitiser before the Christmas rush
29	Times May 10, 2009 Are	hand	sanitisers winning the war on
30	Families > Health News Sales of	hand	sanitizers surging ahead of flu

from. So in addition to general corpora, more specific corpora also provide valuable data. The concordance lines for *hand* shown above were retrieved using WebCorp, a corpus search engine searching the web for occurrences of a word. WebCorp allows you to focus on a selection of texts that can be regarded as a 'specific' corpus. In this case, the search was limited to British broadsheet newspapers, and more specifically, to sites that were updated in the six months before writing this section. Examples such as *hand gels/ sanitisation /sanitisers* reflect the topicality of the newspaper articles they are taken from: the repeated occurrence of these examples is to some extent due to references to swine flu – the pandemic that hit the world in 2009.

A characteristic feature of corpus work is that it is comparative. When you analyze a concordance you compare the individual lines to find patterns, but it is also possible to compare the distribution of words across different corpora. Even for a word with a seemingly straightforward meaning such as *hand*, patterns vary according to genre and can even be specific to individual texts. If you search for *hand* in *Our Mutual Friend*, a novel by Charles Dickens, you will find the pattern *his hand to his forehead* characterizing the character Twemlow. To investigate patterns that cannot be identified on the basis of repetitions of words alone, corpora can be annotated. Annotation is information on linguistic categories that is added to a corpus, e.g. words can be annotated for word class, or for the semantic field they belong to, or for the paragraph they occur in. Such annotation can then be used to find out how many adjectives a text contains, or whether a word has a tendency to occur in the first paragraph of a text.

The area where corpus linguistics seems to have had the greatest impact so far is lexicography. Since the pioneering work of John Sinclair and his team in the 1980s, most major dictionaries are now informed by corpus data. Frequencies of words can serve as an indication of what items to include in a dictionary and the patterns that are observable in concordances can help to describe meanings and provide examples of actual language use. With the great potential of creating different corpora for different purposes, corpus approaches can support linguistic analysis in a variety of fields such as sociolinguistics, forensic linguistics, historical linguistics, language teaching, translation studies or literary stylistics. Basically, corpora can be useful in any field that deals with the analysis of natural language.

An example of a project you may find useful to explore some corpus methods is the following:

> Study the language that was used to talk about the British Prime Minister and the leader of the opposition in the weeks leading up to the general election in 2010. To tackle this problem you could compile two corpora collecting newspaper articles from the web. One corpus would contain articles focusing on Gordon Brown and one would contain articles focusing on David Cameron. With the help of the key words procedure you can identify 'key words', i.e. words that are relatively more frequent in the 'Gordon Brown corpus' compared to the 'David Cameron corpus'. You could then also analyze concordances for selected key words to get a more detailed picture of the kind of language that characterizes each of the corpora.

Readings

Baker, Paul (2010) *Sociolinguistics and Corpus Linguistics.* Edinburgh: Edinburgh University Press.

Hoey, Michael, Mahlberg, Michaela, Stubbs, Michael, Teubert, Wolfgang (2007) *Text, Discourse and Corpora: Theory and Analysis.* London: Continuum.

Scott, Mike and Tribble, Christopher (2006) *Textual Patterns: Key Words and Corpus Analysis in Language Education.* Amsterdam: John Benjamins.

Sinclair, John (2004) *Trust the Text: Language, Corpus and Discourse.* London: Routledge.

Wynne, Martin (2005) *Developing Linguistic Corpora: A Guide to Good Practice.* Oxford and Oakville: Oxbow.

8.6   Critical Discourse Analysis

Thomas Bloor, Visiting Fellow, School of Languages and Social Sciences, Aston University

Critical Discourse Analysis (CDA, also known as Critical Discourse Studies, Critical Language Study and Critical Linguistics) is an *applied* field of study with explicit social motivations that go beyond pure description and theoretical explanation, though these are also important. CDA attempts to get to grips with inequalities in society, particularly as they are implemented through spoken and written discourse. It is a campaigning activity inspired by a desire for a fairer, more equal world. CDA is a highly eclectic field, drawing on many disciplines: including linguistics (in the narrow sense but more especially in the broad sense – as in the title of the present volume), sociology, literary studies, politics, philosophy of language and possibly more. As its name indicates, it is clearly a branch – or rather an aspect – of discourse analysis, which is itself eclectic. Because it is essentially concerned with human communication in social settings, the type of linguistics preferred by most CD analysts is functional linguistics and especially Systemic Functional Linguistics (see Chapter 3). Cognitive Linguistics (see this chapter) is also important for some practitioners.

The word 'critical' in this context does not necessarily have negative connotations. CDA is critical in the sense in which we speak of literary criticism or film criticism, which may be favourable, unfavourable or equivocal. Although it is probably true that CDA is mostly hard on the subjects of its enquiry, exposing the concealed motivations or tactics of the enemy, it can be used more benignly to show how an approved ideology informs and determines admirable discourse. A notable example of this is James Martin's (2004) positive analysis of discourses around the theme of reconciliation with indigenous people in Australia.

Issues that attract the attention of CD analysts include unequal power relations determined by differences in sex, ethnicity, nationality, age, wealth, education, and culture. Not only does discourse reflect and illustrate these inequalities; it creates them. To take a very obvious example, the law of the land is created and implemented linguistically in courtroom dialogue, written statutes and other texts. The legality or illegality of slavery, say, is determined through such textual processes. This is true regardless of whether legal decisions are based primarily on a written constitution, as in the USA and France, or on legal precedent, as in Britain. Less obviously, the phenomenon of racism is inseparable from its textual manifestations. True, in a world without language, a lynching would be no less horrific than it is in ours and the victim would be just as dead, but a lynching based on racism would be impossible in such a world, as would all forms of social discrimination or, indeed, virtually all social life. And there is no such world.

An important concept in CDA is *ideology*. Some idea of the complexity of this notion can be gained from the fact that, at the outset of his book on the subject, Teun van Dijk (1998: vii) says of 'ideology': 'its definition is as elusive as ever.' (Van Dijk 1998: vii.) However, to give a rough idea, I will – rashly perhaps – quote the definition given in the glossary of an introduction to CDA:

> **Ideology:** set of beliefs and attitudes consciously or unconsciously held by a social group. (Bloor and Bloor 2007: 174)

CD analysts believe that ideology underpins most discourse and that, in order to critically deconstruct a text, it is necessary to make the ideology explicit. Consciously or not, text-producers usually have an axe to grind, and part of the analyst's job is to show what it is: to put it in colloquial terms, we need to ask where the author (or speaker) is coming from and what he or she is getting at.

Take the example of a text on the topic of immigration, say a newspaper article. If it is produced by a spokesperson for an avowedly anti-immigrant political party, the task of exposing the reflexes of the ideology is made easier, though it may still be worth doing. The analysis may be even more productive when the producer claims to have a neutral or objective stance, or even a pro-immigrant stance, yet makes a case against immigration. It is a well-known fact that racist utterances are often prefaced by a denial of bigotry ('I'm not a racist but ...'), and sometimes this denial and the expression of prejudice it accompanies can take a much more subtle form.

A CD analysis may examine any features of the text that will shed light on its meaning, especially on those aspects of its meaning that are conveyed surreptitiously. Such features may include all or any of the following: lexical choices, presuppositions, implicatures, metaphors (literary, grammatical and cognitive), cohesive ties, politeness phenomena and facework, grammatical options, stance and appraisal. The purpose of the analysis is to reveal what the text producers are up to and the linguistic means by which they attempt to achieve their aims, and this is where linguistics analytical skills are so important.

For the most part, most fields of serious language study since the beginning of the twentieth century have attempted to adhere to the convention of objectivity in research, a position which is taken by most sciences. The assumption is that scientific research proceeds independently of the personal attitudes and beliefs of the individuals implementing the research. The field of Critical Discourse Analysis (CDA) is one of the first where the researchers involved deny the possibility of full objectivity and are prepared to admit to motivations other than a commitment to dispassionate investigation and theory construction. Of course, the usual requirement applies: claims must be supported by evidence rather than unfounded speculation, but CDA practitioners recommend the open admission of bias regarding the issues under investigation. Indeed, this is often evident in the work regardless of any explicit declaration. The CDA position is that, just as analysts seek to expose the underlying presuppositions and prejudices of the texts that they examine, so they should be open about their own ideological stance.

Major studies of racism and related forms of discrimination have been carried out by, among others, Teun Van Dijk and Ruth Wodak. The political field has been forcefully targeted by Paul Chilton (2004) and also by Norman Fairclough (1989), who has more recently declared economic globalization to be an area demanding critical investigation. There have been critical analyses (by Fairclough, among others) of the commercialization of education as implemented through university promotional and management discourse in advertisements, brochures, speeches, memos, on the internet and elsewhere. Gender studies have also flourished. In the legal context, researchers have exposed discourse-based injustices systematically suffered by women plaintiffs in rape cases, child victims of molestation, and aboriginal Australians charged with crimes or even called as witnesses. (This takes us into the more specialized field of forensic linguistics; see this chapter.) Advertising and all forms of promotion of goods and services (cold-calling, circular letters, internet information sites, and so on) provide plenty of scope for CDA. Also, some very interesting work has been done on the murky world of pharmaceuticals and the promotion or suppression of diseases. Yes, even the identification of a disease is a textual matter, at least in part. These are just a few examples of the scope of CDA.

Readings

Bloor, Meriel and Bloor, Thomas (2007) *The Practice of Critical Discourse Analysis: An Introduction*. London: Hodder Education.

Chilton, Paul (2004) *Analysing Political Discourse: Theory and Practice*. London and New York: Routledge.

Fairclough, Norman (1989) *Language and Power*. Harlow and New York: Longman.

Martin, James R. (2004) Positive discourse analysis: solidarity and change. *Revista Canaria de Estudios Ingleses* (Special Issue on Discourse Analysis at Work: Recent Perspectives in the Study of Language and Social Practice) 49: 179–200. [Reprinted in *The Journal of English Studies* (Special Issue on Discourse Analysis). Guest Editor: Huang Guowen). Vol.4(14): 21–35. Sichuan International Studies University, Chongqing, China. 2006.]

van Dijk, Teun A. (1998) *Ideology: A Multidisciplinary Approach.* London and Thousand Oaks, CA: Sage.

8.7   Educational Linguistics

Frances Christie, Emeritus Professor of Language and Literacy Education, the University of Melbourne; Honorary Professor of Linguistics at the University of Sydney

Educational Linguistics, a term first used by Bernard Spolsky in the 1970s, is the application of linguistic theory towards an understanding of the role of language in learning and teaching. It has become an established field, with a number of graduate programs around the world, and applications have been carried out in a wide variety of educational contexts.

While educational linguists vary in their approaches, many of the insights into the role of language in education have come from systemic functional linguistics (see Chapter 3). Indeed, one of the most compelling observations M. A. K. Halliday made about children and their learning is that 'learning language is learning how to mean' (Halliday 1975). That is to say, language is a tool or a resource which the young child learns as a necessary part of learning about the world and about human relationships. Language is the major resource with which children learn, and nowhere is this more apparent than in schools, where language mediates all areas of teaching and learning. Systemic functional linguistics allows analysts to make explicit just how that mediation takes place in education.

In the study of classroom talk, the functional grammar allows one to examine not only who is talking and when they talk, but also what kinds of meanings are negotiated in talk. Since classroom discourse covers written language as well, the grammar allows us to examine the nature of the written texts students read and write and the relationship of these to what they talk about.

As for children's writing development, the SF grammar allows us to examine the kinds of written texts first produced and then to trace developmental changes in control of the grammar of writing throughout childhood and adolescence. Moreover, the grammar allows us to tease out the differences between the discourses of subject English, history and science, for example, addressing the 'subject specific literacies' of the different school subjects.

The SF grammar is a wonderful tool for analysis, capable of being used in exploring a multitude of areas of school learning. For example, using the grammar, I (Christie 2002) have researched classroom talk on the one hand, and on the other hand, I have recently completed a study with a colleague (Christie and Derewianka 2008) of children's writing development from about age 6, when they enter school, to about age 17 or 18 when they leave school.

Readings

Christie, Frances (2002) *Classroom Discourse Analysis: A Functional Perspective.* London and NY: Continuum.
Christie, Frances and Derewianka, Beverly (2008) *School Discourse: Learning to Write Across the Years of Schooling.* London and NY: Continuum.
Halliday, M. A. K. (1975) *Learning How to Mean: Explorations in the Development of Language.* London: Arnold.
Halliday, M. A. K. and Matthiessen, Christian (2004) *An Introduction to Functional Grammar: Third Edition.* London: Arnold.
Spolsky, Bernard (1999) *Concise Encyclopedia of Educational Linguistics.* Amsterdam: Esevier Science Ltd. Pergamon.

8.8   Forensic Linguistics

Malcolm Coulthard, Professor of Forensic Linguistics, Aston University, Birmingham UK

Forensic Linguistics is one of the newest and, I think, the most interesting addition to the field of Applied Linguistics. The discipline has recently come of age: it now has its own association, The International Association of Forensic Linguists, founded in 1993, its own journal *The International Journal of Speech, Language and the Law,* founded in 1994, and a biennial international conference. There are three major introductory textbooks – Coulthard and Johnson (2007), Gibbons (2003) and Olsson (2008) – and a growing number of specialist monographs. Modules in forensic linguistics or language and the law are taught to undergraduate and masters level students in a rapidly increasing number of universities worldwide; and, at the time of writing, there are two annual summer schools and specialist Masters courses offered at three universities: Aston, Barcelona (Pompeu Fabra) and Cardiff.

Forensic linguistics can usefully be divided into three sub-areas:

1. the language of legal texts, where linguists are interested in the arcane vocabulary, complicated grammar and rare punctuation which typifies many legal texts (see Tiersma 1999);

2. the language of the legal process, where linguists examine the nature of police interviews with suspects and the specialized rules which govern interaction in courts of law (see Heffer 2005); and

3. the work of the linguist as expert witness, to which I will now devote the rest of this section, (see Coulthard and Johnson 2007).

Two major areas in which forensic linguists work as experts are trademarks and authorship. There are no specific descriptive tools; each case requires a different selection from the toolbox which any competent student of language already possesses.

Roger Shuy (2002: 95–109) reports his contribution to the case of McDonald's Corporation vs. Quality Inns International, Inc, which revolved around whether McDonald's could claim ownership not simply of the name McDonald's but also of the initial morpheme 'Mc', and thereby prevent its use in other trademarks. The case began in 1987 when Quality Inns announced that they were going to create a chain of basic hotels called McSleep. McDonald's decided to challenge the McSleep mark, claiming it was a deliberate attempt to draw on the goodwill and reputation of the McDonald's brand.

In supporting their case McDonald's pointed out that they had deliberately set out, in one advertising campaign, to create a 'McLanguage' with Ronald McDonald teaching children how to 'Mc-ise' the standard vocabulary of generic words to create 'McFries', McFish', McShakes' and even 'McBest'. Quality Inns' lawyers asked Shuy to help with two linguistic arguments, first, that the morpheme 'Mc' was in common use productively in contexts where it was not seen to be linked in any way to McDonald's and second, that such examples showed that the prefix had become generic and thus now had a meaning of its own, which was recognizably distinct from both of the other major meanings, 'son of' and 'associated with the McDonald's company'.

Shuy used a corpus linguistics approach and searched to find instances of what one might call 'Mcmorphemes'. Among the 56 examples he found were general terms like McArt, McCinema, McSurgery and McPrisons, as well as items already being used commercially such as the McThrift Motor Inn, a budget motel with a Scottish motif and McTek a computer discount store which specialized in Apple Mac computer products. On the basis of such examples, Shuy argued that the prefix had become, in the language at large, an independent lexical item with its own meaning of 'basic, convenient, inexpensive and standardized'. Rather than resort to corpus evidence themselves, McDonald's hired market researchers to access the public's perception of the prefix directly and to do so through interview and questionnaire. Their experts reported unsurprisingly that their tests confirmed that consumers did indeed associate the prefix with McDonald's, as well as with reliability, speed, convenience and cheapness. Faced with this conflicting evidence, the judge ruled in favour of McDonald's, thereby giving them massive control over the use of the morpheme Mc.

A new area of study within forensic linguistics is the investigation of the authorship of text messages. Text messaging is a very interesting linguistic phenomenon because there is a great deal of freedom in encoding, the abbreviations are not yet fixed and so even small samples of usage can be distinctive. Thus, as is happening in a growing number of murder cases, a linguist can express an opinion on the probability of the authorship of a message or messages sent from the deceased's phone after the supposed time of death. In my latest case (http://www.royalgazette.com/rg/Article/article.jsp?sectionId=60&articleId=7d9893330030001), suspect text messages included the items 'I will', 'yes', 'come' and 'home' when, in frequent messages sent in the previous three days the owner of the cellphone preferred the forms 'ill', 'ya', 'com', and 'hme'.

One interesting area of authorship attribution, particularly in an academic context, is student plagiarism. One of my colleagues, David Woolls, has developed a computer program which can compare large numbers of student assignments very quickly and detect if two or more are more similar than they should be if produced independently. This program is now being used by UCAS, the agency through which all English students apply to university. As part of the application process, everyone has to write a personal statement, some of which are, sadly, not sufficiently personal. In 2007 an investigation found that 234 personal statements, submitted by applicants for medical degrees, related a dramatic incident involving 'burning a hole in pyjamas at age eight', which was based on a model answer on a website.

For those interested in a little more information about forensic linguistics, I recommend two short Youtube videos: 'The Linguist as Detective and Expert Witness', http://www.youtube.com/watch?v=4z6Krsjwc84 and 'The Work of the Forensic Linguist', www.tinyurl.com/forensic-linguist. For those who would like to read in depth, I recommend Coulthard and Johnson (2007) or Gibbons (2003).

For anyone who would like to undertake a small research project, analysing text messages is always rewarding. One suggestion is to collect ten messages from several friends and ten others from several family members from the previous generation. Analyse them to see if there are any significant gender and/or age differences. Could you distinguish some or all of the second group of ten from the first linguistically?

Readings

Coulthard, Malcolm and Johnson, Alison (2007) *An Introduction to Forensic Linguistics: Language in Evidence*. London: Routledge.

Gibbons, John (2003) *Forensic Linguistics: An Introduction to Language in the Justice System*. Oxford: Blackwell.

Heffer, Chris (2005) *The Language of Jury Trial*. London: Palgrave.

Olsson John (2008) *Forensic Linguistics: An Introduction to Language Crime and the Law. Second Edition*. London: Continuum.

Shuy, Roger (2002) *Linguistic Battles in Trademark Disputes*. New York: Palgrave.

8.9   Formal Linguistics

Amaya Mendikoetxea, Universidad Autónoma de Madrid

Formal linguistics endeavours to identify the formal properties which underlie the architecture of grammar. Since the late 1950s this research agenda has been identified with a framework known as 'Generative Grammar' and, particularly, with the work carried out by Noam Chomsky and his associates. In contrast to previous formal approaches (traditional grammar and structuralism), Chomsky adopts a cognitive approach to the study of grammar: language is understood as a system of knowledge in the mind/brain (see Chapter 4). The generative linguist seeks to determine what the nature of that knowledge is: what native speakers *know* about their language that enables them to speak and understand the language. This knowledge is implicit and unconscious: just as people can drive cars without understanding the inner workings of the engine, so can speakers use a language to form and interpret words, phrases and sentences without conscious knowledge of their internal structure.

The linguist's task is to devise a model of that knowledge (i.e. linguistic competence) by building grammars, where 'grammar' should not be understood in the traditional sense, as a volume containing a set of prescriptive or descriptive rules, but as a complex system of abstract principles governing grammatical categories, their internal structure and the way they combine into larger units (words, phrases, clauses and sentences). The goal of the generative linguist is to characterize the nature of this internalized linguistic system: a mental state of linguistic competence ('I'nternal)-language' in Chomsky's (1986: 19–56) terminology). Creativity is the most striking aspect of linguistic competence and the fundamental motivation behind the generative enterprise. In devising a model of linguistic competence, linguists must account for the fact that speakers of a language are able to form and interpret an infinitely large number of sentences they have never encountered before. A generative grammar is basically a finite system of rules/ principles that will generate an infinite set of well-formed structures.

The ultimate goal is to devise a theory of Universal Grammar (UG), a generalization from the grammars of particular I-languages to the grammars of all possible natural languages -- highly abstract principles which characterize the nature of possible human language grammars, are common to all languages and are thought to be innate. UG is crucial for what some linguists consider to be the fundamental problem of linguistics: language acquisition. How does language arise in the mind/brain? How is it that children can learn such an intricate system of knowledge in a remarkably short period of time? In Chomsky's view, this is possible because humans are biologically endowed with an innate language faculty, which incorporates a UG that enables the child to acquire quickly a grammar of any natural language on the basis of sufficient linguistic experience (input).

Formal linguists are mostly interested with aspects of language form (phonology, morphology and syntax) and meaning (semantics). In recent years there has been an increasing interest in how the language faculty interacts with performance systems (systems for the articulation-perception of sounds and for the interpretation of strings generated by the grammar) and, thus, attention has been turned to interface areas: syntax-phonology, lexicon-syntax, syntax-discourse and so on, in what some generativists have called 'the end of syntax' (see Marantz 1997). Research into all those areas relies on speakers' intuitions about grammaticality/acceptability of strings and interpretation (often those of the researcher) and is often based on a much smaller data subset than that of other linguistic disciplines. The focus is not on empirical coverage but on linguistic facts that can be revealing to illustrate a particular rule or principle and to explore the limits of a theoretical construct.

Research on formal linguistics can take a variety of forms. What formal linguistics is good at is providing highly detailed in-depth analyses of specific areas of the syntax, morphology, phonology, and so on, of particular languages, sometimes focusing on aspects that had not received much attention from linguists before. Thus, researchers may focus on a construction or a set of constructions in a particular language or they may undertake comparative work, mostly focusing on what apparently very diverse languages have in common and how the grammar can account for the differences observed in a constrained way. Data for this kind of research comes from grammaticality/acceptability judgements. Research may also be highly abstract, with focus on proving or disproving a particular hypothesis or theorem, refining generalizations and linguistic constructs. Evidence for this kind of work is often of a theoretical nature, rather than empirically based.

Although unfounded optimism and unrealistic expectations about the usefulness of the Chomskyan approach for areas such as language teaching, computer generated language and so on led a lot of linguists to abandon this paradigm in the late 1960s and 1970s, it cannot be denied that the field is still very much alive and that we have witnessed more than half a century of unprecedented advances in our knowledge of the structure of language due mainly to the success of Generative Grammar. Attention has focused on data previously neglected, new analyses have led to the viewing of grammatical problems in a new light and and/or to the discovery of grammatical properties that had gone unnoticed. Distinctions have been established among grammatical categories and structures traditionally grouped together and, conversely, generalizations have been made covering constructions often considered to be very different, both within the grammar of a particular language and crosslinguistically. As a result, we have much more detailed grammars of particular languages and a much deeper understanding of principles of structure building shared by all languages. In short, we are much closer to uncovering the defining characteristics of human language, and, hence of human cognition. As Jackendoff (1990: 7–8) puts it 'to the extent that generative linguistics has indeed been successful in increasing our understanding of the human language capacity, the choice of I-language as the object of inquiry has been vindicated.'

Readings

Jackendoff, Ray (1990) *Semantic Structures*. Cambridge, MA: MIT Press.
Marantz, Alec (1997) No escape from syntax. Don't try morphological analysis in the privacy of your own lexicon. *UPenn Working Papers in Linguistics*, 4: 202–225.

Seminal works

Chomsky, Noam (1957) *Syntactic Structures*. Cambridge, MA: MIT Press.
Chomsky, Noam (1965) *Aspects of the Theory of Syntax*. Cambridge, MA: MIT Press.
Chomsky, Noam (1981) *Lectures on Government and Binding*, Dordrecht: Foris.
Chomsky, Noam (1986) *Knowledge of Language: Its Nature, Origins and Use*. New York: Praeger.
Chomsky, Noam (1995) *The Minimalist Program*. Cambridge, MA: MIT Press.
Chomsky, Noam (2000) Minimalist inquiries. In Roger Martin, David Michaels and Juan Uriagereka (eds) *Step by Step: Essays on Minimalist Syntax in Honor of Howard Lasnik* 89–156. Cambridge, MA: MIT Press.
Chomsky, Noam (2005) Three factors in language design. *Linguistic Inquiry* 36, 1–22.

Textbooks

Adger, David (2003) *Core Syntax: A Minimalist Approach*. Oxford: Oxford University Press.

Carnie, Andrew (2001) *Syntax*. Oxford: Blackwell.

Culicover, Peter W. (1997) *Principles and Parameters: An Introduction to Syntactic Theory*. Oxford: Oxford University Press.

Haegeman, Liliane (1994) *Introduction to Government and Binding Theory: Second Edition*. Oxford: Blackwell.

Haegeman, Liliane (2006) *Thinking Syntactically: A Guide to Argumentation and Analysis*. Oxford: Blackwell.

Radford, Andrew (1988) *Transformational Grammar*. Cambridge: Cambridge University Press.

Radford, Andrew (2004) *Minimalist Syntax*. Cambridge: Cambridge University Press.

Roberts, Ian (1997) *Comparative Syntax*. London: Edwin Arnold.

8.10 Functional linguistics

Christopher S. Butler, Honorary Professor, Swansea University, UK, Visiting Professor, University of Huddersfield, UK and Visiting Fellow, Centre for Translation Studies, University of Leeds, UK

If someone asked you what you think language is, you might be a bit puzzled at first, since we tend to take language for granted, but my guess is that when you'd thought about it for a bit, you'd say something about language being a tool for communication between human beings. This is in fact the starting point for a group of linguistic theories which go under the general name of **functional linguistics**. This type of approach to language is sometimes contrasted with **formal linguistics**, typified by the work of Noam Chomsky, which is less interested in language as communication than in the abstract properties which are claimed to be valid for all human languages. Functionalists believe not only that language is first and foremost an instrument for communication, but also that the forms which languages take are intimately related to their communicative role, in three ways.

First, the properties of languages are related to the functions which communication serves in our everyday lives. One of the most important functions is to enable us to talk (and, for literate societies, also to write) about the world outside and inside us: we constantly refer to people, objects and abstractions, and to their qualities, and we build these references into descriptions of who is doing what to whom, and under what circumstances. A second function, which is sometimes even more important than the first, is to enact social relationships through the speech acts that we perform and the assessments of situations that we provide to our hearers. Functionalists have shown how these two fundamental functions, which normally operate together, are actually built into the structures of languages. They have also been concerned with how we create coherent stretches of discourse, which 'hang together' rather than being disjointed.

Second, the properties of languages are related to the physical and cognitive properties of the biological systems involved in communication. An example of the influence of physical properties is that the vowel systems found in languages are constrained by the physical characteristics of the human vocal tract. An instance of a cognitive constraint can be seen in the principle that languages tend to prefer to put long, 'heavy' constituents of sentences late in the sentence. For example, we would normally say *It's a pity that Mary can't come to the party at John's house next Saturday* rather than *That Mary can't come to the party at John's house on Saturday is a pity*, even though English prefers the Subject (which here is the long clause *that Mary can't come to the party at John's house on Saturday*) to be in first position in a declarative (i.e. the kind of sentence which is most usually used to make a statement). The reasons are concerned with processing mechanisms: the preferred ordering is easier to process than the dispreferred one.

Third, the properties of languages are related to the material and social conditions under which communication occurs. All languages have ways of indicating social relationships, for instance concerned with power, authority or degree of acquaintance. In languages such as French, Spanish, Italian, German and Dutch, there is a distinction between 'familiar' and 'formal' forms of pronouns (and also verb forms), so that in French we can say *tu achètes* or *vous achetez* to mean 'you buy', depending on our relationship with the addressee. In other languages, such as Japanese and Javanese, there are systems of honorifics which can be used to indicate the speaker's relationship not only with the addressee, but often also with third persons. Languages also have different levels of vocabulary, the use of which correlates with social factors: in an informal environment we could say *The cops have arrested three kids*, whereas in a more formal context we might say *The police have arrested three children*.

There are many functional approaches to language, just as there are different formal approaches. Different functional theories may emphasize different things: for instance, at the most radically functionalist end of the spectrum we find an approach (Emergent Grammar/Interactional Linguistics) which claims that grammar is not a stable, isolable entity at all, but emerges from the dictates of discourse phenomena, whereas at the more formal end of the spectrum we have theories (e.g. Role and Reference Grammar,

Functional Discourse Grammar) which are concerned only with the grammar itself, in the sense of the word which includes semantics, phonology and some aspects of discourse pragmatics as well as morphosyntax. Systemic Functional Linguistics (see Chapter 3) lies between the two extremes, though closer to the radical functional end. Finally, some functional approaches (e.g. Word Grammar) are closely related to theories (e.g. Cognitive Grammar, Cognitive Construction Grammar) which go under the general name of Cognitive Linguistics (see Section 8.2, this chapter).

Readings
General discussions of functionalism

Butler, Christopher S. (2003) *Structure and Function: A Guide to Three Major Structural-Functional Theories. Part 1: Approaches to the Simplex Clause. Part 2: From Clause to Discourse and Beyond.* Amsterdam and Philadelphia, PA: John Benjamins.
Butler, Christopher S. (2005) Functional approaches to language. In Christopher S. Butler, María L. A. Gómez-González and Susana Doval-Suárez (eds) *The Dynamics of Language Use: Functional and Contrastive Perspectives* 3–17. Amsterdam and Philadelphia, PA: John Benjamins.
Butler, Christopher S. (2006a) Functionalist theories of language. In Keith Brown (ed.) *The Encyclopedia of Language and Linguistics, Second Edition: Volume 4* 696–704. Oxford: Elsevier.
Butler, Christopher S. (2006b) On functionalism and formalism: A reply to Newmeyer. *Functions of Language* 13(2): 197–227.

Functional Discourse Grammar

Hengeveld, Kees and Mackenzie, J. Lachlan (2008) *Functional Discourse Grammar: A Typologically-Based Theory of Language Structure.* Oxford: Oxford University Press.

Role and Reference Grammar

Van Valin, Robert D., Jr. (2005) *Exploring the Syntax-Semantics Interface.* Cambridge: Cambridge University Press.

Systemic Functional Linguistics

(for more SFL references, see Chapter 3)
Fawcett, Robin P. (2008) *Invitation to Systemic Functional Linguistics through the Cardiff Grammar: An Extension and Simplification of Halliday's Systemic Functional Grammar.* London: Equinox.
Halliday, M. A. K. and Matthiessen, Christian M. I. M. (1999) *Construing Experience through Meaning.* London: Continuum.

Word Grammar

Hudson, Richard A. (2007) *Language Networks: The New Word Grammar*. Oxford: Oxford University Press.

Emergent Grammar/Interactional Linguistics

Ford, Cecilia, E., Fox, Barbara A. and Thompson, Sandra A. (2003) Social interaction and grammar. In Michael Tomasello (ed.) *The New Psychology of Language, Volume 2* 119–143. Mahwah, NJ: Lawrence Erlbaum.

8.11 Historical Linguistics

Michael Cummings, Department of English, York University, Toronto

Historical linguistics concerns itself with changes in language over time. English for example has changed enormously since it was first recorded. In this century we might write of a fondly remembered ruler, 'That was a good king.' Ten centuries ago an English speaker wrote 'þæt wæs god cyning' (*Beowulf*, line 11). Historical linguistics attempts to find out how a language like English has changed over the centuries, and why it has changed. Historical linguistics also wants to know why languages of all kinds always change.

To find the answers to these questions, the historical linguist must examine all of the levels of a language at different stages in its chronology. Comparisons across the timeline have to be made in the areas of phonetics and phonology, morphology and syntax, lexis and semantics. For example an examination of the evidence for pronunciation across time reveals that English words underwent a radical change in the phonetics of their vowels roughly from 1400 to 1600, while at the same time the general phonological structure of the language was preserved. Exactly why this happened when it did is still an unresolved question, although many interesting theories have been proposed, chiefly from the viewpoints of articulatory phonetics and sociolinguistics.

Over great stretches of time, a language may change so much that it has become a different language altogether. The colloquial Latin of the Roman Empire changed into the different Romance languages of the modern world. The common Indo-European tongue of some 5000–7000 years ago has evolved and fragmented into many great families of languages in modern Europe and Asia. The study of language evolution has given rise to an analytic tool called the comparative method. This method attempts to identify languages which are related through a common ancestor language.

Sets of words from different languages are identified which are similar both in phonetics and in semantics, like Sp. *caballo*, It. *cavallo,* and Fr. *cheval* (horse), separately evolving from colloquial Latin *caballus*; or like Eng. *father*, Lat. *pater*, ancient Gk. *patēr*, Sanskrit *pitar-*, evolving from Indo-European **pətēr*. Other tools to assist the tasks of historical linguistics include the ancillary disciplines of paleography (the study of manuscript hands), linguistics (including phonetics, phonology, grammar and semantics), mathematics and statistics.

Some of the findings of historical linguistics are very famous, like the discovery of the Latin origin of the Romance languages, or the discovery and partial reconstruction of the Indo-European substratum for some of the European and Asiatic language families. Other types of results include the reconstruction of the pronunciations of historical dialects of modern languages, the description of the historical evolution of grammar patterns from lexical idiom in various languages (grammaticalization), the discovery of the origins of language families other than the Romance and Indo-European, the etymologies of individual words, the dating and evolution of borrowed words, and the measurement of rates of change in individual languages.

Here are a couple of projects that could serve to acquaint you with some of the materials of historical linguistics:

1. Find and use some etymological dictionaries to work out the proportions of vocabulary from different source languages in some short texts from different genres of writing, like narrative, scientific exposition, spoken discourse.
2. Find and compare the same short text in related languages, e.g., the Lord's Prayer in Old English, Old High German, Old Norse, modern English, modern High German, modern Icelandic, etc., for the differences and similarities in vocabulary and grammar.

Readings

Brinton, Laurel J., and Arnovick, Leslie K. (2006) *The English Language: A Linguistic History*. Don Mills, Ontario: Oxford University Press Canada.

Hopper, Paul J. and Traugott, Elizabeth Closs (1993) *Grammaticalization*. Cambridge: Cambridge University Press.

Lehman, Winfred P. (1992) *Historical Linguistics: An Introduction. Third Edition*. New York: Routledge.

Millward, Celia M. (1996) *A Biography of the English Language. Second Edition*. New York: Holt, Rinehart and Winston.

8.12 Psycholinguistics

Amanda Miller, Psychology Department, University of Denver

Whether conversing with a friend, reading the newspaper, or watching a movie, we are constantly immersed in language. Language use is typically a seamless, effortless process that goes unnoticed and that most people take for granted. Psycholinguists appreciate the complexity of human language use, and their primary aim is to understand the cognitive processes involved in acquiring, producing, and comprehending language.

Psycholinguistics is a very diverse area of study. One major focus of psycholinguistics is the study of how children acquire language. Language acquisition is an amazingly complex process that happens in a very brief period of time – by age five, the average child has already acquired a vocabulary of 10,000 words! (see Chapter 7). Developmental psycholinguists study many aspects of language development, including how infants learn to distinguish one speech sound from another, how old they are when they reach language milestones (e.g., babbling, first word, first phrase), how they learn to apply grammatical rules, and how they create novel sentences. Studying language development in children provides insight into 'big picture' questions that interest psycholinguists, such as whether the capacity for language is a skill that is built into the brain or whether language acquisition is experience-driven and easily acquired by the human brain because it is well-suited for such a feat.

Not only do psycholinguists study how individuals acquire their native language, but they also examine the processes involved in acquiring a second or foreign language. If you have tried to learn a foreign language as an adult, you know that it is no easy task! Perhaps you have noticed that while you struggle with each foreign word, young children seem to learn foreign languages with relative ease. Such age of acquisition effects is one aspect of foreign language learning that is of interest to psycholinguists. Psycholinguists also explore how individuals' native and foreign languages are processed in the brain. Do the two languages activate the same regions of the brain or different ones? Additionally, psycholinguists study the relationship between language and thought. Languages vary in a variety of aspects, and a number of very interesting studies suggest that linguistic differences play a role in shaping the cognition and behavior of cultures in surprising ways.

While many psycholinguists explore the cognitive processes involved in successfully acquiring, producing, and comprehending language, other psycholinguists examine the instances when these processes go awry. These psycholinguists use an individual differences approach: they study factors such as reading ability, attention, working memory, and vocabulary that affect language processing. By examining such individual differences, psycholinguists are better able to understand each of the individual components that are involved in successful (and unsuccessful) language processing. For example, by assessing the reading comprehension skills of children with Attention Deficit Hyperactivity Disorder, who have problems sustaining their attention, psycholinguists can gain insight into the role of attention in reading comprehension.

A variety of methods are used in the study of Psycholinguistics. Traditionally, behavioral measures have dominated the field. Such measures often calculate the reaction time required to complete specific tasks that involve language processing, such as making decisions about a word's semantics, phonology, or orthography. The field has made tremendous progress in the last decade, thanks to advances in non-invasive neuroimaging techniques, such as functional Magnetic Resonance Imaging (fMRI) and event-related potentials (ERP). These tools allow psycholinguists to gain insight into the specific areas of the brain that are active while language is being processed, as well as obtain a precise estimate of the timing at which these processes occur.

As you can see, psycholinguists explore a wide variety of exciting topics. They seek to solve the mysteries surrounding how we acquire, use, and comprehend the priceless language that allows us to engage in society and to learn about the world.

Readings

Cutler, Anne (2005) *Twenty-First Century Psycholinguistics: Four Cornerstones*. Mahwah, NJ: Lawrence Erlbaum Associates Publishers.

Gernsbacher, Morton Ann (1994) *Handbook of Psycholinguistics*. San Diego, CA: Academic Press.

Hernandez, Arturo, Li, Ping and MacWhinney, Brian (2005) The emergence of competing modules in bilingualism, *Trends in Cognitive Sciences*, 9(5), 220–225.

MacWhinney, Brian (2005). A unified model of language acquisition. In Judith. F. Kroll and Annette M. de Groot (eds) *Handbook of Bilingualism: Psycholinguistic Approaches* 49–67. New York, NY: Oxford University Press.

Pinker, Steven (2007) *The Stuff of Thought: Language as a Window into Human Nature*. New York: Viking.

Whorf, Benjamin (1956) *Language, Thought, and Reality*. Cambridge, MA: MIT Press.

8.13 Sociolinguistics

Jeffrey Reaser, Department of English, North Carolina State University

Imagine sitting in your favorite restaurant and overhearing a heated conversation between two people in the booth behind you. You are curious to know about these people, but you don't want to be caught staring at them as they argue. Instead, you listen carefully to their voices to create a mental image of who they are and what they are like. Some attributes are easy to determine, such as gender. You then ponder other, slightly more difficult to discern, characteristics, such as their regional origins, nationalities, body sizes, etc. You may even reach conclusions about how intelligent or educated they may be based solely on their voices (in fact, judgments about intelligence or education tend to more accurately catalog a person's socioeconomic upbringing). We give away an incredible amount of personal information about ourselves every time we open our mouths. While we are acutely aware about the fallacies of prejudging people based on physical characteristics, people rarely see judging people based on their speech as problematic. Thus, language has the power to either draw people together or push them apart. As such, how language works ought to be seen as a topic of focused scientific study.

Sociolinguists investigate the correlations between language use and social/regional variation with the goal of uncovering the social meaning of that variation. For example, one might research how language use in a speech community varies across socioeconomic lines. While it may not be surprising to find that, in general, the lower the socioeconomic background of a speaker, the less standard he or she is, it may be surprising to uncover that some lower socioeconomic speakers use a highly vernacular means of speaking as a means of projecting to the world who they are or who they want to be seen as. On one level, sociolinguistics is straight forward: it seeks to find correlations between social categories and linguistic use. More often, sociolinguists are interested in the ways in which a speaker uses language as a tool of identity. That is, the how and why of why a lower socioeconomic speaker may be using his speech as a means of asserting a particular persona, e.g., hyper-masculine, someone worthy of deference, etc. To research such questions, sociolinguists often employ methodologies from related fields, such as sociology, psychology, ethnography, or anthropology. They also rely on historical research and often employ sophisticated statistical analysis.

The popular view of language is that it reflects where you came from and how much effort you have spent learning it. In other words, speaking a vernacular dialect is tantamount to failure to learn the standard. The reality is that vernacular dialects persist because they are useful for personal identity; local, regional, or social group affiliation; and for gaining access to local goods and services in certain speech communities. Locally, it may be the standard variety that is less useful than local varieties. Common but incorrect assumptions about language and language usage have important ramifications in the educational and professional world. Sociolinguists are increasingly seeking ways to apply their knowledge of language to fight discrimination in housing, occupational situations, and educational settings.

My own research focuses on educational settings. It is important to note that no study has effectively demonstrated that any language or dialect in and of itself constitutes a barrier to academic success. Instead, it is the schools' and teachers' treatment of students and their language varieties that is the ultimate source of language-related academic failure. Sociolinguists examine the effect of one's dialect on reading, writing, and speaking, and pedagogical strategies to help students master the standard variety. My work takes a different but complementary track. Instead of assessing and remediating vernacular speaking students, I aim to introduce all students to linguistic and sociolinguistic knowledge so that they and their teachers have a better sense of how language works linguistically and socially. I believe that as students learn that everyone speaks a dialect, about the history of dialects, the patterns of some dialect features, and the roles dialects play in local heritage, they become more tolerant of other ways of speaking. This tolerance is crucial for all speakers, especially students who are lucky enough to have been raised speaking an empowered or mainstream variety. As a means of spreading such information, I have collaborated to create a free, national, language awareness curriculum to accompany the PBS documentary, *Do You Speak American?* and a curriculum specifically for public schools in North Carolina. The latter curriculum has been tested with great success throughout the state, and has recently become the first state-based curriculum on language variation endorsed by the local department of education.

Readings

Chambers, J. K., Trudgill, Peter and Schilling-Estes, Natalie (eds) (2002). *The Handbook of Language Variation and Change*. Malden, MA: Blackwell Publishing.

Craig, Holly K. and Washington, Julie A. (2006) *Malik Goes to School: Examining the Language Skills of African American Students from Preschool-5th Grade*. Mahwah, NJ: Lawrence Erlbaum Associates.

Lippi-Green, Rosina (1997) *English with an Accent: Language, Ideology, and Discrimination in the United States*. London and New York: Routledge.

Rickford, John Russell and Rickford, Russell John (2000) *Spoken Soul: The Story of Black English*. New York: John Wiley.

Smitherman, Geneva (2000) *Talkin' That Talk: Language, Culture, and Education in African America*. London and New York: Routledge.

Wardhaugh, Ronald (2009) *An Introduction to Sociolinguistics. Sixth Edition*. New York: Wiley-Blackwell.

Wolfram, Walt and Ward, Ben (eds.) (2006) *American Voices: How Dialects Differ from Coast to Coast*. Malden, MA: Blackwell Publishing.

Glossary

Acronyms Words which have been formed by using the initial letters of each word in a phrase, such as *scuba* (for *self-contained underwater breathing apparatus*).

Actor A term used in Systemic Functional Linguistics to refer to a participant in a material process, such as *John built the cabin.*

Adjacency pairs A set of utterances in which the articulation of the first (the first-pair part, or the first turn) provokes the response of the second (the second-pair part, or the second turn), such as greeting-greeting or compliment-acknowledgment.

Adjective A member of a class of words which serve as modifiers of a noun or of a nominal referent; adjectives provide attributes of nouns, such as *the tall man; John is tall.*

Adjunct As used in Systemic Functional Linguistics, an optional element of the clause which expresses either a circumstance, such as how or when the action in the clause occurred as in *in the morning* or *at school* (circumstantial Adjuncts), or a relationship of the clause to the surrounding text, such as *in addition* or *therefore* (conjunctive Adjuncts or a perspective on the proposition in the clause, such as *in my opinion* or *clearly* (modal Adjuncts).

Adverbs A member of a class of words which function as modifiers of verbs or clauses, as in *she ran quickly, she runs often*, and as modifiers of adjectives or other adverbs or adverbial phrases, such as *he gave me a wonderfully useful gift; she ran very quickly.*

Affix A bound morpheme which can attach at the beginning of a root or stem morpheme (**prefix**), at the end (**suffix**), in the middle (**infix**), or simultaneously at the beginning and at the end (**circumfix**); **transfixes** refer to morphemes which are discontinuous, and which are attached to discontinuous roots.

Affricate Type of consonant that begins as a plosive and ends as a fricative.

Agent A term used in semantics to refer to a participant in the sentence who represents the 'doer' of the action, as in *John kicked the ball.*

Agglutinating languages Languages whose morphosyntax relies on the addition of grammatical morphemes with differing meanings to roots and stems, often resulting in the buildup of long words of many morphemes.

Agrammatisim Refers to the inability to speak using syntactically acceptable sentences, due to a brain lesion.

Allophones One of the alternative phonetic realizations of a phoneme, as in [p] and [pʰ].

Allophonic Quality of a speech sound that is not distinctive in a given language.

Amelioration Said of a word or expression which has moved from having a negative connotation to having a positive one, such as *wicked*.

Aphasia A language disorder caused by brain lesions which have been brought about for any number of reasons, such as strokes, tumors, infections, and traumas.

Approximants Consonant sounds which are produced with only a partial obstruction of the air flow, creating some turbulence, such as [j] (as in you̱r), and [w] (as in w̱ild).

Articulatory phonetics The study of how speech sounds are produced by the vocal apparatus.

Assimilation rules Rules that make it easier to articulate strings of sound; the modification of a sound that makes it more like a nearby sound, for example, when the vowel in *pin* is nasalized due to the following nasal consonant; assimilation can be progressive (when the sound becomes more like a preceding one) or regressive (when it becomes more like a following one).

Attribute A term used in Systemic Functional Linguistics to refer a participant in a relational process which provides a characteristic or attribute of the Carrier, as in *John is tall; John has a piano*.

Babbling A stage of child language development, usually beginning around age 5 or 6 months, the sounds of which are 'language-like': open syllables, or consonants followed by vowels, with no ending consonant.

Back-formation The creation of a new word by removing an affix from an already existing word, as in *edit* which came from *editor*.

Behaver A term used in Systemic Functional Linguistics to refer to the main participant in a behavioral process, as in *John sneezed*.

Blend A combination of parts of two words into one, as in *smog* or *brunch*; the resulting words are also known as portmanteau words.

Broca's area An area of the brain identified by Paul Broca as having a role to play in the understanding and production of syntax.

Buzzword Usually a pejorative term for jargon in the business and political world which become highly popular for a short-lived period of time.

Carrier A term used in Systemic Functional Linguistics to refer to the main participant in a relational process, the participant to which we can ascribe an Attribute, as in *John* is tall; *John* has a piano.

Categorical perception The ability to perceive differences in sensory phenomena, such as the ability to categorize phonemes.

Child-directed speech A way of speaking which is directed at infants and small children, features of which include high pitch, exaggerated intonation, repetition, short phrases, and a sing-song rhythm.

Circumstance In Systemic Functional Linguistics, a term used to refer to a transitivity function in the clause, which serves to express location, extent, cause, manner, contingency, accompaniment, matter, angle or role, usually realized by prepositional phrases or adverbial phrases, such as *In the morning, Throughout Europe*.

Classifier A term used in Systemic Functional Linguistics to refer to an element of the nominal group which serves as a pre-modifier of the Head noun, and which serves to indicate 'what kind', as in a *baseball cap*.

Clicks A speech sound produced by a velaric airstream mechanism in which the back of the tongue makes a closure at the velum, and a second contact is made further forward in the oral cavity, creating an enclosed space so that when the second closure is then released, air flows inwards creating a clicking noise.

Client A term used in Systemic Functional Linguistics to refer to a participant in a material process for whom the action is carried out, as in *John made a basket for Mary*.

Clipping The creation of a new word by using part of a word for the whole, such as *gas* for *gasoline*, or *perp* for *perpetrator*.

Close (or high) vowels Vowels whose pronunciation means that the tongue comes closest to the roof of the mouth, without direct contact.

Code-switching Use of more than one language or variety within the same conversation or text.

Colligation The grammatical company a word tends to keep; the grammatical environment a word tends to appear in; for example, *surprising, amazing* and *astonishing* all mean roughly the same thing, although we can only use *surprising* in the *it's not* _____ *that* pattern.

Collocation The lexical company a word tends to keep; for example, we tend to say *This tea is very strong* but not *This tea is very powerful*, as *tea* collocates, or co-occurs within 4 or 5 word positions, with *strong* in a way which is statistically more significant than chance would predict, but it does not with *powerful*.

Comparative method The search for regularities in changes of and similarities across languages in order to establish common ancestry.

Competence The underlying mental knowledge and processes which we draw on to carry out our production of language.

Complement Elements in the clause which could be Subjects, but which are not, and which answer the questions 'who(m) or what' related to the Predicator as in *John backed Mary a cake*. What did John bake? *a cake*. For whom did he bake a cake? *for Mary*.

Complementary distribution Condition of two speech sounds which do not share any environments of occurrence; where one sound occurs, the other will not occur, as with allophones of the same phoneme.

Compound The joining together of two free morphemes into one single unit, to form a new word, such as *blackboard* and *user-friendly*.

Consonant A speech sound produced with a narrowing or closure which causes an obstruction of air flow at some point in the vocal tract.

Content words A word, typically a noun, verb, adjective, or adverb, which carries semantic content, bearing reference to the world independently of its use within a particular sentence (distinguished from *function words*).

Contrastive Refers to a sound feature which is distinctive in a language; for example, [p] and [b] are both bilabial plosives, but they occur in the exact same contexts (e.g. *pat* and *bat*) so we know that the voicedness of the [b] is contrastive.

Conversation analysis The field that studies the ways in which people construct conversations, for example, the way turn-taking is organized.

Conversational implicature An inference that can be drawn from an utterance, as from one that is seemingly illogical or irrelevant, by examining the degree to which it conforms to the canons of normal conversation and the way it functions pragmatically within the situation, as when 'The phone is ringing,' said in a situation where both speaker and listener can clearly hear the phone, can be taken as a suggestion to answer the phone.

Conversion Process of changing the class of a word without changing its form, e.g. *Google* (noun) → *to google* (verb).

Cooperative principle The principle formulated by H. P. Grice that speech interactants assume that they are each behaving rationally and cooperatively; this principle underlies the way people understand the intended meaning of an utterance.

Coreferential When two different expressions (often with different senses) refer to the same thing (e.g. *the house on the corner and the red house* could refer to the same house).

Creole A language which has developed out of a pidgin, and which becomes the first language of a generation or generations of speakers.

Declarative (mood) Said of clauses/sentences which express statements or assertions, in which the order of elements in English is Subject^Finite.

Deictic Said of a word or expression part or all of whose meaning can be derived only by attending to the context in which it is uttered, as with *you, he, we, that book*. In Systemic Functional Linguistics, a term used to refer to one of the functional slots of the nominal group, and which serves to root the Thing (the main focus of the nominal group) in the speech context.

Diachronic variation Refers to changes in a language over a period of time.

Diacritic A mark added to a phonetic symbol to indicate some further quality of the speech sound, such as ^{h} to indicate aspiration, $\sim$ to indicate nasalization, and to indicate primary stress.

Dialect A variety of a language which is used in a specific social or geographical speech community.

Diglossia Situation in which two languages or varieties coexist in a society, where one of the languages constitutes the high variety (language of government and education) and the other the low variety (language used in everyday situations).

Diphthongs Combinations of vowel sounds within the same syllable where the sound begins in one place and positioning in the mouth and glides towards another.

Direct speech act A speech act in which the grammatical form directly indicates the type of act; for example, in English a question would be expressed as a direct speech act by use of a grammatical form like *Is she going?*

Discourse The totality of interaction between humans within a given sphere or context. For example, political discourse includes everything from speeches, political cartoons, editorials in newspapers, books about politics and comments by politicians in public arenas. It includes the gestures they use, symbols which refer to political parties and movements, statistics, slogans, etc.

Discourse markers Any of a set of particles, conjunctions, or conjunctive adjuncts which help to indicate the flow of discourse and the relevance of an upcoming utterance to the surrounding discourse.

Dispreferred second-pair part A term used in Conversation Analysis for a response which is delayed or mitigated, or whose reception is linguistically or paralinguistically marked as unexpected.

Distinctive/contrastive sounds Sounds which are phonemic, or meaningful, in a language, such as [p] and [b] in English.

Egressive pulmonic airstream An airstream produced by forcing air from the lungs out of the vocal tract; most of the world's languages rely heavily on this airstream to produce their sounds.

Ellipsis The omission from a sentence or other construction of one or more words that would complete or clarify the construction, as the omission of *who are* or *while I am* from *I like to interview people sitting down*.

End weight Principle of arranging the elements of a clause or clause complex in such a way that lengthier elements with more information appear later in the clause or clause complex.

Epithet In Systemic Functional Linguistics, a term used to refer to one of the functional slots of the nominal group, and which serves to indicate some quality of the Thing (the main focus of the nominal group), either an objective property, or some expression of the speaker's attitude towards it, such as *John is happy*.

Eponyms Words formed from real or fictitious names, such as *google* and *sandwich*

Existent A term used in Systemic Functional Linguistics to refer to the main participant in an existential process, such as *There are many people in the room*.

Face In interaction, refers to the positive social awareness that people would like for others to award their enacted role, and which people also award to others.

Field The subject matter at hand that is referred to in interaction in terms of experience, real or imagined.

Finite A function of the clause which indicates the aspect, polarity modality and/or tense of the main verb.

First-pair parts (See adjacency pairs)

Foot A rhythmic unit of speech which consists of a set of syllables, the first of which is stressed, unless there is a **silent ictus**, and which lasts until the next stressed syllable.

Fricative Type of consonant in which air flow is never completely obstructed, rather air is forced steadily through the articulation point.

Frontness How far forward or back in the mouth the tongue is positioned upon producing a vowel.

Function words A word, as a preposition, article, auxiliary, or pronoun, that chiefly expresses grammatical relationships, has little semantic content of its own, and belongs to a small, closed class of words whose membership is relatively fixed (distinguished from *content words*).

Fusional languages (Also called inflectional languages) Languages whose morphosyntax relies mainly on the addition to roots and stems of morphemes that often include more than one aspect of meaning (e.g. person, number <u>and</u> tense), or on morphemes which are difficult to separate out from the root or stem.

Generalization When a word takes on a broader meaning, such as *navigate* widening to refer to non-acquatic contexts, such as *navigate your way around the city*, or *navigate the Web*.

Genre A staged, purposeful linguistic interaction arising from repeated occurrences of a shared activity in a given culture.

Gist Allows for clearing up any possible misunderstanding in terms of meaning of the language used, in order for the social action to continue unfolding.

Goal In Systemic Functional Linguistics, a term used to refer to a participant in a material process which is affected by the action in the verb, as in John *squashed <u>the pumpkin</u>*.

Grammatical metaphor A term used in Systemic Functional Linguistics to refer to meanings which are expressed via non-congruent or un-typical ways, as when a process is expressed by a nominal group rather than by a verbal group.

Head The dominant functional element in a group; e.g. the Head of a nominal group is typically a noun.

Height of the tongue Used to describe the position of the tongue in the production of vowels. See **frontness, roundedness.**

Heteronyms Words which are spelled the same but have different pronunciations (e.g. *bow* and *bow, read* and *read.*

Homonyms Words which sound the same but have different meanings (e.g. *bear, bear* and *bare*)

Hyponyms A specialized instance of a more general word; e.g. *chair* is a hyponym of *furniture*.

Identified A term used in Systemic Functional Linguistics to refer to a participant in a relational process whose identity is specified by the **Identifier**, as in <u>*John*</u> *is the leader*.

Identifier A term used in Systemic Functional Linguistics to refer to a participant in a relational process which functions to provide the identity of the participant **Identified**, as in *John is the <u>leader</u>*.

Idiolect Our own individual way of using language, which includes our pronunciation and typical lexico-grammatical choices when speaking or writing.

Illocutionary act The act of doing something by saying something.

Illocutionary force The speech act performed by a speaker in making an utterance, for example, promise, command, request, or warning.

Imperative (mood) Noting or pertaining to the mood of the verb typically used in commands, requests, etc., as in *Listen! Go!*, and which is expressed in English by leaving off the Subject.

Implosives A speech sound produced by an ingressive glottalic airstream, in which air is sucked in.

Indicative (mood) Noting or pertaining to the mood of the verb when it is not imperative; refers to both **declarative** and **interrogative** mood.

Indirect speech act An utterance whose mood does not explicity reflect its communicative purpose, for example, *I have no money* used as a request for a loan.

Indo-European A family of languages which consists of most of the languages of Europe, Iran, the Indian subcontinent, and other parts of Asia.

Inflectional languages (see **Fusional languages**)

Ingressive airstream mechanism An airstream produced by drawing air into the oral or nasal cavity. The ingressive airstream may be used when speaking while taking a breath; it is also used with the glottalic and velaric airstreams in the formation of implosives and clicks.

Innateness hypothesis A theoretical stance which holds that we are born with a special ability to acquire syntax, with some pre-existing knowledge of or specific ability for language.

Insertion sequences A sequence of turns that intervenes between the first and second parts of an adjacency pair.

Instrument A term used in semantics to refer to the thing used to perform an action in a sentence, as in <u>*The key*</u> *opened the door*.

International Phonetic Alphabet (IPA) The alphabet of the International Phonetic Association designed to represent the sounds of all of the world's languages.

Interrogative (mood) Of, relating to, or being an element or construction used to ask a question.

Intonation The relative rise and fall of voice pitch.

Intonation contours (or **patterns**) The way in which we vary our pitch at the end of phrases, usually divided into four different types: rising, rising-falling, falling-rising, or falling.

Isolating languages Languages which rely mainly on morphemes that are separate words, rather than inflections, to convey morphosyntactic relations

Jargon Ways of using language which are specific to an occupational community or other specialized group

Language acquisition device A hypothetical mechanism in the brain posited by Noam Chomsky, present in humans at birth, which aids in the acquisition of syntax.

Langue The grammatical system of forms of a language, which is a collective social product

Lexico-grammar (lexicogrammatical) Refers to both the vocabulary and grammar of language; a term from Systemic Functional Linguistics, which suggests that vocabulary and grammar are arranged along a cline, where meanings are construed as more specific at the lexical end, while meanings are construed as more general at the more grammatical end.

Loanwords Words imported from other languages, such as *patio, canyon* and *anchovy* in English.

Locutionary act The act of saying something.

Manner of articulation The way in which the airstream is obstructed and modified as it passes through the constriction in the vocal tract in the production of a consonant.

Manner The maxim or convention formulated by H. P. Grice which states that a speaker's contribution to conversation should be orderly, and should avoid obscurity and ambiguity.

Meta-language Any language or symbolic system used to discuss, describe, or analyze another language or symbolic system.

Metaphor The extension of the meaning of a word to other concepts that have shared properties with the initial word, such as *branch* of a tree to *branch* of a bank or library

Metonymy The extension of a meaning of a word to something which is contiguous or related, as in using *the crown* to refer to the king or queen.

Mid vowels Vowels whose pronunciation means that the tongue is neither close to nor far from the roof of the mouth.

Minimal pairs Two words that are identical except for a single phoneme, for example, *pin* and *bin* in English.

Modality The expression of obligation/usuality with respect to the verb of a clause.

Mode The channel of communication, e.g. written, spoken, etc.

Mondegreens Homophonic phrases which are heard as a different set of words and meaning than that originally intended.

Mood The system of choices of finite clauses: **indicative (declarative** and **interrogative)** or **imperative**, realized in English by the configuration of the Subject and the Finite.

Morpheme The smallest linguistic unit of meaning; **free** morphemes are those which can stand alone (e.g. *pin*) and **bound** morphemes are those which cannot (e.g. *un* in *unpin*). **Root** morphemes are morphemes which cannot be broken down into smaller units, and **stem** morphemes are root morphemes with any attached affixes. **Inflectional** morphemes are used for syntactic purposes, to indicate for example tense, gender, number or case. **Derivational** morphemes are used to change meaning or to change the part of speech.

Morphology The study of the structural ways in which morphemes combine into larger units such as words.

Morphophonemics The study of the changes in pronunciation of morphemes, which occur due to the surrounding speech sounds (e.g. [əz], [z] or [s] for the plural noun morpheme in English.

Morphosyntax (morphosyntactic) The study of the combination of linguistic units which have morphological and syntactic categories.

Move A term used by John Swales within genre analysis to refer to a distinctly staged rhetorical maneuver in a text.

Nasal Type of consonant that redirects air flow through the nose, e.g. [m], [n], [ŋ].

Negative politeness strategies Instances of communication in which interlocutors attempt to mitigate face-threatening acts by appealing to the others' need for their own space and their desire to avoid being imposed upon.

Nonce A word that is coined for one particular occasion, and not used again.

Noncontrastive sounds Similar speech sounds that do not change the meaning of a word or make up two different words, such as [p] and [phʰ].

Noun A member of a class of words that can function as Subject or Complement (object) of a clause or as an object of a prepositional phrase, and which share properties, such as the ability to be modified.

Numerative In Systemic Functional Linguistics, a term used to refer to one of the functional slots of the nominal group, and which serves to indicate 'how many' of the Thing.

One-word stage Period of child language development, typically beginning at the end of the first year or at the beginning of the second year, and lasting until around the end of the second year, in which the child uses one-word phrases to communicate a range of meanings.

Open (or low) vowels Vowels whose pronunciation means that the tongue is farthest from the roof of the mouth.

Other initiated repair When a listener works toward solving problems in understanding in a conversation by correcting the speaker.

Paradigmatic Refers to the relationship of linguistic units (a phone, phoneme, morpheme, word, group, phrase, etc.) which can be substituted for another within the same structure, resulting in a different meaning, such as [h] and [b] before *at* to form *hat* and *bat*, or *I want* _____ where we can fill in the blank with several kinds of paradigmatic choices, such as nominal groups (*chocolate, some hot soup*).

Parole The actual use of language by individual speakers.

Participant In Systemic Functional Linguistics, a term used to refer to a transitivity function in the clause, usually realized by a nominal group, and which serves to specify who, whom and what with relation to the process, such as *John bought bagels*.

Patient A term used in semantics to refer to the entity changed by action expressed in the verb (compare with Goal in Systemic Functional Linguistics), as in *John kicked the ball*.

Pejoration Said of a word which has taken on negative connotations, such as *aggressive* in describing people, and *spinster* in describing single women.

Performance Actual language use (compare with **competence**).

Performatives Sentences that are used to *do* things, rather than declare or state something. They indicate their speech-act value explicitly, such as *I now pronounce you man and wife*.

Perlocutionary act The act of achieving something by saying something.

Phenomenon In Systemic Functional Linguistics, a term used to refer to a participant in a mental process, one which refers to the sensory input which affects or which is perceived by the Sensor, as in *John saw the accident*.

Phonemes A minimal meaning-making unit in the phonology of a language; a distinctive phone.

Phonemic inventory Inventory of phonemes, of speech sounds that are distinctive and meaningful in a language.

Phonemic Speech sounds that are contrastive.

Phones Speech sounds; smallest phonetic segment that can be isolated in a stream of speech, for example [pʰ].

Phonetic features Features of speech sounds, including points and manners of articulation.

Phonetics The scientific study of speech sounds and their production, transmission, and reception, as well as their analysis, classification, and transcription.

Phonology The sound system of a language, including the inventory of phonemes and their paradigmatic and syntagmatic patterning; also the study of the sound systems of languages.

Pidgin A form of language, often a combination of two languages, which comes into existence for specific communicative needs across speech communities; pidgins tend to have a restricted set of lexical items, few grammatical rules, and are not learned as a first language.

Plosive/stop Type of consonant when air is completely stopped and then released.

Polarity Positive or negative character of words, phrases, or sentences. Refers to the 'yes/no' dimension of clauses.

Polysemy Ability of a word to have separate but related meanings, e.g. *paint* (n) and *paint* (v), or *wood* (lumber) and *wood* (group of trees).

Positive politeness strategies Instances of communication in which interlocutors attempt to mitigate face-threatening acts by appealing to the others' desire to be liked and accepted.

Post-deictic In Systemic Functional Linguistics, a term used to refer to one of the functional slots of the nominal group, and which serves to further identify the Thing, such as *the same book*.

Post-modifier An element in the nominal group which follows the noun and which provides further specification; realized by a **Qualifier**, as in *The boy with the bike*.

Pragmatics The study of language in use, where meaning is inferred not just from the language itself, but from the context in which the language is used.

Predicator A function of the clause which serves to express the main process; the verb without the Finite.

Preferred second-pair parts Preferred responses, usually brief and straightforward in adjacency pairs. The response that is expected.

Premodifier An element in the nominal group which precedes the noun and which provides further specification; Deictics, Post-deictics, Numeratives, Epithets and Classifiers all function as Pre-modifiers in the nominal group.

Preposition group A group of words with a preposition as Head; it may consist solely of a preposition (*in, on, down, under*), or it may be modified, as in *straight up* or *right behind*.

Prepositional phrase A phrase which combines a **preposition group** with a **nominal group**.

Preposition A member of a class of words that typically express a spatial, temporal, or other relationship, as in *in, on, by, to,* and *since*.

Presequences An utterance or set of utterances serving as a precursor to subsequent action, as in *Guess what? What?* Often they are used to avoid face-threatening acts, as in *Are you free this weekend?*

Presupposition Something that must be assumed true for a sentence to be appropriately uttered; for example, *Have some more tea* presupposes the addressee has already had some tea.

Process The ideational meaning expressed by the verb of the clause, which may be material ('doing'), relational ('being', 'having'), mental ('seeing', 'thinking', wanting'), verbal ('saying'), behavioral ('behaving': unconscious process), existential ('existing': *there is*)

Proto-Indo-European (PIE) A pre-historic unrecorded language, thought to be the common ancestor of all of the **Indo-European** languages; a constructed language based on all of the Indo-European languages.

Proto-linguistic Refers to aspects of communication which exist prior to the existence of human language as known in its full extent of symbolic representation through phonology, syntax and semantics.

Qualifier In Systemic Functional Linguistics, a term used to refer to one of the functional slots of the nominal group, which serves to further specify the Thing, and which realizes the Post-modifier in English, as in *The boy with the bike*.

Quality The maxim formulated by H. P. Grice which states that a speaker's contribution to conversation is understood to be truthful and not backed by unsupported claims.

Quantity The maxim formulated by H. P. Grice which states that a speaker's utterance is understood to be neither less nor more informative than required at its point in a conversation.

Quoted A term used in Systemic Functional Linguistics to refer to a participant in a verbal process, namely the material that appears between quotes; the exact words someone says as in *He said 'Now that's a good idea!'*

Rank A hierarchy of linguistic units such as *clause→phrase→group →word→morpheme*.

Receiver A term used in Systemic Functional Linguistics to refer to a participant in a verbal process to whom the information is addressed, as in *John asked him a question*.

Recipient A term used in Systemic Functional Linguistics to refer to a participant in a material process, one who receives the benefit of the action, as in *John gave him the book*.

Redundant/noncontrastive sounds Non-meaningful sounds in a language; renditions of a phoneme which occur because of the surrounding speech environment, but which do not have additional meaning, as in aspiration of voiced stops at the beginning of a syllable, e.g. [pʰæt].

Reduplication A form of affixation which in which a syllable is repeated to change the meaning or class of a word.

Register The context of situation of a text, constituted by the variables of **field, mode** and **tenor**.

Relation The maxim formulated by H. P. Grice which states that a speaker's utterance is understood to be relevant to the topic being discussed.

Repair The way in which interlocutors work towards solving problems in understanding in conversation. See **self-initiated repair, other initiated repair**.

Reported A term used in Systemic Functional Linguistics to refer to a participant in a verbal process, namely the gist of the words of the sayer, as in *He said that it was a good idea*.

Rheme The rest of the clause which is not **Theme**; together with the Theme it constructs the functional unit of message; the Rheme typically (although not always) provides new information in the clause.

Rhoticized vowel sounds R-colored vowel sounds or r-like speech sounds.

Roundedness The shape of the lips upon the production of a vowel.

Sayer A term used in Systemic Functional Linguistics to refer to a participant in a verbal process who utters or reports the words spoken, as in *John said that he would call*.

Schwa A mid-central neutral vowel, typically occurring in unstressed syllables, as the final vowel of English *sofa.*

Scope A term used in Systemic Functional Linguistics to refer to a participant in a material process over which the process extends, as in *They sang a <u>song</u>.*

Second-pair parts See **adjacency pairs, preferred second-pair parts,** and **dispreferred second-pair parts.**

Self-initiated repair A term used in Conversation Analysis to refer to the attempt made by speakers themselves to resolve a problem of understanding caused by their own conversational turn, through, for example, a mistaken choice of words; it can be compared with other-initiated repair in which another speaker attempts to resolve the problem caused through someone else's turn.

Semantic bleaching Said of a word which has lost any specific meaning, such as *thing* or *nice.*

Semantics The study of the linguistic meaning of morphemes, words, phrases, sentences and grammatical relations. Semantic meaning is encoded in linguistic signs and is meaning in a dictionary type sense.

Senser A term used in Systemic Functional Linguistics to refer to a participant in a mental process who perceives or experiences the inner state or does the sensing expressed in the process, as in *<u>John</u> knows the answer.*

Side sequences A sequence of exchanges in which the social action is different from the talk in which it is embedded.

Sign A combination of a thing or concept and its label or icon.

Signified The thing or concept referred to in a **sign.**

Signifier The configuration of sound elements or other linguistic symbols used to refer to a *signified.*

Silent ictus A beat in a foot which would receive stress if a syllable were uttered.

Slang Lively, colloquial use of language which is often considered not standard usage.

Sociolect A variety of language based on social factors, such as socioeconomic status, gender, age and occupation.

Specialization When a word takes on a more restricted meaning, such as *meat* referring only to 'animal flesh' instead of more generally to 'food', as it did in the past.

Speech act theory A philosophical approach to language designed to explain how we use language to achieve action.

Speech community Communities of people whose language defines them as belonging to a group.

Standard (dialect) A variety of a language which is considered by the wider speech community to be the norm.

Stop/plosive Type of consonant whose articulation means that air is completely stopped and then released.

Stress-timed (or foot-timed) Said of languages such as English, which have a rhythm in which stressed syllables tend to occur at regular intervals of time, regardless of the number of intervening unstressed syllables.

Structuralists Linguists that focus on the interrelatedness of linguistic units, the ways they form structures and systems of oppositions.

Subject The noun phrase immediately dominated by the sentence in a phrase structure tree; the nominal group in a clause which determines the agreement of the verb in terms of person, number, and tense, and which can be queried through a question, or mood, tag.

Syllable-timed Said of languages such as Spanish, which have a rhythm in which syllables are approximately equal in duration and thus tend to follow each other at regular intervals of time.

Synchronic variation Used to refer to differences in a language (for example across geographical or socio-economic communities) at any given point of time.

Syntagmatic Refers to the relationship between elements in a chain; the relationship between linguistic units that combine together to make other linguistic units (e.g. the relationship between *the* and *chair* in the nominal group *the chair*).

Syntax The order and arrangement of elements (morphemes, words, groups and phrases) in a clause.

Systemic functional linguistics (SFL) A theory of linguistics which models language as a system of choices which are both constrained by and help construct the context of situation of the language use.

Taboo Said of words whose use is deemed unacceptable in certain social contexts.

Target A term used in Systemic Functional Linguistics to refer to a tangential participant in a verbal process; it does not occur with direct or indirect speech, and includes verbs such as *describe, explain, criticize, flatter* and *blame* as in *John blamed the kids*.

Tenor The relationship between interlocutors.

Text The linguistic outcome of a specific interaction, such as a particular speech (or part of a speech), a book (or a chapter or a paragraph from a book).

Theme The point of departure of the message; in English, the idea represented by the first constituent of a clause in English. Together with the **Rheme** it forms the functional unit of message, and it typically (but not always) expresses given information. There are three types of Theme: textual (a conjunction or conjunctive Adjunct such as *in addition*) and modal (such as *clearly*) Themes (both of which are optional) and ideational Themes, which are obligatory, and which consists of some experiential content: a participant, process or circumstance.

Thing A term used in Systemic Functional Linguistics to refer to the main element in a nominal group.

Tone language A language in which tone is phonemic, as in many languages of Africa, America and South-East Asia.

Tone The contrastive pitch on a syllable.

Transition relevance place (TRP) The moment in a conversation when a transition from one speaker to another is possible.

Transitivity System which displays choices of verb processes and their participants, as well as attending circumstances, in the clause.

Turn allocational component Describes the way in which turns are allocated among participants in a conversation. The three ordered options are: 'current speaker selects next speaker', 'current speaker selects self', or 'next speaker selects self'.

Turn constructional component Describes the basic units out of which turns are fashioned. These basic units are known as *turn constructional units* or TCUs. Unit types include: lexical, clausal, phrasal, and sentential. These are grammatically and pragmatically complete units, meaning that in a particular context they accomplish recognizable social actions.

Turn constructional units (TCUs) See **Turn constructional component**.

Two-word stage Period of child language development which usually begins at some point during the second year, usually around 18 months, in which children put words together in coherent strings, although without inflections for number, person or tense, such as *more milk*, *me go* or *allgone doggie*.

Upshot Allows for clarification of the pragmatic meaning behind the language used.

Vague language Linguistic sign that lacks specificity in meaning, such as *It's kind of odd*.

Verb A member of a class of words which are used to express **processes**.

Verbiage A term used in Systemic Functional Linguistics to refer to a participant in a verbal process, via an encapsulation of words into a label which packages the words reported on into a type, such as *a question, the truth, the facts*, as in *John asked a question*.

Vernacular (dialect) Language varieties which are considered to vary from the standard dialect.

Voiced consonants Consonants like [b] and [v] that are pronounced with the vibration of the vocal cords (compare with [p] and [f]).

Voicing The vibration of the vocal cords.

Wernicke's area An area of the brain identified by Karl Wernicke as having a role to play in the understanding and production of language, especially word production and meaning.

Word A unit of meaning which consists of one or more morphemes.

THE INTERNATIONAL PHONETIC ALPHABET (2005)

CONSONANTS (PULMONIC)

	LABIAL		CORONAL				DORSAL			RADICAL		LARYNGEAL
	Bilabial	Labio-dental	Dental	Alveolar	Palato-alveolar	Retroflex	Palatal	Velar	Uvular	Pharyngeal	Epi-glottal	Glottal
Nasal	m	ɱ		n		ɳ	ɲ	ŋ	N			
Plosive	p b	ɸ β		t d		ʈ ɖ	c ɟ	k ɡ	q ɢ			ʔ ʔ
Fricative	ɸ β	f v	θ ð	s z	ʃ ʒ	ʂ ʐ	ç ʝ	x ɣ	χ ʁ	ħ ʕ	ʜ ʢ	h ɦ
Approximant		ʋ		ɹ		ɻ	j	ɰ				
Trill	ʙ			r					ʀ		ʀ	
Tap, Flap		ⱱ		ɾ		ɽ						
Lateral fricative				ɬ ɮ		ꞎ	ʎ̝̊	ʟ̝				
Lateral approximant				l		ɭ	ʎ	ʟ				
Lateral flap				ɺ								

Where symbols appear in pairs, the one to the right represents a modally voiced consonant, except for murmured ɦ.
Shaded areas denote articulations judged to be impossible. Light grey letters are unofficial extensions of the IPA.

CONSONANTS (NON-PULMONIC)

Anterior click releases (require posterior stops)	Voiced implosives	Ejectives
ʘ Bilabial fricated	ɓ Bilabial	ʼ Examples:
ǀ Laminal alveolar fricated ("dental")	ɗ Dental or alveolar	pʼ Bilabial
ǃ Apical (post)alveolar abrupt ("retroflex")	ʄ Palatal	tʼ Dental or alveolar
ǂ Laminal postalveolar abrupt ("palatal")	ɠ Velar	kʼ Velar
ǁ Lateral alveolar fricated ("lateral")	ʛ Uvular	sʼ Alveolar fricative

CONSONANTS (CO-ARTICULATED)

ʍ	Voiceless labialized velar approximant
w	Voiced labialized velar approximant
ɥ	Voiced labialized palatal approximant
ɕ	Voiceless palatalized postalveolar (alveolo-palatal) fricative
ʑ	Voiced palatalized postalveolar (alveolo-palatal) fricative
ɧ	Simultaneous x and ʃ (disputed)
k͡p t͡s	Affricates and double articulations may be joined by a tie bar

VOWELS

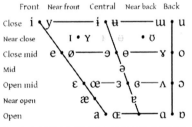

Front   Near front   Central   Near back   Back

Close	i y	ɨ ʉ	ɯ u
Near close	ɪ ʏ		ʊ
Close mid	e ø	ɘ ɵ	ɤ o
Mid		ə	
Open mid	ɛ œ	ɜ ɞ	ʌ ɔ
Near open	æ	ɐ	
Open	a ɶ		ɑ ɒ

Vowels at right & left of bullets are rounded & unrounded.

SUPRASEGMENTALS

ˈ	Primary stress
ˌ	Secondary stress [ˌfoʊnəˈtɪʃən]
eː	Long
eˑ	Half-long
e	Short
ĕ	Extra-short
.	Syllable break
‿	Linking (no break)

INTONATION

ʼ	Extra stress
|	Minor (foot) break
‖	Major (intonation) break
↗	Global rise
↘	Global fall

TONE

Level tones		Contour-tone examples:	
e̋ ˥	Top	ě ˩˥	Rising
é ˦	High	ê ˥˩	Falling
ē ˧	Mid	e᷄ ˦˥	High rising
è ˨	Low	e᷅ ˩˨	Low rising
ȅ ˩	Bottom	ê ˥˧	High falling
Tone terracing		e᷆ ˧˩	Low falling
ꜛ	Upstep	e᷈ ˦˧˦	Peaking
ꜜ	Downstep	ẽ ˧˩˧	Dipping

DIACRITICS

Diacritics may be placed above a symbol with a descender, as ŋ̊. Other IPA symbols may appear as diacritics to represent phonetic detail: tˢ (fricative release), bʱ (breathy voice), ʼa (glottal onset), ᵊ (epenthetic schwa), oʷ (diphthongization).

SYLLABICITY & RELEASES			PHONATION			PRIMARY ARTICULATION			SECONDARY ARTICULATION		
n̩ l̩	Syllabic	n̥ d̥	Voiceless or Slack voice	t̪ b̪	Dental	tʷ dʷ	Labialized	ɔ̜ χ̜	More rounded
e̯ ʊ̯	Non-syllabic	s̬ d̬	Modal voice or Stiff voice	t̺ d̺	Apical	tʲ dʲ	Palatalized	ɔ̹ χ̹ʷ	Less rounded
tʰ hᵗ	(Pre)aspirated	n̤ a̤	Breathy voice	t̻ d̻	Laminal	tˠ dˠ	Velarized	ẽ z̃	Nasalized
dⁿ	Nasal release	n̰ a̰	Creaky voice	ʊ̟ t̟	Advanced	tˤ dˤ	Pharyngealized	ɚ ɝ	Rhoticity
dˡ	Lateral release	n̼ a̼	Strident	i̠ t̠	Retracted	ɫ z̴	Velarized or pharyngealized	e̘ o̘	Advanced tongue root
t̚	No audible release	n̪ d̪	Linguolabial	ä j̈	Centralized	ü	Mid-centralized	e̙ o̙	Retracted tongue root
e̞ β̞	Lowered (β̞ is a bilabial approximant)	e̝ ɹ̝	Raised (ɹ̝ is a voiced alveolar non-sibilant fricative, r̝ a fricative trill)						

Version 1.3, 3 November 2008 Copyright © 2000, 2001, 2002, 2007, 2008 Free Software Foundation, Inc.
http://fsf.org/

Index of Names

Subject Index

CPSIA information can be obtained
at www.ICGtesting.com
Printed in the USA
FFOW01n0415061217
43825683-42764FF

9 781845 534264